As a character from the
inimitable one might
sign, Your 'umble servant,

10/28/96

DICKENS STUDIES ANNUAL
Essays on Victorian Fiction

DICKENS STUDIES ANNUAL
Essays on Victorian Fiction

EDITORS

Michael Timko
Edward Guiliano

DICKENS STUDIES ANNUAL

Essays on Victorian Fiction

VOLUME
24

Edited by
Michael Timko and Edward Guiliano

AMS PRESS
NEW YORK

DICKENS STUDIES ANNUAL
ISSN 0084-9812

International Standard Book Number
Series: 0-404-18520-7
Vol. 24:0-404-18544-4

Dickens Studies Annual: Essays on Victorian Fiction welcomes essay and monograph-length contributions on Dickens as well as other Victorian novelists and on the history of aesthetics of Victorian fiction. All manuscripts should be double-spaced, including footnotes, which should be grouped at the end of the submission, and should be prepared according to the format used in this journal. An editorial decision can usually be reached more quickly if two copies are submitted. The preferred editions for citations from Dickens' works are the Clarendon and the Norton Critical when available, otherwise the Oxford Illustrated or the Penguin.

Please send submissions to the Editors, *Dickens Studies Annual,* Room 1522, Graduate School and University Center, City University of New York, 33 West 42nd Street, New York, N.Y, 10036; please send subscription inquiries to AMS Press, Inc., 56 East 13th Street, New York, N.Y. 10003.

Manufactured in the United States of America

Contents

List of Illustrations

Preface

Once again we express our thanks to the many people who enable us to bring out this annual volume. To the members of our editorial and advisory boards we express our appreciation, and to our colleagues who read and evaluate the essays we give special thanks. Those scholars and critics who give freely of their time deserve special commendation. We also want to note our special debt to those colleagues who have written the comprehensive review essays, the importance of which needs no elaboration.

With the publication of this volume perhaps it is appropriate to reiterate what has always been the primary purpose of the journal. The editors have always set out to publish the best of what is being thought, said, and written about the most admired novelist England ever produced and his contemporaries. With that goal in mind, we can only emphasize the one standard we have always sought to uphold: we have always sought to publish the most interesting and informative essays dealing with the work of Charles Dickens and other nineteenth-century novelists. Upholding this standard entails making certain that we publish not only what might be regarded as long-recognized scholarly approaches to the various aspects of these authors and their works (literary, biographical, social, political, and historical), but also those that reflect contemporary critical ones, including structuralism and semiotics, post-structuralism, Marxist, psychological, feminist, gay and lesbian, and reader-response criticism. It is only by being as openly receptive as possible to all views that *Dickens Studies Annual* can continue to maintain its relevance and appeal to scholars, critics, and students of Victorian fiction and its place as a premier publication in its area.

We again express our gratitude to those in administrative posts in different institutions who continue to provide various kinds of support: Chancellor W. Ann Reynolds, CUNY; President Frances Degen Horowitz; Provost Geoffrey Marshall; Executive Officer Joseph Wittreich; Vice President for Academic Affairs, King Cheek, New York Institute of Technology; Dean Raymond Erickson; Provost John Thorpe; and Chair, Department of English, Charles Molesworth, Queens College, CUNY; and Gabriel Hornstein, president, and our irreplaceable editor, Jack Hopper, AMS Press. Special thanks to our DSA Editorial Assistant, Kathleen Geier.

—MICHAEL TIMKO
—EDWARD GUILIANO

Notes on Contributors

MARGARET SOENSER BREEN is an assistant professor of English at Hartwick College. She is particularly interested in realist representations of female progress. In addition to her piece on Brontë, she has written articles on Bunyan, George Eliot, Jane Rule, and Yeats.

JEROME H. BUCKLEY, Gurney Professor of English Literature, Emeritus, Harvard University, is author of *The Victorian Temper, The Triumph of Time,* and other studies in nineteenth-century literary and intellectual history. He has written of Dickens' relation to the tradition of the Bildungsroman in *Season of Youth* and has edited the Norton Critical *David Copperfield.*

ELIZABETH CAMPBELL is an associate professor of English at Oregon State University where she teaches Victorian literature and the novel. The essay in this volume and "Minding the Wheel: Women's Time in Victorian Narrative," *Rocky Mountain Review* 48 (1994), are part of a book-in-progress entitled *Fortune's Wheel: Of Time and the Female in Dickens' Novels.*

MARK CRONIN is the director of Academic Advisement at Saint Anselm College, where he also teaches in the English department. He has previously published on Dickens and Thackeray in the *Dickens Quarterly;* he has also published articles on Kipling.

RODNEY STENNING EDGECOMBE, associate professor of English at the University of Cape Town, took his M.A. cum laude at Rhodes University and his Ph.D. at the University of Cambridge, where he was also awarded the Members' English Prize for 1978/79. He has produced books on Herbert, Crabbe, Gray, Leigh Hunt, Patrick White, and Muriel Spark, and over eighty articles on a wide variety of topics, including the history and aesthetics of classical ballet. Two further books—on Richard Wilbur and on the poetry of Keble and Newman—are in press.

Laura Fasick teaches at Moorhead State University in Minnesota. She has published articles on a number of eighteenth- and nineteenth-century authors, including Samuel Richardson, Thackeray, and Charles Kingsley. Her current project is a study of representations of women's bodies in selected English novels from Richardson to D. H. Lawrence.

K. J. Fielding is Emeritus Saintsbury Professor of English literature at the University of Edinburgh; author of *Charles Dickens: A Critical Introduction* (1958); editor of *The Speeches of Charles Dickens* (Oxford, 1960; Harvester-Wheatsheaf, 1988); co-editor of the Pilgrim Dickens *Letters,* volumes 1 and 5 (Oxford, 1965, 1981); senior co-editor of the *Carlyle Letters* (1970–), volumes 1–24; author of other works and articles mainly on Dickens and the Carlyles.

Jan B. Gordon, a professor of Anglo-American studies at Tokyo University of Foreign Studies, has previously appeared in DSA 11. His *Echo's (') Econo-mies: Gossip and Subversion in Nineteenth-Century British Fiction,* with an extensive discussion of *Bleak House,* is forthcoming from Macmillan.

Jonathan H. Grossman is a graduate student at the University of Pennsylvania. His dissertation is about the relationship between the English novel and the law courts as two interdependent storytelling forums.

Anne Humphreys is a Professor at Lehman College and the Graduate School, City University of New York. She is the author of *Travels into the Poor Man's Country: The Work of Henry Mayhew* as well as articles on the nineteenth-century press, popular culture, and the Victorian novel, including several essays on Dickens, including "Carker the Manager" for *Nineteenth-Century Fiction* (1980), "Generic Stands and Urban Twists: The Victorian Mysteries Novel" (*Victorian Studies,* 1991), which includes a discussion of *Bleak House,* as well as papers about *Oliver Twist* and *Hard Times* for The Dickens Universe. She is currently working on a book on the Victorian divorce novel.

Caroline McCracken-Flesher is an associate professor at the University of Wyoming, and specializes in the nineteenth century, the novel, and their intersection with film. She has published numerous articles on Scotland's literary nationalism (e.g., "Thinking Nationally, Writing Colonially? Scott, Stevenson and England," in *Novel* 24:3). some on the theoretical questions behind the transposition of literature into film, but this is her first foray into Dickens studies.

DAVID PARKER is curator of the Dickens House Museum at 48 Doughty Street in London. He has taught for the University of Sheffield, the University of Malaya, and the Open University, and is the author of numerous articles on literary topics, in recent years especially on Dickens and on literary museums. He has lectured on these topics in many countries.

BARRY QUALLS teaches English at Rutgers University in New Brunswick, New Jersey.

EDWARD L. TUCKER professor of English at Virginia Polytechnic Institute and State University (Virginia Tech), has published three books and thirty articles, mostly in the field of American literature, especially Southern literature. His book, *The Shaping of Longfellow's "John Endicott,"* was awarded the emblem of the Center for Scholarly Editions of the Modern Language Association.

DAVID WILKES is a lecturer at the University of Rhode Island. He has published articles on Dickens and Robert Browning, and is currently writing a book on Dickensian Neopastoralism.

Dickens and the Political Economy of the Eye

Jan B. Gordon

> The same opportunity served me for noticing that Mr. Pumblechook appeared to conduct his business by looking across the street at the saddler, who appeared to transact *his* business by keeping his eye on the coach-maker, who appeared to get on in life by putting his hands in his pockets and contemplating the baker, who in his turn folded his arms and stared at the grocer, who stood at his door and yawned at the chemist. The watch-maker, always poring over a little desk with a magnifying glass at his eye, and always inspected by a group of smock-frocks poring over him through the glass of his shop-window, seemed to be about the only person in the High-street whose trade engaged his attention.
>
> *(GE* 8, 84)

Immediately prior to his initial departure for Satis House, Pip looks upon a community where looking itself assumes the form of a failed commodity transaction. In an arena of diminished economic activity, the mutual investment of gazes—but a gaze which is transmitted rather than precisely reproduced or reciprocated—usurps business activity as a simulated trade. The gaze is in effect "passed on," but only in the sense that the eye is the agency of what in another context, might be termed a "chain gaze," to borrow a concept more often used to denote epistolarity. Or, to put a different emphasis upon the same activity, the gaze is, even etymologically, part of a *spec*ulation, combining "looking" with passive investment. Trapped within something that bears an uncanny resemblance to the so-called hermeneutic "circle," the participants of the scheme stockpile time, one definition of boredom, even as they engage in the ocular wager of speculation. Symbolically even the watchmaker, the guardian of time who measures it with his own "loupe," is himself maintained within the visual loop of other spectators, so that life itself is structured as a visual *penetralium*, from which no one can escape.

This scene of the de-centered gaze occurs early on in *Great Expectations*, at approximately the same time that Pip is launched upon his visionary pro*spects*. Initially encountering Estella as Rapunzel, leaning out from the solitary "eye" of a Satis House window, Pip revises his view to "see" the opening as only partially a window, in fact "rustily barred" amidst a row of "walled up" windows (*GE* 8, 84–85). He has symbolically, but only symbolically, abandoned the forge, where locks and files are made (and people are brought up!) by hand, in favor of an Estella who holds keys to secrets and scorns his working-class hands. Pip's expectations appear then, as not only a closely guarded secret, but a secret that subjects his secrets to surveillance even as the iron windows and key bear a relationship to a life he had presumably left. In making the fairy princess of his dreams yet one more turnkey of Dickens' ubiquitous prisons, the orphan's prospects are made to appear *always-already* foreclosed. Pip simultaneously *sees* Satis House for what it is and does not see it. This characteristic mode of seeing as a repressed revisionary activity occurs repeatedly in *Great Expectations*, but perhaps most memorably in Pip's first observation of Miss Havisham's chamber and (originally) white wedding dress which quickly becomes something else:

> It was not in the first few moments that I saw all these things, though I saw more of them in the first moments than might be supposed. But, I saw that everything within my view which ought to be white, had been white long ago, and had lost its lustre, and was faded and yellow. I saw that the bride within the bridal dress had withered like the dress, and like the flowers, and had no brightness left but the brightness of her sunken eyes. I saw that the dress had been put upon the rounded figure of a young woman, and that the figure upon which it now hung loose, had shrunk to skin and bone.   (*GE* 8, 87)

What the narrator had previously seen—a bride dressed in white beside a wedding cake—is subverted by a second "viewing," with the result that *all* seeing henceforth becomes provisional. Every revisionary seeing constitutes nothing less than the cancellation of some first *impression* in which the reader had initially placed his *credit*.

If the eye is involved in this (enchained) double gesture in which it is constantly *seeing through* first impressions, then the constant devaluing and revaluing would constitute an *economy*: one vision compensates for the loss of another. Were this to be the case, then the economy would surely condition the way in which Dickens' characters view each other. Yet, one question would appear to loom very large: does this unique way of seeing constitute a form of social control—in which case traditionl French "gaze theory" might provide a model—or, conversely, does the revisionary potentially liberate the ocular object from confining social (or material) positions? Is identity fixed or freed by imagining it as part of a visual economy?

In at least one remarkable passage in *A Tale of Two Cities*, Dickens, in observing passengers within a stagecoach bundled up so as to avoid social intercourse, described identity itself as a secret:

> A wonderful fact to reflect upon that every human creature is constituted to be that profound secret and mystery to every other. A solemn consideration, when I enter a great city at night, that every one of those clustered houses encloses its own secret; that every room in every one of them encloses its own secret; that every beating heart in the hundreds of thousands of breasts there, is in some of its imaginings, a secret to the heart nearest it! Something of the awfulness, even of Death itself, is referable to this. No more can I turn the leaves of this dear book that I loved, and vainly hope in time to read it all. . . . It was appointed that the book should shut with a spring, for ever and for ever, when I had read but a page. It was appointed that the water should be locked in an eternal frost, when the light playing on its surface, and I, stood in ignorance on the shore. (*TTC* 3, 44)

Because each being is so "constituted," secrecy is the ontic condition of all objects in the universe. It is as if some God "in the beginning" had said, "let there be darkness" and henceforth, each created object harbored this first darkness, albeit individuated so that it simultaneously makes me what I am. No matter how far I descend on the chain of created objects, each is divisible into a smaller one which harbors its own secret, as part of a collective share. Insofar as it resembles death itself, this secret is simultaneously what makes and unmakes the individual. It is noteworthy that long before many of Dickens' characters are in fact imprisoned or come into contact with incarceration, each is *always-already* imprisoned in his own private darkness.

And yet, were my unique secret to *secrete*, as it often does in Dickens, there would occur a hemorrhage of the self, like that which had already afflicted John Carker in *Dombey and Son* who, upon having a secret "found out" before his twenty-second birthday, "from all men's society . . . died" (*DS* 13, 179). My identity is a knowledge which, paradoxically, can never be known to others without resulting in an alternative radical loss of self as a consequence of having this unique self-knowledge "trafficked." The irony should not be lost on us. The secret of my being is either permanently "banked," in its invulnerability to others' knowledge or, conversely, it is released for a public consumption in which the self is devalued in the speculations of others which vehicularize it. In either case, the metaphoric equivalent of a life sentence for indebtedness is the consequence. Whether perpetually on deposit or leaked, the secret assumes some of the characteristics of money.

For only then can someone like James Carker, the manager of Dombey and Son, when reminded of his infallible memory by his employer, comment, "It's the only capital of a man like *me*" (DS 13, 172). A memory so sophisticated as to inductively determine the secrets of others, is one avenue by which the lower social orders can approach the condition of being self-made, without the benefit of family wealth or silent partner. In accumulating knowledge of the secrets or secret life of others, one is able to "call" upon the other financially as well as personally. The individual thereby becomes "open," transparent to the advancement of future claims. It is this promise which is made abundantly clear during Arthur Clennam's first visit to the Marshalsea:

> As they eyed the stranger in passing, they eyed him with borrowing eyes hungry, sharp, speculative as to his softness if they were accredited to him, and the likelihood of his standing something handsome. (*LD* I, 9, 131)

Upon entering the prison Clennam shares in the perspective of a double vision. For the prison is a perfect metaphor for a life simultaneously closed and open, in the sense that it is totally introverted and yet an entirely public institution devoid of any semblance of private space. It is not merely that the Marshalsea is a debtor's prison, and hence literally the locus of failed economic transactions, but that there is no reciprocity in either the individuated or the "universal stare [which] made the eyes ache" (*LD* I, 1, 39) and which conditions the novel's instantiating moment as well as that of Amy Dorrit.

This intensive scrutiny likened to that of the Mediterranean sun is surely founded upon two unusual presuppositions in Dickens: (1) there is a market, a future, as it were, for secrets that necessitates precise "timing" by the bearer in order to optimize his profit and, (2) an excess of demand over supply, that is to say, an environment chronically short of the information that these secrets might provide. Hence the secret itself tends to have two kinds of existence. In one instance, it is contained within a more liquid asset which simultaneously *preserves* it, and renders it vulnerable to exchange—an effect that initially seems contradictory. These more substantial (yet more liquid) "carriers" of the secret allow it a depository, but furnishes the depository with a vulnerability to liquidation. Mrs. Bumble's gold locket engraved with the name "Agnes" on the inside, which is the secret of Oliver Twist's birth and the watch given Arthur Clennam by his dying father would both qualify, for they contain secrets which nullify the "face" value of the commodity which bears them. The secrets of birth (and hence history itself) can be *denominated*, though for the now adult child to assume a rightful *nomination*, the recipient/viewer of the asset must read beyond or behind its monetarization. The locket and watch must be devalued as jewelry in the same reading by which they are revalued in terms of establishing a hitherto obscured *relationship*.

In the other instance, the body itself can become a liquid asset which the recipient/viewer again must *look through* or behind, inducing a material transparency. This may well account for the studied gaze with which one character, say a Jaggers on the stairs at Satis House, holds Pip's head in his hands—as if to read its presence in another relationship which is not materially present. The unforgettable individuating physical features of many of Dickens' characters—the clicking sound in Magwitch's voice when he speaks; Sleary's linguistic "slides" in *Hard Times*; Bradley Headstone's nosebleeds in *Our Mutual Friend*; Jagger's compulsive washing of his hands in *Great Expectations*—have charmed generations of readers. Yet, in each instance, the role of these features in individuation must be strategically forgotten in order to see them not as individuating, but as linking that character with another (relationship or theme) from which it initially would have separated him. In Magwitch's case, the "clicking sound" which identifies him (even years later), also de-individuates him by linking him as a mysterious "double" who initially appears as an imaginary avenger to the frightened Pip in the graveyard, but later becomes a real avenger, stalking Magwitch himself, not Pip. Jagger's scented hands nominate him as a gentleman (to the Pip who has dirty hands in Estella's eyes), but de-nominate him from that position when Pip learns that they are compulsively washed—which means that they are compulsively dirty, like his own. The same gesture which had seemed to separate Jaggers and Pip, in the revisionary mode, is seen to bind them in a relationship which transcends the apparent difference. In some sense the reader *of* Dickens' novels must come to read like the characters *in* the novels in order to solve the puzzle of a relationship which is not immediately visible.

Given its corporeal transparency which is often represented as a flexibility, one model of the body habitually subjected to the obtrusive eye would be that of the physically defective or insufficient. Although a number of critics have recently read the crippled or maimed as symbolic manifestations of a specialized complex of persecution and social attitudes, if it is assumed that each individual is defined by a private secret, then that secret would constitute both my being and my share in a universal handicap. Even those not visibly maimed are in fact maimed *in situ*. And in fact, several of Dickens' novels at their margins have characters who are either scavengers of the body or traffic in body parts. This would suggest what Harmon-Rokesmith's life does in *Our Mutual Friend*, notably that the individual and its composite parts are quite interchangeable, one for the other.

Perhaps this could be more clearly visualized if we thought about the "stain" of some private secret as part of a process analogous to the printing of money: an illegitimate birth would constitute a "false" impression or "bad" mark, insofar as it designated a counterfeit specimen. Because a knowledge of this inauthenticity might result in the inauguration of new or competing claims upon an estate in the event of death, the secrets associated with births would have a "life" beyond death. Easily monetarized, the "impression" of a name would thus come to embody both an ontology and potentially, a form of transcendence. In *Oliver Twist, Great Expectations, Bleak House*, and *Little Dorrit*, the plot is resolved under the question of paternity, the origin of a name. And in *Our Mutual Friend* and *The Mystery of Edwin Drood*, one of the characters abandons his name willingly (rather than existing from the outset as an abandoned name!) in order to gain control over his own rebirth, and hence his own naming. Re-naming oneself becomes the sole mode of escaping the determined life, as Dickens allows the trope of a bad name (illegitimacy) to trope itself: the historically constrained individual gains control of his life by figuratively "fathering" himself—biologically impossible, but neither fictionally nor fiscally (especially in an age of inflation) impossible. The possibility that the "self-made" man was no longer imaginary—either physically or fiscally—may be suggested in this notion of the *exchange*-ability of bodies, names, and identities, their openness to "over-printing." One consequence would be the suspicion that humanity is a palimpsest. Esther Summerson is "Dame Durden" as well as "Mother Hubbard" in *Bleak House*, and an accurate list of the characters' names in Dickens' novels would have to accommodate this overlay into such hyphenations as "Harmon-Rokesmith," "Drood-Datchery," and "Pip-Handel." "Character" comes to be an accumulation of values from different discursive or imaginative systems as one remedy to the discontinuity which J. Hillis Miller has observed among the author's orphans.[1]

Were the monetary model to be deployed, "character," like the secrets which comprise its essence, could be seen as an agent of both union and separation, the same way that money is in Marx's thought. There the so-called "use-value" is determined by the physical properties of the sign (the commodity, in Marx's scheme). The "exchange-value," to the contrary, is a permanent ground, which is founded on the effacement of any empirical determination.[2] In other words, money (in my model, the Dickensian secret) can approach the form of a general equivalent only when it is itself excluded by all other signs (commodities) as an equivalent. Money ceases to be paper when it becomes a transactional measure: a form of forgetfulness occurs. In much the same way, secrets are never exchanged for goods in Dickens, but rather for additional information. Value in exchange is thus acquired, "added on" to something already defined as complete—the exchange of one commodity for another—in order to facilitate circulation in a different register, in much the same way that nicknames are "added on" in Dickens. Once introduced as a general equivalent in an economy of exchange, the secret comes to dominate the process, dislocating value away from other commodities (signs) and locating itself at the centre of circulation. This occurs when the value of the "secret" usurps that of its putative "carrier": Arthur Clennam's father's watch is usurped in value by the "value" that it gives his relationship to Amy Dorrit in the same way that in *Our Mutual Friend*, Harmon's second will makes the Dutch bottle buried in the mounds worthless to Weg's elaborate plans for extortion (and indirectly to the reader's attention to that portion of the plot).

The archetypal Dickens plot involves the discovery of a presumably authentic source (an instantiating moment) behind a proliferation of copies or facsimiles. In its privileging of recuperation, this plot is perfectly appropriate to the illegitimate child on a quest for his paternity. One will lies behind another in *Bleak House* which takes its very name from one of two identically-named dwellings. The Father of the Marshalsea is the honorary head of a family which both grounds and competes with William Dorrit's failure to be an adequate genealogical father. Magwitch in *Great Expectations* assumes the role of the absent father of the opening scene in the graveyard whose place was occupied by an inscription that the young Pip reads as an exact physical representation, forcing language to do what it can never do: "stand in" for the absentee. The very ease with which wills, dwellings, fathers, and even children become substitutes for some absent antecedent in Dickens' plots subverts the very notion that "value" inheres in *position* or *substance*. One will comes to be valued over another, or other "versions," less by virtue of what it in fact distributes, than by virtue of some *relationship* with another will (chronologically prior, dictated rather than copied, authentic rather than forged) which it in all other ways resembles. What is really being elaborated is the value which lies in simulation, those qualities which allow a substance or a document or a person to become a substitute for another. Hence, characters as well as objects tend to exist, like Dickens' characters with more than one name, on multiple registers. They exist *for* themselves and potentially *as* another, and must be read—subjected to an ocular investment—in order to discover a relationship that may be hidden in its material "value."

Magwitch in *Great Expectations* has no value whatsoever to the society which has transported him as a criminal, but his value to Pip is acquired because he so easily simulates the role of an absent father to an orphan: "Look'ee here, Pip. I'm your second father. You're my son—more to me nor any son. I've put away my money, only for you to spend . . ." (*GE* 39, 337). He has value as a "general equivalent," a surrogate for a cancelled relationship. And yet, the plot centers upon the fact that the two Magwitches follow each other about in Pip's imagination, just as do "use-value" and "exchange-value" in Marx or Goux: the criminal is inseparable from the rich benefactor (as "Abel" is from "Provis") in such a way that each is denominated by the other. Money is materially worthless to Magwitch; it has value only insofar as it allows him to assume a relationship that is biologically impossible.[3] The same pattern regularly recurs in Dickens: child brides to aging husbands (*David Copperfield*); mental ten-year-olds who become "mothers" (*Little Dorrit*); or an "Aged P." to whom one reads newspapers and nods as if he were a child (*Great Expectations*). These surrogate relationships are possible only after the *real*, in the sense of material, relationship has been nullified, for in order to function as a general equivalent, an object or sign must have a certain pliability, a softness which enables it to parasitically attach itself and then become indistinguishable from another. For example, in transforming a financial relationship into a surrogate biological one, Magwitch's actions allow money to circulate in ways analogous to sperm. For one way of thinking of the will in Dickens is to imagine it as a kind of post-mortem contraceptive/fertility device which, enabling an author (father) to abbreviate or enlarge his family through an "inscripted affection" metaphorically permits him the luxury of deleting or extending paternity after traditional engendering is no longer possible. The will itself represents a second chance, a supplementary form of patriarchy in an age which limited divorce and access to contraception, even as material patriarchy is subverted.

Often in Dickens, the univocity of the family itself is what is being nullified, so that members belong to more than one family "unit" at the same time. In *Great Expectations*, for example, Compeyson is (structurally) the absentee partner as both potential financial investor (to Magwitch) and potential sexual investor (to Miss Havisham). Those two forms of familial investment exist in a relationship of similitude, perhaps best illustrated in the activity of Jaggers, who distributes Magwitch's money to Pip and his baby to Miss Havisham re-enforcing the economic analogy:

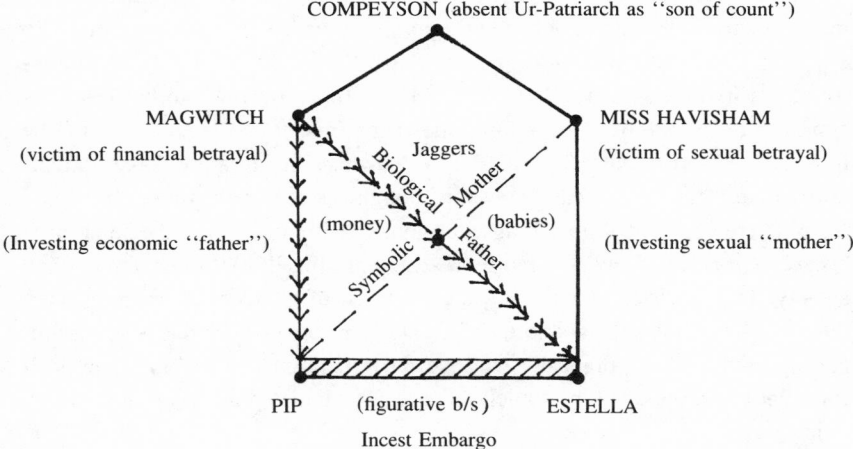

Magwitch's emotional "share" in this economy of Compeyson's betrayal is banishment to a distant land (homelessness); Miss Havisham's "share" is banishment to the perpetual enclosure of a ruined house (too much house), so that her victimization seems the obverse of his. Similarly, both Magwitch and Miss Havisham suffer from alternative symptoms of an eating disorder: one, the "heavy grubber" (*GE* 40, 346) who devours with a knife; the other, a woman never seen to eat. Although not materially related by Dickens' plot—they never meet and never would, given the exigencies of class, gender, and social environment—the values of social and sexual betrayal, respectively, are made analogous through an economy of "circulation." Both lose money as a preamble to losing self-worth to the same absentee father. But it is surely noteworthy that the same simulational model also demands that we consider the ways in which social betrayal at the hands of society is *different* from sexual betrayal at the hands of a lover: one can temporarily succeed in disguising his criminal "past," but the other must forever "live" the moment of her abandonment, as an internalization.

This second *relational*, as opposed to *material*, family is especially vulnerable to a unique form of surveillance. In the first sense, they are both "created," standing in a relationship to a father-author. Hence, Pip comes to participate in the dual-life that art objects have for their creators, being both *proper* and *improper* simultaneously to the question of authorial intention: he reproduces

Magwitch's original investment, without representing Magwitch, that is, bearing his name.[4] As with the headstones in the graveyard, once again the notion of inscripted representation becomes problematic. No wonder that as Pip's "second" father, Magwitch takes a long, hard look, before acknowledging that his ocular pleasure is dependent upon the secrecy of the investment: "to know in secret that I was making a gentleman" (*GE* 39, 339). "The singularity of his fixed look at me" (*GE* 39, 334) initially startles Pip because it is simultaneously one of recognition ("he is my investment") and denial ("he is what I as a criminal can never be"). Nowhere in literature, save perhaps in extreme forms of radical Protestant thought, is the created more alienated from its creator. Every time Magwitch looks at Pip he sees at the same time his social reproduction and what represents not himself, but his revenge upon society. This intense, voyeuristic gaze—"an air of wondering pleasure" (*GE* 39, 333)—embodies the economy of passive participation, and it is so disconcerting to the youth, precisely because only then, can he recognize himself for what he *is*, the agent by which the socially alienated relates to that which is forbidden.

This process is not all that different from what characterizes a money economy, where the circulation of one commodity or sign is denominated by another without losing the trace of self-sameness that permits simulation to occur. In traditional readings, *Great Expectations* is a cautionary *bildungsroman*, teaching an ever-chastened Pip that his fantasy of a gentleman's life with Estella is just that and nothing more, a reading that privileges the pastoral life at the Forge. But the critic more attuned to the operational economy of voyeurism might see how a "money economy" and a "genetic economy" are being denominated in terms of each other. Since Magwitch is the author of both "illegitimacies," Pip and Estella, they are in some sense destined to fall in love. Both financially and biologically, the convict is a creator who has retreated after the act of investment (duplicating what his "partner," Compeyson had done to him earlier) in order to participate passively. The "child" of capitalist investment is interchangeable with the abandoned child. Hence the marriage of Pip and Estella—Dickens' more romantic of two possible endings (which, as with wills and fathers, suggests that narrative closure too is in a relationship of dependency to some prior or originary)—would be in some sense incestuous. Sharing the same metaphoric father, Pip and Estella are in a relationship which binds at the same time that it is irrevocably prohibited. Both Pip's sexual as well as his monetary "expectations" are made to appear what in some sense he *already is*.

Absolute self-sameness would leave no room for the simulation upon which so much of the plot is dependent. Although one must not exaggerate this aspect of Dickens' achievement, a number of the novels skirt incest—defined as the absolute end of difference—in order to put limits upon the subtle differentiations which fuel this oppressive economy of the eye. The tendency toward the marriage of older males to "child-brides" in *David Copperfield, Little Dorrit,* and *Our Mutual Friend* may well be part of an impulse to restrict the economy of "giving" and "being given in" marriage by endorsing the possibility of a self-valorizing relationship that could not be subsumed within the traditional homologies of capitalist logic: sociality, the representation of collective productivity, or the measure and signs of patrimony.

If symbolic incest would represent one possible limit of the subtle differentiations upon which simulation, and hence a transactional, economy has its basis, there are also other instances in which the subjection of the subject, its openness to a censoring gaze, occurs at the margins of Dickens' novels. One example might be the economic subject's characteristic anonymity. The "gentleman" in *Great Expectation* or the Clennam family trading house in *Little Dorrit* are both the creations of some "silent partner" who occupies the position of an economic subject with none of the subject's characteristic liabilities. Hence, Pip is "bound" to someone who has a guarantee of deniability in the same way that the trading house (in both *Little Dorrit* and *Dombey and Son*) is, doubly, a "Ltd.," totally dependent upon capital that is anonymous.[5] It is, ironically, a cruel parody of the way in which Pip is initially "bound," as an apprentice to a master (Joe Gargery) who cannot sign his name, albeit for different reasons. Both the concept of the "gentleman" and that of the successful trading house—stalwart institutions of nineteenth-century Britain—are in every sense fictional insofar as the subject is either imaginary or otherwise irrecoverable by virtue of its infinite regress.

The economic subject's characteristic anonymity in Dickens' plots surely contributes to recurrent patterns of social formation and observation in the novels. Because neither the author nor the occasion of authorship—be it imagined as biological, literary, or capitalist—can be identified with certainty by the victim/beneficiary in Dickens, their social position often appears as entirely arbitrary. They are born to good fortune in the same way that the victims of class oppression seem born to bad fortune. Furthermore, the energies needed to protect the anonymity of the subject increase exponentially with increased economic interdependence in the novels. Sooner or later, everyone in a Dickens novel is touched by money or some dubious scheme to share in the benefits of an estate or company which subjects both to exposure. The

Nadgett of *Martin Chuzzlewit* shares with the later Bucket of *Bleak House* the lack of a Christian name, the euphonics of a diminutive family name, and the ability to combine disappearance with a kind of eternal wakefulness. He is one for whom "every button on his coat might have been an eye: he saw so much" (*MC* 38, 662). Those who are touched by money are ultimately "marked" so that they can be placed under surveillance, *read*. In certain of the novels, like *Bleak House*, the metaphor for this exposure to criminal fraud (misrepresentation) is the exposure to disease which spreads through the classes, marking members of diverse social strata who, under ordinary circumstances, would remain mutually invisible. Dr. Allan Woodcourt and Bucket appear as (ultimately state-sponsored) allies in this surveillance—nothing less than the bureaucratization of the gaze—so as to determine the distributional networks along which microbes and money pass.[6] And like the Nadgett who sends himself unmailed letters as memoranda and arranges meetings with fictional people, surveillance in Dickens assumes the same absentee, intrasitive posture as do other forms of "instantiating" patriarchy.

For even those not literally orphaned in Dickens often find themselves *abandoned* to a pre-existent narrative whose "author" is either obscure or resistant to intimate knowledge. Hence, they exist under the illusion of being *always/already* objects of surveillance, even though no one is watching. Arthur Clennam of *Little Dorrit* and Eugene Wrayburn of *Our Mutual Friend* are engaged in professions that have been chosen for them. Clennam's belated return to England after years in China is the return to a decaying business house headed by a partially paralyzed mother. Now a secondary forwarder of shipping documents, Arthur's role in the family firm is that of an agent of agents of agents! Similarly, Eugene Wrayburn has had his profession chosen for him by a father who has made all the choices for three sons upon their births. In his case, he is to "represent" his family at law, but representation, the "standing in" for another which it simulates at the same time it dissimulates, is imagined as a kind of guardianship over vague interests. Both exist as simultaneously attached (to a family which has pre-determined the course of life) and detached (to any motives other than familial expectations). Absentee father/authors reproduce a variant of the guardian.[7]

This condition of ontic neutrality has a number of crucial implications for their lives. Perhaps primary among them is boredom: insofar as they "merely" represent their fathers' hopes, both Clennam and Wrayburn in some sense "store time," in Walter Benjamin's striking simile.[8] They have nothing to do when we first encounter them, imprisoned as they are within a narrative in which they have no share. Wrayburn already exists as what he will ultimately *become* in the plot of *Our Mutual Friend*: floatsam upon the river of time, "unilluminated by a ray of hope" (*OMF* 12, 159). The other side of that dissimulative metaphor, however, is a parasitical ease of "attachment"; being drifters, both Clennam and Wrayburn are constrained and free *at the same time*. Nor does gender seem to be a determining factor in this economy. Bella Wilfer of *Our Mutual Friend* describes the antinomy of her status perfectly, as a "widow who never was married" (*OMF* 4, 36) and Rosabud in *The Mystery of Edwin Drood* similarly laments, "It *is* so absurd to be an engaged orphan" (*MED* 3, 54). For all of these characters, everyday existence assumes the very form of a *simulation*, acting out what has been pre-scribed, usually in the will of a patriarch. If indeed this situation is one wherein no light can ever enter, as Wrayburn describes his hopelessness, then daily life, even for heirs, is little different from life within one of Dickens' ubiquitous prisons. No wonder that Wrayburn fantasizes about maintaining a lighthouse rather than sharing a solicitor's chambers with *Light*wood. Were that possible, Wrayburn could provide his own, self-determining illumination within the enclosure of history. Keeping an eye on the family business by being metaphorized as "keeping the light up" (*OMF* 12, 145), incorporates two contradictory gestures: guardianship of interests, a basically defensive posture, is combined with the image of a searching, voyeuristic eye that ferrets out the secrets of the night while remaining publicly inaccessible save in its affect. The scanning beacon of Wrayburn's fantasy lighthouse bears an uncanny resemblance to Bucket's real "bull's eye" in *Bleak House* which sees into all of the novel's corners.

Would the *similar*ity (both ideologically and structurally) of subjects and objects in this "economy of the eye" suggest that the characteristic gaze is easily—too easily—reproducible? If the victims of some Other's gaze—to borrow the nomenclature of so-called French gaze theory—can achieve self-sufficiency only by making themselves into a (detached) illumination, then the Dickens' world is the scene of an ocular Darwinism. Liberation from an absent patriarch's gaze or will (the synecdoche of the gaze) would result only in the subjection of an Other to an equally absent gaze.[9] To be sure, at first glance (which could never describe the gaze!), the deployment of the searching eye seems entirely in keeping with the complicated notion of *play* (jouissance) which voyeurism occupies in the thought of Barthes and Kristeva, perhaps nowhere more pointedly than in John Chivery's adolescent love for Amy Dorrit:

> When he had played with her in the yard, his favourite game had been to counterfeit locking her up in corners, and to counterfeit letting her out for real

kisses. When he grew tall enough to peep through the keyhole of the great lock of the main door, he had divers times set down his father's dinner, or supper, to get on as it might on the outer side thereof, while he stood taking cold in one eye by dint of peeping at her through that airy perspective.

(*LD* I, 18, 255)

What conditions this characteristic attitude of the voyeur is precisely the extent to which it involves a double simulation. Although regarded as a "game," Chivery's activity is not that at all, since it is entirely dependent upon the absence of reciprocity, upon which any game, in its disjunctive determination of winners and losers, depends.[10] It is rather a ritual, disguising itself as a game in order to create the illusion of an Other to be overcome. Since Amy Dorrit and her erstwhile lover are entirely free to enter and leave the Marshalsea at will, the imaginary sequence of imprisonment and release is an attempt to bond love and rescue, to force her to need him, thereby controlling the conditions of her freedom.

But, paradoxically, the maintenance of the "game," is a function of *his* secrecy; once let out for real—as opposed to counterfeit—kisses, the "game" would be up. Or stated another way, the game is possible only when one or both of its participants is a non-participant. Once there exists a keyhole to be seen *through* for Chivery, a wonderful metaphor for puberty, there would be no *outside* in any case, but only a simulated outside. His gaze simulates her liberation, but at the price of his own imprisonment. In retrospect, Chivery's voyeurism seems not to conform to the traditional models of the mode of imaginative viewing, any more than does Miss Havisham's request that she be allowed to *look* at Pip's humiliations at the hands of Estella. In both instances, any mastery is compromised by its absorption within a ritual which confines the subject of the gaze: the young Chivery catches an ocular cold and Miss Havisham, after delighting in Pip's losses at cards, concludes the "game," by rehearsing her imprisonment in the guided walks about the solitary room that is her life. Visual domination is subtly democratized, so that the *voyeur in situ* is herself enmeshed within some larger economy of the eye. The youth's speculative stare in *Little Dorrit* is a simulation of that larger, "universal stare" (*LD* I, 1, 39) embodied in the sun that had "made the eye's ache" in the novel's opening chapter, illuminating a dark prison even as it shadows Rigaud's curious misogyny.

In so many of the novels Dickens is suggesting that love is possible only when an entirely simulated barrier—whose very simulation is suggested by a gossamer porosity that makes it into an absence—is erected so as to create a mediated, negotiable gaze. The barrier is both an obstruction and a channel for transmission of information, not unlike the trembling veils which Eve Sedgwick has located at the edges of conventional Gothic narratives.[11] Any transaction *across* the veil is determined by a *relationship* between absence and presence that is strategically obscured. The "economy" of production and consumption of the gaze is made possible by a (symbolic) porosity like that of paper money which allows us to "see" what is putatively "behind" it to some imaginary "ground." Yet, what occupies the position of the subject of the gaze, is already its object.

Hence, many of the social spaces which seem to be defined by walls or boundaries, when scrutinized more carefully, are truly defined by the *illusion* of inpenetrability, like the apparently barred windows of Satis House which, on second glance, are an "opening" in which Estella's welcoming eye appears. In fact, the ubiquitous prison in Dickens' work may participate in this problematic of the wall, since in reality, they too are porous. People can come and go easily into the Marshalsea from Bleeding Heart Yard, and it in fact functions as an "out-prisoner" prison. Magwitch escapes from the Hulks in *Great Expectations* and is just as easily recaptured. In *A Tale of Two Cities* even the dreaded Bastille is not at all impervious, if a Sydney Carton can easily deceive the guards and wives can signal messages to inmates. Newgate Prison, as horrible as it is, provides remarkably easy access to the outside world, since Jaggers must continually wash his hands precisely because the taint of the prison is as transportable as are its inmates. Some system of *compensation* would in fact seem to be operative. Acquitted of a potential capital offence by Jaggers's legal legerdemain, Molly, his servant, must have her symbolically manacled wrists on display for guests. To be freed is only to have the form of imprisonment changed. Could the prison itself, then, possibly be a fiction, a structure really no different from Wemmick's castle, say, with its defensive armor and repetitive practices? That which is structurally or legally "inside" is not readily distinguishable from the "outside," as Amy Dorrit quickly learns upon gaining her ostensible freedom:

> It appeared on the whole, to Little Dorrit herself, that this same society in which they lived, greatly resembled a superior sort of Marshalsea. Numbers of people seemed to come abroad, pretty much as people had come into the prison; through debt, through idleness, relationship, curiosity, and general unfitness for getting on at home. They were brought into these foreign towns in the custody of couriers and local followers, just as the debtors had been brought into the prison. They prowled about the churches and picture-galleries, much in the old, dreary, prison-yard manner. . . . They paid high for poor accommodation, and disparaged a place while they pretended to like it: which was exactly the Marshalsea custom. (*LD* II, 7, 565)

If the prison, that most thematically interior of Dickens' spaces, were a simulation, differentiable but only barely so, from other social enclosures, then the traditional notions of voyeurism and surveillance—some outside "standing in" so as to bracket an object—must be modified, so as to comprise an economy of exchange. In fact Michael Ignatieff has recently suggested that, contrary to the social pit that is our traditional view of the Dickens' prison, that institution by mid-nineteenth century had been fully appropriated by the ideals and disciplinary practices of industrial capitalism with the introduction of hard labor, self-maintenance, and above all, demand production at very low wages.[12] If accurate, then by 1850 the prison experience was not radically different from the most extreme conditions of working class life during the same period: hard labor at long hours; subsistence wages; lack of adequate ventilation and sanitation; and chronic overcrowding. Therefore, Betty Higden's pride aside, the outside was only barely differentiable from the inside no matter what one's class allegiances. If the prison only *simulates* a prison, then pride becomes a form of social censorship just as walls are.

If walls are really but simulated walls erected by the individual or society, then how are we to understand their role? Like many instances of opacity in Dickens, most present a surface upon which some channel is inscribed. Like writing itself (equally opaque in its environments like Chancery and its adjoining warren of legal copyists), most barriers are in fact tablets for repeated re-inscription. This "always-already reproduced" quality of spatial dividers endows them with the status of the palimpsest. Plornish's parlor wall would be a case in point; it is an already demarcated "marker: "

> This poetical heightening of the parlour consisted in the wall being painted to represent the exterior of a thatched cottage; the artist having introduced (in as effective a manner as he found compatible with their highly disproportionate dimensions) the real door and window. The modest sunflower and hollyhock were depicted as flourishing with great luxuriance on this rustic dwelling, while a quantity of dense smoke issuing from the chimney indicated good cheer within, and also, perhaps, that it had not been lately swept. A faithful dog was represented as flying at the legs of the friendly visitor, from the threshold; and a circular pigeon-house, enveloped in a cloud of pigeons, arose from behind the garden-paling. On the door (when it was shut), appeared the semblance of a brass-plate, presenting the inscription, Happy Cottage, T. and M. Plornish. . . .
>
> (*LD* II, 14, 630)

In place of the familiar sampler with "God Bless Our Home," the parlour wall is the space of a simulation upon which a fantasy is inscribed which converts the interior into a landscape.

Similarly, in both *Great Expectations* and *Little Dorrit*, the first product created by wealth is a simulation which reproduces the very form of money, a denominated surface negotiating between power and metonymic linkage. Pip's superficial "polish" is desired by the newly freed William Dorrit who tells his daughter, Amy, "I wish you, under the auspices of Mrs. General, to form a—hum—a surface" (*LD* II, 5, 533). Representation, in other words, does not come after objectivity or meaning as something supplementary. The designation by the human mind of a domain of objectivity requires representation and the condition of ideality is dependent upon representation. But, linguistic representation is constituted by and as a set of differences wherein each substantive term is constituted through an interrelation with other terms in the system and, because language is inseparable from a pragmatic context, language units refer to each other. Baudrillard's persuasive model attempts to substitute the notion of a "circulation" of signs which allows them to function referentially rather than as a set of objective correspondences between signs and things.[13] This accelerated flow of circulating signifiers is nowhere better illustrated than in Mrs. General's deportment drills involving the precise enunciation of "prunes" and "prisms" so as to contour her students' faces into the surface of a sound. "Prunes" and "prisms" share no material relationship, save a shape incurred upon production. Hence, the reader, like her students, is in the position of always "looking for" a relationship not immediately or fully accessible, not unlike the "What *larks*!" messages which Biddy transcribes in the letters from Joe to Pip.

The effects of simulation are nowhere better illustrated than in the spaces inhabited by the poor, which appear curiously "packaged" to the eye of the outsider. For they give every appearance of being as artfuly mimetic (and hence crafted as a resemblance to some model) as say, Magwitch's or Noah Claypole's idea of a gentleman. The simulational character of this extra-simulational reality, the extent to which its "outsideness" or "otherness" is shaped by a representational power that expels such majorities into an undemocratic silence, is surely one of Dickens' concerns. For social "position" is itself revealed as largely a rhetorical or simulational procedure of which Mrs. General's pronunciation drills would be exemplary. Banished from any prospect of self-determination, the poor in his novels are often both victims and manipulators of metonymic substitutions, displacements which illuminate their ontic status. Visible and invisible at the same time, the reader must gaze upon their spaces twice, for they are prey to a constant mutation, as make*shifts*:

> Genteel blinds and makeshifts were more or less observable as soon as their doors were opened; screens not half high enough, which made dining-rooms out of arched passages, and warded off obscure corners where footboys slept at nights with their heads among the knives and forks; curtains which called upon you to believe that they didn't hide anything; panes of glass which requested you not to see them; many objects of various forms, feigning to have no connection with their guilty secret, a bed; disguised traps in walls, which were clearly coal-cellars; affectations of no thoroughfares, which were evidently doors to little kitchens. . . .   (*LD* I, 26, 359)

So many of Dickens' notorious "no thoroughfares"—those geographic and psychological obstructions to passage to which Ned Lukacher has called our attention—are not real obstacles, but precisely what Dickens says they are, "affectations," simulated closures which call attention to their provisionality.[14]

One of these affective barriers "frames" a recruitment for Fagin in *Oliver Twist*. Following the defections of Oliver and Nancy, Fagin travels to the Cripples, an appropriately named public house, where he "sees" Noah Claypole and Charlotte, his companion. The scene is in some sense a "double" of one of the most memorably terrifying scenes in the novel, when Monks and the Jew gaze upon a recuperating Oliver through the lattice-window of Maylie's richly furnished bedroom and he awakens from a dream to see their faces. Here, Fagin hides behind a curtain which is not a curtain insofar as it conceals a channel, a pane of glass:

> He again applied his eye to the glass, and turning his ear to the partition, listened attentively: with a subtle and eager look upon his face, that might have appertained to some old goblin.
>
> "So I mean to be a gentleman," said Mr Claypole, kicking out his legs, and continuing a conversation, the commencement of which Fagin had arrived too late to hear. "No more jolly old coffins, Charlotte, but a gentleman's life for me: and, if yer like yer shall be a lady."   (*OT*, 42, 380)

Just as Magwitch seems visually possessed as he utters the incessant refrain, "Look'ee here!" (*GE* 39, 338) while fingering Pip and the material accessories he has "made," so Fagin, at the very moment that Noah Claypole simulates the gentleman, dis-simulates him in a double sense. Observed through the glass partition, Noah is bracketed and blackmailed (another kind of bordered narrative?), for Fagin learns that Noah's down payment on gentility, a twenty-pound note, has been stolen and payment stopped. In other words it is denominated as having been already discounted, part of an antecedent narrative that marks the hapless Claypole as in fact what so many of Dickens' would-be heirs are—agents or "carriers." By threatening to circulate that information (a form of over-writing that would foreclose the "currency" of Noah's currency by displacing it as gossip), Fagin instantiates the counterplot that subverts a simulated gentleman's plans. Fagin's spying dislodges Claypole from both his proper social position as well as his simulated position at the same time that Fagin becomes aware that criminality is both taught (in an established pedagogy) and learned, even when one thought he knew it all. Once having been so "viewed," Noah Claypole, like so many other characters in Dickens, becomes unwittingly an "Informer" (*OT* 53, 477).[15]

Obviously this particular visual economy has a number of ethical and philosophical implications. In the first instance, the body is a transparency, like money.[16] Intricated in simulation, both are vulnerable to being placed *under glass*, subject to a scrutiny by which we determine the counterfeit from the authentic. Just as Noah Claypole becomes a text for his potential recruiter who *reads* him as part of a larger narrative—which he can call upon later—so William Dorrit at one of Merdle's infamous dinner parties comes to see himself as the object of a reading by a lowly Chief Butler who "had him in his supercilious eye, even when that eye was on the plate and other table-garniture; and he never let him out of it" (*LD* II, 16, 678). Even those among the nether orders, who may not be literate, can or can be imagined to engage in, other types of ocular "readings" by the self-conscious. If one is always-already vulnerable to a reading by another which then may be circulated, then any notion of a private, detached self, is in jeopardy.

If my secret is like a monetary debt insofar as it must ultimately be settled or balanced under circumstances over which I may have limited control, then one is always on call (view). Public opinion, imagined as Nadgett's myriad eyes, becomes a mode of access to lives whose privileges are always in danger of being revealed as simulated. The traditional consumers of commodities or ideas are suddenly vulnerable to a newly empowered consumerism which tends to be less discriminating its voracious tastes, long pent up.[17] The socially elite can be levelled, even miniaturized, in what appears to be a "peek-a-boo" game, but which is in fact *work*, like that of the Doll's-Maker in *Our Mutual Friend*, carried out from beneath the carriages of the rich. If both bodies and money are hosts to a potential simulation, then a counterfeit note would find its corresponding palimpsest in the idea of criminality or illegitimacy. Clearly, the traditional puritan imagery of the "stain" carried by all of us as our share in Original Sin, could be easily absorbed within the monetarist model. Estella's dirty hands (the condition of both her birth and being "passed on" by Jaggers) is different from Pip's only because that "mark" is temporarily invisible in the novel's plot. Social *acceptance* is determined only after a *reading* that may displace one from *prop*-riety, even etymologically: the sense of self-sameness.

One can avoid a counterfeit circulation (or circulation-as-counterfeit) in Dickens in a variety of ways familiar to the most casual reader. A character can forcibly undergo a radical removal of the mark, the stain, by a cleaning like that offered the murderer, Sikes, in *Oliver Twist* when, bedaubed by Nancy's blood, he enters a public house only to be assaulted by the sales pitch of an itinerant stain-remover, the antidote to circulating stains:

> 'Wine-stains, fruit-stains, beer-stains, water-stains, paint-stains, pitch-stains, any stains, all come out at one rub with the infallible and invaluable composition. If a lady stains her honour, she has only need to swallow one cake and she's cured at once—for it's poison. If a gentleman wants to prove this, he has only to bolt one little square, and he has put it beyond question—for it's quite as satisfactory as a pistol-bullet. . . .' (*OT* 48, 426)

Or, alternatively, one can deflect the stain so that it can be read only as an absence, like the smear which Krook "becomes" under spontaneous combustion in *Bleak House*:

> "Ah!" returns Mr. Guppy. "See how the soot's falling. See here, on my arm! See again, on the table here! Confound the stuff, it won't blow off—smears, like black fat!" (*BH* 32, 505)

Perhaps the most elaborate solution to the problem of moral or financial staining in Dickens' political economy would be the transformation of one's own private stain or mark into something *readable*, over which he has some control. This is achieved by the Esther Summerson of *Bleak House* who, in a novel where everything from the megalasaurus in the antediluvian mud of the novel's opening pages, to Mrs. Jellyby's inky fingers, to Lady Dedlock herself, has an obsessive concern with the "stain and blot upon this place" (*BH* 41, 634), somehow manages to transform the stain of an illegitimate birth into a *text of her own*, that exists as a pleat within Dickens' more public, omniscient narrative. Her diary comes to approximate the rhythms and periodicity of speech rather than writing, and exists as a simulation of the polyphonic. The provisional quality of Esther's diary—it incessantly points to itself as a discourse under construction—seems to rival other instances of simulation:

> "Her close little sitting-room was prepared for a visit; and there was a portrait of her son in it, which, *I had almost written here*, was more like than life. . . ."
> (*BH* 38, 597, italics added)

Dickens' novel can only be totalized as a reproduction of a sequence of reproductions, a palimpsest under constant revision. From one perspective, Esther Summerson's diary represents the attempt to maintain the privacy of her stain in a novel where inscription and copying (and counterfeiting the copy) are so over-determined that even an inquest becomes an "Inkwhich" (*BH* 16, 276) to Jo the Crossing-Sweeper. In a novel where the referential antecedents of both people and writing are under continual pressures—Jarndyce versus Jarndyce has been under continuance for so long, that the instantiators of the original suit can neither recover nor be recovered—Esther tries ultimately unsuccessfully, to keep her corporeal and inscriptive *marking* private, so that one becomes synecdoche of the other.

If the body, money, and the author's paper are similar scenes of inscription, marked by stains and scratches which de-nominate them as ultimately recursive narratives that some voyeur stares *through* in order to read the past, Dickens' novels also, logically enough, pose the relationship between and among them as a problematic. Gaffer Hexam in *Our Mutual Friend*, accused by his former partner, Rogue Riderhood, of not merely reclaiming money from the bodies of the dead, but under cover, taking money from live bodies before killing them, poses this problematic as an economic question, one that resonates throughout Dickens' works:

> "Has a dead man any use for money? Is it possible for a dead man to have money? . . . How can money be a corpse's? Can a corpse own it, want it, spend it, claim it, miss it?" (*OMF* I, 1, 4)

Although superficially these questions would all invoke a negative response, the novel leaves the determination open to question.[18] The elder Harmon's will, as do the provisions of all wills, mandates the possession of money by a dead body, deployed so as to shape the lives of offspring as an authored narrative. What John Harmon-Rokesmith—having been apparently "killed for his money"—achieves by his counter-plot of dying into the eternal wakefulness of voyeurism through an assumed identity, is nothing less than the attempted separation of monetary value from flesh and blood. This is achieved by an inverse gesture to those we have been examining: notably, displacing the body from the center of an economic model which the novel originally proposes.

The elder Harmon's death-dealing, the symbolic re-animation of inorganic matter (the Dustmounds) into gold, is really of a part with Venus' "articulation" of human remains into the prosthesis of Weg or Gaffer's scavenging of the depths for the "meat and drink" of his children. The dead body *is* money and in the early part of the novel, wealth is either death-centered or concentrated in human remains. The *apparent death* of the voyeur-figure thereupon becomes the only direct access to real value, for it is the condition of both story-telling and the regenerative change that *creates* value. Like any good omnipotent narrator, John Harmon can in advance read the complete pattern and realize its "worth" by adding value. By remaining "dead" as the affianced John Harmon, he can win the affection of a mercenary Bella Wilfer who would otherwise have married him only for money. But it is surely worth noting that the voyeur hidden behind the veil of a simulated identity in one sense, supplants the absentee (dead) father as the capitalist investor in a marital project, but in another mimes his position. Voyeurism thus becomes a metaphor for "management" (both narrative and financial) from a distance, but a "management" which must ultimately identify itself by disclosing its cover. John Harmon's plot suggests then, that real value, that of life as opposed to death, is only discernible from some vantage point outside the body. Thus a novel that commenced by identifying the human body as the source of economic value and both scientific and police enquiry, concludes with the radical suggestion that only a state of suspended animation—a human life held temporarily "dormant" (*OMF* II, 3, 445) or in a condition such that, in the words of Harmon, "there was no such thing as I, within my knowledge" (*OMF* II, 12, 369)—which characterizes the successive immersions of Harmon, Rogue Riderhood, and Eugene Wrayburn, can induce a "life" to assume a value in exchange: the giving and receiving of love.

If we must read the voyeur in two antithetical ways (as a form of escape from a determining patriarch and as a supplementary, *simi*lar patriarch) and if the figure itself reads others "otherwise" (as both in themselves and as detached carriers of information), then the figure of the attached/detached eye in Dickens' political economy is paradigmatic of the ways we read. Reading with the pre-established assumption that the character (or work) is part of a larger whole that is coherent and well-structured has recently come under attack as a critical strategy that privileges strongly ideological interpretations, erases disturbing or "incoherent" details that might not "fit," and imposes on the text a conception of unity that may be neither relevant nor appropriate.[19] This kind of reading often colonizes or erases the marginal, by *seeing* them only as "clues" to some larger, that is, transcendent, concept of meaning. Considered in this light, the voyeuristic gaze in Dickens would seem to be accompanied by an understood (but unstated) query, like "Where have I seen him before?''—a question as likely to emanate from Dickens' late twentieth-century critics, with our obsessive interest in patterns of repetition, as from Merdle's Chief Butler. It is part of the disturbing effort to read *through* detail, in the process, of course, establishing textual desires as simulations of material desires, sharing a denial of the ''merely'' contingent.

Were poverty to become an entirely open text in this way, it would exist statistically in a form everyone could read, even those otherwise immune from the sights, sounds, and smells of the unwashed. And, in fact, mid-nineteenth-century England was in some sense deluged by the textualization of poverty exemplified in the proliferation of parliamentary reports and commissions bearing the names of men like Chadwick and Hutchinson, which subjected the poor to a new discursive, but only discursive, legibility. In *Bleak House*, the poor are similarly ''written in'' to the proceedings of Chancery, but are so distant from actually having their grievances heard, that the proceeds are consumed in the proceedings. Again, money would appear to be afflicted by the same entropic pressures as is *writing*: one gets no closer to a recovery of an original issue/claim. The role of mountains of writing in repressing, by infinitely postponing,[20] the ad*vocacy* of the disestablished is surely suggested both in the slow demise of a Gridley demanding to speak between the submission of affidavits, and in the blood which gushes from the space usually reserved for orality during Richard's attack. In Dickens' novels, as we have seen, to exist as a text-for-the-Other, behind the veils of writing, is often to cease to exist *in fact*. If one can be read at the expense of being experienced and vice versa, then to be ''open'' to an institutionally-mandated reading is, from another perspective, to be hidden.

The voyeur, however, can remove an object from circulation, re-insert him back into a regime of signs that might liberate him from some a priori experiential, ideological, or class position, or, do both simultaneously. Hence the best eyes *in* the novels—as one suspects, the best readers *of* Dickens—must come to read analogously to the way in which Inspector Bucket reads Jo the Crossing-Sweeper. For he neither patronizes Jo by attempting to buy off his attentions (Lady Dedlock), nor urges him to continually ''move on'' (the police), nor regards him as only or exclusively a threat to public health and safety (Dr. Allan Woodcourt). In Bucket's eyes he becomes a more or less permanent object of social and individual *attention*, intimately ''connected'' to a variety of social and ideological interests—in fact, as well-connected as the Dedlocks and their numerous relatives. Bucket is more aware than most that to conceive of the body as a disposable term, an object to be held in position, as a term of subservience, or in submission, is to bracket out the transformative capacity that the body possesses through work. Although Jo, as is true of so many victims of the voyeur's gaze, is inserted into the given institutions, he also forms those institutions, subjecting them to endless revision, and in *Bleak House*, even modifying them. What traditional instrumentalist deployments of the image (voyeurism) cannot afford to admit is a volatility or unpredictability of a body that it must ostensibly control by supplying its work with a goal towards which its movements and "productivity" must be directed, "plotted."

For Jo the Crossing-Sweeper, Bucket approaches the limits of Dickens' omniscient narrator in the sense that "he's in all manner of places, all at wunst" (*BH* 46, 690), but then so in his own way is Jo! The fact that "nothing escapes" (*BH* 53, 770) the ubiquitous eye of the abstraction that is Bucket, gives him a certain kinship with the state bureaucracy which employs him. For Bucket has been recruited, as members of the bureaucracy invariably are, from the middle and lower social strata which thereby detaches part of its membership from the rest of the population and links their fate to that of the dominant class. This might be exemplified in Sir Leicester Dedlock's easy appropriation of the inspector's services despite the fact that he is employed by the state. By an "adaptability to all grades" (*BH* 53, 777), even though the son of a footman and the brother and brother-in-law of those similarly in "service" (*BH* 53,777), Bucket represents not only a new kind of police surveillance, but a new social order, a genuine civil *service*.[21]

The great landed families, like the one which has controlled Chesney Wold for generations, enjoyed a monopoly of the production and reproduction of both genteel blood and British law (in their capacities as Members of Parliament), but it now gradually yields to those who will have a monopoly of information. In a Marxist analysis, the bureaucrat strives for the highest position so that the work itself is often subordinated to the attainment or maintenance of personal status, in such a way that the bureaucracy appears as a vast *network* of personal contacts and informants whose relationships of dependence are substitutes for relationships objectively defined by the division of labor or social class. This could again appear as similar to what exists among the criminal orders. It is in Bucket's interests to insure deniability for the very plot which he has authorised. But the deniability is combined, curiously enough, as part and parcel of the man's incredible adaptability to a plethora of social environments from Bagnet's parties, to Tulkinghorn's chambers, to public houses, to Sir Leicester's library and its sherry. In other words, state surveillance, a kind of institutionalized voyeurism, has some of the characteristic postures of the very over-determined patriarchy which its "findings" will ultimately subvert. In a novel filled with counterfeit wills, illegitimate children, and other stained reproductions, Bucket derives his power from the paradoxical modality of an absentee presence: "Time and place cannot bind Mr. Bucket. Like man in the abstract, he is here today and gone tomorrow—but, very unlike man indeed, he is here again the next day" (*BH* 53, 769).

In a novel where everyone appears to be defined by his or her relatioship to the recovery of an antecedent text (as producer, transcriber, interpreter, or beneficiary), Bucket dedicates himself almost exclusively to the metonymic, as opposed to the metaphoric, register, context-dependent and therefore unpredictable and indeterminate in his social "connections." He never writes anything down, but can form a near perfect imitation of Hortense's French accent. Again like Nadgett, his precursor in *Martin Chuzzlewit*, who as an absentee landlord keeps watch over a chaotic, phantom library at which Tom Pinch is "employed" as a cataloguer, so Bucket gains easy access to Tulkinghorn's secretive chambers, the titles of whose obscure books seem to have withdrawn into their bindings (*BH* 10, 182). Both use society's tendency to privilege values of the letter—closure, dedicated to the recovery of antecedence, iterable—to subvert the criminality or motives for criminality which it obscures. Bucket eschews both production and consumption of the written word, confessing that he is not poetical "except in a vocal way" (*BH* 57, 832). He is in fact so sensitive to sound that the "unusual slowness" and "curious trouble in the beginning" (*BH* 54, 784) which comes to typify Sir Leicester Dedlock's speech, denoting the onset of a stroke, is apparent to his ears long before any of the other characters are aware of the impediment.

It is altogether fitting that his network of informants is also largely oral. Within the compressed, densely populated lanes of Tom-all-Alone's, the narrow warren of copyist's streets adjacent to Chancery, or the equally recessed libraries within libraries which constitute the *cloture* of Tulkinghorn's services, the advent of a professional, institutionalized voyeur and the delivery system which he administers, disperses people and ideas along a "grid." This articulation of information as a "train" or "trail," Michel de Certeau, in another context, has termed a "local authority."[22] For, it forms a crack, like young Chivery's opening in the gate of the Marshalsea or Esther Summerson's diary under construction in the textually saturated *Bleak House*, in a system of enclosure. And, this subversive openness is narrated as a transparency to Bucket's eye (reception) or its symbolic antipode, the "bull's eye" (illumination):

"He had gone into every late or early public-house where there was light (there were not a few at that time, the road being then much frequented by drovers), and had got down to talk to the turnpike-keepers. I had heard him ordering drink, and chinking money, and making himself agreeable and merry everywhere; but whenever he took his seat upon the box again, his face resumed its watchful steady look. . . .'   (*BH* 57, 829)

Looking through the partially drawn blinds of a window at the guests of Tulkinghorn's large funeral, the city becomes a precursor of Mondrian's modern "grid-city," insofar as no space is any longer special or "proper." As Bucket and Esther Summerson cross, re-cross, and criss-cross the darkest suburbs, the optical economy is itself submitted to a code, translated into the plus and minus of a movement, not of sensation, but of cognition—in short, a moment of pure *relationship*:

"I know so much about so many characters, high and low, that a piece of information more or less, don't signify a straw. I don't suppose there's a move on the board that would surprise *me*. . . ."   (*BH* 54, 782)

Toward the end of so many of his novels, Dickens' "field" in some sense comes to be structured by signals, perhaps nowhere more obviously than in the concluding chapters of *Great Expectations* where disguises, wigs, household blinds, and even innocuous activities, like rowing on the Thames become part of a signalling apparatus designed to protect Magwitch from those in pursuit. Space exists as a consequence of the operations that orient it, situate it, and abet or hinder it in a polyvalence of conflictual programs or contractual proximities and agreements.[23]

If *Bleak House* begins as a novel of a singular place, even in its title, a place defined by and as "representative" inscription, it ends as a novel of space, a space like that in fact of the word when it is *caught*, like the train of thought or ideas, in the ambiguity of actualization. It no longer possesses any of the univocity or recoverability of a "proper": there are *really*, two Bleak Houses, two wills, two Pips. Hence the polycentrism of communicational, geographic, and personal coordinates in Dickens' novel would *appear* to lend its field some of the attributes of a state bureaucracy, which, as the possessor of "an unlimited number of eyes" (*BH* 22, 368), forms strategic bonds with certain institutions in alliance with which it works to prevent the formation of class or special interest unity. For, even were some provisional unity to be attained, the bureaucracy would preserve the principle of indetermination which characterizes a Nadgett or Bucket's movements. The "drift" in and out of consciousness both watchful and the object of a watchfulness to which Garrett Stewart has called attention in another context in Dickens, would describe Eugene Wrayburn or John Harmon-Rokesmith, but would not characterize either the young Chivery or Miss Havisham's voyeurism at all.[24] Neither Bucket, nor Nadgett, nor Harmon-Rokesmith would appear to have an objective existence separable from the *social* rather than merely ocular, form of power: "Pervad[ing] a vast number of houses, and stroll[ing] about an infinity of streets" (*BH* 53, 768). Assuming that for all these viewers, there is a tendency to transform the world into a totalized image constituted by the logic of its own "frame" (of exclusion), the implication would be that the "field" becomes one of ideological construction. Even if not a system of economically-determined domination, those charged with surveillance would constitute a sort of *I*nstitutional *S*tate *A*pparatus "avant la lettre," to pun on Althusser's intriguing nomenclature.[25]

But is the putative framing procedure an accurate description of the voyeur's production of the image? Instead of defending a "proper" interiority sealed off from an exteriority of social and cultural discourse—shared by the prison, a landed patriarchy, Bella Wilfer, or, say the "self" as a free agent with guaranteed rights that various liberalisms might advance—the concept of the subject is imagined as a complex of differential boundary relations where an internal subjectivity and an external social environment are tied together in a way that precludes a clear demarcation between the two. Because the material conditions of "viewing" are always changing, that thought to be external is revealed as internalized components of self-identity (cultural representations, institutional practices, social conventions like that of the *filiative* family). The presence of the "double" or shadow figure in Dickens, like the Doege Orlick of *Great Expectations*, is really a material em*bodi*ment of a "seam" in Pip himself, who exists a simultaneously self-identical and as Joe and Biddy's "second" Pip which "our" Pip wishes to adopt. The "self" internalizes its relations to others as he grows so that one's mature life is determined by refigurations of these internalized, inter-subjective relations.[26] This world of heightened differential relationships—physical, economic, narrative, insofar as it might embody the provisionality of point-of-view—would imply that the "other" is *always-already* contained within the self. If the concept of differential boundary relations in fact replaces the individual as a primary category of social life in Dickens' novels, then the deployment of figuration, the *re*visionary rhetoric of an ever-present eye, privileges situational as opposed to the "given" relationships of family or class. This constant refiguration signals a persistent materiality in any metaphoric ideal. The figural cannot escape a literality that is reproduced as a sequence of "false positions," for the propriety of the ideal is always questioned by the instrumentality or "agency" which communicates it.

Though wills and affidavits, and just perhaps Miss Havisham, can be in a "false position," neither Bucket nor Harmon-Rokesmith remain so for long. Even Dickens' least admirable voyeurs like the James Carker of *Dombey and Son* straddles representation (as an amanuensis for Paul Dombey, he writes letters over the owner's signature) and reproduction (of himself as a spy in others). Having installed the unfortunate Rob the Grinder (literally under the table) at Sol Gills' instrument shop, the truant reciprocates the surveillance as "he [Carker] suddenly encountered the round eyes of the sleek-headed Rob instantly fixed upon his face as if they had never been taken off" (*DS* 22, 308). Later asked to intercede for the elder Dombey in rebuking his wife, Edith, for her unwelcome strength of will, Carker, the ever-willing agent, dismisses even the possibility of being placed in a false position, by his employer's strange request: "*I* in a false position! . . . I shall be proud—delighted—to execute your trust" (*DS* 42, 599). And then, as if to show the mastery of an exchange economy, shared by most of Dickens' spies, the accountant "elopes" with Edith to the continent, duplicating the same gesture by which the elder Dombey had used a false love to effect the rescue of a woman unhappy in her family ties. Estrangement is reproduced as a second (false) marriage, but in such a way that marriage and separation are revealed as metonymic equivalents. In Carker's case, to execute a trust is to duplicate the trust, not to be an outsider at all: repetition is subversion.

How is it possible that a self-described voyeur can *never* be (structurally) in a false position, for almost by definition, that form of ocular investment appears as the "outsider looking in"? Dickens' earlier Nadgett may in fact ironically provide the clue rather than reading it. For in *Martin Chuzzlewit* the homeless itinerant who has "never closed my eyes" in his pursuit of Jonas Chuzzlewit as a perpetrator of a double murder, upon solving the mystery at a typical gathering of suspects and family members, points a finger to a man beside the window and in a loud voice,

'Murder,' said Nadgett, looking round on the astonished group. 'Let no one interfere.'

The sounding street repeated Murder; barbarous and dreadful Murder; Murder; Murder; Murder. Rolling on from house to house, and echoing from stone to stone, until the voices died away into the distant hum, which seemed to utter the same word!

They all stood silent: listening, and *gazing* in each other's faces, as the noise passed on. (*MC* 51, 866, italics added)

It would be impossible for knowledge to spread so quickly and return (constituting in effect a cycle, like the chain gaze in *Great Expectations*), unless it was in some sense *always-already* known. The spy's special kind of knowledge appears inseparable for *public opinion*.

Were this indeed the case, then the simultaneous freedom and imprisonment of the voyeur-figure in Dickens becomes more reasonable. Through his eyes, everyone and everything is potentially an informant, but once so regarded then the viewer too is limited, constrained to being a *representative* eye. At the beginning of *Bleak House*, Lady Dedlock's elusive movements and long vacations are a secret even to her husband and personal retainers, but not to the village merchants who cater to her taste in fashionable apparel and recognize that she has been abroad. They are understandably delighted to receive her custom, but in exchange, she becomes a subject of their discussion—what Dickens terms the "fashionable intelligence." At the end of the novel, tradesmen's gossip is reproduced in Bucket as *state intelligence*. Public opinion leads Bucket to a stain—a variant of what Lady Dedlock has termed "the stain and blot upon this place" (*BH* 41, 634)—which would suggest a confidence that the false reproduction of her life can remain enclosed, separated from public knowledge. Yet, from another perspective, public opinion *is* the stain, inseparable even in the novel's imagery, from the dripping weather, mud, and ink which touch everyone sooner or later.

Public opinion is both outside and inside "weather" in Dickens, apparently, whose career (and whose voyeurs) seem to bear a certain resemblance to that abstraction in John Stuart Mill's thought. Early on, Mill was the champion of the voice of public opinion as a potential liberating influence from the dominance of one or another social "estate." Free speech, its active ingredient, should never be embargoed, for unrestrained discourse alone was the guarantee of liberty for all. But, at some point, public opinion could detach itself from an anti-hegemonistic posture. Mill was perhaps less than entirely lucid regarding the causes of this transformation from a discourse, the exercise of which was a guarantee of freedom, to a discourse so overwhelming, that it threatened to stifle all minority opinion. His solution, however, was to attempt a benign control of public opinion by *subject*ing it to representation: this might explain the movement from *On Liberty* to *Representative Govenment*. Public opinion could detect a stain obscured by history or *stain* all that lies in its path. Oscillating between a metaphysical, determining ground and a discourse to be subjected to representation (counterfeited?) so as to "guide" it, public opinion participates in a political economy of the eye, insofar as it can either separate itself from an accepted *view* or *form* an acceptable judgment.[27]

Perhaps this accounts for the remarkable ability of eyes like those of Nadgett, Bucket, Harmon-Rokesmith, or even Eugene Wrayburn to form *a-filiative* "alliances" so easily. They either have no history or are attempting to escape it. Though none are "family men" in any sense, all nonetheless have an easy familiarity with either children or the down-trodden as well as the ability to gain the confidence of both the idle and the wealthy. Their distrust of writing, at least in its transitive manifestations, in favor of orality gives each the ability to join, circulate within, and exit from groups informally as a kind of *currency*, without referential appeals. Both synchronically and diachronically, they are not bound to traditional beginnings and endings, not unlike gossip itself.

To be sure, all of this suggests a certain relationship between the secret or the stain, considered in all of its ideological and discursive richness, as illegitimacy (a leaky penis), counterfeit (a leaky pen), a false entry into an accounting leger (a leak from respectability to living at the "margin"), or a written text riddled with gaps and seams, and the presence of the voyeur's eye. For all would embody the potential hemorrhage of subjects across barriers. If the stain is a mark that cannot quite be read, then the voyeur's is an eye that does not quite see; yet, both stain and eye constitute the presence of an absence. Both signal an oozing that is the potential exposure of the subject as not itself, and hence the possibility of infinite refiguration. Surely, the staining of inscriptive authority and the incriminating eye of the outsider-cum insider-cum outsider is the counter-plot *carried* within all of Dickens' plots, much, one suspects, as the stains of Warren's Blacking Factory are held within his more readable secrets.

In a seminal essay, Stephen Marcus has assigned the origins of Dickens' fear of being seen and its formative role in his novels to a specific childhood exposure to a father's gaze, a father who was simultaneously a figure of shame and a betrayer of his son's educational hopes.[28] And surely, the child in some "false position," be it intricated in a variant of the Freudian "primal scene" or otherwise, is a familiar trope in Dickens, as are adults forced to become children. The voyeur-figure, however, would represent one possible antidote, given his mastery of the simulation which defines social barriers: value is extra-familial, extra-corporeal and therefore always makeshift. The Dickens who was quite an accomplished amateur magician in later life learned to use simulation to deceive the eye into believing what it had not actually seen by a well-placed "blink."

At Warren's Blacking Factory, the scene of that youthful humiliation, the young Dickens was employed tying labels to pots of shoe polish, a product which removes the stains, scuffs, and knicks or work of social class, by . . . - *staining*. The same company, as one of the ironies of commercial history would have it, was among the first makers of household products in mid-nineteenth-century England to launch what we would now call a public advertising campaign, by imbedding posters into sidewalks. The placards, like the shoe polish, covered the stains of life's passageways, in a simulation of its application to human surfaces. The viewer had to look at his shoes when participating in the public discourse that was both censorship and an escape from censorship: not the Ghost's Walk, but close.

NOTES

The author wishes to acknowledge the assistance of John Jordan, Director of the Dickens Summer School at the University of California/Santa Cruz, who provided the venue where portions of this essay were originally delivered.

1. J. Hillis Miller, *Charles Dickens: The World of His Novels* (Cambridge, Mass.: Harvard UP, 1959).
2. Karl Marx, *Economic and Philosophical Manuscripts*, translated by Martin Milligan (New York: International, 1964), p. 167 ff. In Marx's succinct analysis paper money in fact appears as a "shadow" of its "ground," first forming a combination with and then detaching itself from what lies metaphorically "behind" it. A fiscal exchange system would thus depend upon simulations and dis-simulations.
3. Jean-Joseph Goux, *Freud, Marx: Economie et symbolique* (Paris: Editions de Seuil, 1973), pp. 53–56 explores an analogy between the "imaginary" in Marx and in Freud, where both fuel an economy of "compensation."
4. It is often forgotten that the conditions which Magwitch sets upon Pip's expectations include the demand that he "always bear the name of Pip" (*GE* 18, 165). Since Pip has in fact named himself by combining "Phillip" and "Pirrip," a clear impossibility since no one ever names himself, it is Magwitch's proviso as much as his money which forces the orphan to live a double life. His imaginary self is fixed, made permanent ("you will never become anyone else") at the same time that his expectations are constituted as a Future Imaginary ("you will become a gentleman"). Hence, he is held in the double bind of two contradictory simulations, a technique often used by artists like Aubrey Beardsley to engage a special kind of viewing.
5. Jacques Derrida, "Signature, Event, Context" in *Limited Inc* (Evanston: Northwestern UP, 1988), pp. 1–27. In Derrida's thought, writing retains its functioning, its "readability," despite the disappearance of any receiver. The presupposition of an iterability extending beyond *absence* gives it a continuity not defined by subject considered beyond *presence*. Paradoxically, this is often precisely the condition of Dickens' orphans who are, "engaged," without having any subjectiv-ity.

6. The ease with which *exposure* (even etymologically, "the putting outside of what is inside") unites simultaneously the "money plot" (the sudden openness to risk); the "public health plot" (Esther Summerson's vulnerability to smallpox) and the so-called genealogical plot (the revelation of paternity in unexpected places) would suggest that life beyond the gaze is not really to have a private life, but to have a public life not yet metastasized. The paradox of the analogy should not be lost on those interested in Dickens' social critique: our immunity to social illness is a false immunity, "acquired" by visually limited exposure (a kind of blindness). Only with complete public exposure, can the illness be controlled. In other words, Dickens' analogy has the effect of making *immunity* and *illness* simulacra of each other.

7. George Levine has, alternatively, addressed this combination of attention and detachment by identifying it as a tradition involving the so-called, cynical dilettante whom he associates with the rising interest in scientific observation instead of my emphasis on the abstraction of an indifferent personality. See George Levine, "The Hero as Dilettante: *Middlemarch* and *Nostromo*," in *George Eliot: Centenary Essays and an Unpublished Fragment*, ed. Anne Smith (London: Vision, 1980), pp. 152–80.

8. I am making a distiction between the flaneur or "gambler" as one who "plays" with time, as opposed to the bored individual who "loads" or stores time in the hopes that he might tap a hidden reservoir. In Dickens' works, the voyeur-figure often appears saturated, and this "waiting" often exists not as "waiting for," but "waiting in." See Walter Benjamin, *Gesammelte Schriften* (Frankfurt: Suhrkamp, 1972–85), eds. Rolf Tiedemann and Herman Shweppenhauser, Vol. 5, 1, 162–64.

9. Because "gaze theory" has recently been deployed (especially in gender criticism) in the analysis of forms of gender dominance and submission, it may be useful to reread the appropriate sections of *The Four Fundamental Concepts of Psychoanalysis*, trans. Alan Sheridan (New York: Norton, 1977). For Lacan, the gaze was useful in demonstrating a dialectic between the deictic and the distich, between pointing and screen. In the context of the space of the luminous, the viewer is not the surveyor—standing at some point outside the pyramid of vision—but caught within the onrush of light, the viewer is what blocks the light, interrupting its flow. In this interruption the "viewer," invisible to himself, enters the "picture" created by this light as a "stain" or blind spot, as the shadow cast by the light, its trace of deictic mark. From this place, the subject can neither see himself nor see the source of light: his position is that of dependence upon an illumination that both marks him (the deictic) and escapes his grasp (the distich).

10. I am here using Claude Levi-Strauss' distinction in *The Savage Mind* between *games* (which disjoin participants into winners and losers at the conclusion of a contest in which they had been equals) and *rituals* (which conjoin by assisting an "unequal" pre-initiate into a condition of equality with some priest or medicine man). The latter, insofar as it is mimetic ("do what I conduct and you will become a Christian") is ultimately more democratic.

11. Eve Kosovsky Sedgwick, "The Character of the Veil: Imagery of the Surface in the Gothic Novel," *PMLA* 96, no. 1 (March 1981), 255–70. The veil is a common device in Dickens' novels, perhaps most memorably used to create the false resemblance between Lady Dedlock and Hortense in *Bleak House* and again in the same novel, to "half hide" (but also half disclose) Esther Summerson's disease-ravaged face from/to her lover, Dr. Allan Woodcourt.

12. Michael Ignatieff, *A Just Measure of Pain: The Penitentiary in the Industrial Revolution 1750–1850* (Harmondsworth: Penguin, 1978), pp. 174–207.

13. Jean Baudrillard, *Simulacres et simulation* (Paris: Editions Galilee, 1981), pp. 48ff. Baudrillard finds a gradual evolution in the role of capital which in his analysis substitutes the structural form of value for the commodity form of value. In this new situation, the individual's labor power, body, unconscious, etc. are no longer primarily productive forces in a society, but rather "operational variables" mobilized by social institutions. One consequence is the birth of a kind of semiological idealism, whereby signs and the codes and structural dimensions that they deploy, gain some degree of autonomy.

14. Ned Lukacher, *Primal Scenes: Literature, Philosophy, Psychoanalysis* (Ithaca: Cornell UP, 1986), pp. 226–80.

15. Alexander Welsh, *Strong Representations: Narrative and Circumstantial in England* (Baltimore and London: Johns Hopkins UP, 1992) argues that the development of deductive logic as a philosophical discipline in the first quarter of the nineteenth century enhanced the status of circumstantial evidence, in the process transforming the linear spaces of the Victorian novel. Everyone exists both for himself and as a place-holder in some "master narrative" of which he is unconscious. In my analysis, this would constitute a *simulation* of mass production, industrial economies where "alienation" from some totalized product would constitute everyday life.

16. The frequency with which scarred or maimed bodies is encountered in Dickens' work is the subject of a marvelous essay by Helena Michie, " 'Who is this in Pain?': Scarring, Disfigurement, and Female Identity in *Bleak House* and *Our Mutual Friend*," *Novel: A Forum of Fiction.* Vol 22. 2 (Winter 1989): 199–212. Whereas in Michie's analysis, the scarred body becomes a metaphor of universal, non-corporeal pain, in mine the trope would suggest the provisionality of the *body* itself which is always "under construction," "articulated," to borrow Venus' own description of his work in *Our Mutual Friend*.

17. Harry Stone, *The Night Side of Dickens: Cannibalism, Passion, Necessity* (Columbus: Ohio State UP, 1992), especially pp. 246 ff. draws a relationship between cannibalism and Dickens' evolving interest in philosophies of necessity. Often in Dickens the recipients of payment in metal specie bite the particular coin in order to determine its authenticity. The circulation of bodies and its confusion (both as money and as a source of money) with food is a common motif, especially in *Our Mutual Friend*.

18. See Catherine Gallagher, "The Bio-Economics of *Our Mutual Friend*" in *Fragments for a History of the Human Body* III, ed. Michel Feher with Ramona Naddaff and Nadia Tazi (Zone: New York, 1989), 345–65. It is not obvious, however, that it is only men who have some extra-corporeal identity that enables them to remain "dormant" as potential voyeurs which would implicate misogyny in "doubling," since Miss Wade (*LD*) and Estella (*GE*) can similarly escape their bodies in reproducing the dependency which had previously defined their relationship to an Other.

19. Mieke Bal, "De-Disciplining the Eye," *Critical Inquiry* 16 (Spring, 1990): 506–31.

20. The proliferation of the "copy" may function both metaphysically and materially in Dickens, for copying and printing trades were reservoirs of vast pools of unskilled labor at wages often less than that of navvies. In 1861, almost one-fourth of London's lowest paid labor constituted this nether world stained by ink. See Gareth Steadman Jones, *Outcast London: A Study in the Relationship Between Classes in Victorian Society* (Harmondsworth: Penguin, 1971, pp. 21–25, 69–70.

There are many scenes in Dickens where the author's putative "share" in the production of writing is questioned, most memorably in *David Copperfield* where the mature David must "arrange" to have the passive Dora contribute by bringing him his pens and ink.

21. See D. A. Miller, "Discipline in Different Voices: Bureaucracy, Police, Family, and *Bleak House*," in *The Novel and the Police* (Berkeley: U of California P, 1988), pp. 58–106. In my analysis, Bucket is, like public opinion, both a public figure, and easily privatized which serves to make of him both an embodied and disembodied figure of discipline.

22. Michel de Certau, *The Practice of Everyday Life*, trans. by Stephen Rendall (Berkeley: U of California P, 1988), pp. 105–08.

23. In all of the attention directed to Dickens' "city" and its attendant spaces, no critic to my knowledge has suggested the extent to which the voyeur-figure is part and parcel of some post-modernist reconfiguration. In his work, the not-ground is a field or background that rises to the surface of the novel to become exactly coincident with its foreground. It is as if the field were ingested by the novel as a figure.

24. Garrett Stewart, *Dickens and the Trials of the Imagination* (Cambridge, Mass.: Harvard UP, 1974), is remarkably perceptive in discussing the representations of transcendence in Dickens' "death" scenes.

25. Louis Althusser, "Ideology and Ideological State Apparatuses," in *Essays on Ideology* (London: Verso, 1984), pp. 1–61. In Althusser, the knowledge process is viewed not as cognition, but as the production of "intellectual instruments." Theoretical ideology is a knowledge, but it exists only in the form of recognition (one "knows" the presence of the state only when he perceives himself as "hailed" by it in the way an innocent by stander is addressed by the police) rather than cognition. Hence the disappearance of the knower in knowledge or the speaker in language, a characteristic feature of Althusserian Marxism, lends it a remarkable applicability in the analysis of Dickens' voyeurs.

26. One of the best treatments of the figure of the "double" as the exteriorization of some internal conflict is that of Julian Moynihan, "The Hero's Guilt: The Case of *Great Expectations*," *Essays in Criticism* 10 (1960): 60–79.

27. Jurgen Habermas's work remains the best commentary upon the changing configurations of public opinion in Europe in the eighteenth and nineteenth centuries. His most concise elaboration is in *The Structural Transformation of the Public Sphere: An Inquiry Into a Category of Bourgeois Society*, trans. Thomas Burger with the assistance of Frederic Lawrence (Cambridge, Mass.: MIT P, 1991), pp. 121–38.

28. Stephen Marcus, "Who is Fagin?" in *Dickens: From Pickwick to Dombey* (London: Chatto and Windus, 1965), pp. 358–78, calls attention to a crucial scene in Dickens' childhood when one day, while at work affixing labels at the blacking warehouse (where a man named Fagin partially protected him as the son of a gentleman), beside a window open to the street, the sad youth beheld his father *looking* at him. In Marcus' psychoanalytically-inspired reading, the frequency of "hypnagogic" phenomena (that "dormant" condition between wakefulness and sleep) is partially explained by its deployment as a "screen memory" in situations where a child is simultaneously ashamed of being seen and protective of a "seer" who has in some sense betrayed him.

WORKS CITED

All citations from Dickens' novels, in the order of their appearance in the text, are from the following editions, designated by the appropriate abbreviation, followed by chapter and page number.

GE Great Expectations, ed. Angus Calder. Harmondsworth: Penguin, 1965.

TTC A Tale of Two Cities, ed. George Woodcock. Harmondsworth: Penguin, 1970.

DS Dombey and Son, introd. H. W. Garrod. Oxford: Oxford UP, 1964.

LD Little Dorrit, ed. John Holloway. Harmondsworth: Penguin, 1967.

MC Martin Chuzzlewit, ed. P. N. Furbank. Harmondsworth: Penguin, 1968.

OMF Our Mutual Friend, introd. E. Salter Davies. Oxford: Oxford UP, 1967.

MED The Mystery of Edwin Drood, ed. Arthur J. Cox with an introduction by Angus Wilson. Harmondsworth: Penguin, 1985.

OT Oliver Twist, ed. Peter Fairclough with an introd. Angus Wilson. Harmondsworth: Penguin, 1985.

BH Bleak House, ed. Norman Page with an introd. J. Hillis Miller. Harmondsworth: Penguin, 1985.

The Absent Jew in Dickens: Narrators in *Oliver Twist, Our Mutual Friend,* and *A Christmas Carol*

Jonathan H. Grossman

> The Jew is one whom other men consider a Jew: that is the simple truth from which we must start. . . . for it is the anti-Semite who *makes* the Jew.
> Jean-Paul Sartre, *Anti-Semite and Jew*

From Fagin in *Oliver Twist* (1837–39) to Riah in *Our Mutual Friend* (1864–65), Dickens' depiction of Jews has been seen as proceeding from an anti-Semitic stereotype to an apology.[1] However, this understanding of Dickens' Jews elides how Dickens' *narrators* engage the problem of narrating this racial and religious other. This elision has most obviously resulted in an institutionalized disregard for Dickens' final 1867 revision of *Oliver Twist*, in which he only selectively deleted the term "the Jew." Even the recent Norton Critical edition of *Oliver Twist* treats the 1846 edition of the text as authoritative, following the precedent established by the variorum Clarendon edition in 1966. If Riah is often misconstrued as the end point of Dickens' treatment of Jews, it is because Dickens' Jews have been mistakenly judged solely on mimetic grounds. In his novels, Dickens never constructs a Jewish character like his other more mimetic characters, who exist in context, which, in Dickens, means within a home or a community. In his scattered allusions to Jews, like the one waiting for Mr. Jaggers in chapter 20 of *Great Expectations*, the Jew is invariably in a public place.

In his extended depictions, Dickens explores Jewish identity not by attempting to depict Jewish life as George Eliot does in *Daniel Deronda*, but rather by constructing and deconstructing the problem of narrating (representing) a Jew. He repeatedly poses what Michael Ragussis calls "a question of the *representation* of the Jew and thereby recognizes the immense power of representation in shaping the English response to Jews."[2] Dickens' exploration of Jewish identity eventually comes to center not on his Jewish characters, but on his middle-class Christian characters and, finally, on his narrators' interaction with the represented Jew, on the narrating itself.

I

In *Oliver Twist*, the narrator introduces Fagin as "a very old shrivelled Jew, whose villainous-looking and repulsive face was obscured by a quantity of matted red hair."[3] Beyond physically characterizing Fagin as a villain, this introduction labels Fagin a "Jew" and then conjures up the evil stage Jew through the metonymic cue "red-hair," effectively directing the reader to a stereotype. Though Fagin is finally too complicated a character to be equated with the simplified stage Jew, the anti-Semitic sentiment persists with the narrator's incessant repetition of the epithet "the Jew" for the demonic Fagin. "Fagin, I fear, admits only of one interpretation," wrote Eliza Davis, an Anglo-Jew, to Dickens.[4] She left it to the literary critics to consider the nuances of this interpretation, which has generally meant pondering questions such as how Fagin relates to the possibility that Dickens himself might be anti-Semitic or how Fagin fits the Jewish stereotype or breaks with it. It almost seems tautological to say that the interpretations of Fagin as Jew invariably focus on Fagin. Yet, this critical assumption that Fagin should be the subject under inspection elides the differentiated dynamics of anti-Semitism within the novel, as presented by the rest of the characters, including the narrator. If Fagin admits only one interpretation, *Oliver Twist* as a whole presents a different textual problem for the interpretation of "the Jew." Beginning with an examination that applies to all the editions, including Dickens' 1867 revision, I will argue that *Oliver Twist* presents a system of anti-Semitism in which what is at stake is the naming of Fagin as "the Jew," rather than any references to what this label might mean.

At that same moment when Fagin is first introduced to the reader as a red-headed Jew, he is also frying sausages over a fire in his den, while several ·boys smoke and drink at the table. While the devilish toasting fork with which he cooks might reenforce a certain Jewish stereotype, the sausages distance Fagin from kosher Judaism. As it turns out, Dickens separates Judaism as a religion from Fagin's character.[5] More importantly, the odd, but cozy domesticity of the scene indicates how Fagin, in his "little community" (OT, 293) is not defined against the (underworld) society in which he lives. In contrast, other fictional Jews, such as Shakespeare's Shylock, Scott's Isaac, or even Dickens' Riah, are sharply defined as Jews by being outsiders to a Christian community. Fagin also never particularly identifies with other Jews. When the Jewish character Barney first appears, Fagin carries on silent communication with him as if they were in league, but, then, in the same scene, Fagin performs similarly covert signalling to Nancy (OT, 94–95). In fact, the lack of connection and association (only physical) between Barney and Fagin underscores Fagin's distance from a Jewish world. For Edgar Rosenberg, the distance of Fagin from a Jewish context dehistoricizes Fagin, making him timelessly terrifying, a "more nearly archetypal Jew-villain."[6] We might, however, also say that the distance between Fagin and Jewishness makes Fagin less Jewish, and therefore less an archetypal Jewish villain, than a Jewish cypher.

Filling in this cypher, this blank, the narrator employs the term "the Jew" to mean "Fagin." The narrator's perpetual references to Fagin as "the Jew" overwhelmingly outnumber the times Fagin is called by his actual name, so that by dint of repetition, the narrator effectively renames Fagin with this epithet.[7] Even though throughout the novel the narrator often modifies "the Jew" with denigrating adjectives like "wily" (OT, 120), the narrator circumscribes the Jewish renaming of Fagin to "the Jew," never straying into related tags for Fagin's Hebraism. Most importantly, Dickens restricts the term "the Jew" almost completely to the province of the narrator. The underworld characters call Fagin by his name. When Sikes first appears in the novel after being soaked offstage by a pitcher of beer, he growls out the one and only vocalization of the narrator's standard name for Fagin in the first thirty-five chapters:

> I might have know'd, as nobody but an infernal, rich, plundering, thundering, old Jew could afford to throw away any drink but water; and not that, unless he done the River Company every quarter. Wot's it all about, Fagin? (OT, 76)

Sikes uses "the Jew" here as his lead-off oath, rather than as a renaming per se. In contrast to the narrator, the term carries no more weight with Sikes, who never uses it again, than his many other curses of Fagin. For Sikes, "the Jew" is one descriptive term among endless derogatory and entertaining variations, not an alias. For the first thirty-five chapters, *Oliver Twist* establishes "the Jew" as a name for Fagin shared particularly between the narrator and the reader, indicative of a privileged, knowledgeable viewpoint (over the more limited viewpoint of the characters). Through repetition and limited circulation, the narrator's renaming of Fagin as "the Jew" becomes a charged, meaningful act, not because it particularly describes Fagin, but because it connotes an authoritative viewpoint, power.

"The Jew! the Jew!" (OT, 229) a frightened Oliver bawls after Fagin in the beginning of chapter 35. He has just seen Fagin spying in the window of the Maylie's country home. By this point in the novel, Oliver has already been kidnapped by Fagin once and has reason for his terror of "the hideous old man" (OT, 228). Oliver's terrified cry—"The Jew! the Jew!"—hardly surprises the reader; we understand his fear, and we know, through the narrator, who he means. Yet, when Oliver yells after Fagin "The Jew! the Jew!" what has been restricted for thirty-five chapters to the authoritative and omniscient province of the narrator prominently and loudly crosses over into the characters' milieu. Oliver, like the narrator, renames Fagin. Certainly, this slippage between the narrator's and Oliver's discourse reflects the narrator's close alignment with Oliver's perspective. More importantly, however, Oliver's cry reveals that he has knowledge without any apparent source, much like Oliver's knowledge of standard English. Until this point in the text, Oliver has only called Fagin "sir," and none of the other characters have referred to Fagin as Jewish, or "the Jew," in Oliver's presence. Yet, Oliver knows Fagin is Jewish, and he knows to rename Fagin as "the Jew." With his denomination of Fagin as "the Jew," Oliver claims his position in the middle class, with Mr. Brownlow, who also later deploys the term "the Jew" rather than Fagin's name.[8]

Responding to Oliver's shout, Harry Maylie "who had heard Oliver's history from his mother, understood it at once" (OT, 229). This understanding suggests either that Oliver called Fagin a Jew at the moment when he told his story earlier to a middle-class audience (consisting of the Doctor, Rose, and Mrs. Maylie) or that he was taught the epithet (by them) when he told his story. In either case, the renaming traces back to the first re-telling of Oliver's story, to its translation into a middle-class narrative for a middle-class audience. The reader is subtly assured that what Oliver recounts to his audience is no different than what the narrator recounts to the reader; in this story, "the Jew" is a token indicating knowledge of the story. When the servant Mr. Giles, who does not know Oliver's story, responds to Oliver's shout, he "was at a loss to comprehend what this outcry meant" (OT, 229). Though admittedly Giles would not have recognized the cry "Fagin!" either, "Fagin!" is not the cry; Giles' failure hinges on not knowing how the epithet "the Jew" functions in Oliver Twist's story. For the middle-class characters, "the Jew" becomes a shibboleth, a token, the possession of which indicates what the Doctor calls "possession of the boy's real story" (OT, 199), privileged knowledge, shared with the narrator.

When the middle-class characters evince their knowing solidarity with the narrator by calling Fagin "the Jew" and thereby announce their privileged possession of Oliver's story, the story, however, presents a mystery for both them and the reader. The mystery, appropriately, is that the cypher Fagin, "the Jew" after whom Oliver cries out, disappears completely. Before Oliver's outcry, at the end of chapter 34, Oliver drifts in that hazy state between sleep and waking, where "reality and imagination becomes so strangly blended that it is afterwards almost a matter of impossibility to separate the two" (OT, 228). With Oliver's perspective in this state of confusion, the narrator separates Oliver's dream from reality for the reader. Using the free indirect style, in which a character's private thoughts spill into the discourse of the narrator, the narrator follows Oliver into what is demarcated as a brief nightmare in which Oliver returns to Fagin's den. At this point, the text then presents two utterances from "the Jew" and "the other man" (Monks) that could either form part of Oliver's dream, or, what seems more likely, be "actual" quotations, which Oliver is incorporating into his dream. Indeed, the narrator reports that when Oliver awakes, "there stood the Jew!" (OT, 228). For the moment, the occurrences of the scene seem to be settled from the reader's perspective: Oliver drifts off into a nightmare and awakes to see Monks and Fagin in the window.

Yet, the first half of chapter 35 is taken up with an extensive description of exactly how impossible Oliver's visions could have been.[9] The evidence accumulates suggesting that Oliver dreamed the entire episode, and the mystery is perfunctorily dismissed by the narrator with the words, "after a few days, the affair began to be forgotten, as most affairs are" (OT, 231). At first, this strange reversal of Oliver's story seems rather pointless. The mystery never returns in the novel, and it is rather feeble to account for the engimatic disappearance of Monks and Fagin as an attempt to portray their extraordinary powerful criminal capabilities. The episode goes on too long and is pursued too minutely, and no argument can support the idea that the novel actually abruptly crosses into the genre of the fantastic here. All that is left is that the reader is uncertain about the truth of the episode. By creating this uncertainty, this little, unexplained "affair" not only casts doubt upon "the accuracy of what [Oliver] said" (OT, 230), but also upon the trustworthiness of the narrator that shares so deeply in Oliver's perspective. It is not that the narrator suddenly becomes untrustworthy. Rather, the narrator subtly signals that what seemed accurate before, might now be reinterpreted as part of Oliver's limited and uncertain perspective. The seemingly incongruous second half of chapter 35 bears out the narrator's shift away from Oliver's perspective, leaping abruptly from Oliver's story to a traditional, sentimental love scene between Rose and Harry. As soon as Oliver and the middle-class characters announce their alignment with the omniscient narrator by renaming Fagin "the Jew," the perspective of the narrator changes, broadening the story of *Oliver Twist* from Oliver Twist's story to a perspective that critically encompasses, rather than identifies with, these middle-class characters.

The middle-class characters continue to refer to Fagin as "the Jew," but now their renaming, rather than just straightforwardly aligning them with the omniscient narrator, also signals the use of "the Jew" as a badge of middle-class authority. When Nancy, an underworld character, meets Brownlow, a middle-class character, the naming of Fagin as "the Jew," "Fagin," "that man," and "this Jew," overtly operates to register the speaker's position:

> "But if—if—" said the gentleman, "he [Monks] cannot be secured, or, if secured, cannot be acted upon as we wish, you must deliver up the Jew."
> "Fagin!" cried the girl, recoiling.
> "That man must be delivered up by you," said the gentleman.
> "I will not do it! I will never do it!"....
> "You will not?" said the gentleman, who seemed fully prepared for this answer.
> "Never!"....
> "Then," said the gentleman, quickly, as if this had been the point he had been aiming to attain; ....
> "Then," pursued the gentleman, "this Jew shall not be brought to justice without your consent...."   (OT, 313–14)

In 1867, Dickens revises only the final "this Jew" to "this Fagin," tellingly leaving the initial occurrence of "the Jew," so that when Brownlow agrees to Nancy's request, he marks his acquiescence to her by referring to Fagin by name, while keeping the distancing modifier "this." These subtle name changes for Fagin underscore the chilling indications that (in any edition) Brownlow is manipulating Nancy here: he is not only "fully prepared" for her answers, it is even "as if this had been the point he had been aiming to attain." While Nancy acts, or rather speaks, in naive good faith, Brownlow uses rhetorical ploys to achieve his aims, wielding his anti-Semitic labels to master Nancy. Moreover, Brownlow's game is not given a moral justification here, as reflected by the neutral tags of "the gentleman" and "the girl" that mark the narrator's perspective. Though the narrator is hardly celebrating the underworld in this scene, the narrator no longer engages in the more dualistic moral judgments that characterize the narrator's earlier alignment with Oliver. Instead, the text explicitly represents the renaming of Fagin as "the Jew" as an act that does not carry any particular meaning in reference to Fagin himself, but rather that marks an authoritative, middle-class discourse of dubious trustworthiness.

In contrast to the middle-class characters, the underworld characters might play with an anti-Semitic stereotype, but they are not concerned with denying Fagin entrance to their drawing room. They do not use "the Jew" as a shibboleth. Earlier, when the middle class and underworld meet amicably for the first time, Nancy uses the epithet "the Jew" twice, but she makes it clear, as she does in the interview with Brownlow discussed above, that "the Jew" is not *her* name for Fagin. First, Nancy identifies herself to Rose as "the girl that dragged little Oliver back to old Fagin's, the Jew's" (OT, 271), apparently employing the term "the Jew" to identify Fagin for Rose. Even this occurrence is, however, excised in 1867, leaving Sikes as the only one of Fagin's intimates to refer to him as a Jew. Later in this conversation, Nancy uses the term "the Jew" when she quotes Monks, an occurrence that is appropriately not revised in 1867: " 'In short, Fagin,' he says, 'Jew as you are, you never laid such snares as I'll contrive for my younger brother, Oliver' " (OT, 272). Monks announces that being a "Jew" is irrelevant here. However, his own use of the term "Jew" (like his almost middle-class English) suggests an alignment with the middle-class characters, betraying his middle-class origin, but his mention of Fagin's name in the same breath serves to solidify his bond with the underworld. In a parallel moment later in the novel, Mr. Brownlow reminds Monks of his "own words to [his] accomplice the Jew" (OT, 336, also not revised in 1867). However, in contrast to Nancy, when Brownlow quotes Monks, the reference to "the Jew" is his own, a renaming and a signal—like the quotation of Monks with which he follows it—of his own perfect knowledge of the story and, thus, his own power over Monks. In contrast to the underworld characters, the middle-class characters use the term "the Jew" as an anti-Semitic badge of both their knowledge of the "truth" about Fagin and their own middle-class identity.

Dickens' revision of "the Jew" in 1867 confirms both the middle-class characters' use of "the Jew" as a shibboleth and the narrator's critical distance from their perspective. It is no accident that Dickens begins his revision with the first occurrence of "the Jew" after Oliver first recounts his story to a middle-class audience, consisting of the Doctor, Rose, and Mrs. Maylie. Dickens begins revising "the Jew" as soon as the middle-class characters share Oliver's story with the narrator and the reader, indicating that from thereon the epithet "the Jew" no longer distinguishes the perspective shared solely between the narrator and the reader. This beginning point shifts the epithet "the Jew" *out* of the narrator's province at the moment when the middle-class characters take possession of it. All the earlier editions depict only the shift of "the Jew" *into* the middle-class characters' discourse beginning with Oliver's cry "The Jew! the Jew!" Appropriately, Dickens refrains from revising any occurrences of "the Jew" at this second moment (of Oliver's cry), when the text depicts the token "the Jew" moving into the middle-class character's discourse, completing the exchange. In general, Dickens' revision of the epithet "the Jew" is not readily apparent in the text until Fagin himself first reappears, in chapter 39, after the shifts in the novel's system of anti-Semitism are already completed. Though the frequent excisions of "the Jew" (and insertions of "Fagin") from thereon do serve to humanize Fagin, they do not result from a change in Fagin, who continues his devilish machinations, such as recruiting Noah Claypole and encouraging Sikes to murder.[10] The change in the narrator's terminology is also certainly not characterized by a sudden shift away from the anti-Semitism of calling Fagin "the Jew" as if an abrupt self-conscious enlightenment occurs. The narrator continues to call Fagin "the Jew" occasionally. Instead, Dickens' 1867 revision confirms how, in all the editions, when Oliver's perspective comes into alignment with the narrator, the narrator removes to a perspective more critical of the middle class.

The most telling revision of 1867 occurs in the famous chapter "Fagin's Last Night alive," previously "The Jew's Last Night alive." In this chapter, which humanizes and complicates the doomed Fagin, Dickens excises every occurrence of "the Jew" except one:

> "Fagin," said the jailer.
> "That's me!" cried the Jew, falling, instantly, into the attitude of listening he had assumed upon his trial. "An old man, my Lord; a very old, old man!"
> "Here," said the turnkey, laying his hand upon his breast to keep him down. "Here's somebody wants to see you, to ask you some questions, I suppose. Fagin, Fagin! Are you a man?"   (OT, 363)

This brief, final, and isolated occurrence of "the Jew" in the novel specifically calls attention to how "the Jew" is not the name of Fagin, not the name the guard calls him and not the name with which Fagin identifies himself. This Jew has, after all, "driven . . . away" and "beat . . . off" the "venerable men of his own persuasion [who] had come to pray beside him" (OT, 361) earlier in this chapter. Instead, the last occurrence of "the Jew" underscores that the use of "the Jew" throughout the novel revolves around those voices, including the narrator's, that tell Fagin's story, not Fagin, who remains a Jewish cypher. As we have seen, the shift in the novel's system of anti-Semitism centers on and occurs between Oliver and the narrator. Through this shift, the narrator creates a new perspective, replacing the perspective that was previously constructed by the shibboleth "the Jew." Not only does the shift to a new perspective sustain the illusion that somehow the whole story is being specially conveyed to the reader by the narrator, but also the new perspective suggests a position outside and above a perspective aligned with Oliver, one with a critical distance from the middle-class perspective. This shift in narrative perspective suggests that Dickens might be using the narrator to draw his middle-class readers away from their own perspective and their own happy ending, to a more self-critical perspective and a more ambivalent ending. After all, the story goes on quite a while after Oliver is rescued, and though the novel's punishment of the underworld might be read simply as the successful completion of a middle-class victory, the narrator's shifted perspective helps elucidate why that punishment hardly seems a victorious celebration or a happy ending.

II

In *Our Mutual Friend*, Riah, "an old Jewish man,"[11] is introduced by the narrator as Fledgeby's secret. The secret, which the reader is let into from the start, is that Fledgeby hides his ownership and control of the Pubsey & Co. counting house behind Riah. By using terms such as a "venerable" and "graceful" to describe Riah, the narrator constructs the initial moral terms of the scenario: mercenary and "mean" (OMF, 328) Fledgeby is exploiting kind and humble Riah, or, more specifically, Riah's obvious Jewishness. By leading the reader into knowledge of Fledgeby's secret, the omniscient narrator allies the reader, implying that the reader, too, is in possession of the truth of this matter. Initially then, Dickens constructs a narrow moral perch from which the reader, aligned with the narrator, must condemn not only the stereotyping of Riah as Jew by Fledgeby's customers, but also the self-conscious exploitation of that stereotype by Fledgeby.[12]

Up until near the end of the third volume, both narrator and narrative contribute to exonerating Riah, opposing a villainous, selfish Fledgeby to a spiritual, altruistic Riah. However, the initial scenario Dickens constructs is ultimately complicated by Riah's complicity in Fledgeby's scheme. The actual moral complexity of the situation is brought to a climax when a reluctant Riah performs his role as ruthless moneylender in front of his young friend Jenny Wren. Jenny Wren is an appropriate audience because she assumes the simple fairy-tale opposition between evil and good, naming Riah her fairy "godmother" (OMF, 492), which has previously marked the narrator's judgment. In this scene, Fledgeby, once again enjoying his "secret joke" (OMF, 484), pretends to beg for clemency for his "friend" Twemlow while actually instructing Riah through word-cues, glances, and other clues that he "meant him to be racked" (OMF, 636). Though Riah searches "for any sign of leave to be easy with Mr Twemlow" (OMF, 636), Riah "read his master's face, and learnt the book" (OMF, 637). At this point, Riah's clear moral position in the novel clouds as he clashes with the reader's and narrator's united moral condemnation of Fledgeby, and he is instead placed in the ambivalent role of a reluctant participant in Fledgeby's crime. The moral terms that have been employed to describe Riah are exposed as simplistic, and Dickens personifies their shallowness in Jenny Wren. Acting as audience to Riah's performance, she presents the one possible reaction based on the old terms by fleeing the scene with the parting words: "You are not the godmother at all! . . . You are the Wolf in the Forest, the wicked Wolf!" (OMF, 638).

The reader, in firm possession of Fledgeby's secret, knows that Jenny Wren's moral outrage is a misreading of the scene. She mistakenly abandons her understanding that Fledgeby is master of Pubsey and Co. and accepts that Riah is acting on his own (evil) behalf. Her reaction to the scene is a mistake, which is pointed out by the narrator, who indicates the injustice of Jenny's outrage by noting that she equates the sympathetic Riah with her unredeemable, drunkard father. Jenny's misreading of the scene cannot then be accepted by the reader, who has trusted to the narrator. The reader is thus left wavering between condemning Riah for his role as front man and exonerating him because he is exploited by Fledgeby.

In order to pose and resolve the reader's question within the text, Dickens shifts Jenny Wren's position. Jenny Wren discovers that Fledgeby is indeed the master of Pubsey and Co., and thus she comes to occupy the same questioning, uneasy space as the reader. She seeks out Riah, "to ask [him] a question or two, to find out whether you are really godmother or really wolf" (OMF, 794), to affirm of the previous scene that "it did look bad; now didn't it?" (OMF, 795). After disappearing from the text for many pages and months (in both serial and narrative time), Riah finally has the opportunity to explain his position before effectively disappearing again from the text. Riah replies, in his longest and most important speech by far:

> "It looked so bad, Jenny," responded the old man, with gravity, "that I will straightway tell you what an impression it wrought upon me. I was hateful in mine own eyes. I was hateful to myself, in being so hateful to the debtor and to you. But more than that, and worse than that, and to pass out far and broad beyond myself—I reflected that evening, sitting alone in my garden on the housetop, that I was doing dishonor to my ancient faith and race. I reflected—clearly reflected for the first time—that in bending my neck to the yoke I was willing to wear, I bent the unwilling necks of the whole Jewish people. For it is not, in Christian countries, with the Jews as with other peoples. Men say, 'This is a bad Greek, but there are good Greeks. This is a bad Turk, but there are good Turks.' Not so with the Jews. Men find the bad among us easily enough—among what people are the bad not easily found?—but they take the worst of us as samples of the best; they take the lowest of us as presentations of the highest; and they say 'All Jews are alike.' If, doing what I was content to do here, because I was grateful for the past and have small need of money now, I had been a Christian, I could have done it, compromising no one but my individual self. But doing it as a Jew, I could not choose but compromise the Jews of all conditions and all countries. It is a little hard upon us, but it is the truth. I would that all our people remembered it! Though I have little right to say so, seeing that it came home so late to me.".... "Thus I reflected, I say, sitting that evening in my garden on the housetop. And passing the painful scene of that day in review before me many times, I always saw that the poor gentleman believed the story readily, because I was one of the Jews—that you believed the story readily, my child, because I was one of the Jews—that the story itself first came into the invention of the originator thereof, because I was one of the Jews. This was the result of my having had you three before me, face to face, and seeing the thing visibly presented as upon a theatre. Wherefore I perceived that the obligation was upon me to leave this service."
>
> (OMF, 795–96)

For this speech and for his resignation from Pubsey and Co., Riah regains the name "godmother" from Jenny Wren. However, her simplistic resolution of the situation now appears as shallow and childish (she is, after all, a child!) as the response she gives to Riah's speech that her "idea" of Riah's situation "is as large now as a pumpkin" (OMF, 796). In fact, she has little idea of the implications of Riah's speech. For in this speech, Riah not only admits his own imperfect morality, his willingness to compromise "his individual self," but also explains how he has had to give up the possibility of acting as an individual and has had to begin performing for what he sees as Christian-prejudiced eyes, which exist even in the apparently unprejudiced Twemlow and Jenny: "I always saw that the poor gentleman believed the story readily, because I was one of the Jews—that you believed the story readily, my child, because I was one of the Jews.'' What Riah discovers is that he must review the scene ''as upon a theatre,'' that he must perform as if in the theater where the image of Shylock and the stage Jew reigns. In other words, he must act in response to a representation. In order to discover this, he has adopted the vision of the Christian onlookers, as suggested by his careful syntax: ''I was hateful to myself in being so hateful to the debtor and to you.'' Moreover, by emphasizing again and again how he has ''reflected'' on the situation, how he has thought it out carefully, alone on his roof-garden, his symbolic spiritual mountaintop, he suggests the depths of his moral reasoning and considerations in *opposition* to Jenny Wren's quick moral conclusions, which grow in quick bounds from the size of a ''marble'' to an ''orange'' to a ''pumpkin'' (OMF, 794–96). Riah's speech tacitly suggests that she and society have failed him, that she has not given proper reflection (in both senses of the term) to his situation, but forced him instead to act, not as a complex individual, but as a character in a fairy tale, as a response to a representation, or, as Riah puts it, a ''sample'' and ''presentation.'' Unlike Pancks in *Little Dorrit*, who, in a similar predicament, rejoins the general community simply by proclaiming in a public square his rejection of the Patriarch's secret rent gouging, Riah cannot simply rejoin the community; he was never part of it.

For Jenny Wren, Riah appears simply to have returned: ''welcome back, dear godmother!'' (OMF, 795). However, as Riah suggests in his speech, he can return only upon the condition that he appease her moral stance, as is quickly underscored when Jenny unwittingly confirms her own prejudices, interrupting Riah as he says ''it is the custom of our people to help—'' with the words ''Oh! Bother your people! . . . If your people don't know better than to go and help Little Eyes [Fledgeby], it's a pity they ever got out of Egypt'' (OMF, 797). Interrupting this ''debating'' (OMF, 797), a messenger brings a malicious, anti-Semitic notice from Fledgeby that Riah is fired. Dickens writes:

> 'Well, godmother,' said Miss Wren, as they remained on the steps together, looking at one another. 'And so you're thrown upon the world!'
> 'It would appear so, Jenny, and somewhat suddenly.'
> 'Where are you going to seek your fortune?' asked Miss Wren.
> The old man smiled, but looked about him with a look of having lost his way in life. . . .   (OMF, 797–98)

What is striking about this conversation, in which Jenny Wren echoes the melodramatics of fairy tales, is that Riah has hardly been ''suddenly'' thrown out, as he says. He has mentioned on just the page or so before that he has resigned and that his last day is, in fact, the very next day (OMF, 796). Thus, Dickens complicates the assumption that it is simply through being suddenly fired that Riah has come to have "a look of having lost his way in life," for by his own account he has been waiting to leave for months. What, perhaps, is sudden and recent for Riah is the loss of Jenny Wren (and by extension Riah's Christian audience), who has failed to understand and rectify the implications of Riah's lengthy speech and with whom the "debating" is now over. What, perhaps, accounts for Riah's lost look is not the loss of his miserable, petty position from which he has already resigned, but rather his conclusion that he must act "as upon a theatre" in accordance with the audience's expectations. Through Riah, Dickens thereby paradoxically reveals that Jewish identity is, in part, formed through a response to (Christian) representations, such as his own.

When Dickens suggests that Riah is doomed to act as a sample, he has, in a sense, constructed within his novel a microcosm of his own literary predicament as an author in relation to the Jews. For much as Fledgeby effectively and authoritatively narrates Riah's actions, creating a fiction of Riah for his Christian audience, Dickens also constructs Riah for the reader. Caught in the same exploitative mode as Fledgeby, Dickens subverts it by portraying it. Dickens does not make a mimetic attempt to construct a Jew, as George Eliot does in *Daniel Deronda* by "realistically" depicting multiple Jewish personalities and milieus. Instead, he personifies his novelistic and linguistic dilemma in Riah. Dickens' audience seems to suffer for it; the common reaction to Riah as a character is that he is hollow and artificial. However, disdaining Riah's artificialness and judging him as unconvincing (unrealistic) misses the point. Paradoxically, Riah's failure to be convincing can be seen as something of a success in terms of Dickens' attempt not to depict a Jew, but rather to represent the impossibility of doing so. Riah, representing Dickens' Jews, will always be both literally and metaphorically in public spaces; the home of the Jews remains off-stage, a vague place where Lizzie Hexam can find refuge, but the narrator cannot follow.

III

Inasmuch as Fagin is a cypher and Riah is a representation of the impossibility of depicting Jews, Dickens does not construct a realistic Jewish character in his novels. It is not that he never depicts some single perfect Jewish character, as if some kind of absolute, essential Jewish character exists, but rather that he never constructs a Jewish character like his mimetic characters, who exist in the context of a home or a community. Unless, perhaps, ironically a Jew at home and in the community is suggested by the character Ebenezer Scrooge.

In *A Christmas Carol*, Scrooge is never referred to as Jewish.[13] Yet, more than just the overall scenario of a conversion at Christmas time suggests that Scrooge's Jewishness might haunt this text. In *The Lives and Times of Ebenezer Scrooge*, Paul Davis quite rightly points out how the naming of the characters links Ebenezer and Jacob to the Old Testament, and the Cratchits to the New Testament.[14] The awkward twists in the text are even more suggestive. For example, in the beginning of *A Christmas Carol*, the following cryptic exchange takes place after Scrooge rudely rejects his nephew's invitation to Christmas dinner:

> "But why?" cried Scrooge's nephew. "Why?"
> "Why did you get married?" said Scrooge.
> "Because I fell in love."
> "Because you fell in love!" growled Scrooge, as if that were the only one thing in the world more ridiculous than a merry Christmas.[15]

In this exchange, Scrooge seems to answer his nephew's question with a non sequitur—"Why did you get married?" However, the exchange makes sense if Scrooge is Jewish: a Jewish uncle sees his (Jewish) nephew's celebration of Christmas dinner as a direct result of his marriage to a Christian. Certainly, missing Christmas dinner was a regular event for Scrooge, who never went home for the Christmas holidays as a child. Though the text suggests that his father's heartlessness kept little Scrooge in school, Scrooge's Jewishness would explain not only why he never went home, but also why he tells the Ghost of Christmas Present that he has *never* celebrated Christmas. Moreover, at that most tragic moment, which is also presumably the most guilty moment for Scrooge as a Jew, when Scrooge enters the Cratchit's home with Christmas Future and the death of the Christ-figure Tiny Tim is revealed, Peter Cratchit is (mis)reading from the Bible:

> " 'And He took a child, and set him in the midst of them.' "
> Where had Scrooge heard those words? He had not dreamed them. The boy must have read them out, as he and the Spirit crossed the threshold. Why did he not go on? (CC, 75)

In this interrupted Biblical quotation, Peter substitutes "He" for the King

James's "Jesus," changing the quotation so that it reads as if it were about God setting Jesus "in the midst" of the Jews, placing Scrooge in the position of the Jew who should profit by it. More to the point, the interruption pointed out by the odd question "Why did he not go on?" is completed:

> And said, Verily I say unto you Except ye be converted and become as little children, ye shall not enter into the kingdom of heaven. (Matthew 18:3)

The instruction off the page is to "be converted." As Marley advises Scrooge in the beginning, suggestively closing the difference between "regions" and religions: "it [comfort] comes from other regions, Ebenezer Scrooge, and is conveyed by other ministers, to other kinds of men" (CC, 20).

The text's suppression of Scrooge's Jewishness would also help to explain why Scrooge's conversion is incomplete. In the end of *A Christmas Carol*, the persistence of Scrooge's dark sense of humor reveals his continued difference, qualifying his supposedly successful conversion. Before his conversion, Scrooge exhibits nervously sarcastic humor, as when he says to Marley's Ghost, "You're particular—for [to] a shade" (CC, 17). This dark sense of humor persists in the end colored only by the fact that if Scrooge is depressive in the beginning, he is manic in the end. His final, frightening, ferocious joke on Bob Cratchit, in which he comes in early to work in order to catch Bob coming in late, reveals just how different he still is from Bob. After "giving Bob such a dig in the waistcoat that he staggered back,"

> Bob trembled, and got a little nearer to the ruler. He had a momentary idea of knocking Scrooge down with it; holding him; and calling to the people in the court for help and a strait-waistcoat. (CC, 86)

Bob is clearly not attuned to Scrooge's merry making. Scrooge's jokes are still not meant for the amusement of others, but rather for himself. His jokes, articulating the uneasy space between himself and society, reflect in their nervous releases how Scrooge's isolation from the novel's community is unbridgeable and, perhaps, partly unwritten. Perhaps because the possibility of Scrooge's Jewishness troubles, but never enters, the narrator's discourse, the narrative cannot fully resolve Scrooge's predicament. For while Scrooge's conversion is supposed to make him one with the Cratchits, in the end, like Riah, he cannot join the community, suggesting that there is more to the narrator's conception of Scrooge's isolation than can be rectified by simply changing his miserly, selfish ways.

IV

Paradoxically, the Jewish figures in Dickens turn out to be more like Jewish silences than Jewish constructions. Yet, the absence of mimetic Jews in Dickens is not a lack, to be mourned as a failure of representation. Dickens' constructions of Jews should be understood as meaningful and complex Jewish silences. When Fagin acts as Jewish cypher, his silent Jewishness forms the center for an entire structure of anti-Semitism. When Riah acts as Jewish sample, his apparently loud Jewishness actually announces Dickens' complex silence on Jewishness, his paradoxical inability to portray a Jew, even as he portrays a Jew. The possibility of Scrooge's Jewishness exists only under erasure, but this silent Jewishness might haunt the narrator's discourse, complicating Scrooge's "full" conversion. Jewishness does not enter Dickens' text in mimetic form, but rather as silence that generates meaning.

Considering Dickens' treatment of the Jew chronologically reveals an increasingly sophisticated use of a narrator who paradoxically does not narrate the Jew. Certainly, the original edition of *Oliver Twist* (1837–39) shows Dickens at his most unsophisticated; despite the complex circulation of the token "the Jew," it still serves as a persistent, racist label for Fagin. Then, in 1843 in *A Christmas Carol*, traces and hints of Dickens' suppression of a racist construction of Scrooge perhaps disrupt his narrative. The creation of Riah in *Our Mutual Friend* (1864–65), though traditionally considered merely Dickens' beneficent portrayal of a Jew, actually reveals and portrays Dickens' attempt to confront his own authorial position in relation to portraying exploiting the Jew. Finally, the 1867 revision of *Oliver Twist* suggests that rather than simply saving his narrator (and himself) from charges of racism by excising every occurrence of "the Jew" in the novel, Dickens manipulates the naming and narrating of "the Jew" to construct a system of anti-Semitism within the novel, hinging on a shift in the narrator's perspective that calls attention to this anti-Semitism, to the use of "the Jew," even as it fails to escape it.[16] As a group, these different narrators present increasingly complex representations of the power of narrating a racial and religious other. By returning full circle to the revising of *Oliver Twist*, Dickens ends his major considerations of the Jew with the hopefulness implied by revision. However, he also ends up rather recondition, centered on his narrator, at the level at which representation is constructed. For at the same time that Dickens' novels rightly reveal that the representation of Jews is what shapes British understandings of Jewish identity, they also naively suggest that their readers must pay careful attention to the manufacturing of that representation over the representation itself, to the story of the production of the image over the image, an unlikely focus in the chilling daily economy of anti-Semitism.[17]

NOTES

1. See, for example, Edgar Rosenberg's authoritative work *From Shylock to Svengali* (1960) or Deborah Heller's more recent "Jews in Dickens's *Oliver Twist* and *Our Mutual Friend*"in *Jewish Presences in English Literature* (1990).
2. "Representation, Conversion, and Literary Form: *Harrington* and the Novel of Jewish Identity," 115. In this important article, Ragussis revises the "critical position accepted for several decades now . . . that the tradition of Jewish portraiture in English literature is consistently naive and unself-conscious in its production of stereotypes" (113–14). However, for Ragussis," 'the novel of Jewish identity' attempts to articulate, investigate, and subvert *The Merchant of Venice*'s function as the English master text for representing 'the Jew' " and in doing so "exposes the ideology of conversion, both as literary strategy and cultural institution" (114). I am not concerned here with understanding Dickens' narration of Jews as part of a novelistic tradition that self-consciously re-views Shakespeare's Shylock, nor am I concerned with the trope of conversion, which Ragussis authoritatively explores in *Figures of Conversion,* the book that follows up this article.
3. Charles Dickens, *Oliver Twist*, ed. Kathleen Tillotson (Oxford: Clarendon Press, 1966), 50. All further references will be cited in the text, indicated by an "OT." This edition has the textual variants of different editions footnoted. My quotations and references to chapter numbers will follow the 1846 edition that the Clarendon presents. Though I ignore several very minor differences, such as the omission of the article "a," my quotations of the 1846 edition always appear the same in the 1867 edition, unless I specify otherwise. For my references to Dickens' revisions in 1867, see the footnotes of the Clarendon edition.
4. From Cecil Roth, *Anglo-Jewish Letters*, 305. Ironically, this Jewish woman's criticism of Fagin eventually contributes to Dickens' creation of yet another Jewish man (Riah). Though Riah is called a "godmother," the truly absent Jew in Dickens is female.
5. Dickens points out this separation in his reply to Eliza Davis, writing that Fagin "is called 'The Jew', not because of his religion, but because of his race." See Roth, 306.
6. *From Shylock to Svengali,* 116.
7. I am not claiming that other name substitutions are not made. However, even when the narrator is employing other names, "the Jew" is usually more prominent, as in this passage:

> From this day, Oliver was seldom left alone; but was placed in almost constant communication with the two boys, who played the old game

with the Jew every day: whether for their own improvement or Oliver's, Mr. Fagin best knew. At other times the old man would tell them stories of robberies he had committed in his younger days: mixed up with so much that was droll and curious, that Oliver could not help laughing heartily, and showing that he was amused in spite of all his better feelings.

In short, the wily old Jew had the boy in his toils. Having prepared his mind, by solitude and gloom, to prefer any society to the companionship of his own sad thoughts in such a dreary place, he was now slowly instilling into his soul the poison which he hoped would blacken it, and change its hue for ever.   (OT, 120)

The narrator is literally split into the two voices in the two contrasting paragraphs here, as reflected in the naming of Fagin. Two alternative names for Fagin, "Mr. Fagin" and "old man," overwhelm the term "the Jew" in the first paragraph, but when the narrator re-interprets the picture of Oliver in less sympathetic and less complicated terms in the second paragraph, "the Jew" returns to its dominant position. In this paragraph, the narrator dubs Fagin "the wily old Jew," leaving little doubt as to whether the narrator's use of "the Jew" is anti-Semitic.

8. In a related scene earlier in the novel, Oliver reveals that he understands that middle-class identification is predicated on not just a certain treatment of Jews, but on their exclusion. After Mr. Brownlow marks Oliver entrance into his middle-class home with "a complete new suit, and a new cap, and a new pair of shoes" (OT, 83), Oliver himself establishes his middle-class identity by giving his old clothes "to a servant who had been very kind to him: and ask[ing] her to sell them to a Jew: and keep the money for herself" (OT, 84). As he watches "the Jew" through the "parlour-window," Oliver (mistakenly) feels he is finally safe, his insider status defined by the outsider, Jew (OT, 84). He must, however, still exorcise Fagin, his own Jew.

9. In brief: (1) Fagin and Monks could not have fled without being seen by Harry (OT, 229–230); (2) "in no direction were there any appearances of the trampling of men" (OT, 230); (3) two days of "inquiries" after anyone having seen the men around the neighborhood surprisingly turns up nothing. "It must have been a dream" and "This is strange!" (OT, 230) comments Harry appropriately.

Even George Cruikshank's sketch is situated between the two readings of Oliver's story. Cruikshank draws Oliver *sleeping* at his desk, with Monks and Fagin looking in the window, rather than Oliver actually seeing Monks and Fagin. If his sketch at first seems to confirm the presence of Monks and Fagin while Oliver dreams, by the middle of chapter 35, the picture can only be said to confirm his dreaming.

10. Harry Stone rightly criticizes the idea that Dickens' excisions of "the Jew" were part of an attempt to humanize Fagin that occurs in the chapter "Fagin's Last Night Alive." In "From Fagin to Riah: Jews and the Victorian Novel," he writes:

> Dickens' excisions of "the Jew" were not confined to the penultimate chapter of *Oliver Twist*, but were a consistent feature of his revision from Chapter XXXIX on—almost forty per cent of the chapters in which Fagin takes an active part. As a matter of fact, Dickens was exercising "the Jew" in many of the scenes . . . [regarded] as Fagin's most demoniacal

and archetypal. The changes in the penultimate chapter of *Oliver Twist* therefore have nothing whatever to do with Dickens' supposed shift, in the condemned-cell scene, from an archetype [stereotype of a Jew] to a human figure; either the shift occurred two-thirds of the way through the book (an untenable assumption in the light of Fagin's actions in the last third of the novel) or the changes must be explained by something other. . . .   (251–252)

What matters is not so much that Stone mistakenly suggests that Dickens' revision of "the Jew" begins in chapter 39, an error Tillotson points out in her introduction to the Clarendon edition (OT, xxxix), but that Stone writes of this "something other":

> As for the excision of "the Jew" in *Oliver Twist*, I can give no conclusive explanation of why they suddenly begin when they do, although I suspect the answer is biographical and bibliographical rather than archetypal.
>   (252)

He goes on to "conjecture" about the timing of the printer's proofs and speculate about other incidental possibilities that might have reduced the starting point of Dickens' change to a matter of happenstance. However, he presents no evidence that Dickens began his revision randomly. It is unlikely that Dickens would deem it acceptable to revise radically a random section of his novel, making it inconsistent with the rest of the novel, without some thought as to the placement of his change—even if he only had part of the proofs.

11. Charles Dickens, *Our Mutual Friend* (New York: Penguin, 1981), 328. All further references will be cited in the text, indicated by an "OMF."

12. Some critics, such as Harold Fisch, read Riah as an apology for Dickens' anti-Semitic characters simply by noting that Dickens presents a benevolent Jewish character in Riah. Focussing on the type of relationship Dickens constructs for Fledgby and Riah, Fred Kaplan moves beyond this formulation, pointing out that "Reversing the historical stereotype, [Dickens] depicts Christianity as responsible for the fiction of the materialistic perversion of the Jew in Christian culture" (472). As I will show, the text goes on to complicate even this complex, initial reversal of an anti-Semitic stereotype.

13. Investigating the possibility that Scrooge is a Jewish character lacking only the explicit appellation implies that other characters in Dickens might be thinly veiled caricatures or portraits of Jews, for example, Uriah Heep. However, because characters with stereotypically Jewish traits that are Christian, like Fledgeby, do more to subvert anti-Semitic stereotyping than confirm it, seeing a veiled Jew or a racist portrait in every character with stereotypical Jewish traits is incorrect. Therefore, my consideration of Scrooge avoids equating the stereotype of a Jew with the representation of a Jew. Scrooge's miserly ways are suggestive of a racist Jewish stereotype, but the occasional clues and cues for reading Scrooge as a Jew that the text of *A Christmas Carol* provides are what suggest how this text, like all texts, operates through silence and effacement as well as explicit description.

14. However, in Davis's interpretation, Scrooge is not a Jewish figure, except as "an imitation of Christ," and the story is a "retelling of the original Christmas story" (80, 81).

15. Charles Dickens, *A Christmas Carol* (New York: Bantam Books, 1986), 9. All further references will be cited in the text, indicated by a "CC."
16. I am not actually concerned with the extent to which Dickens was self-aware or simply acting "unconsciously" in his textual manipulations. Whether his progressively complex narrators are a conscious or unconscious product makes little difference, it seems to me. Our unconscious behavior and judgments amount to nothing less than the unquestioned and larger part of our personality and are equally, if not more, that which we call our "selves."
17. I am grateful to Nina Auerbach and Elisa New for their comments on this article.

WORKS CITED

Davis, Paul. *The Life and Times of Ebenezer Scrooge*. New Haven: Yale UP, 1990.

Dickens, Charles. *A Christmas Carol*. New York: Bantam, 1986.

———. *Oliver Twist*. Ed. Kathleen Tillotson. Oxford: Clarendon, 1966.

———. *Our Mutual Friend*. New York: Penguin, 1981.

Fisch, Harold. *The Dual Image*. London: World Jewish Library, 1971.

Heller, Deborah. "Jews in Dickens's *Oliver Twist* and *Our Mutual Friend*." *Jewish Presences in English Literature*. Eds. Derek Cohen and Deborah Heller. Montreal: McGill-Queen's UP, 1990.

Johnson, Edgar. "Dickens, Fagin, and Mr. Riah: The Intention of the Novelist." *Commentary* 9 (1950): 47–50.

Kaplan, Fred. *Dickens, A Biography*. New York: William Morrow, 1988.

Lane, Lauriet. "Dickens' Archetypal Jew." *PMLA* 73 (1958), 94–100.

———. " 'Oliver Twist': A Revision." *Times Literary Supplement* 20 July 1951:460.

Modder, Frank. *The Jew in the Literature of England*. New York: Meridian, 1960.

Naman, Anne. *The Jew in the Victorian Novel*. New York: AMS Press, 1980.

Ragussis, Michael. *Figures of Conversion: "The Jewish Question" and English National Identity*. Durham: Duke UP, 1995.

———. "Representation, Conversion, and Literary Form: Harrington and the Novel of Jewish Identity." *Critical Inquiry* 16 (Autumn 1989), 113–43.

Rosenberg, Edgar. *From Shylock to Svengali: Jewish Stereotypes in English Fiction*. Stanford: Stanford UP, 1960.

Roth, Cecil, ed. *Anglo-Jewish Letters*. London: Soncino P, 304–09, 1938.

Sartre, Jean-Paul. *Anti-Semite and Jew*. Trans. George Becker. New York: Schocken Books, 1965.

Stone, Harry. "From Fagin to Riah: Jews and the Victorian Novel." *Victorian Studies* 2 (1959): 223–253.

Dickens, Bakhtin, and the Neopastoral Shepherd in *Oliver Twist*

David Wilkes

> "Who could continue to exist where there are no cows
> but the cows on the chimeny-pots; nothing redolent of Pan
> but pan-tile; no crop but stone crop?"
> —Mr. Pickwick

At the Middlesex House of Correction near the Saffron Hill district in London—an area notorious for its high murder-rate and dense criminality—prison magistrate Benjamin "Sheep-shearing" Rotch used to insist upon "bringing live sheep into the [Coldbath Fields] prison, day after day, for demonstrations and practice in the art of shearing" (Collins 54, 69). One of the things this odd combination of place and practice suggests is a working relationship between the criminal and the pastoral, a relationship that is clearly inscribed in Dickens' *Oliver Twist*. At the very center of this novel about crime, class, poverty, and apprenticeship is a figure who embodies the mores and habits of Virgilean pastoralism while simultaneously displacing these same values and practices from their traditional literary settings. Thus at the beginning of *Oliver Twist*, we find Fagin caring for his lost sheep, those stray and discarded little boys who would inevitably fall prey to starvation, brutality, disease, and neglect. In taking on the values and practices of the "feminine rural" while residing in the "masculine urban" (Gail David 229), Fagin deploys what Bakhtin might call the power of neopastoralism when he herds, refreshes, and intructs his flock of pickpockets. Such behavior cuts directly across the demarcations of traditional pastoralism and identifies *Oliver Twist* as a text loaded with novelized characters and practices (Bakhtin 3–41). In fact, by the time the novel closes, Fagin has undergone several novelizing transmutations of his own: once a nurturing victimizer who preyed upon helpless lambs,

Fagin eventually becomes a type of neopastoral Lamb who is himself sacrificed in the "struggle of genres" (Bakhtin 5).

I

Critical opinion has long been divided as to where Dickens acquired his pastoral images and characters. Roselee Robison, for example, has asserted that "Dickens' acquaintance with the pastoral mode derives largely from his reading of English authors, notably Shakespeare and Goldsmith" (409). Raymond Williams then adds William Blake to Dickens' list of bucolic influences when he notes the similar way in which both authors transform "pastoral images" into "elements of a general condition. The simplifying contrast between country and city is then decisively transcended" (149). And Rosemarie Bodenheimer has found a number of other critics who have heard "Wordsworthian echoes" and seen "Genesis imagery" in Dickens' novels as well.[1]

Yet there is evidence to suggest that Dickens may have actually taken his initial inspiration and pastoral imagery directly from his own Latin studies, during his impressionable stay at the Wellington House Academy, Hampstead Road, from 1824 to 1827.[2] Under the direction of his Latin master, Dickens had "distinguished himself enough to carry off the Latin prize one year" (Ackroyd 108–09). The significance of this boyhood achievement is often underestimated or even entirely ignored, but perhaps this schoolboy's prize does mark the beginning of a studied fascination with things classical and hence pastoral, for rather than "show[ing] few signs . . . of having been influenced by Roman literature" (Johnson 44), Dickens may have allowed his creative genius to feed upon that early Latin influence. In any case, as Peter Ackroyd has recently chronicled, Dickens is later to be found "consulting the works of Virgil" (109):

No doubt, in the seventh or perhaps eighth volume [of the Pilgrim Edition of *The Letters of Charles Dickens*], Dickens's letter to Frank Stone, dated 31 May, 1855 will be printed; this is the letter in which Dickens refers to his consultation of Vergil and thus proves that he did, after all, study Latin during his school days. (Ackroyd 1095)

Perhaps in addition to studying the requisite sections of Cicero's *de Senectute*, Ovid's *Metamorposes*, and Virgil's *Aeneid*, the young Dickens also read some of Virgil's *Eclogues*, in particular, eclogue seven wherein a singing match between Thyrsis the shepherd and Corydon the goatherd takes place using a plot line with very Dickensian overtones. Additionally, the inventory of books taken from Dickens' library in 1844 suggests that he had an ongoing fascination with Latin texts and ideas, for among the collected neoclassical works of Pope, Dryden, Johnson, and Goldsmith were a copy of Ovid's *Metamorphoses*, a *Dictionary of Latin Phrases* compiled by W. Robertson and dated 1824 (the year Dickens enrolled at Wellington House Academy), a copy of Johnson's *Plautus* translated by Bonell, a Latin dictionary, and an edition of the *Life and Letters of Cicero* (*Pilgrim Edition* 710–26).[3] Thus, although it may be impossible to know the full extent to which Dickens drew upon the images, themes, characters and cadences of Roman literature and language, there can be no doubt of the pastoral outcroppings in his writings, especially since "none of his novels fails at some point to incorporate pastoral imagery" (Burgan 313).

II

David Thuente's assessment of "the generic features of pastoral narratives" will provide an initial point of reference for taking a quantitative look at Dickens' use of pastoral motifs (247). As a genre, traditional pastoralism is centrally informed by "the virtuous nature of the simple life, . . . the harmony between man and nature, . . . [and] the contrast between city and country life" (249). The "psychological root of the pastoral," according to Renato Poggioli, is concurrently said to manifest itself as "a double longing after innocence and happiness" which are "only to be recovered . . . through a retreat" (1). For nineteenth-century British writers in particular, the innocence, happiness and simplicity of the Golden Age are then relocated in a contemporary version of the pleasurable place wherein the harried individual can find relief from the pressures of his or her complex world. More often than not, this pastoral retreat is "set apart in space from the great world beyond, isolated by thick trees or imposing hills that function as agents of circumscription" (Squires 15). Idealized and so "stripped of its coarsest features," the pastoral refuge is "made palatable to urban society" (Squires 18). Dickens certainly does experiment with this type of escapist pastoralism as Pickwick's sojourn at Dingley Dell, Smike's edenic vision in *Nicholas Nickleby*, Nell's bucolic wanderings throughout *The Old Curiosity Shop*, and "Boythorn's rustic retreat" in *Bleak House* all attest to (Deirde David 83). Yet critical opinion has long been mixed regarding the "haven-of-rest quality" engendered by these bowers, edens, alcoves, and retreats (Thuente 249). While some find Dickens' escapist pastoralism believable, others cannot get beyond the "embarrassing falseness" of such "extremely flat and banal" pastoral set-pieces.[4] Referring specifically to *Oliver Twist*, Steven Marcus has concluded that "escape from society into an idealized, non-existent 'little society,' a refuge in the country where it is almost impossible to imagine how life goes on, is the least satisfactory part of the novel" (91). Marcus's comment typifies the critical response to Dickens' placement of flat pastoral characters in beatific worlds very much unlike our own. Moreover, it seems that even Dickens himself was dissatisfied with the strained plausibility of his pastoral images, which may have compelled him to find new ways of incorporating what is good about the pastoral with the writing of his urban novels. And perhaps this dissatisfaction also explains why neopastoral forms began emerging so early in his career, and why they continued to appear as Dickens uses the pastoral as a means of understanding the growing ethical complexities of urban life.

That "a distinctly Victorian transformation of the pastoral genre" produces neopastoral forms is explained, in part, by a process of "absorption and adaption" that fuses "shepherds, flocks, and loci amoeni" with their "contemporary equivalents" (Hunter 3–4). In transforming "the pastoral into the Victorian idyll," Hunter has described the Bakhtinian process of "novelization" wherein a weaker genre is consumed by the more dominant novel in the "struggle of genres" (3–40):[5]

> We have already said that the novel gets on poorly with other genres. There can be no talk of a harmony deriving from mutual limitation and complementariness. The novel parodies other genres (precisely in their role as genres); it exposes the conventionality of their forms and their language; it squeezes out some genres and incorporates others into its own peculiar structure, reformulating and re-accentuating them.   (Bakhtin 5)

Thus, in *Oliver Twist*, it is the aggressive novelization of the pastoral that produces the text's neopastoral outcroppings. It is the reformulation of a genre, and not the mismanagement of its tropes, that deliberately creates the bucolic mutations and hybridizations found time and again in Dickens' novels.

What is more, these novelized results manifest themselves in *Oliver Twist* as odd, pseudo-pastoral scenes, characters, tones, and settings which do not fit neatly into the escapist category represented by the Maylies and their country retreat. Rather, the subsumed genre experiences a new kind of transgeneric movement:

> They become more free and flexible, . . . they become dialogized, permeated with laughter, irony, humor, elements of self-parody and finally . . . the novel

inserts into these other genres an indeterminacy, a certain semantic openended-
ness, a living contact with unfinished, still evolving contemporary reality . . .

(Bakhtin 7)

Set free from the strictures of its own genre, the novelized pastoral or "neopastoral" openly declares itself through the "parodic stylization" of conventional shepherds, sheep, and shepherding practices (Bakhtin 301). There is,
for example, that shepherd of the dead, Mr. Sowerberry, the comic/gothic
undertaker who functions as the final overseer of the Poor Law's gruesome
work. In fact, Sowerberry gathers together those that do not survive "the new
system of feeding" and inters them, although "the prices allowed by the
board are very small" indeed. "So are the coffins" replies Mr. Bumble and
both men enjoy the grave joke (Dickens 23). The pastoral pun on "sour
berry" indeed provides a comedic gloss on the grim reality of the undertaker's
work, wherein the "sower" has to "bury" his dead little "pips" in order to
make a living. Later on in *Martin Chuzzlewit*, Dickens associates the rural
sport of "berrying" with yet another undertaker and his two daughters, the
Misses Mould, who discover that there is more to life than "playing at ber-
ryins" (404). At any rate, Sowerberry's ensuing conversation with Mr. Bumble, another novelized shepherd who abuses the poor while wearing a jacket
with Good Samaritan buttons on it, marks yet another place in the novel
where the reader is satirically confronted with "the plight of children born
into the early phase of the Industrial Revolution" (Paroissien 14). Victimized
by "parish overseers" and "cruel employers" alike, these children often
"fled from the harsh conditions and brutal treatment" of their oppressive
situations into a life of crime (14). What they find in the slums of London is a
"gallows-labyrinth" that offers "a kind of coziness and hospitality otherwise
unavailable. It beckons its victim onward; it also threatens death" (Maxwell
73). At the very heart of this labyrinthine enclave is a genuine provider and
an overseer whose hospitality (a central tenet of the traditional pastoral code)
and "green language" are both parodied by his criminal lifestyle (Williams
127–41). The pastoral activity of playing games is also novelized into a
series of criminal contests wherein Fagin succeeds in coaxing Oliver into
participating. And in Fagin we also find that "crucial tension develop[ing]
between the external and internal man" that further identifies him as the
text's most novelized character, a walking indeterminacy whose presence as
a neopastoral shepherd evolves from provider to twisted Christ-figure as the
struggle of the genres continues to remake his pastoral image (Bakhtin 37).

III

Fagin has long been "one of Dickens's most puzzling characters" (Marcus 358). Yet why has "this demonic, disgusting and monstrous old man . . . [been] so fascinating, so comic, even so winning in his abominable wickedness"? (378). Perhaps Fagin is just a memory or an experience—a "condensation, decomposition, displacement, reversal or multiplication" of the past—that Dickens has successfully transformed "with gusto and delight" into a character in a story (Marcus 375, 378). Or perhaps we are captivated by the "perverse charm" of Fagin's "ambivalent figure" (Duffy 417; Bayley 87); afterall, Dickens himself regarded Fagin "with a loathing so fascinated as to be [a kind of] half horrible enjoyment" (Johnson 1.282). At least part of the fascination stems from what Dickens has called the "attraction of repulsion. . . . [that] law of our moral nature, as gravitation is in the structure of the visible world," that is activated by certain macabre events such as public executions, traumatic accidents, or criminal activities (qtd. in Collins 248). (Dickens later capitalizes on this attraction during his public reading of Nancy's murder and Sikes's "haunted flight and death" [Johnson 552]). When this strange "attraction" is localized in the pastoral shepherd, it creates an irresistible character which Renato Poggioli has identified as the bad "pastor":

> Instead of protecting their herds, or guiding them forward to greener pastures, they mislay and corrupt them. Their worst sin is perhaps their betrayal of the pastoral calling, a calling that demands from them, even more than from other Christians, a life of simplicity and humility, of obscurity and poverty. They replace the Imitation of Christ with the Imitation of Satan and are easily tempted into ambition and cupidity, striving after power and wealth, honor, and pomp. Thus they become both the scourge and the shame of their flock: not shepherds but wolves in sheep's clothing, or black sheep.   (122)

Without question, Fagin is a defiler of souls whose worldly desire for power and wealth causes him to abuse his flock. And his life is brought to a close via the ignominy of the gallows. What is more, the criminal and the pastoral converge here in the image of the corrupt shepherd since lawbreaker and leader-as-black sheep both feed into the "attraction of repulsion" mystique that surrounds Fagin's darker side.[6]

But to see only this sinister dimension is to reduce Fagin to a flat, melodramatic stereotype and thereby skip over his import as a marginalized character. Andrew Ettin has shown that outsiders do occasionally show up in the bucolic mainstream: "They appear infrequently, but the pastoral tradition includes renegades and cagey scoundrels, whose crimes, appropriate to their rank and environment, involve sneakiness and trickery, the small-scale private vices, petit larceny rather than grand theft . . ." (159). But these are type-cast villains, not shepherding protagonists who displace our cultural expectations about good and evil as Fagin does. In fact, it is Fagin's condition as social misfit that engages the reader's interest and, in part, identifies him as a neopastoral shepherd. A man literally among boys, Fagin is a generational outcast who subsequently chooses not to make himself known to anyone at all. Like the treasure box he so cunningly watches over, his inner being is jealously guarded from public view. Equally estranged are Fagin's adult subordinates—Nancy, Betsy, Bill Sikes, and Toby Crackit—all of whom mistrust their overseer, and with good reason: he cleverly manipulates them for his own personal gain. When Harry Stone labels Fagin as a "renegade Jew" who maintains his distance from both the underclass Barney and the "venerable men of his own persuasion," he clearly affirms Fagin's role as an ethnic pariah (235; Dickens 407).[7] In sum, Fagin is a genuine outcast who has no spouse, no lover, no family, no real friends—not even a skulking dog.

In his introduction to *Oliver Twist*, Humphry House discusses how the outsider's sense of alienation is rooted in Dickens' own repressed feelings of abandonment, which stem from the author's well-known childhood experience at Warren's blacking factory. Certainly, Dickens the writer and Fagin the criminal are essentially psychodynamic reflections of the same desire to belong, and no doubt Dickens "knew no security and no tenderness" during his six-month period of loneliness (x). When these repressed feelings find their way into Fagin's own acute sense of alienation, they too feed into the attraction created by Fagin's twisted character: thus it is victimization *and* the lurid life of the criminal that stimulate the reader's curiosity. For Fagin's desire "to belong" to a community—a surrogate family brought together by "the shadow of the gallows" (Maxwell 80)—subsequently lends a ring of authenticity to his creation of a "domicile" for orphaned boys (Dickens 91); and given the alternative world of Bumble and the Patriarchal Board, Fagin's den ultimately translates into more than just a criminal's hideout, and his kindness, into more than just a criminal's ploy.

Similarly, when Fagin offers Nancy the safety of "his own home," he again reveals that side of himself which is strangely compassionate—that "tiny soft place in his black heart" which denotes the "natural Fagin" rather than "the slimy reptile" (Crotch 95; Lucas 51).

> You have a friend in me, Nance; a staunch friend. I have the means at hand,
> quiet and close. If you want revenge on those that treat you like a dog—like a
> dog! worse than his dog . . . come to me. I say, come to me.   (341)

It is certainly true that Fagin has previously used Nancy, and that his hatred
for Sikes has adulterated the "innocence" of his proposition. Yet in spite of
their past (and abusive) relationship, Fagin nonetheless has known Nancy a
very long time and indicates this when he uses the "green" language of
neopastoralism. Tapping into Nancy's "connecting feelings of human warmth
and community, in a time of real dispossession," Fagin appeals to her need
for security (Williams 140). That is to say, Fagin reasserts his role as Nancy's
neopastoral shepherd when he offers the girl his hospitality, "the highest
of all pastoral virtues" (Poggioli 252). True to the Bakhtinian process of
domineering reformulation, love and lechery are seen to coexist in the same
novelized shepherd.

Nor is this the first time that Fagin has extended such hospitality to someone
in need. Several chapters earlier, Fagin had offered "board and lodging, pipes
and spirits" to a couple of complete strangers, Noah Claypole and his comic
lover, Charlotte:

> [You] are as safe as you could be. There is not a safer place in all this town
> than is the Cripples; that is, when I like to make it so. And I have taken a fancy
> to you and the young woman; so I've said the word, and you may make your
> minds easy.   (323)

While "inquir[ing] after some of his young pupils" at the Three Cripples
Inn, Fagin discovers these two countrified strays and subsequently offers them
suitable lodging and sustenance (320). Yet even more significantly, Fagin
offers the weary travellers the security of his presence and the comfort of his
favor bestowed, which again identify him as a neopastoral host who makes
his "guests" feel right at home.

Of course, the stray most affected by Fagin's neopastoral hospitality is
Oliver himself who is first met by one of Fagin's emissaries, the Artful
Dodger. Practicing his mentor's brand of hospitality, Jack Dawkins first sees
the famished Oliver in Barnet's High Street and calls to him by using a
greeting with pastoral overtones: "Hullo, my covey!" As a phrase that is
"used of an intimate or associate" which also suggests "a brood or hatch of
partridges" (and "a family"), this endearing piece of slang is an emotional
meal for the love-starved boy (*Compact OED* 1109). Furthermore, the conversation that follows is chocked full of the pastoralized cant and slang of the

underworld. For example, Oliver is "green" because he does not understand the meaning of "beak" or magistrate; nor is he familiar with the "Stone Jug," that is, Newgate Prison. Before supplying Oliver with some "grub," the Artful Dodger tells him that "I'm at low-water mark myself—only one bob and magpie; but, *as* far *as* it goes, I'll fork out and stump" (Dickens 53).[8] A pauper's feast of bread, ham, and beer then ensues in what is clearly meant to be a gesture of hospitality, despite the ulterior motives, as is the Dodger's offer to take Oliver to London, to "a 'spectable old gentleman as lives there, wot'll give you lodgings for nothink, and never ask for the change—that is, if any genelman he knows interduces you. And don't he know me. . . !" (54). Oliver accepts the Artful's proposal since the "unexpected offer of shelter was too tempting to be resisted" (54). In this brief exchange, Dickens taps into Oliver's longing for security which is met, oddly enough, by a rogue from the city. Rather than leaving the boy in the country (a place that Oliver ironically associates with rootlessness and alienation), Dickens places him in an established London "family" so as to provide "the security and sense of belonging to a community which Oliver has never known before" (Miller 48). It is precisely these two elements, that of safety and inclusion, that mark the den at Saffron Hill as a neopastoral community.

Predictably, Fagin's hideout is not an idyllic bower in any conventional sense since it is *not* an escapist enclave filled with strained images of innocence and simplicity. Rather, it is a parodic place where the need for human warmth and stability are met. As a thematic complex, Fagin's den seems to have emerged at a time when Dickens himself was experiencing instability, as both an adult plagued by the blacking warehouse experience of the past and as a disparaging idealist trying to cope with the present loss of a loved one. For while he was in the very act of writing chapter viii of *Oliver Twist* in May of 1837 (wherein Oliver finds a temporary place in Fagin's "family"), Dickens was stunned by the unexpected death of Mary Hogarth who was living with the Dickenses at the time (Ackroyd 227). Thus it is the loss of a family member and the dying of an ideology that raise the demons of insecurity in Dickens' own life and result in the creation of a place in *Oliver Twist* where he can vicariously enter through Oliver. To an extent, the comforts of the criminal's lair allow both author and character to overcome the pain and disorientation brought on by loss. Real relief, then, is initially found in the city, in Fagin's den, long before any of the stock pastoral scenes ever appear in the novel.

With the *locus amoenus* of traditional pastoralism having been transplanted in the squalor of urbanized London, Fagin becomes a "father-figure to his 'boys' '' by providing his wayward sheep with shelter and sustenance (Kreutz 333).[9] Yet in doing so, this neopastoral shepherd displays a "fervid tenderness" that has also been described in distinctly matriarchal terms (Duffy 407; Marcus 367; Kincaid 72). Gail David has recently noted that femaleness, as expressed in "the male-heroed pastoral romance," is patriarchally inscribed with "feminine" values such as tenderness, submission, and nurturing which are typically associated with the rural landscape of the pastoral (xvi–xvii). That Dickens replaces the stereotypically feminine presence found at the center of the traditional pastoral enclave with a male (and criminal) one is significant because it creates a neopastoral shepherd/space capable of providing "tough" hospitality and security within the hostile environment of inner-city London.

Nowhere is this displacement clearer than in George Cruikshank's well-known illustration entitled "Oliver introduced to the Respectable Old Gentleman." Standing next to the fire with a toasting fork in his right hand and a frying pan in his left, Fagin embodies the warmth and provision of the hearth usually associated with femaleness and the pastoral. Critics, though, are quick to gloss over this signification in favor of the traditional male reading of Fagin as aggressive devil, pointing all the while to the "fork" as the telling icon. Yet as a reformulated image belonging to the neopastoral, the fork becomes an implement of power—a type of shepherd's crook—used to maintain the stability of the den since Fagin applies his "toasting fork [to] the heads and shoulders of the affectionate youths" when they step out of line (57). The frying-pan in Fagin's left hand (a skillet filled with sizzling sausages), however, is not so easily dismissed since it is associated directly with the homey comforts of both the c(r)ook and the den. But instead of being a flawed image improperly borrowed from its traditional pastoral context, the image of Fagin as a nurturing figure instead defines him as a neopastoral shepherd who is only doing his duty: he must feed his sheep.

In the well-known scene that follows Oliver's introduction to the gang, in which Fagin is eventually caught revelling in his "portable property," Dickens again shows the neopastoral shepherd working at the hearth:

> It was late next morning when Oliver awoke, from a sound, long sleep. There was no other person in the room but the old Jew, who was boiling some coffee in a saucepan for breakfast, and whistling softly to himself as he stirred it round and round, with an iron spoon.   (58)

The smell of coffee, the gentle sound of whistling, the clanking of kitchen utensils all suggest familial security and order. That Fagin creates this type of atmosphere, while believing the boy to be asleep, attests to the authenticity of his domestic care. Yet the nurturing placidity of this late morning scene is suddenly ended when Fagin indulges in a form of exhibitionism. Again the conventional image of the pastoral shepherd collapses and mutates under the pressure exerted by the dominant genre of the realistic novel. Purity and innocence give way to avarice as the shepherd begins to finger his loot in a homoerotic gesture that calls to mind young Master Bates, a neopastoral shepherd-in-training. In essence, Fagin exchanges a quiet moment shared with the hypnagogic Oliver for a clandestine act that necessarily excludes the boy, or rather includes him, in a silent but perverse fashion since the exhibitionist needs an audience. Playing with his jewels, Fagin is discovered in the very act of consummating his avaricious desire and now aggressively flies at the intruder who is watching him; the neopastoral community, it seems, has its limits: "He closed the lid of the box with a loud crash; and, laying his hand on a bread knife . . . started furiously up. He trembled very much though; for, even in his terror Oliver could see that the knife quivered in the air. . . . 'What have you seen? Speak out, boy! Quick—quick! for your life'" (59). At this point, the shepherd considers the unnatural act of slaughtering his own "sheep." But before dealing such a rash blow, Fagin manages to regain his emotional balance by pretending that he is only playing a game:

> "Tush, tush, my dear!" said the Jew, abruptly resuming his old manner, and playing with the knife a little, before he laid it down; as if to induce the belief that he had caught it up, in mere sport. (60)

The suggestion that Fagin is merely sporting with the boy again foregrounds the novelization process wherein the traditional pastoral contest, usually defined in terms of poetic competition and game playing, is here redefined in terms of role playing and lie telling. In fact, the "distinctive bucolic subject" of game playing is almost exclusively associated with the underworld in *Oliver Twist* (Halperin 17).[10]

There is, to begin with, the conventional "game of whist" that Tom Chitling consistently fails to win (178). There is the robbery at Mrs. Maylie's which Toby Crackit sees as a contest of wit and skill involving timing and strategy: "The game of that is, that they alway leave [the room-door] open with a catch, so that the dog, who's got a bed in here, may walk up and down the passage when he feels wakeful. Ha! ha! Barney 'ticed him away to-night. So neat!" (163). Fagin and Monks also play a more complicated game of defilement, the full extent of which is revealed by Nancy in her conversation with Rose Maylie: "What a game it would have been [for them] to have brought down the boast of the father's will, by driving [Oliver] through every jail in town, and then hauling him up for some capital felony which Fagin could easily manage, after having made a good profit of him besides" (303). And Charley Bates humorously imagines the "context" that occurs between the Artful Dodger and the Bench: "What a game! What a regular game! All the big-wigs trying to look solemn, and Jack Dawkins addressing of 'em as intimate and comfortable as if he was the judge's own son making a speech after dinner—ha! ha! ha!" (331).

Yet the most significant series of neopastoral contests in the novel occurs inside of Fagin's den and includes the merry old gentleman himself. After breakfast is cleared away, Fagin, Dodger, and Charley Bates "played at a very curious and uncommon game, which was performed in this way" (61). Loading himself up with a snuff-box, a note-case, a watch with a guard chain, a mock diamond pin, a spectacle-case, and a handkerchief, Fagin "trotted up and down the room with a stick, in imitation of the manner in which old gentlemen walk about the streets any hour in the day" (62). Dodger and Charley Bates must then try to retrieve the concealed items, but "If the old gentleman felt a hand in any one of his pockets, he cried out where it was; and then the game began all over again" (62). The dexterous voices of the pastoral singers are here replaced by the quick hands of thieves while the whole lighthearted interplay suggests the "friendly exchange" characteristic of pastoral contests (Toliver 4). The overall effect of such gaming is to make Oliver laugh—a clear sign that he feels comfortable in the group. This display of emotion is significant because it marks the reappropriation of conventional pastoralism through laughter, which has

> the remarkable power of making an object come up close, of drawing it into a zone of crude contact where one can finger it familiarly on all sides. . . . Laughter demolishes fear and piety before an object, before a world, making of it an object of familiar contact and thus clearing the ground for an absolutely free investigation of it. (Bakhtin 23)

This contest and the one to follow (Fagin later invites Oliver to try his hand at "taking the wipe") are clear-cut attempts to provide the boy with an investigative look at an alternative kind of community and security. And it is laughter that specifically puts Oliver in crude contact with the familial side of Fagin's criminal underworld.

Oliver's den experience is cut short, however, when the "wipe" game is subsequently tranferred to the unprotected reality of the streets and Oliver is quickly collared by a real policeman. When Fagin discovers that he has lost his prized sheep, a city-wide search then follows which sends Nancy to the local police station to inquire about the boy—but not before she is tranformed from city drab to neopastoral maiden: "Accordingly, with a clean white apron tied over her gown, and her curl-papers tucked up under a straw bonnet, . . . Miss Nancy prepared to issue forth on her errand" (89). Carrying "a little covered basket," a pastoral prop taken from Fagin's "inexhaustible stock" of clothing and accessories, the neopastoral maiden sets out on her parodic journey.

While inquiring for the boy at the police office, Nancy encounters another novelized pastoral figure,

> a miserable shoeless criminal, who had been taken up for playing the flute, and who, the offence against society having been clearly proved, had been very properly committed by Mr. Fang to the House of Correction for one month; with the appropriate and amusing remark that since he had so much breath to spare, it would be more wholesomely expended on the treadmill than in a musical instrument. He made no answer [to Nancy's inquiry]: being occupied in mentally bewailing the loss of the flute, which had been confiscated for the use of the county . . . (90)

The criminal and the pastoral again converge, this time in the image of the caged fluteplayer. Stripped of his pipe due to the revelries of wine, song, and dance that accompany the intoxicating worship of Dionysus, the jailed flutist laments for his confiscated pipe (a symbol of the irretrievable past) which has been replaced by the grim reality of the treadmill. Here the novel has literally arrested the movement of the pastoral as the Pan-like figure is labeled a criminal solely because of his bucolic behavior.

After speaking with the caged pastoralist, to no avail, Nancy discovers Oliver's general whereabouts and so returns to Fagin's den with her information. Extending himself through his subordinates, Fagin soon finds his parodical son and brings him home: "Oh you naughty boy," cries the bucolic voice, "to make me suffer sich distress on your account! Come home, dear, come. Oh, I've found him. Thank gracious goodness heavins, I've found him!" (107). "Weak . . . stupefied . . . terrified . . . [and] overpowered," Oliver is led back to the fold (108).

> "So you've got the kid," said Sikes . . .
> "Yes, here he is," replied Nancy.
> "Did he come quiet?" inquired Sikes.
> "Like a lamb," rejoind Nancy. (149)

In this dialogue, spoken before Oliver is taken to the Maylie robbery, Dickens again reinforces Oliver's neopastoral role as a young, passive, sheep-like follower. But in bringing the boy back into the underworld, Dickens also begins to dismantle the den by setting the neopastoral maiden's desire to save Oliver against her equally strong desire to preserve the only community and security she has ever known. When Nancy chooses to betray the den, she ultimately transfers Oliver's victimization to herself while also signifying a major novelizational shift from classical imagery to biblical typology. Having set the sacrificial lamb free, Nancy is bludgeoned to death in his place.

The blow that Bill Sikes delivers to Nancy's head becomes the narrative stroke that shatters Fagin's neopastoral community, thus transforming the criminal shepherd into a neopastoral victim who is now defined by Christological imagery, especially during Fagin's arrest and transportation to prison. It is certainly true that the "sympathetic criminal . . . can be made to suggest. . . . Christ as the scapegoat" (Empson 16).[11] In fact, Fagin's new role as neopastoral Christ-figure is clearly described in Tom Chitling's account of his arrest. Just after the flock scatters—Bates escapes, Bolter is caught, and Bet goes off to identify Nancy's body: thus "the sheep of the flock shall be scattered"[12]—Tom Chitling finds his "refuge" on Jacob's Island, along with two other dispossessed sheep, Toby Crackit and Kags, and recalls Fagin's ignominious fall:

> You should have heard the people groan . . . the officers fought like devils, or they'd have torn him away. He was down once, but they made a ring round him, and fought their way along. You should have seen how he looked about him, all muddy and bleeding, and clung to them as if they were his dearest friends.   (384)

The apparent groan of sympathy uttered in the opening line is, in reality, the groan of antipathy expressed by the angry crowd which would like to tear Fagin away (and to pieces). The officers who protect him are described as "devils" thus setting up the ironic contrast between the Christological imagery used and the character of the condemned criminal. Fagin's collapse also recalls Christ slumping to his knees on the way to Calvary which is met, in both cases, with harshness. The "ring" which forms around Fagin to protect him replaces the Roman escort and the enlisted help of Simon of Cyrene. Bloodied and soiled, the weakened outcast clings to his protectors "as if they were his dearest friends."

The latter half of Tom Chitling's account brings Fagin's role as a novelized Christ-figure even more sharply into focus:

I can see 'em now, not able to stand upright with the pressing mob, and dragging him along amongst 'em; I can see the people jumping up, one behind another, and snarling with their teeth and making at him; I can see the blood upon his hair and beard, and hear the cries with which the women worked themselves into the centre of the crowd at the street corner, and swore they'd tear his heart out! (384)

The narrational shift to first person plunges the reader into Fagin's suffering and alienation. Like Oliver, Fagin is now "weak . . . stupefied . . . terrified . . . overpowered" as blood, hair, and beard (all red) seem to elicit sympathetic cries from the women who are watching his arrest: "And there were following Him a great multitude of the people, and of women who were mourning and lamenting Him" (Luke 23:27). Yet these "Daughters of Jerusalem" are not weeping for Fagin; rather, they are crying out for his execution in their desire to "tear his heart out," to have Fagin's death for the death of a lover or friend whom the twisted shepherd had previously sacrificed to the gallows.

In the novel's penultimate chapter, Dickens continues to draw upon the events of Christ's life when he next shows Fagin at his own trial. A combination of Jewish Sanhedrin and Roman Pilate, the English Bench condemns Fagin to death and then washes its hands of him. The death sentence itself is met with "a peal of joy from the populace outside" while Fagin is later "assailed . . . with opprobrious names" and with hissing and screeching as he is being led back to his prison cell (405). Despised and rejected, the victim momentarily turns aggressor as Fagin shakes his fist at the jeering crowd. Yet back in his cell, Fagin bears all the marks of the sacrificial Lamb: The cloth crown of infamy, the tangled red hair, the "bloodless face," the torn beard (an ancient insult), and the eyes that "shone with a terrible light" all suggest the figure of the condemned Shepherd (408).[13]

Yet despite the Christological imagery that defines him, Fagin is still a convicted felon whose reality soon fractures after he finds himself locked up in Newgate prison—an image that recalls the caged pastoralist found earlier in the novel. Time and place lose their referential sequency and stability as Fagin begins to drop in and out of his two roles as Christ-like victim and shepherding victimizer. When Oliver and Mr. Brownlow first enter Fagin's cell in chapter 52, they find that his "mind was evidently wandering to his old life, for he continued to mutter, without appearing conscious of their presence otherwise than as a part of his vision" (409). Like William Dorrit's later reversion to the Father of the Marshalsea, Fagin begins to re-see himself as a neopastoral shepherd when he suddenly calls out "quite the gentleman now—quite the—take that boy away to bed!'' and thus curiously returns to the reclamation of Oliver as lost sheep (4109. Only the intrusive voice of the jailer can temporarily roust Fagin from his past.

When Fagin is asked to supply information regarding the whereabouts of Monks's papers, he again sees Oliver, cries out his name, and instantly slips back into his shepherding role. Thus it is a confused layering of synchronic moments, and not Fagin's repentant heart, that causes him to divulge his secret concerning the hidden papers. Because Fagin senses the severity of his situation without clearly sorting it into categorical realities, he subsequently feels an urgent need to escape but does not understand the context from which he is fleeing. Certain elements such as Oliver and the locked door remain foregrounded while other elements are blocked out, such as the jailer, Mr. Brownlow, and the prison itself. Feeling like a victim yet acting like a victimizer, Fagin pathetically attempts to use Oliver as his means of escape.

Fagin begins his delusory flight by calling to the boy in the shepherding language of the past: ''I want to talk to you, *my dear*. I want to talk to you'' (Emphasis added 411). Once again, he assumes his role as manipulator by ''pushing the boy before him towards the door'' and whispering, ''Say I've gone to sleep—they'll believe you. You can get me out, if you take me so. Now then, now then!'' So distorted is Fagin's perspective that even Oliver's tears of pity are misinterpreted as being signs of obedience—a reinforcement of a previous reality: ''That's right, that's right . . . That'll help us on.'' But the past and present fatally clash when Fagin and the prison guards are brought together, via Oliver as nexus, for one final confrontation:

> The men laid hands upon [Fagin], and disengaging Oliver from his grasp, held him back. He struggled with the power of desperation, for an instant; and, then sent up cry upon cry that penetrated even those massive walls . . .   (411)

This literal separation externalizes the psychological renting of the neopastoral shepherd from his reclaimed authority, for in pulling Oliver out of Fagin's grasp, Dickens yanks away the old man's connection with the past. His final ''cry upon cry'' then becomes a variation on the sacrificial scream ''It is finished'' that acknowledges the shepherd's utter separation.

IV

At the end of *Oliver Twist*, strangely enough, we never actually witness Fagin's execution. The consuming realism of the novel does give us ''the black stage, the cross-beam, the rope, and all the hideous apparatus of death'' but it withholds the body in yet another novelized presentation of the criminal/ shepherd who is ultimately transformed out of existence (411). In fact, the hospitality, the game-playing, even the sacrificial suffering of the Christ-figure are all conspicuously absent as Fagin is suddenly reduced to a scream which fades into silence with the closing of chapter 52. It is certainly true that "humankind / Cannot bear very much reality" and that Dickens himself abhorred public execution, thus explaining, in part, the removal of the hanging scene (Eliot 172). Yet why not carry the sacrifice through to its pathetic end in hopes of eliciting as much public sympathy as possible? Why not depict the neopastoral shepherd as a societal victim so as to chastise those like the disbelieving Alderman cited in the novel's preface who refuse to acknowledge the charismatic presence of the neopastoral shepherd?[14] Partly, of course, the answer is that once Fagin is used to create what Bakhtin calls a ''zone of maximal contact with the present,'' wherein the reader comes close-up with the contemporary reality of the nineteenth-century criminal underclass, he is removed in order to make way for the romanticized semblance of closure that follows in the last chapter (11). *Oliver Twist* would be a very different novel indeed if it were to end with chapter 52, that is, with the ominous image of the gallows clearly fixed in our minds, and with the eerie postmodernist scream of the neopastoral shepherd, novelized into oblivion, still ringing in our ears. Thus, in the end, Fagin must be destroyed because he exerts an ''attraction of repulsion'' influence that cannot be legitimized by a civilized society, even if Fagin's neopastoral transformation from classical to biblical to nullified shepherd is acknowledged. And, of course, the reason is simple: Fagin represents an energy which is far too dangerous for society to accept since it not only exposes the inhumanity of Poor Law bureaucracy but threatens to subvert the very social order which produces all laws in general. While we can do without the criminalization of the poor, we cannot survive without a system for punishing the lawless outsider, even if he is, at times, a compassionate shepherd.

NOTES

1. See "Dickens and the Art of Pastoral," *Centennial Review* 23 (1979): 452–67, footnote 1. Additional, more recent commentators on Dickens and the pastoral include Angus Easson, "John Chivery and the Wounded Strephon: A Pastoral Element in *Little Dorrit*," *Durham University Journal* 36 (1975): 165–169; William Burgan, "Tokens of Winter in Dickens's Pastoral Settings," *MLQ* 36 (1975):

293–315; Roselee Robison, "Dickens' Everlastingly Green Garden," *English Studies* 59 (1978): 409–424; Simon Petch, "*Little Dorrit*: Some Visions of Pastoral," *Sydney Studies in English* 7 (1981–2): 102–114; Gail Finney, "Garden Paradigms in 19th-Century Fiction," *Comparative Literature* 36 (1984): 20–33, and *The Counterfeit Idyll: The Garden Ideal and Social Reality in Nineteenth-Century Fiction* (Tubingen: Niemeyer, 1985); Rosemarie Bodenheimer, *The Politics of Story in Victorian Social Fiction* (Ithaca: Cornell UP, 1988), chapter 3; and Michael Miller, "The Fellowship-Porters and the Veneerings: Setting, Structure and Justice in *Our Mutual Friend*," *Dickensian* 85 (1989): 31–38.

2. Edgar Johnson also notes that Dickens's mother "taught him to read, and later even a little Latin" (18), a statement that follows a descriptive passage of Dickens as "a very little and very sickly boy" whose fragility compelled him to find pleasure in reading and study.

3. Dickens also owned various Greek translations including a copy of Cowper's Homer (containing the *Iliad* and the *Odyssey*, 1802). A Lexicon and a Gradus were also listed among his books.

4. See William Burgan, "Tokens of Winter in Dickens's Pastoral Settings," 306; Angus Easson, "John Chivery and the Wounded Strephon," 167; Barbara Hardy, *The Moral Art of Dickens*, New York: Oxford UP, 1970, 44. Escapist readings tend to dominate the discussion concerning Dickens's use of the pastoral. Joseph Duffy in "Another Version of Pastoral: *Oliver Twist*," 403–21, sees the "pastoral setting of the Maylie residence" as a restorative enclave. F. S. Schwarzbach views the country "as a refuge" which "allows us to experience, or more precisely to re-experience, paradise itself" (*Dickens and the City* [London: Athlone, 1979], 60). Jerome Meckier in "The Faint Image of Eden," *Dickens Studies Annual* 1 (1970): 129–46, claims that the image of Eden functions as a "foretaste of some sort of heaven"—a kind of etherealized retreat (134). Garrett Stewart states that Jenny Wren's internalized pastoral haven allows her to transcend her reality (*Dickens and the Trials of Imagination* [Cambridge, MA: Harvard UP, 1974], 155) while Rosemarie Bodenheimer in *The Politics of Story in Victorian Social Fiction* notes that "Dickens's pastoral is an individualistic middle-class retreat" (117). In *The Counterfeit Idyll*, Gail Finney says that "Riah's rooftop retreat . . . epitomizes the unreality associated with the garden realm throughout literature in its role as the incorporation of an alternative to the social world" (133). Despite their varying conclusions, each reading views the pastoral as a vehicle for escaping something.

5. Raymond Williams has also cataloged some of the complexities of the pastoral's evolving form in *The Country and the City* (Oxford: Oxford UP, 1973). After citing Theocritus, Hesiod, Virgil, and Horace as examples of the "classical pastoral" wherein the "living tensions" of experience are excised (18), Williams then defines the "artificial mode" (22) of the "neo-pastoral" as a type of "artificial eclogue or idyll" (22), spawned by agrarian capitalism, which has located the "perpetual peace and innocence of the neopastoral dream" in the image of the aristocratic country house (26). The neopastoral, as William defines it, is assigned to a particular type of poetry and does not extend to the "modern proletarian industrial novel" (21).

6. W. Walter Crotch, *The Pageant of Dickens* (London: Chapman & Hall, 1915), suggests that "we are compelled to wonder whether even Fagin hasn't a tiny soft place in his black heart when he leaves poor little Oliver, pale as death, to sleep till morning before he delivers him over to Sikes for the burglary. 'Not now,'

said the Jew, turning softly away.'To-morrow—to-morrow.' Had Fagin any pity in his traitorous nature when he warned Oliver: 'Take heed, Oliver! Take heed! . . . Whatever falls out, say nothing and do what he [Sikes] bids you, mind!' Is there reflected in this anything more than a cunning self-interest?'' (95–96). The implied answer, of course, is "yes." John Lucas, on the other hand, sees the division between the "natural Fagin" and the "slimy reptile" as a "flaw," an inconsistency that cannot be reconciled. He then declares that "Fagin is out of focus . . . as I think most readers would acknowledge," implying that Dickens has once again mishandled the pastoral (*The Melancholy Man*, 51–52).

7. See also Lauriat Lane, "Dickens' Archetypal Jew," *PMLA* 73 (1958): 94–100 and Anne Aresty Naman, *The Jew in the Victorian Novel: Some Relationships Between Prejudice and Art* (New York: AMS Press, 1980), chapter 3.

8. Other pastoral-sounding terms with criminal overtones appear throughout the novel. Oliver is said to be from "Greenland" (56); a "jemmy," according to Kathleen Tillotson's "Glossary of Thieves" (see *Oliver Twist* [Oxford: Clarendon, 1966], 401–03), is both "a sheep's head" and "housebreaking implement" (150); to "peach" is to betray one's friends (88) while a "prime plant" is both a victim of a robbery (65) and a disguise worn by Toby Crackit (138). Broader associations between the criminal and the pastoral include Rose Maylie's speculation "that ill-usage and blows, or want of bread, may have driven [Oliver] to herd with men who forced him to guilt" (217), Blather's reference to the "Chickweed" robbery (226), the undeniable and sordid presence of Jacob's Island as fallen *locus amoenus* (382), and the mixing of sheep and thieves at the Smithfield marketplace (153).

9. Perhaps Dickens had Virgil in mind when he created Fagin's den. In Eclogue VII, Thrysis describes his enclave with the following lyric: "here we have a hearth and pitchy brands; here, a good fire ever blazing and door-posts black with never-failing soot. Here we reck as much of the chill blasts of Boreas as the wolf of the number of sheep, or rushing torrents of their banks" (Virgil 53). Upon entering Fagin's den, Oliver sees that "the walls and ceiling of the room were perfectly black, with age and dirt. There was a deal table before the fire: upon which were a candle, stuck in a ginger-beer bottle: two or three pewter pots, a loaf and butter, and a plate. In a frying-pan, which was on the fire, and which was secured to the mantelshelf by a string, some sausages were cooking" (56).

10. Harold Toliver, in *Pastoral Forms and Attitudes* (Berkeley: U of California P, 1971), defines the contest further when he says that "a pastoral society . . . is non-competitive or else converts a limited competition into such games and ceremonies as the friendly exchange of rival singers" (4). While being novelized, the contest in *Oliver Twist* takes on all the earmarks of inner city life.

11. Empson's statement (*Some Versions of Pastoral* [London: Chatto and Windus, 1935, rpt. 1974]) is not made with reference to Dickens. J. Hillis Miller (*Charles Dickens: The World of His Novels* [Oxford: Oxford UP, 1958]) has remarked that "Fagin dies 'for' Oliver the death he would have died," if the boy had been a real thief, yet Miller never labels Fagin as a Christ-figure (66). Janet Larson (*Dickens and the Broken Scriptures* [Athens: U of Georgia P, 1986]) calls Fagin "the Bad Samaritan" (60) while Dennis Walder (*Dickens and Religion* [London: George Allen and Unwin, 1981]) refers to him as "the old devil" (60).

12. Gospel of St. Matthew 26:31, *Ryrie Study Bible* (Chicago: Moody Press, 1978). All subsequent biblical references are made to this text.

13. Fagin's dishevelled red hair is usually taken as a stereotypical sign of his "jewish villainy" (see, for example, Lauriat Lane [p. 95] and Harry Stone ["Dickens and

the Jews," p. 233]). Yet red hair is also found on Greek and Hebrew shepherds: see Menalcas and Daphnis in "Idyll 8: Second Pastoral Song" in *The Idylls of Theocritus*, trans. Thelma Sargent (New York: Norton, 1982), 35; see also David in I Samuel 16:12 and Essau in Genesis 25:25. The markings of the criminal and the shepherd are coterminus in Fagin's case.

14. As recently as November 1, 1993, in Los Angeles two "modern-day Fagins" were persuading "young boys . . . to invade banks with automatic weapons, terrorize patrons and tellers and flee with money in high-speed freeway getaways in stolen cars" (*The Providence Journal Bulletin*). These "appalling corrupters of youth" more than likely provided their "disadvantaged and miserable teenagers" with all the provisions of a Saffron Hill community in order to win their support and teach them the ins and outs of "takeover robberies."

WORKS CITED

Ackroyd, Peter. *Dickens*. New York: Harper-Collins, 1990.

Bakhtin, M. M. *The Dialogic Imagination*. Trans. Caryl Emerson and Michael Holquist. Austin: U of Texas P, 1981.

Bayley, John. "Oliver Twist: 'Things as They Really Are.' " 83–96 in *Dickens: A Collection of Critical Essays*, ed., Martin Price. Englewood Cliffs, NJ: Prentice-Hall, 1967.

Bodenheimer, Rosemarie. *The Politics of Story in Victorian Social Fiction*. Ithaca: Cornell UP, 1988.

Burgan, William. "Tokens of Winter in Dickens's Pastoral Settings." *Modern Language Quarterly* 36 (1975): 293–315.

Collins, Philip. *Dickens and Crime*. London: Macmillan, 1962.

"Covey." *Compact Edition of the Oxford English Dictionary*. 1971.

Crotch, W. Walter. *The Pageant of Dickens*. London: Chapman & Hall, 1915.

David, Deirde. *Fictions of Resolution in Three Victorian Novels*. New York: Columbia UP, 1981.

David, Gail. *Female Heroism in the Pastoral*. New York: Garland, 1991.

Dickens, Charles. *The Pilgrim Edition of the Letters of Charles Dickens*. Eds. Graham Storey and K. J. Fielding. 6 vols. Oxford: Clarendon, 1981.

———. *Oliver Twist*. 1838. Oxford: Oxford UP, 1949.

Duffy, Joseph M. "Another Version of Pastoral: Oliver Twist." *ELH* 35 (1968): 403–21.

Ettin, Andrew. *Literature and the Pastoral*. New Haven: Yale UP, 1984.

Eliot, T. S. *The Complete Poems and Plays of T. S. Eliot.* London: Faber & Faber, 1978.

Halperin, David M. *Before Pastoral: Theocritus and the Ancient Tradition of Bucolic Poetry.* New Haven: Yale UP, 1983.

House, Humphry. Introduction. *Oliver Twist.* By Charles Dickens. Oxford: Oxford UP, 1949. v–xiv.

Hunter, Shelagh. *Victorian Idyllic Fiction: Pastoral Strategies.* Atlantic Highlands, NJ: Humanities Press, 1984.

Johnson, Edgar. Charles Dickens: *His Tragedy and Triumph.* New York: Penguin, 1980.

Kincaid, James. *Dickens and the Rhetoric of Laughter.* Oxford: Clarendon, 1971.

Kreutz, Irving W. ''Sly of Manner, Sharp of Tooth: A Study of Dickens's Villains.'' *Nineteenth-Century Fiction* 22 (1968): 331–48.

Lucas, John. *The Melancholy Man: A Study of Dickens's Novels.* London: Methuen, 1970.

Marcus, Steven. *From Pickwick to Dombey.* New York: Simon and Schuster, 1965.

Maxwell, Richard. ''Knotting the Maze in Oliver Twist'' in *The Mysteries of Paris and London.* Charlottesville: UP of Virginia, 1992.

Miller, J. Hillis. *Charles Dickens: The World of His Novels.* Oxford: Oxford UP, 1958.

Paroissien, David. ''*Oliver Twist* and the Contours of Early Victorian England.'' *The Victorian Newsletter* 83 (Spring 1993): 14–17.

Poggioli, Renato. *The Oaten Flute: Essays on Pastoral Poetry and the Pastoral Ideal.* Cambridge, MA: Harvard UP, 1975.

Robison, Roselee. ''Dickens' Everlastingly Green Garden.'' *English Studies* 59 (1978): 409–24.

Squires, Michael. *The Pastoral Novel: Studies in George Eliot, Thomas Hardy, and D. H. Lawrence.* Charlottesville: UP of Virginia, 1974.

Stone, Harry. ''Dickens and the Jews.'' *Victorian Studies* 2 (1958–59): 223–53.

Thuente, David Raphael. ''Pastoral Narratives: A Review of Criticism.'' *Genre* 14 (1981): 247–67.

Toliver, Harold. *Pastoral Forms and Attitudes.* Berkeley: U of California P, 1971.

Williams, Raymond. *The Country and the City.* Oxford: Oxford UP, 1973.

Little Nell's Curious Grandfather

Jerome H. Buckley

The Old Curiosity Shop is a curious novel, both in itself and by reputation. Like the times described at the beginning of *A Tale of Two Cities*, it has been rated in the extremes of "best" and "worst," as if readers shared the odd compulsion Dickens ascribed to the "noisiest authorities" on the French Revolution, who insisted on that period's "being received for good or for evil in the superlative degree of comparison only." What seemed to its first public, thanks largely to little Nell, a masterpiece of true pathos to be ranked with *King Lear* became to later generations, thanks again to Nell, a mere sentimental embarrassment. Carlyle and other rigorous Victorians warmed to Nell's ineffable goodness much as Bret Harte's rough miners filled with tearful reverence for "the book wherein the Master / Had writ of 'Little Nell,' "[1] Oscar Wilde, on the other hand, declared it difficult to imagine anyone so hard of heart not to laugh at Nell's death, and Aldous Huxley railed at Nell's "vulgarity." But Dick Swiveller and the Marchioness and the horrendous Mr. Quilp have vigorously survived both the praise and blame of Nell's novel, and the oddity of the fiction remains more than a matter of conflicting reader-response. It inheres, I suggest, in the curious framing of the text, the relation of the initial setting to the theme, and the depiction of Nell's counterpart, the grandfather who is central to the plot but too often ignored in evaluation of the narrative.

The Old Curiosity Shop, we should remember, first appeared as a fiction within a fiction, but few of us return to *Master Humphrey's Clock*, its cumbersome vehicle for weekly serialization. Designed as a miscellany of curious lore, exotic travel sketches, historical anecdotes, strange tales of ghosts and giants, the periodical in its brief run summons up Mr. Pickwick and the Wellers to hear these stories read aloud. Master Humphrey, the host of the reading group and the principal narrator, clings to one name only (is it a given name or a surname?) and carefully conceals his address, though he describes in affectionate detail the cobwebby residence that for many years has been his retreat from an undisclosed past. He is a self-confessed aged eccentric, solitary but not misanthropic—in Dickens' words to Forster, "this old file in the queer house" (*Letters* II, 4). And his dearest "friend" is his "old cheerful companionable Clock, . . . a quaint old thing in a huge oaken case curiously and richly carved" (*Clock* I, 4). This large dark clockcase becomes the depository of "piles of dusty papers," including the manuscript of *The Old Curiosity Shop*, here listed under the heading *Personal Adventures of Master Humphrey*—appropriately enough, for the narrative begins from Humphrey's point of view, and not till the end of Chapter III does Humphrey "for the convenience of the narrative detach [himself] from its further course, and leave those who have prominent and necessary parts in it to speak and act for themselves" (I, 90). When the story is complete, Master Humphrey, returning in the first person, justifies the "fictitious" form of his narrative, but nonetheless identifies himself with the "single gentleman," Nell's grandfather's long-lost younger brother, and so, to the great surprise of his auditors, reveals his own "share, . . . no light or trivial one—in the pages [he has] read" (I, 224).[2]

Master Humphrey's capacious clock was apparently inspired by a similar product of the London clock-maker Thomas Humphreys or of his son William, either or both of whom no doubt suggested to Dickens his character's name (*Letters* II, 5 n.). But the clock of the title was probably a composite of several, and Dickens was at pains to deny its actual existence. "There is no such clock!" he told an inquirer; "If there were I should be its owner" (*Letters* II, 439). The clock then has become a fictitious curio in Humphrey's queer house, an item that grandfather Trent would have welcomed to his own odd collection.

Curiosity shops, however, like his but larger and more successful ventures, were surely real enough and common, too, in London up through the early nineteenth century. One of the more pretentious of the 1780s, Richard Altick reports, was the establishment of George Humphrey (of which, I assume, the young Dickens may well have heard), known as Humphrey's Grand Museum or the Museum Humfredianum (Altick, 428). Such showrooms for "curios" and "rarities" were often, we are told, "nothing more than junk shops" (Altick, 428), and old Trent's moldy emporium is certainly no better. Later London dealers, eager to claim an antique charm, have striven to associate their business with the original Dickensian Old Curiosity Shop. But there is really very little of the quaint or charming to be emulated in the dingy jumble of Trent's treasures. The narrator Humphrey, himself a collector of oddities, on first entry into the shop, discovers only a dreary place of dust, rust, and misshapen ugliness,

> one of those receptacles for old and curious things which seem to crouch in odd corners of this town and to hide their musty treasures from the public eye in jealousy and distrust. There were suits of mail standing like ghosts in armour, here and there; fantastic carvings brought from monkish cloisters, rusty weapons of various kinds; distorted figures in china, and wood, and iron, and ivory; tapestry, and strange furniture that might have been designed in dreams.
>
> (I, 40)

Before long, however, the murky shop recedes from view, until late in the novel Kit Nubbles comes upon its deserted ruins. By the end even Kit cannot surely identify the site, for the shop has perished in its decrepitude and been carried off to make room for a spacious new roadway.

Indeed, after engaging our early attention, the shop may seem merely peripheral to the larger fiction. We encounter no interested curio-buyers, we witness no sales or transactions, though we gather that Mr. Quilp as dispossessor eventually disposes of the wares at some profit to himself. Edgar Allan Poe, who greatly admired much of *The Old Curiosity Shop*, complained that its title was inappropriate—evidence, he felt, that Dickens in the course of writing had changed his focus, since "the shop itself is a thing of an altogether collateral interest, and is spoken of merely in the beginning" (Ford and Lane 16). Actually, however, Dickens' concern with the "curious" in objects, character, and conduct extends far beyond the initial setting. Thomas Hood apparently perceived a symbolic significance at the outset in the contrast between the luminous innocence of Nell and the "old dark murky room" in which she sleeps (and to which, we might add, her grandfather's mismanagement has consigned her); the illustration in the serial of the scene ending Chapter I was, he wrote, "like an allegory" (*Letters* II, 221n.). Pleased by Hood's interpretation, Dickens added four paragraphs at this point to the book version, playing off the "unusual," "uncouth," and even sinister surroundings against the radiance of the child, who now "seemed to exist in a kind of allegory" (*OCS* 56).[3] The narrator of the addition then entertains the "curious speculation" that Nell may some day be forced to hold "her solitary way among a crowd of wild, grotesque companions"—a fancy which echoes the intention announced by Dickens' preface, "to surround the lonely figure of the child with grotesque and wild, but not impossible, companions, . . . associates as strange and uncongenial as the grim objects that are about her bed when her history is first foreshadowed" (*OCS*, 429. The curiosity shop accordingly serves by design as an expressionistic symbol of the wildness pitted more or less allegorically against Nell's innocence. And even at the last, when the evil is defeated, something of the curious Gothic imagery remains to describe the still monastic relics among which Nell comes to rest.

Several of the principal characters in the fiction relate explicitly by stated comparison or contrast to Trent's curiosities or to similar odd artifacts. The demonic Quilp, whose "horribly grotesque and distorted face" (*Clock* I, 105) leers from Mrs. Quilp's mirror, eventually engages battle with a huge curio, an antique ship's figure-head, which he savagely bludgeons to vent his hatred of Kit Nubbles. Quilp's agent, Sampson Brass, assigned to guard "the store-room of old curiosities," is said to be "the ugliest piece of goods in all the stock" (I, 155). The "single gentleman" retains the "many peculiarities" of Master Humphrey, among which is his delight in an ingenious breakfast-making machine—though this is an efficient contraption of a Rube Goldberg complexity rather than a moldy curio. The children welcoming Mrs. Jarley's caravan to their town are surely mistaken to suppose Nell "to be an important item of the curiosities" (I, 249), but they are not so much in error when they regard Nell's grandfather at his most listless as "a cunning device in wax."

More than all others indeed, more even than Quilp, old Trent is defined from the beginning by the curious objects he has amassed:

> The haggard aspect of the little old man was wonderfully suited to the place; he might have groped among old churches, and tombs, and deserted houses, and gathered all the spoils with his own hands. There was nothing in the whole collection but was in keeping with himself; nothing that looked older or more worn than he. (I, 40)

So in this first scene the grandfather fixes a dominant theme and a recurrent imagery for the narrative that follows, the central story where he is either a passive presence or an oppressive burden. Overshadowed by more vigorous characters, he is still the most elusive and enigmatic of all, an old man too curious to be overlooked.

The fact that Dickens considered calling his novel *The Old Curiosity Dealer and the Child* (*Letters* II, 42) suggests both the grandfather's original primary role and the essential conflict of the plot, the disparity between helpless age and hopeful youth. Though already fourteen years old (close, that is, in early nineteenth-century society, to adulthood) and hardly naive in her perceptions, Nell is constantly referred to as "the child." Yet "the old man" confesses at the outset, "It is true that in many respects I am the child, and she the grown person" (I, 44), and the narrator later, when Trent's dotage is apparent, digresses at some length on the difference between childishness and the spirit of true childhood: ''Send forth the child and childish man together, and blush for the pride that libels our own old happy state, and gives its title to an ugly and distorted image'' (I, 152–53). Many of the paintings inspired by *The Old Curiosity Shop*[4] and some illustrations of the text depict a bright-eyed Nell with a dependent but mild and generally harmless charge.[4] But the grandfather, as Dickens presents him—with far less pity and sentiment than that lavished upon Nell,—is scarcely a benign figure; whatever his declared affection, he is in effect the real antagonist of the plot, the one whose misjudgments, foolish ambition, and unconquerable obsession lead to inevitable disaster.

As his brother tells us, Trent has from boyhood been intent on gathering ''curious ancient things,'' from the vending of which he gained for a while ''an anxious and precarious subsistence'' (II, 199). Though always, we gather, an inept tradesman, he seems, when we first meet him, obsessed with the acquisition of money to the extent of bitterly blaming God for not prospering him. His express purpose in life is to amass riches enough to make Nell ''a fine lady'' and to leave her ''what would place her beyond the reach of want forever, . . . no pittance, but a fortune'' (I, 41, 89), such wealth as the more adroit Abel Magwitch will one day bestow upon his ''gentleman'' Pip. In his lust for money the old man neglects Nell, deprives her of a happy childhood, exploits her as a household drudge, exposes her to the perils of the London night—and for all this lack of consideration earns the just rebuke of Master Humphrey. If his misguided plans for Nell's future can be credited as well-meaning, he is meanwhile impercipient, selfish, self-deluded, and full of self-pity. Later, when Mrs. Jarley offers to find ''a good situation'' for Nell, he can think only of himself and his fears of abandonment: ''What,'' he asked, ''would become of me without her'' (I, 244).[5]

From the beginning, like Balzac's Père Goriot, he leads a double life, mysterious and misconstrued. Since he is perpetually muttering of money and worrying aloud about it, both his shiftless grandson and Mr. Quilp mistake him for a miser with a secret cache of gold, and Master Humphrey at first shares their suspicion that he is ''one of those miserable wretches who, having made gain the sole end and object of their lives, and having succeeded in amassing their riches, are constantly tortured by the dread of poverty, and beset by fears of loss and ruin'' (I, 89). But he is in truth as destitute as he claims to be, and his improvidence has brought ''ruin'' upon himself and the child. For his secret is his compulsive gambling, an addiction which Dickens renders, though briefly, with a quite Balzacian intensity.[6] In the beginning Trent appears abstracted and evasive, affirming rather than demonstrating his affection for Nell, but after his serious illness he seems drained altogether of love and vitality, listless and withdrawn, his "vacant smile" betokening a sad senility. Yet the mere mention of a gambling-table quickly restores a gleam to his eyes and a resolution to continue "tempting fortune" (I, 139) in the abject confidence that his luck is always about to change. When he sees an opportunity to join the card-players at the tavern, he is at once aroused, "flushed and eager," inflamed with fevered desire, and fiercely impatient with Nell, who seeks to restrain him. Later that night, in the novel's most melodramatic scene, he comes, like a predatory animal, on all fours, to rob the apparently sleeping child of the few pennies she has held in reserve, and Nell shudders at the transformation:

> the man she had seen that night, wrapped in the game of chance, lurking in her room, and counting the money by the glimmering light, seemed like another creature in his shape, a monstrous distortion of his image, a something to recoil from, and be the more afraid of, because it bore a likeness to him, and kept close about her as he did. She could scarcely connect her own affectionate companion, save by his loss, with this old man, so like yet so unlike him. She had wept to see him dull and quiet. How much greater cause she had for weeping now! (I, 265)

The gentle dependent, in short, has become for a spell the aggressive beast, a Mr. Hyde, as grotesque and menacing as Mr. Quilp. The consequence now is the determination to steal Mrs. Jarley's cash-box, a project which Nell strenuously foils—at the cost of returning the old man to his innocuous torpor.

For the rest of their pilgrimage the grandfather remains self-absorbed, content to be led, greedy for the bits of food Nell has foraged and largely indifferent to *her* hunger and exhaustion. But finally arrived at their place of refuge and tranquilized by the security of a new routine, he achieves a measure of perspective, undergoing a sort of conversion, quieter but no less complete than Scrooge's change of heart. At last sensing the misery he has inflicted, he regards Nell with a new "solicitude": "Never, no, never once, in one unguarded moment from that time to the end, did any care for himself, any thought of his own comfort, any selfish consideration or regard, distract his thoughts from the gentle object of his love" (II, 104). His moral awakening, of course, comes far too late to be of great avail, but we are asked nonetheless to accept its validity. His obsession and sustenance now is the presence of Nell herself rather than a gambling for Nell's imagined future. In his transformation he has become for a time what some Victorians saw in him, a shadowy Lear grieving for Cordelia. And when Nell lies dead, he deludes himself like Lear that she is only asleep, for she has been his last hold on life. At this stage he has no interest at all, virtually no awareness, of the brother who has come to rescue him; the money he craved for speculation no longer tempts him, and the security now proferred him seems of no consequence.

A mystery to Master Humphrey in the beginning, Nell's grandfather thus still eludes the naive goodwill of the "single gentleman," whom the framing *Clock* identifies with Humphrey. Never, except when gaming, the most animated character in *The Old Curiosity Shop,* he is, I believe, the most complex psychologically. With his inveterate compulsions, delusions, and private fantasies, a changeable man, moving in and out of sensibility, fear, and affection, he rewards attention as an intricate intruder upon the simpler allegorical elements of Nell's story. As one of the early Dickens' studies of a troubled subjective life, he remains more curious than all the objects at first invoked to describe him.

NOTES

1. Bret Harte's memorial verses, "Dickens in Camp" (1870), single out Nell's story from all Dickens' works. Ford traces the shifting fortunes of *OCS* in Chapter 4 of *Dickens and his Readers*: "Little Nell: the Limits of Explanatory Criticism." Ford and Lane (*The Dickens Critics*) reprint Poe's 1841 review of *OCS* and Huxley's essay, "The Vulgarity of Little Nell." Fielding (64–65) comments on the Victorian response to *OCS*, and Senelick evaluates the "pathos" of the novel.
2. But there is a serious problem in identifying Master Humphrey with "the single gentleman." If the two are one and the same, why does Humphrey, present in the first three chapters, not reveal himself as the old man's younger brother immediately, instead of spending the last half of the novel as the anonymous "single gentleman," trying to track down Trent, who from the beginning has urgently needed his help? Besides, Michael Steig (*Dickens Studies Notes*, 4 (1973), 40) has questioned the name "Trent" as properly belonging only to the profligate grandson and to Nell; if Humphrey is a surname and he is indeed "the single gentleman," then the grandfather's surname must also be Humphrey. Nonetheless, I have chosen for convenience to follow what has long been usual practice, referring to the grandfather as "old Trent."
3. A *kind* of allegory? *OCS*, of course, is only intermittently allegorical. Nell often seems to incarnate saintly goodness and forbearance, and Quilp (at least as Mrs. Nubbles sees him, ch. 48) is explicitly equated with the "Evil Power" and repeatedly associated with hellish fire and brimstone. But the subplots, invoking a domestic sentimentalism and a starker social realism, have but little allegorical connotation, and some of the principal characters, especially the grandfather, are too much a mixture of human elements to be seen as abstractions of vice or virtue. John W. Gibson describes the allegorical component in the *Dickensian*, 60 (1964), 78 f. Fielding (65–68) makes a case for *OCS* as "a kind of fairy-tale." In his introduction to the Penguin *OCS* (29), Malcolm Andrews finds a parallel between the coming of the three to Nell's deathbed and the journey of the Magi.

Illustrations of the serial *Old Curiosity Shop* from
Master Humphrey's Clock

Nell living in ''a kind of allegory'' (Chap. 1)

Grandfather ruined

Grandfather distrait (Chap. 15)

Grandfather's obsession (Chap. 30)

Grandfather betrayed (Chap. 42)

Grandfather penitent (Chap. 54)

4. Richard Altick in his *Painting from Books: Art and Literature, 1760–1900* (Columbus: Ohio State UP, 1985), 465–66, declares *OCS* "by a substantial margin the most popular of Dickens's novels as far as the art world was concerned"; he has discovered more than forty paintings from the novel, "most of them . . . starring little Nell, . . . often with her undependable grandfather."

5. The grandfather in fact is quite right to fear commitment to an asylum for the feeble or senile. T. W. Hill (*Dickensian*, 49 (1953), 92) comments that the old man surely "knew that some of the 'curative' measures employed in lunatic asylums included: lashes ordered by the doctors, surprise baths (hot), rotating chairs, high walled enclosed courts, or yards for exercise, etc."

6. Alexander Welsh describes the possible relationship between Père Goriot, Nell's grandfather, and King Lear. I am here concerned with similarities between Balzac and Dickens in the depiction of obsessive conduct. The compulsive gambling of old Trent also suggests to me the ruinous addiction of Balthazar Claës to the alchemist's pursuit, in *La Recheche de l'absolu* (1834), though I have no reason to believe that Dickens knew that novel.

WORKS CITED

Altick, Richard D. *The Shows of London*. Cambridge: Harvard UP, 1978.

Dickens, Charles. *The Letters*. Pilgrim Edition, eds. Madeline House and Graham Storey. Oxford: Clarendon, 1969), II (1840–41).

Dickens, Charles. *Master Humphrey's Clock* (2 vols. bound together containing first text of OCS). London: Chapman and Hall, 1840.

Dickens, Charles. *The Old Curiosity Shop*. Ed., Angus Eason; introduction by Malcolm Andrews. Penguin, 1972.

Fielding, K. J. *Charles Dickens*. Boston: Houghton Mifflin, 1965.

Ford, George H. *Dickens and his Readers*. Princeton: Princeton UP, 1955.

Ford, George H., and Lauriat Lane, Jr., eds. *The Dickens Critics*. Ithaca: Cornell UP, 1961.

Harte, Bret. *Poetical Works*. "Dickens in Camp," 202. Boston: Houghton Mifflin, 1882.

Senelick, Laurence P. "Little Nell and the Prurience of Sentimentality." *Dickens Studies*, 3 (1967), 148–59.

Welsh, Alexander. "King Lear, Père Goriot, and Nell's Grandfather." *Literary Theory and Criticism: Festschrift Presented to René Wellek*, ed. Joseph P. Strelker. New York: Peter Lang, 1984, II, 1405–25.

The Incorporation of *A Christmas Carol*: A Tale of Seasonal Screening

Caroline McCracken-Flesher

In February 1844, just a few months after *A Christmas Carol*'s publication, Thackeray called the book "a national benefit, and to every man or woman who reads it a personal kindness" (Collins 149). Dickens' tale certainly has proved a national benefit, but not, perhaps, as he would have hoped or as Thackeray meant. In Britian, and particularly in America, it has benefited not so much national morality, as the national economy. From Russell Baker's perspective, the germ of "the secular mass-marketing exercise that Americans celebrate nowadays" lies in "The Christmases Dickens admired Scrooge for keeping ever afterward." "Scrooge," Baker writes, "stood on the threshold of the modern Christmas—a 'festival of consumption' . . . —in which a monthlong celebration takes place not in the church, but in the department store" (Baker 23). And without doubt, *A Christmas Carol* stands central not just to our experience of Christmas, but to the season's commercial success. As I will argue, in fact, and as television and cinema versions of Dickens' tale will demonstrate, *A Christmas Carol* has become conflated with our culture's dominant economic narrative, the Christmas narrative of corporate sales.

Of course, Dickens did not single-handedly or even deliberately transform Christmas into a festival of giving and getting capable of boosting year-end sales receipts. Neither, indeed, was he solely responsible for the holiday's recovery after its post-Reformation decline, nor for its consolidation from related seasonal festivities into the unified celebration we now know (Pimlott;

This article is dedicated to Roger Henkle, Dickensian, 1935–1991. He liked the movies, too.

Golby and Purdue). In 1836, seven years before *A Christmas Carol* appeared, Thomas K. Hervey published *The Book of Christmas*, with illustrations from Dickens' ill-fated collaborator, Robert Seymour. This text elegizes the various, supposedly moribund seasonal holidays—from St. Thomas's Day (21 December) to St. Distaff's Day (7 January). Crucially, however, *The Book of Christmas* asserts itself as a product available for renewed Christmas giving. It thus manifests the recuperation of Christmas as a scene for spiritual and pecuniary transactions well before Dickens' venture into the Christmas market (*see Figure 1*).

Still, if Dickens did not initiate the recuperation of Christmas, it is nonetheless his text that has come to represent the holiday's vigorous continuance. Almost every year since the tale's publication, as H. Philip Bolton has documented, a new stage production, radio performance, television show or movie has served to demarcate the month of December as ritual space reserved for Christmas. (By 1987, Bolton's count stood at 357; Bolton 234–67. My count for that period includes a further, 1959 version, Vincent Price narrating). More importantly, however, although *A Christmas Carol* apparently marks off sacred time, recurrently, it sets that time apart for secular spending. As *Figure 2* demonstrates, the tale has become a sign invoked by commercial interests to stimulate consumerism, an icon through which the spiritually needy (pun intended) are coerced to participate in transactions redeeming primarily to corporate and national economies.

But how can *A Christmas Carol* have come to serve interests that we might consider those of the unreformed Scrooge? Bernard Darwin and E. W. F. Tomlin each have detailed the appropriation of Dickens texts and characters and even of the author himself to enhance sales as far back as *Pickwick Papers* (Darwin; Tomlin 264–72). However, that widespread advertising phenomenon has long since passed away. In 1930, Darwin noted the decline of the "Nickleby pen," and the "Pickwick" nib, whose jingle he glibly quoted ("They come as a boon and a blessing to men, / The Pickwick, the Owl and the Waverley pen"), has gone the way of the Nickelby pen—as has general audience recognition of both Dickens texts and characters (Darwin 9). Of all the possible Dickensian icons, *A Christmas Carol* alone remains the advertising agency's delight.

Could Dickens' investment in his texts' money-making potential somehow have pressed *A Christmas Carol*, in particular, into service for commercial interests? It is a commonplace, after all, that although Dickens told his brother "there is not a successful man in the world who attaches less importance to the possession of money, or less disparagement to the want of it, than I do,"

Christmas Presents.

Figure 1: Product placement: *The Book of Christmas* creates the conditions for its own reproduction, figuring centrally within itself as a gift available for future years (*The Book of Christmas* 214). Photograph by Cedric Reverand.

Figure 2: A Christmas Present: Gordon's Christmas Spirits as Christmas Spirit (*Time* 4 December 1989:82 b). Photograph by Cedric Reverand.

"Behind all the lofty principles," as Robert L. Patten points out, "Dickens was no paragon: he did covet the power and position that wealth could secure" (Patten 14 and 13). Further, it is undeniable that the publishing history of *A Christmas Carol* reveals the author's conflicted involvement in capitalism and consumerism. In his recent book *The Lives and Times of Ebenezer Scrooge*, Paul Davis notes that "The book itself represented . . . bourgeois values. Its hand-tinted illustrations and the gold leaf on the binding attested to the success and authority of its creator. At the same time Dickens also wanted to speak for the urban poor and reach a working-class audience" (Davis 5–12, esp. 11). Davis stresses both Dickens' generous concern that the book be widely available, and his rage at its dissemination through piracy—his equal obsessions that it perform a social work, and make money. Nonetheless, *A Christmas Carol* must have become a marketing miracle independent of Dickens' interests, for we cannot logically blame the tale's ongoing appropriation to serve capitalist ends on an authorial or publishing history that remains invisible and thus uninfluential to most readers.

Nor can we easily blame the tale itself for its fate, for whatever Dickens' inconsistencies as public benefactor and beneficiary, in *A Christmas Carol* Scrooge gains personal redemption not from getting, as a capitalist narrative would require, but from giving. And this radical shift in the character's exchange processes—from getting to giving—is manifested not through his indulgence in a spontaneous burst of consumerism, an orgy of purchasing, but by his anonymous purchase and distribution of a turkey, and the modest redistribution of his wealth. He sends the boy he hails on Christmas morning to buy and deliver the bird to the Cratchits; he whispers his donation to the charity collectors he had dismissed the previous day; on Boxing Day he raises Bob's salary some amount modestly hidden from the reader. (British employers traditionally gave employees their "Christmas Boxes," their bonuses, on "Boxing Day"—the first working day after Christmas.) Although Don Richard Cox has intriguingly argued that "The 'conversion' . . . Scrooge experiences is not a holy revelation but an economic [one]," and that "Scrooge simply exchanges one set of economic values for another [coming to] the rather secular conclusion that it is not money that brings happiness in life, but rather what money can buy" (Cox Letter), Elliot L. Gilbert has tellingly asked in return: "What . . . is to be said of a critic who appears to believe that, because the decision to buy a turkey and the decision not to buy a turkey both involve financial considerations, there is therefore no important difference in the end between having a turkey and not having a turkey?" Pushing the point home, Gilbert continues: "Surely only someone with the most austerely abstract notions of spirituality could be as careless as this about the distinction between eating and starving'' (Gilbert Letter). Obviously, Scrooge shifts from getting to spending money, but he does so to participate in a carefully modulated exercise of unostentatious giving, and of giving according to need.

Yet, could not the images of excess against which Scrooge's miserliness is contrasted and his redemption played out somehow have invited appropriation of *A Christmas Carol* for the purposes of commerce? The tale foregrounds plenitude, after all. The narrator droolingly reports:

> The poulterers' shops were still half open, and the fruiterers' were radiant in their glory. There were great round, pot-bellied baskets of chestnuts, shaped like the waistcoats of jolly old gentlemen, lolling at the doors, and tumbling out into the street in their apoplectic opulence. There were ruddy, brown-faced, broad-girthed Spanish Onions, shining in the fatness of their growth like Spanish Friars; and winking from their shelves in wanton slyness at the girls as they went by, and glanced demurely at the hung-up mistletoe. There were pears and apples, clustered high in blooming pyramids; there were bunches of grapes, made in the shopkeepers' benevolence to dangle from conspicuous hooks, that people's mouths might water gratis as they passed; there were piles of filberts, mossy and brown . . . there were Norfolk Biffins [apples], squab and swarthy, setting off the yellow of the oranges and lemons, and, in the great compactness of their juicy persons, urgently entreating and beseeching to be carried home in paper bags and eaten after dinner. (Dickens 89–90)

But "the steeples called good people all, to church and chapel, and away they came, flocking through the streets in their best clothes, and with their gayest faces.'' Church calls away the purchasers, and these affluent classes who can afford the plentiful yet rare raisins, the extremely white almonds, the long, straight sticks of cinnamon, are succeeded by the poor, who emerge "from scores of bye streets, lanes, and nameless turnings . . . carrying their dinners to the bakers' shops'' (Dickens 91). This celebration of culinary delights implies no excess for all. Just as Scrooge's redemptive gesture recognizes the necessity only for repletion, not for surfeit, here, plenty abounds, yet is nonetheless distributed with restraint, according to wealth and status. So Dickens provides no template for the conspicuous and excessive consumption the twentieth century considers necessary to drive corporate and thus national economies, and that *A Christmas Carol* now serves to promote.

What, then, precipitated *A Christmas Carol*'s transmutation into a tool for corporate enrichment? I suggest it was Dickens' very care *not* to recommend gluttonous consumption, his care that Scrooge give to each, individually, according to their needs. Dickens emphasized the social integration and the spiritual benefit that devolved upon Scrooge through his thoughtful, measured giving to Bob Cratchit and the charity collectors; by doing so, he sentimental-ized and sanctified the exchange of money and goods at Christmas. Of course, following Arthur Krock, the conservative critic Jeffrey St. John has found here the origin of Roosevelt's New Deal, and what, for him, is the perversion inherent in social programs. He writes in *The New American*, "[Scrooge's salvation] is an unconditional sharing of his wealth with the less fortunate in exchange for being accepted by his fellow-men—not out of any Christian principles of love and charity. What Mr. Scrooge earned by his own effort is automatically open to claim by those who have less. . . . Today [this] is known as the forced transfer of income from the "haves" to the "have nots" (Krock and St. John 30). However by foregrounding the spiritual profit available through gift giving, Dickens equally—though unwittingly—served the inter-ests St. John defends: he offered corporate culture an icon that could be invoked every Christmas to ennoble exchange not between the affluent indi-vidual and the needy poor, but between the purchaser and the corporation that creates and supplies his or her needs.

Further, as this article will demonstrate, because it celebrates individual spirituality, yet links that spirituality to a material generosity dependent on and supportive of retail sales, *A Christmas Carol* has been thoroughly co-opted by corporate culture; it has become in/corporated, in the fullest sense of the word. Certainly, advertisers continue to deploy Dickens' tale to arouse consumer sympathy for products little related to it. Gordon's Gin, for instance, relates to Dickens' tale only through an unfortunate but irresistible pun on "Christmas Spirit." Yet more strikingly, in its television and cinema manifes-tations, Dickens' tale has been conflated with the narratives of the corporations exploiting it and even with those of the media concerns presenting it. In its telling, the tale has no function other than to generate corporate sales. Such sales, in fact, obviate the need for it to stimulate exchange on any more personal level; they pre-empt the possibility of spiritual transcendence through thoughtful gift giving. Christopher Hudson tacitly observed this phenomenon in his acid comment on *Scrooge*, the story's 1970 adaptation. He writes: "It is difficult to be miserly about *Scrooge* . . . which will give a lot of pleasure to countless children and a lot of money to that notable pauper Twentieth Century-Fox" (Hudson). To view a recent adaptation of *A Christmas Carol* is to be divorced from the tale itself, but incorporated alongside it into the capitalist narrative with which it has coalesced.

Paul Davis has ably detailed the operations of *A Christmas Carol* as what he terms a "culture text" (Davis 4). He has traced the tale's occupation by successive cultural moments (Davis 13–14). "The Victorian Carol," he writes, "revealed a new urban world infused with spirit(s), and so it became a kind of scripture." "Victorians of the 1870s," he adds, "read [Dickens'] Christmas story as retelling of the biblical Christmas story." "In the decade preceding World War I," Davis continues, "the Carol was treated for the first time as a children's story," whereas "Before and after the stock market crash of 1929, some saw the Carol as a denunciation of capitalism, but most read it as a way to escape oppressive economic realities." Here, Davis distinguishes between British and American intepretations of Dickens' tale. "The British," he points out, "denied the depression by reaffirming a traditional Carol, but in America a revolutionary version of the Carol emerged that made Cratchit the protagonist." Davis goes on to note that "Restored to his central role in the sixties, Scrooge becomes himself a kind of revolutionary. . . . In therapy with the Christmas spirits, he learns to enjoy life in the here and now." Finally, Davis points out, "If there was joy in the streets of the sixties, in the eighties there is hunger and homelessness. Scrooge is again a social figure placed in the center of unsettling economic realities." He concludes: "The contradiction between self-interest and selflessness that inspired the *Carol* in 1843 [now] prompts its contemporary retelling and produces a Carol that makes the unreformed Scrooge its hero." This last observation, concerning *A Christmas Carol*'s political appropriation in the Reagan era, brings Davis close to recognizing the corporate dynamic that has progressively invaded Dickens' tale. Davis recalls "Edwinezer Meese," and his 1983 defense of the unregenerate Scrooge and thus of corporate profits (Davis 221). But for Davis, *A Christmas Carol* is first and foremost a culture text, not a corporate text. That is to say, Davis recognizes the inscription of shared but personal anxieties across Dickens' tale. For him, it manifests the Victorian's participation in the search for a secular basis for religion, or the Depression era sufferer's desire for a sense of personal power, albeit alongside his fellow sufferers. Even in *Scrooged*, Davis hears an individual voice speaking for humanity. He writes: "The moviegoer is left with the reality of the theater . . . and the voice of the satirist desperately pleading, 'It would help if people treated each other with more consideration—you know it as well as I do' " (Davis 238).

What is equally striking to me, however, is that of the thirteen films, three television movies, and ten teleplays of *A Christmas Carol* presented to date, eight out of the eleven I have viewed on tape, including all seven of those produced in America, map the tale's shift away from personal needs—from Bob Cratchit's need for a turkey; from Scrooge's need for redemption—to the needs of a corporate or national economy (my count adds to Bolton's the 1959 version with Price, *Scrooged, Black Adder's A Christmas Carol*, and *The Muppet Christmas Carol*). For example, the 1938 American movie, starring Reginald Owen, boosts consumerism by focusing not on Scrooge's consider- ate supplementation of Bob's diet and salary, but on his joy in indiscriminate purchasing. Scrooge arrives at the Cratchits' bearing a turkey and sundry mysterious packages; he exclaims to his nephew: ''Everything for everybody, eh Fred?'' And this scene is not elided but augmented in the 1970 British musical, *Scrooge*, a film produced, like its contemporary, *Oliver!* to seduce money from English and American pockets alike. (Consider Oliver's com- modification of his surroundings for local and international consumption in his plaint ''Who will buy this wonderful morning?'' [Bart 99–107].) Here, Scrooge (Albert Finney) runs wild in a series of shops. Then, dressed as Santa Claus—a being who, according to J. A. R. Pimlott, did not usurp Father Christmas in England until the 1870s—and even more anachronistically, sporting the red and white colors marking Santa's function as Coca-Cola advertisement, he parades the streets to the accompaniment of massed voices that celebrate the joys of buying and getting (Pimlott 111–19; Golby and Purdue 71–75; Pendergrast 181). They carol:

> Every Christmas,
> Father Christmas
> Puts a great big sack
> On his dear old back
> 'Cos he loves us all
> And he shows it!
>
> . . . .
>
> In the morning—
> Christmas morning—
> If you lift your eyes
> There's a big surprise!
> On your bed you'll see
> There's a gift from Father Christmas
> From Father Christmas!
> That's how Christmas ought to be!

Eventually, supported by his all-singing all-dancing entourage, Scrooge bursts in upon the bemused Cratchits to distribute largesse willy-nilly—though sig- nificantly, he almost forgets Tiny Tim.

A 1950s television production of Dickens' tale for the Chrysler ''Shower of Stars'' series on CBS reveals most clearly this shift in emphasis from

Figure 3: Old Christmas persists in Britain (*The Book of Christmas* 22). Photograph by Cedric Reverand.

Figure 4:   Coca-Cola's jolly, red-coated Santa beats out the opposition (*The Ladies' Home Journal* December 1931; 96). Photograph by Cedric Reverand.

Figure 5: Scrooge, a jolly red Coca-Cola advertisement, distributes largesse in *Scrooge*, 1970. Courtesy of the Museum of Modern Art Film Stills Archive.

giving to frenzied purchasing and acquiring, this appropriation of *A Christmas Carol* to serve corporate and national economic needs.[1] Indeed, the CBS/Chrysler version of Dickens' story reveals the large degree to which, by 1955, the tale had become invaded by and embedded within the machinery of the corporate narrative. But before we turn to the show itself, some background information will help us understand what motivated Chrysler in its dependence on a television program to boost its corporate balance sheet, and thus to understand the particular type of appropriation suffered here by Dickens' tale. According to Michael Moritz and Barrett Seaman, during the war years Chrysler did very well. Moritz and Seaman observe: "Chrysler marched into the Second World War and emerged decked with a five-star reputation for meeting, and beating, deadlines on all sorts of military paraphernalia" (Moritz and Barrett 45). But in the years following the war, they argue, Chrysler squandered its gains. Management was stodgy and incompetent; the workers became disaffected; production decisions were uniformly poor. Moritz and Seaman point out that:

> At a time when the public was fast becoming convinced that there was little else but style to separate the labels that rolled off the end of the Detroit lines [the Chrysler chairman held to his old-fashioned concerns]. General Motors and Ford lengthened hoods and puffed up fenders while Chrysler actually shortened their 1953 cars. A mere eight weeks after introduction, dealers began to bootleg the cars to secondhand merchants. The first of Chrysler's many years of reckoning was 1953. Although sales increased, earnings were down by 5 percent and the stock price slumped from $96^1/4$ to $56^1/4$ as Chrysler forever lost its hold on second place. (Moritz and Seaman 52)

By the mid fifties, therefore, Chrysler was exerting major efforts to recoup its fortunes. The company restyled its cars, and initiated a major advertising campaign. Moritz and Seaman write:

> At the 1955 preview, Colbert [the president], along with his chief stylist, Virgil Exner, attempted to curb Chrysler's accelerating weakness with an elaborate show of "new fashions in motion." Inspired by a McCann-Erickson campaign dubbed "The Forward Look," the new platoon [of cars] outmeasured the opposition in practically every way. The Plymouth was stretched $10^1/2$ inches to 204 inches (compared with 198 for Ford and 196 for Chevrolet) while the Dodge lined 212 inches of curb. The cars, which rolled out in 173 two-tone and even some three-tone combinations, sported automatic transmissions on the dashboard and temporarily boosted Chrysler's market share to 16.8 percent (from 12.9 percent in 1954). (Moritz and Seaman 56)

"Shower of Stars" showcased the cars of "The Forward Look." To do so, according to Brooks and Marsh, it "offered viewers light entertainment featuring some of the biggest names in comedy and music. . . . most of the telecasts were musical-comedy revues" (Brooks and Marsh 709). But the entertainment chosen as a vehicle for Chrysler sales at Christmas, that peak selling period, had to be such that in experiencing it, viewers should stand simultaneously inscribed within the company's economic plot; they should feel compelled to empty their pockets in favor of that notable pauper, Chrysler (if I may borrow Hudson's apt phrase). That is, the Christmas broadcast should meld with the corporate narrative, and with its readers, grow incorporate not into the Holy Spirit, exactly, but into Chrysler. A Christmas Carol, though first shown in 1954, was rerun in 1955 and 1956. Evidently, in Dickens' text, Chrysler found the perfect incorporable and incorporating tale, the tale that could be coalesced with that of corporate profits and thus could locate its viewers within Chrysler's overarching economic narrative.

Evidence of A Christmas Carol's incorporation forces itself on the viewer even as the "Shower of Stars" production's opening credits roll. Here, oddly, although Dickens' tale presumably will be used to sentimentalize and sanctify the purchase of Chryslers, it is not invoked until two corporate logos, the stars, the cars, and the series host all have put in their appearance. Moreover, these each receive an introduction far beyond that accorded to the text when it finally does appear. One of those full-throated, steak-eating, football-playing, male announcers' voices declares:

Fredric March!
Basil Rathbone!
Ray Middleton!
Bob Sweeney!
Starring in: "Shower of Stars!"
Hollywood's brightest stars making their television appearance in full color.
Brought to you by Chrysler Corporation—maker of these five great cars:
Plymouth!
Dodge!
DeSoto!
Chrysler!
And the exclusive Imperial!

The stars nod and simper at us, the cars speed toward us, fenders a-gleam. Do we have here the equivalent of the drum-roll, the indication that the "really important stuff" is about to come? I think not. Rather, corporations, stars and cars clash in a flurry of mutual authorization that swells to fill the as yet invisible text, blocking any interpretive gap through which A Christmas

Carol's more humane concerns might subsequently call into question its corporate appropriation, its role in padding Chrysler's year-end sales figures.

And this presentation of *A Christmas Carol* not only seeks to embed Dickens' tale in the corporate sign system, it actually struggles to inscribe the corporate narrative as always and already within the tale, as always and already sentimentalized and sanctified, always and already authorized. The most obvious examples of this phenomenon occur in the production's two advertising breaks. Of course, all network offerings suffer commercial breaks, and in these breaks we expect to find advertisers scrambling to elide the space between image and product, between gorgeous hunk of man and odorous scent for women, for instance, but here we find Chrysler trying to identify the corporation with the program that surrounds the advertising space. At the end of Marley's visit, the audience expects to move into Christmas Past; when Scrooge returns from Christmas Yet to Come, we expect to enter a redeemed Christmas Present. Instead, in each case we find ourselves precipitated into the corporate narrative. Marley's visit gives way to a snow scene—Christmas past, surely—no: Chrysler present.

In these advertisements, painstakingly constituted as additional movements in Scrooge's progress and in the progress of the audience, Chrysler's advertisers forge a spiritual link between the joys of giving and of purchasing. In the first break, as gleaming Chryslers pull up to disgorge the fur-clad and the high-heeled for a New England Christmas, the choir carols: "Now is the time for joyful giving. / To give is the way to joyful living." During the second break, the host informs us that *A Christmas Carol* inspired this little ditty, "The Spirit of Christmas," and that it was "written especially for our show tonight." In the meantime, lest we should miss the point, he dangles a tinseled key before us and exclaims: "what better way to combine the time for joyful giving, the way to joyful living, than a gift of one of these superb new stationwagons of The Forward Look '56? For here, truly, is the gift that keeps giving in year round driving pleasure."

But the corporate narrative whose happy ending depends on ceaseless purchasing does not stop even at conflating itself with Dickens' tale; it actually usurps the text—and invites the viewing/buying public's complicity in so doing. Fezziwig's ball, and Scrooge's relations with his fiancée, frequently are expanded in film versions of *A Christmas Carol*, but seldom like this. In his story, Dickens shows Belle in the moment when she parts from Scrooge, and again in her happy, married life. In the 1951 British film, we see Scrooge become engaged to "Alice," we witness their parting, and in Christmas Present, we catch a glimpse of Alice's subsequent, charitable life. In the 1970 musical, the fiancée is Fezziwig's daughter, and her name is Isabel. Scrooge, watching her in Christmas Past, sings his way into an extended memory sequence where we see them rowing, practicing archery, and riding—and getting engaged—in a gig. We also see their parting. In all cases, Dickens' original and our 1955 adaptation included, Scrooge and his love part because of his undue involvement in business. Here, however, the fiancée seems equally implicated in the corporate dynamic. It is she who asks the question that can be answered completely only by a consumerist and Chrysler response. At Fezziwig's party, in an expanded scene that follows the first commercial break and that together with her dismissal of Scrooge makes up Christmas Past, she sings: "What shall I give my lad for Christmas?" She suggests "A bird on the wing and a song to sing / And an answer to three words carved in a golden ring." Or perhaps, she choruses with Ebenezer, "The rattle of rain on the window pane / And the ground floor plan of a castle in Spain." The viewer, who by this point in the production has assimilated *A Christmas Carol* as corporate narrative, suffers an agony of deferred gratification; primed by the sight of more tangible delights, we burn to cry out: "A Chrysler—no, two Chryslers—a Chrysler each!"

And in fact, this version of *A Christmas Carol* works to incorporate all of its participants, to construct its characters, and especially its viewers, as potential purchasing subjects. Everyone can enter the newly humanized corporate narrative; everyone can afford a Chrysler. Consider: Scrooge carries no turkey to the Cratchits, though he shares in their dinner. Why this aberration in turkey mythology? The Cratchits don't need a turkey, thank you very much. As Mrs. Cratchit explains early in the show, the Cratchit bird is larger than the average goose and will take longer to cook—and daughter Martha actually bemoans its size. Moreover, these Cratchits are reasonably well off. Bob stresses that they are only a few shillings a week from affording health care for Tiny Tim. With the largesse we know Bob is destined to receive from Scrooge, surely he too will be able to aspire to a car of "The Forward Look." But perhaps even more striking, the program is so constructed that Bob's needs notwithstanding, the viewer has always and already been economically and *morally* affluent enough to buy a car. The segue from the program's incorporating envelope to the dramatization itself went through the standard appropriative gesture of showing *A Christmas Carol*'s book jacket and title page. But it went further, showing the book buyer, and further still, showing the buyer meeting with and contributing to the Charity collectors before they headed to Scrooge's office. As viewers, we have looked through the book-buyer's eyes, we have delved into his pocket twice, first to purchase the book, second, effectively, to buy off the Charity collectors. From the program's opening scene we have defrayed our debts to the poor; the money left jingling in our pockets is our own. So we too can afford that dream machine; we too can serve the narrative of corporate gain.

CBS/Chrysler's *A Christmas Carol*, then, demonstrates how, and how far, Dickens' text has been co-opted to serve corporate culture and the national economy. Appropriated, conflated and usurped, the story now validates the exchange of money and goods *not* between the haves and the have-nots, but rather between the haves—reconstituted as all working individuals—and the corporate "have lots." The message is no longer the expansive "give so that you shall receive spiritual absolution," but the somewhat circular "buy a Chrysler so that you shall receive one."

Paradoxically, however, *A Christmas Carol*'s extensive incorporation actually has made it subject to critique in the corporate media. In their 1988 movie, *Scrooged*, scriptwriters and "Saturday Night Live" alumni Mitch Glazer and Michael O'Donoghue embed a thoroughly commercialized *Christmas Carol* within an updated and ultimately rehumanized version of the tale. Frank Cross (Bill Murray), youngest network president in history, presides over a Christmas Eve broadcast of Dickens' story, but as a Scrooge surrogate, he participates in his own version of *A Christmas Carol*. In the course of the movie, the *Christmas Carol* Frank produces (titled *Scrooge*) is measured against the one in which he lives. Frank's salvation lies in his ability to recognize the discrepancy between the televised *Carol* and the one in which he is inscribed, in his ability to step out of the appropriated, incorporated tale, and into his own life figured as *A Christmas Carol*.

Yet despite their strenuous efforts—and the always strenuous efforts of their star—Glazer and O'Donoghue fail to transcend the commercialized *Scrooge* by means of Frank's more humanized tale that surrounds it. Paul Davis argues that "If it is to become *Scrooged*, [*Scrooge*] must enter the real world and become history. When Frank leaves the studio for the streets," Davis writes, "he seeks the transforming truths that will save him from narcissistic self-destruction and make his life a Carol." For Davis, the fact that "When the streets come to the studio during the production of *Scrooge*, they threaten and eventually halt the performance," signals the commendable usurpation of television and cinema by life (Davis, 237–38). I suggest, by contrast, that although Glazer, O'Donoghue, director Richard Donner, and star Bill Murray certainly fight to bury the corporate narrative under the Dickensian tale's more social concerns, their movie demonstrates the impossibility of accomplishing that aim within a corporate medium.

Where does the film's problem lie? Certainly not in any reluctance to critique, as the opening scenes make clear. Here, the film invites the viewer to recognize and reject the televised incorporation of *A Christmas Carol*. In a promotional clip for the IBC network's forthcoming production of Dickens' tale, the appropriative and incorporative gestures that we experienced in the Chrysler production are pushed to their deconstructive limit. There is the same attempt to elide the space between Dickensian and corporate narratives: the clip begins with a short of the IBC logo, which then circles to become the imprint on a leather-bound copy of *A Christmas Carol*—here denominated *Scrooge*. There is the same frenzy of name-dropping, the same attempt to bind the text in a web of authoritative, incorporative, and incorporated terms. John Housman narrates the production (by virtue of his role, Frank scathingly notes, as "America's favorite old fart"). The program stars Jamie Farr (otherwise, Corporal Klinger), in some suitably undetermined role, Buddy Hackett, and, in these days when athletes leap from the mat to the podium to the screen, Mary Lou Retton—straight from her back-flipping battery commercials—as Tiny Tim. The show even stands authorized by star venues. For some never explained reason, it will be presented from "New York, Bethlehem, Helsinki, West Berlin, and the Great Barrier Reef!"

Indeed, Glazer et al. construct *Scrooged* to make critique unavoidable for the viewer. Lest we should mistake the system through which to read the IBC show's excess of authorization, the clip for *Scrooge* is preceded by another, more ridiculous one that provides us with an interpretive paradigm. Here, villains I can only describe as the "Ninja/SAS" attack Santa's workshop, blasting "The Night Before Christmas" into *The Night the Reindeer Died*! But not to worry. The man in the white suit arrives to rescue the man in red—spouting strangely familiar lines from another man in white (Rick, in *Casablanca*): "It don't matter a hill of beans what happens to me, but the world couldn't afford it if anything happened to you." In a flurry of inappropriate authorizaton, Santa is validated by his rescuer's status, and the rescuer is validated by Santa's recognition of him in terms that reach beyond the show—beyond even the movie—to merge the actor and his outside, authorizing role. As the white-parkaed knight leaps from his snowmobile to the rescue, Santa exclaims in awe: "It's Lee Majors, the Six Million Dollar Man!"

Scrooged actually goes so far as to stress that the corporate appropriation of Dickens' tale aims to achieve, and requires for its success, the simultaneous incorporation of the viewer. In the Chrysler production of the novel, Dickens' tale served not only to sentimentalize and sanctify the exchange of goods and money between buyer and corporate seller, but also to situate the viewer within the corporate narrative. In *Scrooged*, Frank's problems arise from his subjection to television, to the corporate medium, at a tender age. When Christmas Past returns Frank to his childhood, we see him compensating for an imperfect upbringing by turning to television. The results are two-fold: first, Frank's childhood has been entirely displaced by scenes from *Little House on the Prairie* and *The Courtship of Eddie's Father*—Frank cannot distinguish famous moments in television from genuine personal memories. Second, Frank has been constructed as the perfect viewing subject. A product of television, he's now network president, and in producing shows he constantly reinscribes himself within, and draws others into, the corporate narrative.

But even as *Scrooged* attains this deconstructive moment, its very critique becomes absorbed into the "Paramount" narrative. The movie's opening scenes have emphasized television as a vampiric medium, incorporating and sucking dry viewers who in turn incorporate and suck dry one another. Frank is only television's most visible victim. The executive Frank fires for questioning his preferred *Scrooge* commercial ends up donating blood so that his veins may flow with Christmas Spirit in the fullest sense, that is, with booze (thereby boosting another corporation). And the violent advertisement that Frank prefers dries up the lifeblood in one unfortunate viewer, who suffers a heart attack while watching it. That viewer, as a consequence, becomes the subject of a second version of Frank's promotional clip. Frank fears no liability suit when he hears of the viewer's death: rather, he exclaims: "This is terrific! I knew that ad worked. You can't buy publicity like this! I want that promo run every half hour—I want a disclaimer at the top: 'Anyone with a heart condition must leave the room!' " Now, however, the movie abruptly reinscribes television as a carnivalesque space there individuals are not destroyed but celebrated, where community is not prevented but promoted—a space where the network can reach out and touch its viewers, infusing each and all with genuine Christmas Spirit.

This recuperation of television as the communicative medium gains force from the fact that its prime movers are Christmas Past and Christmas Yet To Come (renamed "Christmas Future"), the spirits who demonstrate Frank's problematic subjection to the television image. While each implicitly criticizes television, each also participates in it, communicating with Frank across the television screen. For instance, Christmas Past carries Frank to Christmas 1971 where his younger self, invested in his role as "Frisbee the Dog," abandons his one true love to court the boss. Christmas Past suddenly disappears, reappearing to hail Frank from the studio monitor that last showed him as Frisbee. "What's going on?" Frank yells. "So long sucker!" Christmas Past replies, as the camera pulls back to reveal that he leans not from the monitor, but from his cab window. The cab then drives out of the picture to reveal on the monitor a scene from the dress rehearsal for IBC's *Scrooge*. Now the camera pulls back even further, including Frank in the shot, and Frank, as producer, turns to interrupt the rehearsal, arguing his own problems across Dickens' dialogue. Christmas Past, then, accomplishes communication not by stepping out of the televised space, as we might expect, but by placing himself and Frank within it. And the strategy remains the same for Christmas Future. "He" initially emerges from the television; his image swells to fill a bank of monitors in Frank's office. But then he reaches out a skeletal hand to draw the unsuspecting network president to an education *through* the screen. Further, Christmas Future bears not a face but a monitor that reflects and refracts successive images of Frank's laughing face and his skull beneath the skin. Indeed, Frank eventually enters his dreadful yet redeeming future on the Spirit's facial monitor. Christmas Future, then, reconstructs television as a medium whose occulted images are not inherently negative, but which need to be read aright.

The closing scene in Frank's life as Scrooge clarifies this reconstruction of television as communicative medium. Here, the reformed Frank re-enters the world and recuperates Dickens' message by invading the televised space of the incorporated tale. The television Scrooge throws a coin to the boy on Christmas morning; the camera pans to show it slowly fall. Suddenly, however, the shot cuts and Frank reaches in to catch the money. Then he addresses the camera. Revoicing Dickens' message, he calls upon the audience within the movie, relocating them within the liberated television space, and the space of Dickens' tale as lived by himself. A series of shots of Frank disrupting the *Scrooge* set are interrupted by a series of reverse shots showing the reacting, viewing public: Frank's boss, his brother, the homeless. These fragments of American society meet across a third set of shots, images of Frank, displayed on television and in monitors. Television becomes a medium in the spiritual sense: a force that mediates between America's varied populations, a space where society's disparate pieces can meet to form a whole.

Perhaps it is inevitable that Glazer and O'Donoghue should produce a critique that serves only the interests of television, since they themselves are writers heavily dependent on that medium. But the most interesting aspect of their concluding recuperation of television is the way it suggests a deeper, preliminary incorporation for both *Scrooged* and the movie-goers who have participated in it. Whether criticizing or recuperating television, like Dickens'

Figure 6:   Frank Cross takes a ride with channel-surfing Christmas Past. Courtesy of Paramount Pictures.

A Christmas Carol, and in its role as *A Christmas Carol, Scrooged* always and already has been fully incorporated by virtue of its articulation through the cinematic medium, and it always and already has incorporated its viewers.

This becomes evident when Glazer and O'Donoghue seek to extend their paean to communication beyond the television space and into the cinema itself. At the end of the movie, as the casts of *Scrooge* and *Scrooged* join to carol, "Think of your fellow man / Lend him a helping hand / Put a little Love in your heart," cameras, monitors, and so on all pull back to open a channel for Frank to the cinema audience. He steps forward, drawing in the audience, in its fragmented groups, for this modernized version of the Dickens message. He invites "The men. . . . the *real* men," then "the women. . . . the *real* women," to join in his global sing-a-long. But when Frank steps from the television screen into the cinematic space and thence into the cinema itself, he leaves the charmed, celluloid circle, steps out of his role as Frank Cross, and becomes Bill Murray. And as Bill Murray, even in the moment when he draws us into the feel-good space *Scrooged* has reconstructed for *A Christmas Carol*, he pulls us, along with Dickens' tale, into the orbit of the cinema industry. Moreover, he reveals that we have been there all along, for this is, after all, the Bill Murray who has been paid for his performance, the Bill Murray who already is involved in some other commercial venture; this is the actor who has left his shadow to please us, to incorporate us by teasing the money out of our pockets and into the coffers of Paramount USA—whatever the avowed message of his movie.

And the movie's final images confirm its subtext. First, even as Bill Murray incites the audience to "Think of your fellow man," to escape the corporate narrative and remember Bob Cratchit, the credits roll, once more entangling the viewer and *A Christmas Carol* in the corporate project. Next, we see the Paramount logo—and remember that we entered the cinema space through Paramount's circling stars. (The movie's opening shots swooped the audience between the Paramount stars to the North Pole, where Santa awaited rescue by Lee Majors in *The Night the Reindeer Died!*) *Scrooged* always has been a creature of Paramount's creation; it always has served the corporation—as have we, by viewing it. Finally, we see Bill Murray, still dancing, but now looking down to brush away the letters of the word "Scrooged," written across the screen. The unreformed Frank told his erstwhile girlfriend to "scrape off" the poor; now that *A Christmas Carol* has accomplished its task of transferring the viewer's money to the corporation, it can be scraped off. And since the viewer has fulfilled her seasonal responsibility by hearing the message of Dickens' incorporated tale, indeed, since she has always and

Figure 7:   Bill Murray brushes off his *Christmas Carol*. Video still by permission of Paramount Pictures.

already accepted her incorporation by buying her ticket at the door, she too can brush off the poor. Together with the rancid popcorn and the scattered remnants of the word "Scrooged," they can be swept out at the end of the performance.

Thus, appropriated, conflated and usurped, *A Christmas Carol* stands co-present with, but subjected to the transcendent narrative of our times, that of corporate economics. Thoroughly incorporated through Dickens' tale, the viewer can only wonder what to do with that spare cash, those pennies saved from the poor. Perhaps this year's *Christmas Carol*?

NOTES

1. Paul Davis asserts that the program was first broadcast in 1954 (Davis 266). The videocassette screens the same date, but includes commercials for Chrysler's 1956 models. Since, according to *The Complete Directory of Prime Time Network TV Shows: 1946–Present*, "Shower of Stars" ran from 1954 to 58 and broadcast *A Christmas Carol* "live" three straight years, and since the host on the cassette mentions Chrysler's pleasure at bringing Dickens' tale to the screen "again this year," it seems likely that the program was presented in 1954, and again in 1955 (presumably, also in 1956), with advertisements appropriate to the year. My argument pertains to the show as it appears on the videocassette, that is, to the 1955 repeat, complete with that year's commercials.

WORKS CITED

Films

A Christmas Carol. Dir. Edwin L. Marin. With Reginald Owen. Loews, 1938; colorized videocassette: MGM/UA.

A Christmas Carol. Dir. Brian Desmond Hurst. With Alastair Sim. United Artists, 1951; videocassette: United Home Video.

A Christmas Carol. Dir. Ralph Levy. With Fredric March. CBS/Desilu, 1954/5 (see footnote 1): videocassette: Carousel Film and Video.

A Christmas Carol. Dir. Clive Donner. With George C. Scott. Entertainment Partners, 1984.

Black Adder's A Christmas Carol. Dir. Richard Boden. With Rowan Atkinson. BBC, 1991; videocassette: BBC Enterprises Ltd.

Casablanca. Dir. Michael Curtiz. With Humphrey Bogart. Warner, 1942.

Charles Dickens' "The Christmas Carol." Dir. Arthur Pierson. Narrated by Vincent Price; with Taylor Holmes. Paramount, 1959; musically enhanced videocassette: Burbank Video.

Mickey's Christmas Carol. Dir. Burny Mattinson. Walt Disney Productions, 1983; videocassette: Walt Disney Home Video.

Mister Magoo's Christmas Carol. Dir. Abe Levitow. UPA Pictures, 1962; videocassette: Paramount.

The Muppet Christmas Carol. Dir. Brian Henson. Jim Henson Productions, 1992; videocassette: Jim Henson Video.

Oliver. Dir. Carol Reed. With Mark Lester. Columbia Pictures, 1969; videocassette: RCA/Columbia Pictures Home Video.

Scrooge. Dir. Henry Edwards. With Sir Seymour Hicks. Paramount, 1935; videocassette: Viking Video Classics.

Scrooge. Dir. Ronald Neame. With Albert Finney. Cinema Center Films, 1970; videocassette: CBS/Fox Video.

Scrooged. Dir. Richard Donner. With Bill Murray. Paramount, 1988; videocassette: Paramount.

Texts

Baker, Russell. "Dickens Stacks The Deck." *New York Times* 24 December 1983:23.

Bart, Lionel. Libretto. *Oliver!* London: Lakeview Music Publishing, 1960. (First performance 1960.)

Bolton, H. Philip. *Dickens Dramatized.* Boston: G. K. Hall, 1987.

Brooks, Tim, and Earle Marsh. *The Complete Directory to Prime Time Network TV Shows: 1946—Present.* 4th ed. New York: Ballantine, 1988.

Collins, Philip, ed. *Dickens: The Critical Heritage.* London: Routledge and Kegan Paul, 1971.

Cox, Don Richard. Letter. *PMLA* 90 (1975): 922–23.

Darwin, Bernard, ed. *The Dickens Advertiser: A Collection of the Advertisements in the Original Parts of Novels by Charles Dickens.* London: Elkin Mathews & Marrot, 1930.

Davis, Paul. *The Lives and Times of Ebenezer Scrooge.* New Haven: Yale UP, 1990.

Dickens, Charles. *A Christmas Carol.* 1843. Harmondsworth: Penguin, 1971. Vol. 1 of *The Christmas Books.* Ed. Michael Slater, 2 vols. 1971.

Gilbert, Elliot L. "The Ceremony of Innocence: Charles Dickens' *A Christmas Carol.*" *PMLA* 90 (1975): 22–31.

———. Letter. *PMLA* 90 (1975): 923–24.

Golby, J. M., and A. W. Purdue. *The Making of the Modern Christmas.* Athens: U of Georgia P, 1986.

Hervey, Thomas K. *The Book of Christmas.* London: William Spooner, 1836.

Hudson, Christopher. "Cashing in on Christmas." *The Spectator* 5 December 1970, 736.

Krock, Arthur. "In Washington: Scrooge and New Deal Ghosts Adorn a Christmas Tale." *New York Times* 25 December 1934:22.

Moritz, Michael, and Barrett Seaman. *Going for Broke: The Chrysler Story.* Garden City, NY: Doubleday, 1981.

Patten, Robert L. *Charles Dickens and His Publishers.* Oxford: Clarendon, 1978.

Pendergrast, Mark. *For God, Country and Coca-Cola.* New York: Charles Scribner's, 1993.

Pimlott, J. A. R. *The Englishman's Christmas.* Hassocks, England: Harvester P, 1978.

"Scrooged Again." *Time* 26 December 1955:46.

St. John, Jeffrey. "In Defense of Scrooge: A Second Look at *A Christmas Carol.*" *The New American* 23 December 1985:27–31.

Tomlin, E. W. F., ed. *Charles Dickens 1812–1870.* New York: Simon and Schuster, 1969.

Bleak House and Dickens' Originals: 'The Romantic Side of Familiar Things'

When Somerset Maugham returned to Malaysia, aged about eighty-six, he found himself unpopular. *The Straits Budget* reported that he had accepted hospitality, picked up local scandals, and "dished them up" in his short stories (Sherry 133). But to those who complained about his drawing characters from life, Maugham replied: "One might suppose that no one had ever done this before. That is nonsense. It is a universal custom." It was a poor excuse, but true. Chaucer, so we are told, had done it; so had Scott, George Eliot, Thomas Hardy, and certainly Dickens. Maugham had discussed the practice before in *The Summing Up*: "I should say that the practice of drawing characters from actual models is not only universal but necessary. I do not see why any writer should be ashamed to acknowledge it. As Turgenev said, it is only if you have a definite person in your mind that you can give vitality and idiosyncrasy to your own creation" (Maugham 217–18). What is interesting about Dickens' practice is that once we have established the facts as far as we can, we should feel free to go on to see what to make of them.

For some reason (and often for good reason) this belongs to the shady side of Dickens criticism. George Ford, in the admirable Norton critical edition of *Bleak House*, is rather cagey about the question, and suggests that we should not think about it if we do not like it. Some readers, he explains, find the search for Dickens' " 'real-life' originals" actually "offensive," because "they contend that to identify a prototype is somehow to cast a slur on the artist's imaginative capacities and his originality" (891); and Ford is stating a general view though he also gives a valuable guide to "originals" or "persons and places." There are other, usually unexpressed, objections: first, that the identification and comparisons are often made so badly. Secondly, they

119

frequently bring in irrelevancies or, as Ford says, suggest likenesses that are "faint . . . far-fetched or pointless." Thirdly, the identification is often made by those who treat art as a shadow, and less important than "real life"—not my *choice* of term. Yet, though all this may be true, if we were to avoid discussing this well-developed feature of Dickens' fiction just because we do not "like it" and because past enquiries took a wrong turning, it would be absurdly faint-hearted.

There are larger critical questions, chiefly a matter of emphasis rather than principle, which I will mainly postpone. It may be that they can be seen as related to the final, somewhat mysterious remark in Dickens' Preface that: "in *Bleak House*, I have purposely dwelt on the romantic side of familiar things." For the present we may agree with George Ford that "such identifications" at least "harmlessly provide materials for interesting comparisons" or "glimpses into the shaping power of the novelist's imagination" which suggest much more. Certainly Dickens himself was always willing to admit the possibility, as in letters cited in the Norton edition. While writing the novel, for example, he mildly replied to a Mrs J. S. Cumming, on 7 September 1852:

> You will, I hope, consider it a sufficient reply to your enquiry if I answer that I presume most writers of fiction write, partly from their imagination; and partly from their experience; and that in the work to which you refer, I have had recourse to both sources   (*Bleak House* 891).[1]

On 4 April 1868 he answered a Miss Palfrey in the United States to explain where she could find the "original" of Jo's burial-ground:

> Convey yourself back to London by the agency of that powerful Locomotive, your imagination, and walk through the centre avenue of Covent Garden Market from West to East . . . Keep straight along the side of the Theatre, and about halfway down, on the left side of the way, behind the houses, is a closely hemmed-in grave yard . . . When I was a boy it was to be got at by a low covered passage under a house, and was guarded by a rusty iron gate. In that churchyard I long afterwards buried the "Nemo" of *Bleak House*.   (894).[2]

In fact, in this instance, the actual and fictional were so close that Dickens used the same phrase as the novel for the "*hemmed-in* churchyard, pestiferous and obscene" (11, 137).

There is a further problem in the division between writers like Kingsley Amis, who are deeply reluctant to admit to originals in anyone's work and even more in their own, and others who are too easily attracted by the idea, such as William Amos in his *The Originals, Who's Really Who in Fiction*.[3] To Kingsley Amis, not unreasonably, to say that a novelist was "really" writing about someone comes close to "concluding that he was 'only' doing so." Yet William Amos has no compunction in declaring that Alderman Cute in Dickens' *The Chimes* is Sir Peter Laurie, Mrs Nickleby "was" Dickens' mother, and even that Master Humphrey, of *Master Humphrey's Clock* "is Thomas Humphreys . . . of Barnard Castle." Yet, though short on evidence, his book is full of good stories which help to dispose of any refusal to accept that there have been fictional "originals," which clearly show how strong a wish there is to believe in them; and this itself suggests something about the nature of fiction—the desire to relate the real and fictional worlds.

Yet many novelists are anxious to throw the reader off the track (as Dickens is at times), or eager to explain that using an original is entirely different from thinking it "the same" as the fictional character. Certainly the term "original" implies that the fiction is a copy, though Maugham agrees (in *The Summing Up*) that the writer "does not copy from his originals; he takes what he wants from them." They remark, like Charlotte Brontë: "You are not to suppose any of the characters in *Shirley* intended as literal portraits. It would not suit the rules of art"; or, like George Eliot, "*There is not a single portrait in Adam Bede* . . . Everything is a combination from widely sundered elements of experience."[4] In fact can anyone ever believe that the original and the fiction *are* "the same" or even that one is an exact "portrait" of the other, except in fanciful exaggeration, as with Dickens himself writing of his mother: "Mrs. Nickleby herself once asked me, as you know, if I really believed there ever was such a woman?"[5]

Maybe we need to remind ourselves of the facts, and before this, to think about what is meant by a character's "original," for not only can there never be an identity between the actual person and the fiction, who live in different dimensions, but the word is so loosely used. It can be found in the *Life* of Dickens by John Forster, who was often consulted by Dickens about the practice and who could use the term with authority. Dickens, himself, wrote to Forster at one point that he had told his illustrator H. K. Browne to make sure that the first illustration of Skimpole in *Bleak House* was "singularly unlike the great original," Leigh Hunt (Pilgrim 6, 623).

Yet, after Dickens had finished the final number, his old friend, the Hon. Mrs. Richard Watson, asked him point-blank about Hunt and Skimpole. Dickens had already told her, "between ourselves," that Boythorn was 'a most exact portrait in words' of Landor (Pilgrim 6, 666). Now he declared:

> I must not forget Skimpole . . . I suppose that his is the most exact portrait that was ever painted in words! I have very seldom, if ever, done such a thing. But the likeness is most astonishing. I don't think he could posible be more like himself. It is so awfully true, that I make a bargain with myself, "never to do so, any more". There is not an atom of exaggeration or suppression. It is an absolute reproduction of a real man. Of course, I have been careful to keep the outward figure away from the fact; but in all else it is Life itself. This is in confidential reply to your enquiry. (Rolfe 194)

This cannot have been wrong about his intention, in spite of later denials. But the story was muted by Forster; this particular paragraph was left out of the Nonesuch Letters, and even the note on Skimpole in the Pilgrim edition is peculiarly exculpatory and does not refer forward to this frank boast to Mrs. Watson. Yet Dickens was evidently not only tempted by his power but surprised by it.

Nor was Forster completely frank about how Dickens broke the bargain with himself when he came to *Little Dorrit* three years later, though maybe as open as decently possible. Early in his account he had explained how the "real" Dora Copperfield (Dickens' first love) was to reappear in his life in 1855 (F, 1, 3, 49). This was Maria Beadnell, by then Mrs Winter. Failing to live up to Dickens' expectations, she was recreated as the ridiculous Flora Finching, as he wrote to the Duke of Devonshire: 'It came into my head one day that we all have our Floras (mine is living and extremely fat), and that it was a half serious half ridiculous truth which has never been told' (Nonesuch 2, 785). She may not have recognised herself when *Little Dorrit* was published, but she outlived Dickens by sixteen years and the connection was cruelly precise in Forster's biography (F, 8, 1, 625).

Whatever the exact meaning, Dickens and Forster believed in "originals," and they were aware of precedents set by Scott and eighteenth-century novelists. They thought of them in the obvious sense of being real people who had suggested recognisable characters; and Forster's discussion is often bound up with excuses for personal betrayal, because such instances were often so close that they are distinct from satire or recognisable figures in a roman à clef. That sense of betrayal, which they found in Scott as well, may even have combined with the shock of recognition and helped to give Dickens' vibrant creativeness its peculiarly potent charge. These are what can be called "true originals," unquestionably derived from and directed at real life, such as the Bow Street magistrate Fang (*Oliver Twist*, Mr. Laing), Wackford Squeers (*Nickleby*, William Shaw), admittedly satiric; Mrs. Pipchin (*Dombey*, Mrs. Roylance), Micawber and Miss Mowcher (*Copperfield*, John Dickens and

Mrs. Seymour Hill), and so on.[6] And to complicate the matter, there are various lesser originals, in which the connection is much less direct, as those for Miss Flite, or Turveydrop in *Bleak House*.[7] We can already see that there is a problem in distinguishing different kinds.

It was made more difficult by the first book on the subject, Edwin Pugh's *Dickens Originals*, which helped to bring it into disrepute. It is typical of weaker studies of the sort in operating in a borderland of tenuous possibilities, often dependent on random association and without discrimination or a sense of evidence. Yet it is precisely this that is needed. For, in fact, almost everything depends on analytically discriminating. It is not only that the truth of such ascriptions needs to be questioned reasonably, but we need to see that we are faced with different kinds of connection between fact and fiction. So-called *originals* can range from likenesses confirmed by the author, his subject and their common friends, to purely whimsical identifications; and, within these extremes, authors may be quite justified in claiming that they have based a character on a single characteristic or more than one person. Then, we ought to recognise that all that an original and the fiction can possibly share are common characteristics such as ways of speech, quirks of behaviour, details of appearance, similar names or circumstances, a locality or occupation. The originals may either come from shared experience or passing observation, or derive from a verbal report, childhood memories, or even minor written allusions without direct knowledge, like any other source. Lastly, when we come back to the evidence (usually best if contemporary with the novel), before a likeness can be reasonably discussed, we have to have some authority for ascription other than the repetition of an old tale. For there is also a large class of "phoney originals," which rest on nothing but someone's say-so, and which go *against* the evidence. For example, John Camden Hotten's remark that Mrs. Jellyby was derived from Harriet Martineau, or the recent statement that Esther Summerson comes from Dickens' sister-in-law, Georgina Hogarth, which simply cannot be substantiated.[8] It slides into gossip and confuses the discussion of almost every question, such as one that I would like to put forward, about whether (at the time of writing of *Bleak House*) the whole practice was growing on him, and why.

Once again, this may be borne in on us if we return to Forster, who was closely involved with the genesis of most of the novels. It is a suggestion that has been stoutly resisted; yet in spite of some of Forster's bad habits as a biographer, it was something that he knew about. He can be read as explaining that the practice grew on Dickens because his writing became less spontaneous so that, particularly after his relative ease in writing *David Copperfield* (where he profited from the autobiographical form), he was drawn even more strongly to using originals. As we have seen, there were certainly real-life prototypes in the early novels; but they proliferate in *Copperfield*, not only in Creakle who was perhaps something like Dickens' own old headmaster Mr. Jones, Rosa Dartle (in one respect like Dickens' friend Mrs. Hannah Brown), Creakle-as-magistrate like the real magistrate Benjamin Rotch, Ham Peggotty with a touch of James Sharman of Great Yarmouth, the adult Traddles (shadowing Dickens' friend Talfourd), and numerous characters from those parts of David's childhood taken from the manuscript of Dickens' lost autobiography.[9]

There is one particular instance in the novel, in which we can watch Dickens at work: a Mrs. Jane Seymour Hill, who is known to have been the original Miss Mowcher. She was a dwarf 'corn-cutter' or chiropodist, a near neighbour of Dickens, who must have met her. She wrote him a moving letter protesting at the recognizable way in which she figured in the ninth number:

> All know that you have drawn my portrait—I admit it but the vulgar slang of language I deny. May your Widow and Children never meet with such Blighting wit . . . Should your Book be dramatised and I not protected madness will be the result.   (Fielding, "The Making" also *Pilgrim* 5, 674).

Dickens' illustrator is said to have produced a likeness from the author's description;[10] the novel *was* dramatized; and what Mrs. Hill most bitterly objected to was the moral character of Miss Mowcher, who was evidently to have been Steerforth's procuress. She is a special case because, though Dickens answered as one might expect, denying the exact resemblance and saying that the character had a composite origin, his private letters show that he was elated at the triumphant likeness. Forster gives his friend's immediate response: "I have had the greatest adventure this morning, the receipt of the enclosed from Miss Mowcher. It is serio-comic [why comic?] but there is no doubt that one is wrong in being tempted to such a use of power" (Pilgrim 6, 676). On consideration, Dickens undertook to alter the character's nature in its development, yet refused to be hurried in changing 'the natural progress and current of the story' (Pilgrim 5, 677). One notices how, in private, he saw Mrs. Hill as just "Miss Mowcher" and that Forster (probably echoing him) calls her a "grotesque little oddity" (F 6, 7, 548), as if she were a puppet tugging at her strings. Only by the eleventh number did Dickens tell Miss Coutts,"I am at present repairing Miss Mowcher's injury—with a very bad grace and in a very ill humour'' (Pilgrim 6, 35), possibly joking but not without resentment.

Yet with *Bleak House*, the significance of Mrs. Hill may appear even more clearly when compared with similar instances of originals. We find the same delight at fictionalizing reality combined with reluctance to change, not only because of the part that the characters play in the plot but (as I suggest) because they may have been needed to develop his meaning. Such grotesques may have been chance trouvailles, but Dickens found them stimulating because they fitted the central ideas of a novel. Miss Mowcher's later transformation (in Mrs. Hill's interests) into a good-hearted minor heroine offended against his first inspiration and was made to fit ''the current of the story'' only because the second half of the whole novel slips towards conventionality.

No doubt the use of originals in writing *Copperfield* was a source of inspiration when Dickens was also managing amateur theatricals, starting his new periodical *Household Words*, and busy with other journalism. And this is just when Forster writes of Dickens' decline in spontaneity. He compares *Bleak House* with its predecessor: ''Ingenuity is more apparent than freshness, the invention is neither easy nor unrestrained, and although the old marvellous power over the real is again abundantly manifest, there is some alloy of the artificial'' (F 7, 1, 599). He sees it as ''inferior'' to *Copperfield* (F 6, 7, 552). Later, *Little Dorrit* is said to show signs of ''a droop in invention'' as ''in portions of *Bleak House*'' (F 8, 1, 623); just as Dickens wrote to him of *Our Mutual Friend*,'' I have been wanting in invention'' (F 9, 5, 742).

It is a judgment Forster returns to: for example, on coming to his chapter about Dickens' separation from his wife, he repeats that the ''strain'' on his ''invention,'' was felt with *Dorrit*, just as it had been present ''in a modified form . . . during the later portions of *Bleak House*'' (F 8, 2, 636). Hence he says of Dickens' resort to a small ''Memoranda'' notebook of suggestions for characters and incidents in writing: ''Never before had his teeming fancy seemed to need such help.'' The book, he explains, was used till *Our Mutual Friend* was finished: a work which ''wearied'' Dickens somewhat with the labor of invention which had not been so free or self-sustained as in the old facile and fertile days'.

More recent criticism has not been willing to accept this, because it thinks highly of the later novels. Yet that is not in question. The difficulties that drove Dickens to a greater intensity were nonetheless there; and there is no doubt that, under the pressure of all his other activities, on top of writing three or four chapters a month, strictly to time, for over eighteen months,

Dickens increasingly resorted to looking about him and turning to fresh experience. Originals often had the advantage of bringing with them a social context and given appearance, often essential to Dickens' characters who chiefly exist in that way.[11] Dickens resorted to life as a stimulus to "vitality" (like Turgenev), as a help to invention, because it gave him a sense of power, and was of the essence in writing fiction—and for other reasons. As it happens, little of this shows up in the number-plans for the novels, which never refer to major originals and rarely to minor ones.[12] Yet, without his leaving us a plain trail, there are signs that one reason why Dickens fastened on his originals was because they could be associated with underlying themes. This may be partly supposition: but it would help to explain why he kept to the practice so tenaciously, and how it happened that the integrity of the novels was unaffected. It equally suggests that we may learn by arguing from the originals to the theme as well as happily confining ourselves to a text and disregarding how it was written.

It may be found in many instances; but, for example, in turning more squarely to *Bleak House*, it has been noticed how three of its most remarkable figures are Skimpole (Leigh Hunt), Boythorn (Walter Savage Landor), and—as now argued—Smallweed (Samuel Rogers) at least in outward appearance. Only Skimpole is a writer and artist in the novel. Yet not only did Dickens develop Skimpole as someone who raised questions about the responsibility of writers and artists, but he was so personally involved with the issue that Landor and Rogers were drawn in by association. For if we look for a reason for the combination, it surely lies in the way that the novel was "Dedicated / As a Remembrance of our Friendly Union, / To My Companions / in the / Guild of Literature and Art": a dedication which many modern reprints (such as the Norton edition) omit. For even before the appearance of the latest volumes of the Pilgrim *Letters*, it was clear that the work for the Guild was central to Dickens' concern while he was writing *Bleak House*. He had made a tremendous effort to organize an association of writers and artists who were to help others and themselves by an insurance or friendly society, which would provide for illness and retirement and assist those in need. And, as well as requiring regular subscriptions from all who could be persuaded to take part, Dickens also managed his amateur theatrical company, and arranged its appearances in order to raise funds.

It was an enormous task, besides which Dickens managed every detail and held together a company incompletely devoted to its aims. He also had to arrange the administrative and legal foundation of the Guild. As it happens, he should have had more assistance, since the wording of the charter establishing it was bungled, and after delays the scheme largely fizzled out.

Both Forster and Dickens, however, blamed their fellow writers for failing to support it. They were probably justified, and Leigh Hunt came to see that his own lack of interest lost him Dickens' sympathy. Yet he has been personally shielded in his time and ours, though it is clear that he was a bad debtor, took for granted the help that Dickens organized for him, and was even ready to reject it at the critical moment in favor of support from the Whig government which the members of the Guild scorned for its reluctance to help literature in general. There were probably other reasons for Dickens' annoyance, such as Hunt's crawling wish to be Poet Laureate, when he had once shone as a martyred radical for his satire of the Prince Regent.[13]

Even so, Skimpole is both a personal satire and the type of artist willing to surrender independence in return for patronage, and constantly willing to be helped out of debt. Dickens' later denials that he meant Hunt to be recognizable seem to have been accepted by recent biographers,[14] but contemporaries were unconvinced. Macaulay wrote: "An odd declaration by Dickens . . . He owns he took the light externals . . . from Hunt, and surely it is by those light externals that the bulk of mankind will always recognise character. Besides . . . the vices of Skimpole are those to which Hunt had, to say the least, some little leaning" (*Diary*, 23 December 1859). Others agreed, such as John Stores Smith, who found Skimpole an "exact moral photograph," a "portrait . . . daguerreotyped to the life . . . despite Mr. Dickens's denial":[15] It is arguable, therefore, that Skimpole's introduction in the second number was a fundamental step in the novel's progress and development; and, once we see this, it is clear why Dickens so obstinately resistd the efforts of Forster and other friends to change it when they were shown advance proofs. Skimpole's weaknesses and attitudes to money, rank, and patronage, were essential; all that *could* be done was to change him from fat to thin and alter his original Christian name from Leonard to Harold. Even so, Dickens was so concerned about the integrity of his novel that, when he accidentally let "Leonard" creep back in a later chapter, he kept to his usual practice and pointedly called attention to it on an errata slip prefixed to every bound volume.

All this may help to explain how Dickens chose to balance him with Landor as Boythorn, as if a corrupt writer who largely belonged to the past Romantic period must be paired with one who compelled Dickens' admiration. (There is also a link in that both figures were even closer friends of Forster, whose loyalties were sharply strained over Hunt.) In fact, Boythorn now seems unconvincing as one of a matching pair and appears chiefly as an eccentric with only a slight connection with the novel's themes of responsibility and radicalism. But for contemporaries who knew him better he was renowned for his radical republicanism and welcome for the revolutions of 1848. He was equally noted for his scorn for any kind of patronage. In 1848, for example, he had written for the *Examiner* under Forster's editorship (18 November):

> Dependent on no party, influenced by none, abstaining from society and conversation of the few public men I happen to be acquainted with, for no other reason than because they are in power and office, I shall continue, so long as I live, to notice the politics and politicians which may promote or impede the public welfare.

Hence his and Skimpole's pointedly contrasting attitudes of hostility and servility to Sir Leicester Dedlock in chapter 18. The degree to which Grandfather Smallweed is like the banker and poet Samuel Rogers is less substantial (Alexander 67–73). The argument for likeness lies in the way they were both illustrated, their state of decrepitude, bad temper, and their treatment of their close relatives; and I fancy we cannot set much store on any connection between Smallweed's usury and Rogers' former banking. In spite of all three literary originals being ''Romantic'' poets of a kind, Smallweed's presence in the trio may come less from the literary association than the novelist's simply being able to turn to someone conveniently familiar.

To discuss all the novel's originals would take too long. The clearest example of one with a central place in the design is Jo, the crossing-sweeper and rejected witness. His examination by the coroner in chapter 11 is taken from a report of George Ruby (also a crossing-sweeper), on 8 January 1850, before an alderman at the Guildhall. His is not a ''putative likeness'' or mere 'reputed original'' (Norton), but a close correspondence. The report had appeared at least twice in the first number of Dickens' *Household Narrative*, at least once in *Household Words*, and in a series of articles about such cases in the *Examiner* to which Dickens is known to have contributed. All of which has long been argued out, as perhaps has the way in which Jo's honest doubt is so typical of the 1850s that other contemporaries chose to comment on Ruby.[16] If we can accept this, the interesting result is to see what Dickens made of him, and how he takes his place in a novel about faith and doubt (among much else) and false teachers such as Chadband. Forster tells us that at first Jo was meant to have had a much larger part to play, but even so he is left with a central one connecting the various classes. If George Ruby could conceivably have joined Mrs. Hill in her objections, Dickens would have been unable to alter his past.

Other figures may, or may not, be almost identical. Plausible originals have been found for such characters as Miss Flite, or Mr. Turveydrop, who is pointedly shown imitating the Prince Regent but may have been prompted by George IV's former tailor, John Henry Shelton. The case of Gridley comes from a pamphlet on Chancery, sent Dickens by a Staffordshire solicitor *after* the novel began to appear (F 7, 1, 564; Pilgrim 6, 623–24). The Jellybys' disorderly home may have been suggested by Mrs. Caroline Chisholm: "I dream of" her "and her house-keeping," Dickens told Miss Courts. "The dirty faces of her children are my constant companions."[17] Inspector Bucket obviously had a definite original in Inspector Charles Frederick Field, although Dickens wrote to *The Times* to deny it, and we can track Field through articles in *Household Words* transparently figuring as Inspector Wield. Yet Dickens clearly reconsidered and transformed such figures; and, as he obviously knew, they had taken on another form of reality in fiction, in which—if space allowed—they could be shown developing a new life.

Others are in a different category, such a Mademoiselle Hortense, who, it is fair to say, is often thought of, or said to have been, based on the sordid and mercenary murderess Mrs. Maria Manning.[18] Some of the evidence is open to question; for although, for example, it has been said that Dickens attended her trial in 1849, it is almost certainly wrong. No doubt he went to her execution. Before drawing conclusions, this needs further investigation; and it is arguable that, as it stands, a simple identification suggests a sensationalism at odds with the deeper implications of the novel. She is remarkable for showing how Dickens wanted a character who challenged his own fictional conception of women as the weaker sex, and this may have been Mrs. Manning's value for him. But he equally wanted a romantic *frisson*, as in the incident when Mademoiselle Hortense cools her jealousy by kicking off her shoes to walk "through the wet grass" as if it were blood (18, p. 231). Again he contrasts the brutality of Tulkinghorn's murder (shot like Manning's victim) with Hortense's bolder and more passionate crime, by introducing it with a lengthy passage about the moon rising over the wilderness as, shining over the city, the Thames winds on to London:

> Its steeples and towers, and its one great dome grow more ethereal; its smoky house-tops lose their grossness, in the pale effulgence . . . In these fields of Mr. Tulkinghorn's inhabiting, where the shepherds play on Chancery pipes that have no stop, and keep their sheep in the fold by hook and by crook until they have shorn them exceeding close, every noise is merged, this moonlight night, into a distant ringing hum, as if the city were a vast glass, vibrating.

What's that? Who fired a gun or pistol? Where was it?

It is romantic, not just in the associations with Wordsworth's sonnet, or perhaps Shelley, or the grand manner, but in distancing itself from the action through elaboration of style.[19]

Dickens means to have it both ways: to root his action in reality, but to treat it romantically. That is to say, to make it wonderful and strange, to play with it linguistically, to involve it in a plot of striking coincidences, and yet avoid harsh unpleasantness. Yet all the while reality was also in view. For what is clear throughout is that, so far as readers were aware of originals, they helped to place the characters and their context in the contemporary scene. This is consistent with the novel's topicality. Jo, for example, is significant of the outcast children of London; Bucket as the sole state functionary who is paid to keep them in order; and all the characters correspond to a visible English population to which our attention is explicitly drawn. Such figures then lead us towards another category which is not fictional at all. Guster's upbringing at a pauper school in Tooting was one shared by over 150 children who had recently died of cholera. Charley Neckett does not exactly have even a "reputed original," though Dickens may have had in mind some recent notorious cases of ill-treatment of young servants. Similarly, the originals of the Bagnets are not exactly to be found in "Soldiers' Wives" (*Household Words*, 6 September 1851), any more than Allan Woodcourt had an original because Dickens' choice of profession presumable arose from contemporary controversy about naval surgeons' pay.[20] These topics actually belong to the *real* world, which it is the aim of the novel to recreate with a difference.

They are from the "familiar" side; and Forster, and some earlier writers on Dickens, were not only source-spotters but ready to take this into account in their criticism. They could, in fact, also go back (as Dickens himself probably did) and think of them in terms of earlier writers. A contrast between writing about the everyday and the "romantic" was familiar in the criticism, for example, of Sir Walter Scott. Scott had written about romantic effects in the work of Mrs. Radcliffe in his *Lives of the Novelists*, delighting in her as "the first poetess of romantic fiction," while he recognized that Jane Austen's "new style of novel," substituted "the art of copying nature as she really exists . . . instead of splendid scenes of the imaginary world."[21] We see Dickens as combining the two approaches, and the inclination to look to the originals as a wish to "copy nature," while being ready to romanticise unpleasant actualities.

There is another sense in which his observation of life is both romantic and familiar. Elements which link his fictional characters with their originals are often associated with touches of nature: Skimpole's playful selfishness, Squeers' comic brutality, Micawber's brand of optimism, and the famished Jo's inability to accept food as the shadow of death falls on him,[23] may all have been linked with this truth to nature. It comes less from external observation than seeing our common humanity. It may even lie in something as ridiculous as the natural way in which Mrs. Gamp relieves her long hours as a night-nurse by gently rubbing her nose along the smooth rail of a high fender—a detail said to have come to Dickens from Miss Coutts, who had observed it in her own night-nurse (F 4, 1, 294; Pilgrim 3, 520). It is often related to an absurd fidelity to life as, in writing about some of his own descriptions, Dickens once said: "Some . . . tickle me very much; but that may be in great part because I know the originals, and delight in their fantastic fidelity" (F 9, 1,726).

It is not new, therefore, to say that Dickens' genius lay in his humanity or "his fellow feeling with his race" (F 7, 1, 562). Novelty should not be in question. But though there is much to be learned from earlier criticism, our answer cannot lie in simply turning back to it. Yet if we can inform ourselves about the way in which he went about his writing, we may be able to go further than John Forster. Certainly we should be able to appreciate that when Dickens drew from life it was seldom for the sake of mere mimicry or making "exact portraits." He looks within. That is why I am so uneasy when Humphry House lays down, in the Introduction to *The Dickens World*, that the "proper interest" of discovering originals "lies only in their relevance" to Dickens' biography or to "the social history behind his novels." Impressive as this sounds, he does not seem to care about how they affected Dickens' writing, and he is bewildering about the whole question, miscalling William Shaw (Squeers' original) "Stone," and professing to find Hotten's blunder about Harriet Martineau and Mrs. Jellyby potentially full of "fruitful sense." For it is not *true* to Dickens. Of course, there is no single critical conclusion that can be drawn from re-examining Dickens and his originals, and there can be no end to discussion if we see him as meaning to return to nature. Mostly I see myself as a crossing-sweeper, clearing the path so that there will be less "tripping . . . on slippery precedents."

NOTES

1. *The Letters of Charles Dickens*, (Oxford: Pilgrim edition; hereafter Pilgrim) 5:755.
2. *The Letters of Charles Dickens*, (London: Nonesuch edition, hereafter Nonesuch) 3:642; given more fully than in the Norton edition.

3. For Amis see Amos and Amis's review of Jacqueline McDonnell, *Waugh on Women* (*Observer*, 9 February 1986). Amos also guards himself with the customary formulas, "it is believed," "reputed," "a possible prototype," and "supposedly part-inspired," etc., but is both acute and misleading.

4. The comments on Charlotte Brontë and George Eliot are from "No Portraits" in Miriam Allott, *Novelists on the Novel*, 279–87, which gives other disclaimers. Mrs Gaskell, for example, more directly says that in *Shirley* "the idea of most" of her friend's "characters" was "taken from life," and that the novelist mistakenly "thought she could draw from the real without detection." See *Life of Charlotte Brontë*, A. Shelston (ed.) (London, 1975), 378.

5. John Forster, *Life of Charles Dickens* 6:6:151; hereafter F., with references, by book chapter, and page.

6. A good deal has been written about these originals, but the main authority for them can be found in Forster.

7. See W. J. Carlton, 521–22; and John Butt, 303; Lionel Stevenson, *Dickensian* (hereafter D), 44 (1947/8), 39–41.

8. J. C. Hotten, 214. "Miss Martineau came forward in her own person to take the cap of Mrs. Jellaby," which is simply incorrect; the Norton "dictionary" suggests Miss Hogarth as Esther's "reputed original," citing Adrian, 33–34, where the proposal is made as an unsubstantiated suggestion, since apart from their sex they seem to have nothing in common. At least it is better than Dickens' friend, Percy Fitzgerald, *The Life of Charles Dickens* 2, p. 134, who once claimed that Esther Summerson was related to the real Esther Elton, daughter of a non-existent 'Dr. Elton', apparently on the basis that they shared a Christian name. Fitzgerald has a long, inadequate chapter on 'Portraits from Life'.

9. Again substantiated by Forster, also Nina Burgis; see also Philip Collins, 86–91; and K. J. Fielding, "David Copperfield and Dialect," citing L. A. Meall, *The Guide to Great Yarmouth*, "The prototype of the brave Ham is—JAMES SHARMAN."

10. Edgar Browne, *Phiz and Dickens*, who knew Mrs Hill, says that his father never saw her but that his illustration gave "a very good general impression," being taken from Dickens' description, though whether as given in the novel or according to his directions to the artist he neither knows nor says.

11. A striking example occurred in the writing of *Our Mutual Friend*, when Dickens felt his invention "stifled and carkened," and his illustrator led him to the "original shop" in St. Giles, which prompted the entire conception of Mr Venus the taxidermist (F 9, 5, 971, and Marcus Stone's memoirs, MS, Dickens House).

12. Minor characters are referred to in the note about "Cole," and the "third gentleman" of *Hard Times*, ch. 2, a jotting with a wealth of allusion; also in the simple note about uncle Frederick Dorrit in the fourth number of *Little Dorrit*: "Ruined brother—(the clarinet-player I saw at the Ambigu in Paris)." These are exceptional, and suggest that Dickens' part-plans may often conceal as much as they reveal.

13. Pilgrim, 5:78, and British Library, Add. MSS.

14. The most recent is Fred Kaplan, *Dickens: a Biography*, 315, generally sceptical, but believing that Dickens' forced an equation . . . when consciously he meant the resemblance only as the loosest starting point."

15. From Smith's anon. "Personal Reminiscences," *Freelance* (Manchester, 4, 11 and 25 April 1968), 109–10, 111–15, 13–35, quoted in Fielding, "Skimpole and Leigh Hunt Again," 174–75.

16. Fielding "The Dickens World Revisited" Joanne Shattock (ed), and citations there including Humphry House, *The Dickens World,* and Fielding and Brice, "Charles Dickens and the Exclusion of Evidence," I and II, *Dickensian,* 64 (1968): 131–40, and 65 (1969): 39–41, etc.
17. Edgar Johnson, 4 March 1850: "It is clear that her domestic arrangements suggested those of Mrs. Jellyby" (166); and "partly inspired Mrs. Jellyby" (15). No comment in Pilgrim.
18. See, for example, B. B. Valentine, declares that "she was intended as a portrait," 21–22; but also Philip Hale "the supposition seems far-fetched," ibid., 22–23.
19. "On Westminster Bridge" and Shelley "Adonais," stanza 52. For Dickens' overt romanticism see also Susan Shatto, 8 and 296–67.
20. For all of which see Susan Shatto's *Companion.*
21. *Lives of the Novelists,* 305; in "Modern Novels," 352–76.
22. In commenting on evidence about the death of one of the pauper boys from Tooting, who refused food before he died, Dickens spoke of it "as of a peculiarly affecting kind, such as the masters of pathos have rarely excelled in fiction"; quoted by Brice and Fielding, "Dickens and the Tooting Disaster," *Victorian Studies,* 12 (1968): 243.

WORKS CITED

Adrian, Arthur. *Georgina Hogarth and the Dickens Circle.* London: Oxford UP, 1957.

Alexander, Doris. "The Poet in Grandfather Smallweed." *Dickensian* 80:1984.

Allott, Miriam. *Novelists on the Novel.* London: Routledge & Kegan Paul, 1959.

Amos, William. *The Originals: Who's Really Who in Fiction.* London: 1985.

Brice, and K. J. Fielding. 'Dickens and the Tooting Disaster." *Victorian Studies* 12:1968).

Browne, Edgar. *Phiz and Dickens as They Appeared to Edgar Browne.* London: J. Nisbet, 1913,

Burgis, Nina. Introduction. *David Copperfield.* By Charles Dickens. Clarendon ed. Oxford: Oxford University Press, 1981.

Butt, John. "Bleak House Once More." *Critical Inquiry* 1:1959.

Carlton, W. J. "Miss Fray and Miss Flite." *Notes and Queries* 196 (Nov. 1951).

Collins, Philip. "The Middlesex Magistrate in *David Copperfield." Notes and Queries* 206:1961.

Dickens, Charles. *Bleak House.* Ed. George Ford and Sylvère Monod. Norton Critical Edition. New York: Norton, 1977.

———. *The Letters of Charles Dickens.* Ed. Walter Dexter. Nonesuch edition. London: Nonesuch, 1938.

————. The Pilgrim Edition of *The Letters of Charles Dickens*. Eds. Graham Storey, Kathleen Tillotson, K. J. Fielding, et al. Oxford: Clarendon P, 1965–.

Fielding, K. J. "David Copperfield and Dialect." *TLS* 30 Apr. 1949.

————. "The Making of David Copperfield." *Listener* 19 July 1951.

————. "Skimpole and Leigh Hunt Again." *Notes and Queries* 200 (Apr. 1955)

Fitzgerald, Percy. *The Life of Charles Dickens as Revealed in His Writings*. London: Chatto & Windus, 1905.

Forster, John. *Life of Charles Dickens*. Ed. J. W. T. Ley. London: Cecil Palmer, 1927.

Hotten, John C. *Charles Dickens: The Story of His Life*. London: John Camden Hotten, 1970.

House, Humphry. *The Dickens World*. Oxford: Oxford UP, 1941.

Johnson, Edgar, ed. *Letters from Charles Dickens to Angela Burdett-Coutts 1841–65*. London: Jonathan Cape, 1953.

Kaplan, Fred. *Dickens: A Biography*. New York: Morrow, 1988.

Maugham, Somerset. *The Summing Up*. London: Heinemann, 1938.

Meall, L. A. *The Guide to Great Yarmouth*. 6th edition. London: 1854.

Pugh, Edwin. *Dickens Originals*. Edinburgh, 1913.

Rolfe, Franklin P. "More Letters to the Watsons." *Dickensian* 38 (1942).

Scott, Sir Walter. *Lives of the Novelists*. London: 1906.

————. "Modern Novels." *Quarterly Review* 24 (1820).

Shattock, Joanne, ed. *Dickens and Other Victorians: Essays in Honour of Philip Collins*. New York: St. Martin's, 1988.

Shatto, Susan. *The Companion to "Bleak House."* London: Unwin-Hyman, 1988.

Sherry, Norman. "Maugham's Last Trip to the East." *KM 80, A Birthday Album for Kenneth Muir*. Liverpool: 1987.

Stevenson, Lionel. "Who Was Mr. Turveydrop?" *Dickensian* 44:1947–48.

Valentine, B. B. "The Original of Hortense and the Trial of Maria Manning for Murder." *Dickensian* 19:1923.

Dickens and the Diseased Body in *Bleak House*

Laura Fasick

In both life and his fiction, Dickens responded with typical energy to the chief charitable movements of his time. Norris Pope has admirably documented Dickens' philanthropic endeavors, as well as his ambivalent relationship with two opposed perspectives that were particularly important in discussions about the poor and their living conditions. On the one hand, conservative Christianity emphasized individual responsibility and typically spoke of poverty as God's just punishment for the culpable (Pope 5–7). From this perspective, the poor's most urgent need was for moral and religious elevation. By improving themselves spiritually, or, more likely, by being improved through instruction from their social superiors, the poor could lift themselves from the curse (God's curse) of poverty. On the other hand, throughout the nineteenth century there was a growing awareness of and horror at the squalid living conditions of the poor. Even clergymen (Charles Kingsley, for one) and staunch Evangelicals (Ashley, for instance) were powerfully enough affected by the nauseating details of slum life to declare that environmental reforms were a prerequisite for moral ones (Pope 200–202). At the same time, the more or less tacit implication that the poor could not be virtuous so long as they lived in misery directly opposed Victorian piety about the efficacy of the individual will and the need for individual responsibility. More disturbingly yet, this assumption that material degradation inevitably led to moral decline could seem a blasphemous contradiction of God's providential plan, in which no circumstances can overcome the soul's capacity for moral choice.[1] The resulting confusion for reformers can be seen in such self-contradictions as Ashley's willingness "tirelessly and courageously . . . to combat the outbreak [of cholera in 1848–9] by direct, physical means" while simultaneously believing it to be a "scourge" from God that demanded "a national day of prayer" (Pope 203).

Dickens' writings provide an especially rich case study of the tension between these two points of view. An examination of the discrepancy between Dickens' public pronouncements on social hygiene and his fictional treatment of disease reveals an underlying ideological split. In order to explore that split, this article first furnishes a brief overview of the background to Dickens' social concerns, then demonstrates the transformation of those concerns in his fiction, specifically *Bleak House*.

Ironically, despite the range of nineteenth-century philanthropic activity, humanitarian benevolence and social justice proved to be not always complementary ideals. Justice might demand simply remedying the physical conditions of the poor en masse, but to do so would necessitate impersonal, because large-scale, activity. Yet charity, theoretically at least, established human relationships between rich and poor.[2] As A. Susan Williams points out, the point of Carlyle's famous story about the Irish widow who falls ill and infects other people after being turned away by supposed social guardians is to demonstrate, and to protest against, the alienation that Carlyle sees as pervading British society, the separation of class from class (50–54).[3]

An admirer of Carlyle, Dickens also so allied himself with the sanitary and environmental reformers that in 1850 he claimed, ''In all my writings, I hope I have taken every available opportunity of showing the want of sanitary improvements in the neglected dwellings of the poor'' (qtd. in Pope 212). Yet in Dickens' novels, as in other Victorian texts, the implications of this environmentalism run directly counter to deeply embedded ideas about the potential of the individual and relationships between the classes. As numerous critics have pointed out, for instance, the same Dickens who waxed compassionate over slum sufferings could dismiss criminals as bad by nature, and, in both his fiction and his private writings, could rejoice in the brutal punishment of malefactors.[4] Icons of goodness like Oliver Twist, meanwhile, miraculously remain pure and virtuous—and irreproachably middle-class in speech and behavior—despite enduring the same conditions that produce lower-class ruffians like Noah Claypole.[5] Dickens never really resolves these contradictions; at best he disguises them—most often, and perhaps most tellingly, by a shift in perspective that transforms both vision and sentiment. Dickens tends to facilitate his move from an environmental to a moral-religious treatment of disease (and of social problems) by what he allows (or does not allow) us to see of the bodies of his characters, both rich and poor, particularly as those bodies suffer the distortion and disfigurement of disease.

Ultimately then, Dickens deflects social criticism through his use of what A. Susan Williams has identified as a common trope of Victorian literature:

disease that originates among the poor and spreads to the upper classes. Usually, Williams claims, this disease illustrates the inevitable interconnectedness of the classes and the harm that comes even to the rich when they allow others to suffer the worst effects of poverty.[6] In Dickens' novels, however, the trope of disease become a way of moving from an emphasis on social responsibility to a celebration of personal goodness. As a corollary of this move, Dickens must shift from an attack on social structure and a call for justice to a focus on the individual and a reliance on human and divine charity.

This shift from body politic to body private takes place despite an animus toward the former that, particularly in the later novels, can easily overshadow the treatment of individual characters. Many critics have commented on Dickens' willingness to show British corruption and materialism as systemic rather than as isolated instances of evil. Yet this indictment of the "system" ironically works against systemic reform by suggesting that any organized movement, let alone any centralized institution, must inevitably partake of the corruption that it sets out to correct.[7] This distrust of collective action appears in Dickens' fiction even for organizations he supported in his life: for example, both Norris Pope and Grahame Smith note the discrepancy between Dickens' approval of the Ragged School movement in his letters and journalism and his scathing depiction of a Ragged School in *Our Mutual Friend*. Similarly, Dickens acknowledged collective efficiency in his sanitary reform work by supporting a centralized Board of Health (Pope 226–27). Yet the logical context of widescale public action is an impersonality that Dickens distrusted. During the Sanitary Association's 1850 inaugural meeting, at which Dickens was a speaker, Lord Ashley declared that the sanitary cause "was an act of justice" rather than "charity . . . [and that] the working people had a right to call upon the Legislature to assist in this great work" (Pope 225). But Peter Scheckner and many other critics have pointed out that for Dickens "workers engaged in class struggle" are as "demonic . . . as the world of industry and capital they protest" (106). Through organizing to demand institutional change, workers disregard the subtle claims of sympathy in favor of an impartial and detached theory of rights. In contrast to this rights-based model of protest, the version of philanthropy that Dickens' fiction endorses most strongly is a sympathetic response to individual cases of suffering: an inevitable result of his apparent unease with ideas of group responsibility.[8]

This focus on individual sympathy implies, however, that improvement, or even palliation, of conditions for the poor must necessarily be piecemeal, since no individual could have the power to effect change for the class as a whole.[9] It also means that the resulting improvement will be more spiritual than physical, since sympathy between an icon of middle-class goodness and a poor person must override merely material concerns. Dickens' poor repeatedly demonstrate their worthiness for sympathy by their refusal to profit materially by that sympathy, as when Nancy refuses to take more than Rose Maylie's handkerchief in *Oliver Twist*, the bricklayer's wife treasures Esther's handkerchief above money in *Bleak House*, and Betty Higden declines money from the wealth Boffins in *Our Mutual Friend*.[10] Ironically, the willingness of the good to recognize the poor as fellow beings deserving of their friendship seems directly opposed to the giving of practical assistance.

Of course, the personal realm of feelings and relationships was that in which women, especially middle- and upper-class women, were supposed to excel. Critics from Nancy Armstrong to Beth Newman to Elizabeth Langland have discussed the way in which the bourgeois lady became the figure whereby the middle classes not only reserved high moral status for themselves, but cast that morality in terms of individual and private affects. As Beth Newman has noted, the lady's body became transparent because her importance was in feelings—her own and those she inspired in others. The effect of poverty, on the other hand, as all middle-class observers agreed, was to make the body disgusting. It is the horrified sense of the gross physicality in which the poor are condemned to live that makes middle-class accounts of visits to slums so surrealistically nightmarish: the repressed Victorian body has returned with a vengeance.[11] But the result is irremediable tension between the vividly visualized problems besetting the corporeal poor and the abstracted solutions of sympathy and fellow feeling.[12] Dickens shows that the corporate/governmental/public body could do little good, but he invests general nurturance abilities in the bodiless figures of ladies. Yet how can ladies cope with the gross bodies of the poor when the female forte is fine feeling? While the nobler of middle-class men may tend to the lower classes' physical condition, it seems to be a woman's duty to alleviate the poor's visible suffering invisibly.

In *Bleak House*, the bodilessness of the lady, here Esther, works to shift the locus of discussion from social wrongs to individual moral stature and even becomes a reproach to the poor. Esther, who glides her way through the book without a single physical description,[13] is early established as the practitioner of the personal touch supreme, a benefactress explicitly contrasted with the institutionalized abstractions of Mrs. Jellyby and the blunderbuss tactlessness of Mrs. Pardiggle. Her superiority is clear because, unlike the two other women, she recognizes that "between us and these people there was an iron barrier'' (159); yet at the same time, she is a moral tutor, whispering Christ's words in a grieving mother's ear (160). Her function in the poor person's household is as arranger and organizer (even to tidying up a dead baby) *and* as religious instructor: she differs from Mrs. Pardiggle only in the sensitivity with which she approaches such responsibilities.[14] But her presence enforces the norm of individual moral culpability. It is possible to sympathize with the bricklayer's tirade against Mrs. Pardiggle in which he implicitly disclaims responsibility for his condition and explicitly blames it on poor living conditions (158), but Esther's presence enforces the necessity of their behaving properly to *her* (and Ada). From then on, it becomes possible to judge them by their behavior to their benefactors, as when one of the bricklayers goes ''out before'' the two young women in order to let them pass (161). Ironically, Esther succeeds partially in effecting the transformation in the family that Mrs. Pardiggle attempts: she is able to make at least the dead child's sister ''ashamed'' of acting improperly (161). Yet she does so by her own self-effacement, by the fact that her ministrations, unlike Mrs. Pardiggle's, are difficult to detect with the naked eye.

Jo's story demonstrates even more strongly the importance of moving from the visible to the felt. Jo begins as an exemplum of the slum ''product'': a hapless repository of disease and suffering too animal-like to be held accountable. His ondition is charged explicitly upon society. In George Ford's estimation, he falls below the line at which it is possible to expect self-help; Jo is one of the truly helpless (94–95). The novel allows a hint or two that Jo possesses a moral nature: he attempts to be an honest witness at Nemo's inquest, and he is grateful for Nemo's kindness to him. Yet the third-person narrator responsible for most of his story consistently treats him as sub-human: ''vermin'' generated by the slums from which he comes (272), Jo ranks below a dog in consciousness (275). Rather than a full person, he is a ''phenomenon'' (Metz, ''Narrative Gesturing'' 17), over the description of which the narrator lingers and to which he returns again and again, embellishing with a richness of digusting detail that contrasts strongly with Esther's invisibility. The reader sees Jo ''in uncompromising colours[, f]rom the sole of [his] foot to the crown of [his] head'' (*Bleak House* 696). We are even told to picture him as being ''like a growth of fungus or any unwholesome excrescence'' (687). Jo can be described in his full physicality precisely because he is almost entirely flesh. As Torsten Pettersson observes of *Oliver Twist*, such reliance on physiological description as characterization brings Dickens close to Zola-esque naturalism (348–49). This implicit naturalism in turn introduces deterministic terms that deny characters like Jo the possibility of free will (Reed 186–87).

This denial of free will, of course, operates in the service of social criticism: even Jo's bestiality is proof of his victimization. Since he is outside the realm of free will that might make him at least partially responsible for his own condition, society must bear the full blame for what he is. Once Jo enters Esther's narrative and Esther's presence, however, both he and the slum-bred disease he carries undergo a shift in meaning for Esther's narrative assumes both the power of the individual will and the providential ordering of the world (Reed 180–81).

Disease up to this point in the novel has been primarily a marker of social wrong: disease among indigents is a disgusting extension and visualization of general slum conditions. As such, it is a vehicle of social protest and a proof that society requires drastic revision. But when disease reaches Esther (and even before her, Charley) it is transfigured into an individual moral test and, overwhelmingly, a demonstration of individual moral worth. With the exception of Skimpole, that parasitic invader of other people's homes, everyone connected with Bleak House rises to the occasion, from Charley to Ada to Mr. Jarndyce to Mr. Boythorn and even to the servants. Esther's bodily weakness, in particular, becomes a way to demonstrate the goodness of those around her, and she is even grateful for the opportunity that sends her this demonstration of people's kindness and their love for her (545). From furnishing an indictment of the larger society of institutions, disease moves to demonstrating the essential health and worthiness of the smaller society of individuals.

The effect is to establish the middle-class home as the site not only of more physical comfort, but of more spiritual potential, than the slum. The pains produced by poverty are degrading morally as well as physical, but illness in the middle-class home reveals angelic spirits. There is therefore a purpose to this suffering—indeed, more than one purpose: it provides examples of nobility for others to follow, gives scope for people's goodness, and reinforces bonds of affection. Esther, Charley's nurse during the latter's illness, records that "[s]o patient she was, so uncomplaining, and inspired by such a gentle fortitude, that very often as I sat by Charley . . . I silently prayed to our Father in heaven that I might not forget the lesson which this little sister taught me" (495). But Charley's virtues during her own sickness are only a prelude to her heroism during Esther's. At that time, she is so deft an attendant that Esther muses she was "sent into the world, surely, to minister to the weak and sick" (545). Esther can find equal utility even in her own pain: her "trivial suffering and change" are "worth" being able "to fill . . . a place" in her guardian's heart (546). All this commentary discovers a meaning, even a positive value, in what could easily seem merely unwarranted misfortune.

Nor is Esther's commentary, shaped as it is by Esther's resolutely hopeful perspective, the only means whereby disease shifts its meaning. It is significant that Charley is able to retain her "gentle qualities" through all the various times . . . in [her] illness" (495). Suffering here lacks the power that Elaine Scarry ascribes it: it cannot make the sufferer's "created world of thought and feeling, all the psychological and mental content that constitutes both one's self and one's world . . . ceas[e] to exist" (30). Above all, it cannot affect the sufferer's will and free choice. Both Charley and Esther remain exemplary moral agents, despite extreme pain and delirium. Indeed, even Esther's feverish delusions provide another illustration of her conscientious nature: reliving each stage of her life simultaneously, she "was not only oppressed by cares and difficulties adapted to each station, but by the great perplexity of endlessly trying to reconcile them" (543). Wishing only to do right, Esther speaks even of her own mortality as though it were an instrument that she could employ as part of her care-taking role. Warning Charley to keep Ada from her sickroom, Esther declares, " 'If you let her in but once, only to look upon me for one moment as I lie here, I shall die' " (497). Here the death of the body is no more than the means for the soul to express its protective love.

Such privileging of the power of the spiritual over that of the physical helps justify the continued effacement of Esther's body. Esther can imagine "nothing definite" of her disfigurement before she actually views herself in a mirror, and even then the reader does not see "anything definite" (559). The only detail we obtain is that Esther's reflection "looked" "placidly" at her, an "encouragement" that allows Esther to keep looking even in the first shock (559). Placid, encouraging: the words could describe Esther's demeanor at any moment in the novel. They establish not that Esther is "very different" from what she had been previously, but that she is the same (559). Indeed, whereas Dickens insists that one must accept Jo's repulsive exterior in order to feel genuine compassion for him, he is equally determined to show in Esther's story that no sympathetic character even notices Esther's changed appearance. There is "nothing" in Ada's "honest face" to show that she does "not find" "her old Esther" in the now-disfigured one: she greets the new countenance with her "old dear look" (573). Even the imperfect but essentially noble Richard recognizes Esther as " '[a]lways the same dear girl' " (575). To Allan Woodcourt, her "scarred face was all unchanged"

(888). Unlike the effort required to empathize with poverty-marred Jo, it is apparently easy to view the disease-marked Esther without repugnance. Esther's facial deterioration does not even diminish Jarndyce's or Woodcourt's sexual love. Both men continue to desire her as a wife, while Guppy's initial recoil from her stamps him as contemptibly shallow. Indeed, even the fact that Guppy later struggles with and subdues his instinctive revulsion is merely the grounds for his comic humiliation and decisive rejection. Dickens is insisting here that people *should* see and that good people *will* see only the "real" Esther, but that involves not seeing her at all in material—and therefore concretely visual—terms. The ambiguity of Woodcourt's final comment about her prettiness therefore neither requires nor repays reduction to a single meaning: whether or not Esther remains scarred is unimportant because Esther's body itself is unimportant. It is not simply that her soul is the most important thing about her: it is virtually the only thing about her, and therefore it receives the priority that scenes with Jo had given to the body.[15]

To insist upon the supreme importance of the soul, however, is to minimize the importance of what happens to bodies. It is also to establish a new priority for well-being, in which material conditions cease to command attention. Esther introduces the language of providence to account for her illness: her appearance will no longer link her to her mother, a divergence in which she traces the merciful hand of God (565). The disease that thus began as an indictment of society now becomes a symbol of God's ultimate and benign ordering of the world, including—apparently—its suffering. And while this attitude belongs to Esther the character, with her limited perspective, the second narrator is never allowed to overturn it.

This vision of the world, however, relies heavily on the presence of the unseen world of Heaven—"[t]he world that sets this right" (927). Such a vision also implicitly defers both justice and mercy for sufferers to that later world. Charley, during her sickness, recalls her prayer after her father's death that he might be "raised up" like one of the Biblical figures restored from the dead. She implores Esther, should she die and her brother likewise long for her immediate resurrection, that Esther "would . . . show Tom how these people of old days had been brought back to life on earth, only that we might know our hope to be restored to Heaven" (495). Here, religious consolation defines itself through immateriality: the body is simply a tool for the soul's instruction. Such an attitude is unexceptional, even commonplace in terms of Christian belief, but by rendering the material ultimately irrelevant, it can lead to treating the material as immediately irrelevant, too.

In the novel's treatment of Jo, for example, we see a shifting emphasis from concern with material social conditions to spiritual and personal ones, a shift from the visible to the invisible that deflects the book's initial impulse toward large-scale social criticism. Jo, during his first encounter with Esther, shows his own lack of spiritual as well as physical health by failing to recognize her transcendent goodness. When she takes him into Bleak House and settles him for the night he responds only with sullen distrust and fear (488). Jo reappears, however, in order to undergo a transformation of his own from social victim to middle-class convert. Once he learns of Esther's infection, he responds with grief, guilt, and an apparent attachment to her that has no foundation in earlier scenes. His very disclaiming of intentionality is an admission of responsibility and his account of Esther's visit chiefly emphasizes her extraordinary generosity in not reproaching him (702). Thus Dicken's mockery in *Our Mutual Friend* of the ludicrousness of expecting slum children to be moved by the virtue of "Little Margery" (242–43) is countered here by Jo's willingness to be moved by the goodness and suffering of Esther. Jo himself, meanwhile, now seems less a victim than Esther; he is at least partially guilty for intruding his gross physicality upon a lady.[16] The tears that Mr. Jarndyce and Allan shed during Esther's visit are tears for her goodness, not his suffering (702). Indeed, for all Allan Woodcourt's later kindness to Jo, his first reaction after realizing the boy's role in Esther's infection is abhorrence and condemnation. He only softens when Jo abundantly establishes his own grief, remorse and sense of guilt (688–89). The focus now is on Esther's individual virtue, not the social conditions responsible for Jo's abjection.

This change in focus also influences the narrator's descriptions of Jo. In earlier accounts of the boy, Dickens, with an almost Brechtian detachment, demands that emotional involvement not preclude full recognition of Jo's grubbiness. He insists on an intense visual presence necessitating real compassion, unlike the easy sentimentality that Mrs. Jellyby devotes to her absent and unseen African "lambs" (696). Seeing Jo as he is entails accepting even his potential threat to the middle classes: the narrator arranges a tableau of Jo sitting beside a dog as a way to warn the reader that slum denizens may one day be ready to "bite" (275).

On his sickbed, however, Jo displays the "virtues" of the poor: gratitude, reverence for those around him, passive acceptance of unavoidable suffering. As this redemption of Jo takes over from social denunciation, Dickens replaces visual metaphors with auditory ones, so that Jo becomes a sound—but not an articulate voice, since his most significant language is breath, not words (703). Here Jo actually approaches Esther's bodilessness, though he can achieve it fully only through death. And the moment of his death draws Dickens from his attack upon a system into an appeal to personal sympathy. "Heavenly compassion" in individual "men and women" (705), not social restructuring, implicitly becomes the force that could have rescued Jo.

If the problem with the socially-minded approach, then, is that it objectifies the slum-dwellers as mere "products" of an environment, even as mere carriers of disease, the problem with the individually-minded approach is that it grants them subjectivity only in relation to the middle classes, the carriers of feeling. For instance, Jenny transfers much of her tenderness for her dead baby to Esther with astonishing ease. She pursues and upbraids Jo for his part in infecting Esther, labelling him " 'a thankless monster' " for inadvertently transmitting his illness (687), and "beginning to rage" as she demands, " 'You ungrateful wretch, do you know that this [Esther's suffering] is all along of you and of her goodness to you?' " (688). Esther, who has only briefly come into contact with Jenny, is here the recipient for whom Jenny implores the Lord's blessing (687); she is "a pretty dear," who even after her disfigurement can be known by her "angel temper, and her pretty shape, and her sweet voice" (688). There is no doubt that Esther is correct when, during the frantic search for the missing Lady Dedlock, she believes that the "very grateful" Jenny "would have resisted no entreaty of mine" (836). In her final reported actions in the novel, Jenny is willing (along with her friend Liz) to succor and aid Lady Dedlock out of sympathy alone (864). By that point, however, she is only an invisible presence. Absent from the bricklayers' dwelling that Esther and Mr. Bucket visit, Jenny has vanished as part of a ploy to help Lady Dedlock. Her feelings, however, link her in grateful service to those above her, an obvious contrast to the crudely visible bricklayers who plot to exploit the misery of their social superiors. Indeed, victims of poverty though the bricklayers are, they appear in this scene primarily as victimizers of the distraught Lady Dedlock and her angelic daughter. Every detail about the men is sordid, violent, or both, from the "shaggy head" of Jenny's husband to the posture of Liz's husband, "eating with a lump of bread and fat in one hand, and his clasp-knife in the other" (834), a posture he changes only when he intimidates his wife by striking "the handle of his knife violently on the table" (934). The "heavy boot" with which the man later kicks his wife, and the "hammer-like hand" with which he threatens to hit her convey a powerful physical presence, but only at the expense of the man's humanity. Again, the poor are at their best when least within view.

In short, it appears that "humanizing" the poor quickly becomes idealizing them. But while social criticism depends upon showing social horrors clearly, idealization opposes vision, or at least any very clear and sharply defined vision of the idealized object. This opposition may help explain Dickens' outraged reaction to John Everett Millais's bold delineation of Western civilization's most famous idealized object in his "Christ in the House of His Parents." Dickens' 1850 denunciation of this painting has been interpreted as proof of his artistic philistinism in not appreciating a new artistic movement (Erickson 35), as class hostility at the image of an apparently working-class Christ, as anti-Catholic and -Tractarian feeling, even as a personally directed attack urged on by enemies of Millais (Leathlean 45–47).[17]

Yet perhaps one of the most striking things about the terms of Dickens' polemic is that he excoriates Millais for what seems to be the visual correlative of his own descriptive style. Millais's use—to some, his abuse—of detail, his mixture of realism and stylization, even what struck many viewers as his grotesquerie, are all reminiscent of Dickens—or at least of Dickens when treating characters other than his idealized heroines.[18] Dickens, however, detests Millais's visual realization of the subject specifically because of the supposed irreverance of visualizing sacred personages in terms so specific, so concrete, so physical. Granted, the vocabulary of class permeates Dickens' discussion, but so does the vocabulary of the body, in particular the diseased, deformed, ugly body. His shock underlines the iconoclasm Victorians saw in giving spirituality a noticeable physical presence. On one hand, Holman Hunt, who modelled the first version of his beloved and etherealized Christ in "The Light of the World" (1853) from two women (Auerbach 77), more acceptably half-hides the divine, feminized incarnation of godhead in shadows; on the other, Millais shows his Christ with a sharpness and clarity that emphasizes the physicality of the body there to be seen. To Dickens, apparently, that intensity of vision makes Christ's suffering human, grotesque, and pointless, not divine and redemptive. As a result, this painting, Dickens suggests, threatens the "faith in which we live and die" (265). That faith, however, is as indefinite as Esther's smallpox scars: it consists of "religious aspirations, . . . elevating thoughts; . . . tender, awful, sorrowful, ennobling, ennobling, sacred . . . associations" (265). The intense but vague feelings that Dickens equates with religion cannot co-exist with that which is obviously physical and therefore visible. The representation—either literary or pictorial—of virtue apparently cannot be too specific.

Thus, despite Dickens' ridicule of Pardiggle's exhortations to the ragged bricklayers and of Chadband's preachments to the ravenous Jo, Dickens himself eschews physicality in favor of a disembodied spirituality when he confronts Millais's painting. That same disembodied spirituality characterizes the truly good, as opposed to officiously philanthropic, inhabitants of Dickens' novels. When tending the poor, the etherealized middle classes can be helpful more to the soul than to the flesh. Esther closes *Bleak House* as the wife of a "medical attendant for the poor' (872), yet her description does not suggest that she and her husband are able to do more than "alleviat[e] pain" and "sooth[e] . . . need" (935). As the sick die, however, they send up "thanks for . . . [the] patient ministration[s]" that have prepared them for death (935). The poor become spiritual in emulation of the classes above them, and as their bodies fade from view, their spirits join in sympathy with those of their middle-class comforters. Perhaps the poor still suffer, but their suffering can no longer be seen.

Yet this erasure of the social causes of physical suffering and ensuing emphasis on personal benevolence could have more than personal results. By binding class to class, religiously inspired feelings of sympathy could ward off the long-threatened social upheaval that might destroy the world the middle classes knew. Thus it presumably is a comfort in more senses than one that Jo, far from developing a "bite," dies saying a prayer taught him by middle-class Allan Woodcourt. Jo's dying words reflect a trend in Victorian fiction in which a providential view of suffering substitutes the redemption of the poor for direct social criticism. Finding purpose and even moral profit in pain, and associating it with a virtuous femininity that seemingly transcends both the physical and the social world, provides a consolation—but not a cure—for institutionalized injustice.

NOTES

I would like to thank William Burgan and—especially—Margaret Goscilo for reading and commenting on earlier versions of this essay.

1. Thomas Vargish traces the interdependence of belief in providence with faith in "human volition" in his *The Providential Aesthetic in Victorian Fiction* (5). Christopher Hamlin, focusing more narrowly, examines the "dilemma that Victorian sanitarians perceived with regard to decomposition" specifically (95) in "Providence and Putrefaction: Victorian Sanitarians and the Natural Theology of Health and Disease."
2. Charles Kingsley, addressing an audience of women in 1855 (a lecture published in 1880), shows the middle-class belief in example when he calls "personal

human intercourse . . . the very thing you have to employ towards the poor, and to call up in them.'' Without "human friendship, trust, affection . . . clubs, societies, alms, lending libraries . . . are but dead machinery'' (5).

3. David Roberts's *Paternalism in Early Victorian England* shows the range of believers in some form of paternalism (25–29), which insisted on personal connection between the rich and poor.

4. Grahame Smith, for example, points out that in characters such as Quilp, "questions of environment seem irrelevant. They represent a principle of total evil which we feel would be unaltered by any circumstances, however softening'' (36). Janet Larson, on the other hand, emphasizes the theological second thoughts that apparently impelled Dickens to revise his statement that criminals like Bill Sikes are "irredeemably bad'' by changing the adverb to "incurably'' (70). This religious soft-pedalling, however, does nothing to alter the "relief'' in *Oliver Twist* "that malefactors can be apprehended'' and that the hellish workhouse can become "the providentially appointed place for Bumble's end'' (70). Graham Storey traces in Dickens' letters the author's anger with "the law's *leniency*" (emphasis in original) (69), while Myron Magnet devotes his entire book-length study to demonstrating that "a coherent structure of belief and feeling'' lies behind the "stern—even truculent—views'' of "the darker Dickens'' (1–4). Philip Collins's *Dickens and Crime* provides a complete overview of the subject.

5. Grahame Smith wryly observes that despite "the misery of the conditions under which Oliver grew up . . . there is no evidence that [Oliver's rescue by Mr. Brownlow] did anything to improve either his grammar or his morality, if only because they already left nothing to be desired'' (30). Janet Larson notes "Oliver's inherent goodness,'' which makes his enemies "strictly external menaces,'' rather than temptations (50–51). Iain Crawford sees in Oliver the "Wordsworthian . . . innocent child,'' to whom Noah Claypole is a "dark counterpart'' aligned with "the human social world,'' rather than Wordsworthian Nature (78–79).

6. F. S. Schwarzbach makes the same point in "*Bleak House*: The Social Pathology of Urban Life,'' as does Michael Gurney in "Disease as Device: The Role of Smallpox in *Bleak House*."

7. Joseph I. Fradin shrewdly analyzed this incongruity in "Will and Society in *Bleak House*." As he points out, Dickens is especially forceful in showing philanthropy as the corruption of "one of the most noble of human impulses, benevolence'' (105). In tracing the "inevitability'' of corruption in 'corporate society'' to "the human will,'' however, Fradin does not explain what can keep the individual will pure. He does imply a gendered difference, however, by declaring that "the strong male personality has few public outlets for its energy which do not distort it'' (105), while Esther's "individual encounters between her goodness and others' need'' are "perfect'' in themselves, although "they carry no larger hope'' (108).

8. As David Roberts shows, this "hostility to philanthropy,'' particularly in its "larger works,'' and preference for private "benevolence,'' was common to orthodox paternalists (34), although Roberts considers Dickens "a humanitarian rather than a paternalist'' (94). Karen Jahn suggests that Dickens' critique of institutionalized charity arises from its subjugation to "natural law'' (376). Large-scale philanthropy would be acceptable, according to Jahn, were it to "evolve [from] the Christian tradition'' (377). D. A. Miller, more pessimistically, considers the novel's structure itself a "promot[ing] . . . a paternalism that, despite the dim view the novel takes of the power structures of the British state, can only be useful in maintaining such structures'' (92).

9. R. Bland Lawson sees evidence of "parallel modes of thinking" between Dickens and Carlyle in both writers' condemnation of "institutions" and their endorsement of the "individual" (24).

10. Michael Cotsell points out this irony in his " 'Do I Never Read in the Newspapers': Dickens' Last Attack on the Poor Law" (82).

11. As A. Susan Williams notes, Victorian sanitary reformers consistently described the poor as a "lower life" on the level of the "pestilence" generated from "putrefaction" (93). Nancy Aycock Metz emphasizes the shock with which "the middle classes . . . discover[ed] the poor" and their living conditions ("Discovering a World of Suffering" 65).

12. Nancy K. Hill lays particular stress on Dickens' visual images of poverty as instruments he used "to instruct, to reform" his readers into realizing "that problems that demanded reform existed in education, in the prisons, in housing, in working conditions" (2). Nancy Aycock Metz likewise emphasizes the importance of "visual impact" ("Narrative Gesturing" 14).

13. Esther, like other Dickens heroines, thus does not support Brian Rosenberg's assertion that "at least in Dickens's case, characters must be *seen* to be effectively revealed and explored" ("Vision into Language" 121). Nor does she fit the model Michael Hollington offers of Dickens as a physiognomer in whose early novels at least characters reveal their inner selves through their features ("Dickens and Cruikshank and Physiognomers in *Oliver Twist*").

14. Elizabeth Langland makes this point in "Nobody's Angels: Domestic Ideology and Middle-Class Women in the Victorian Novel" (297). For an account of contemporary responses to Mrs. Pardiggle and Mrs. Jellyby, however, see Brahma Chaudhuri's "Dickens and the Women of England at Stafford House."

15. Helena Michie offers a different, psychologically oriented view of Esther's illness as a progress toward separation and selfhood in " 'Who is this in Pain?': Scarring, Disfigurement, and Female Identity."

16. Pam Morris provides a sensitive analysis of Jo's movement from a "lack of self-awareness [that] offers a form of freedom from internalized social constraints" into "a willed and willing [sense of] moral guilt" (97–98).

17. Donald Erickson's "*Bleak House* and Victorian Art and Illustration: Charles Dickens's Visual Narrative Style" and Howard Leathlean's "Blood on His Hands: The 'Inimitable Pains' of a Pre-Raphaelite Episode" examine Dickens' response to Millais's painting in more detail.

18. Commentaries on Dickens' visual style, of course, are legion. Examples include Michael Hollington's *Dickens and the Grotesque*, Nancy K. Hill's *A Reformer's Art: Grotesque and Picturesque Imagery in Dickens*, Donald F. Erickson's "*Bleak House* and Victorian Art and Illustration: Charles Dickens's Visual Narrative Style," Brian Rosenberg's "Reading the World: Visual Imagination in Dickens and Ruskin" and "Vision into Language: The Style of Dickens's Characterization," and James R. Kincaid's "Viewing and Blurring in Dickens: The Misrepresentation of Representation."

WORKS CITED

Armstrong, Nancy. *Desire and Domestic Fiction: A Political History of the Novel.* New York: Oxford UP, 1987.

Auerbach, Nina. *Woman and the Demon: The Life of a Victorian Myth.* Cambridge, MA: Harvard UP, 1982.

Chaudhuri, Brahma. "Dickens and the Women of England at Stafford House." *English Language Notes* 25 (1988): 54–60.

Collins, Philip. *Dickens and Crime.* 2nd ed. London: Macmillan, 1964.

Cotsell, Michael. " 'Do I Never Read in the Newspapers': Dickens's Last Attack on the Poor Law." *Dickens Studies Newsletter* 14 (1983): 81–90.

Crawford, Iain. " 'Shades of the Prison House': Religious Romanticism in *Oliver Twist.*" *Dickens Quarterly* 4 (1987): 78–90.

Dickens, Charles. *Bleak House.* Ed. Norman Page. Penguin Classics. Harmonsworth: Penguin, 1986.

———. *Our Mutual Friend.* Signet Classic. New York: NAL, 1964.

———. "Old Lamps for New." *Household Words* 1 (1850): 265–67.

Erickson, Donald H. "*Bleak House* and Victorian Art and Illustration: Charles Dickens's Visual Narrative Style." *The Journal of Narrative Technique* 13 (1983): 31–46.

Ford, George H. "Self-Help and the Helpless in *Bleak House.*" *From Jane Austen to Joseph Conrad: Essays Collected in Memory of James T. Hillhouse.*" Ed. Robert C. Rathburn and Martin Steinmann. Minneapolis: U of Minnesota P, 1958. 92–105.

Fradin, Josseph I. "Will and Society in *Bleak House.*" *PMLA* 81 (1966): 95–109.

Gurney, Michael S. "Disease as Device: The Role of Smallpox in *Bleak House.*" *Literature and Medicine* 9 (1990): 79–92.

Hamlin, Christopher. "Providence and Putrefaction: Victorian Sanitarians and the Natural Theology of Health and Disease." *Energy & Entropy: Science and Culture in Victorian Britain: Essays from* Victorian Studies. Ed. Patrick Brantlinger. Bloomington: Indiana UP, 1989. 93–123.

Hill, Nancy K. *A Reformer's Art: Dickens' Picturesque and Grotesque Imagery.* Athens: Ohio UP, 1981.

Hollington, Michael. *Dickens and the Grotesque.* London: Croom Helm, 1984.

———. "Dickens and Cruikshank as Physiognomers in *Oliver Twist.*" *Dickens Quarterly* 7 (1990): 243–54.

Jahn, Karen. "Fit to Survive: Christian Ethics in *Bleak House.*" *Studies in the Novel* 18 (1986): 367–80.

Kingsley, Charles. "Woman's Work in a Country Parish." 1880. *Sanitary and Social Lectures and Essays.* London: Macmillan, 1889. 3–20.

Langland, Elizabeth. "Nobody's Angles: Domestic Ideology and Middle-Class Women in the Victorian Novel." *PMLA* 107 (1992): 290–304.

Larson, Janet. *Dickens and the Broken Scripture*. Athens: U of Georgia P, 1985.

Lawson, R. Bland. "The 'Condition of England Question': *Past and Present* and *Bleak House*." *The Victorian Newsletter* 79 (1991): 24–27.

Leathlean, Howard. "Blood on His Hands: The 'Inimitable Pains' of a Pre-Raphaelite Episode." *The Journal of Pre-Raphaelite and Aesthetic Studies* 1.2 (1988): 41–53.

Magnet, Myron. *Dickens and the Social Order*. Philadelphia: U of Pennsylvania P, 1985.

Metz. Nancy Aycock. "Narrative Gesturing in *Bleak House*." *The Dickensian* 77 (1981): 12–22.

———. "Discovering a World of Suffering: Fiction and the Rhetoric of Sanitary Reform—1840–1860." *Nineteenth-Century Contexts* 15 (1991): 65–81.

Michie, Helena. " 'Who is This in Pain?': Scarring, Disfigurement, and Female Identity in *Bleak House* and *Our Mutual Friend*." *Novel* 22 (1989): 199–212.

Miller, D. A. *The Novel and the Police*. Berkeley: U of California P, 1988.

Morris, Pam. *Dickens's Class Consciousness*. New York: St. Martin's, 1991.

Newman, Beth. "*Bleak House* and the Body." *Dickens and the Everyday*. MLA Convention. Chicago, 30 Dec. 1990.

Pettersson, Torsten. "Enough to Have Bodies?: Two Incongruities in *Oliver Twist*." *Orbis Literarum* 45 (1990): 341–50.

Pope, Norris. *Dickens and Charity*. New York: Columbia UP, 1978.

Reed, John R. "Freedom, Fate, and the Future in *Bleak House*." *Clio* 8 (1979): 175–94.

Roberts, David. *Paternalism in Early Victorian England*. New Brunswick: Rutgers UP, 1979.

Rosenberg, Brian. "Vision into Language: The Style of Dickens's Characterization." *Dickens Quarterly* 2 (1985): 115–23.

———. "Reading the World: Visual Imagination in Dickens and Ruskin." *The Arnoldian* 11 (1984): 5–13.

Scarry, Elaine. *The Body in Pain: The Making and Unmaking of the World*. New York: Oxford UP, 1985.

Scheckner, Peter. "Chartism, Class, and Social Struggle: A Study of Charles Dickens." *The Midwest Quarterly* 29 (1987): 93–112.

Schwarzbach, F. S. "The Fever of *Bleak House.*" *English Language Notes* 20.3/4 (1983): 21–27.

————. "*Bleak House*: The Social Pathology of Urban Life." *Literature and Medicine* 9 (1990): 93–104.

Smith, Grahame. *Dickens, Money, and Society*. Berkeley: U of California P, 1968.

Storey, Graham. "Dickens in His Letters: The Regress of a Radical." *Dickens and Other Victorians: Essays in Honor of Philip Collins*. Ed. Joanne Shattock. New York: St. Martin's, 1988. 65–74.

Vargish, Thomas. *The Providential Aesthetic in Victorian Fiction*. Charlottesville: UP of Virginia, 1985.

Williams, A. Susan. *The Rich Man and the Diseased Poor in Early Victorian Literature*. Atlantic Highlands: Humanities, 1987.

Great Expectations: Dickens and the Language of Fortune

Elizabeth Campbell

> "You have put yourself in Fortune's power; now you must be content with the ways of your mistress. If you try to stop the force of her turning wheel, you are the most foolish man alive. If it should stop turning, it would cease to be Fortune's wheel."—Lady Philosophy to Boethius, *The Consolation of Philosophy*

By the time Dickens wrote the opening scene of *Great Expectations* for his weekly magazine *All the Year Round* in 1860, his use of inversion had become so familiar that it could have been considered his trademark.[1] Delight in disorder, the sheer pleasure of turning things topsy-turvy, had been a stock device of Dickens' comedy from the start, but in his more recent works—notably in *Little Dorrit*—inversion, representing the relentless cyclicality of fate and the inevitability of its turnings, had taken on a solemn aspect, charged with a somber moral and metaphysical meaning (Stang 140–64). Dickens' most astute readers now knew the serious attention he gave to a first number or installment, particularly to the opening words; and Dickens could trust them to ponder these words with an equally serious attention. It is not surprising, then, that in the short paragraph recalling Pip's first encounter in the church graveyard with Magwitch, Pip's description of the convict's gesture of inversion is fraught with symbolic significance:

> The man, after looking at me for a moment, turned me upside down, and emptied my pockets. There was nothing in them but a piece of bread. When the church came to itself—for he was so sudden and strong that he made it go head over heels before me, and I saw the steeple under my feet—when the church came to itself, I say, I was seated on a high tombstone, trembling, while he ate the bread ravenously. (36; ch. 1)[2]

Both the gesture and Pip's description of it comically visualize for the reader that most Dickensian of themes: the reversal of fortune. From Pickwick on, as the central gesture of plot and the surest test of character, Dickens had been forever turning his protagonists upside down and emptying their pockets. Such a reversal has the effect of reordering one's priorities and changing one's view of things, as Pip realizes immediately, but then must learn several times over during the course of the novel. In other words, the reversal not only inverts Pip, but changes the world and revolutionizes as well Pip's understanding of it.

The gesture is emblematic. It is the kind of detail, reminiscent of Hogarth, for which Dickens had become famous, proof of an imagination that has its source in the visual, that creates a narrative by linking a series of highly graphic scenes or essentially symbolic pictures (Marten 150; Harvey 55). Here the ultimate seriousness of the comic gesture is captured, first, by reference to the upside-down and then upright church, suggesting a complete revolution of belief, a radical upheaval of all that is sacred in the institution at the very heart of the social organism. Second, reference to the child on the tombstone deftly reinforces the fact that Pip, like David Copperfield before him, is a "posthumous child," now reborn to a new consciousness and a new parental order. And finally the high seriousness is conveyed by the stark image of the hungry man, taking communion, as it were, in a graveyard and from the pocket of a trembling boy—rather than in the church and by the grace of a heavenly father. In this upside-down, godforsaken world, Dickens seems to be saying, the old patriarchal order born of the church and sanctified by society has been overturned, indeed buried. Father-figures are either outlaws like Magwitch, or good but ineffectual illiterates like Joe; and children, with neither god nor man to look to as a model, are "naterally wicious" until they can carve out a new morality appropriate to this new, inverted social order.

Magwitch's gesture, more particularly and to my point, evokes an image of "The World Turned Upside Down," a motif traditionally associated with fools' days—carnival or Shrove Tuesday, for example.[3] But since the English civil war in the seventeenth century, WUD (as the motif is called by anthropologists [Babcock 39–94]) was also associated with political and religious revolution—as historian Christopher Hill documents. By the early nineteenth century—the time of Dickens' childhood—this motif was still in currency among the poor, the semiliterate, and their children by way of a popular chapbook (see illustrations). *The World Turned Upside Down or The Folly of Man Exemplified in Twelve Comical Relations Upon Uncommon Subjects*, "Illustrated with Twelve curious Cuts Truly adapted to each Story," was a cheap publication of the sort produced by James Catnach and John Pitts in the Seven Dials section of London and described by Dickens with a tone of nostalgic affection in *Sketches by Boz* (Stone 22–24).[4] The woodcuts, clearly the most salesworthy part of the chapbook, depict "Things quite form'd out of nature's rules," as the accompanying poems tells us. These aberrations include such reversals as an "ox turned butcher," a "roasted cook" and "fishes lords of creation," flying like birds and angling for men. In one cut with a Dickensian theme, children are nursing and punishing adults; and in another (to which I will return later) the reversal "out of nature's rules" is one of gender. In this cut labeled "The Old Soldier Turned Nurse," the male sits holding a distaff and a baby, while the woman paces the room wearing a helmet and sword and toting a rifle.

Two cuts are especially pertinent to Magwitch's gesture, as if Dickens is recalling these quaint and memorable pictures and perhaps expecting that his description will trigger his readers' memories as well. The lead cut shows two jesters holding a ball or globe, from which a man's head and legs protrude upside down; and another shows a village skyline on top and the sun, moon, and stars below. Taken together, these two cuts illustrate inversion moving from the personal to the cosmic in the grotesque reversal of the natural.

What I wish to suggest is that part of the power of the novel's opening scene—and one imaginative source for it—derives from its implied connection to this motif of a reversible world and therefore to a folk and a radical tradition that was largely ignored by official taste in the early nineteenth century, but kept alive through cheap street literature like this chapbook. Dickens's particular genius was to tap into this richly illustrative, semiliterate world and recycle its defining images and themes as part of the official aesthetic of Victorian bourgeois tradition. Perhaps the most explicit and magnificent example of Dickens' use of this topos occurs in *Little Dorrit* as Mr. Plornish's philosophy of life:

> Mr Plornish amiably growled, in his philosophical but not lucid manner, that there was ups you see, and there was downs. It was in vain to ask why ups, why downs; there they was, you know. He had heerd it given as a truth that ... even the best of gentlemen must take his turn of standing with his ed upside down and all his air a flying the wrong way into what you might call Space. Wery well then. . . . That gentleman's ed would come up-ards when his turn come, that gentleman's air would be a pleasure to look upon being all smooth again, and very well then! (799–80; Book II, ch. 27)

Plornish's philosophy, like Magwitch's gesture, seems to find it source in the lead cut from the WUD chapbook.[5]

Considering the highly visual quality of his imagination, it is not surprising that Dickens' phenomenal early success as a writer was partly owing to his shrewd use of illustrations and felicitous partnership with illustrators, whose drawings—especially the cartoon-like designs for the cover wrappers—bear a striking resemblance to chapbook art.[6] It was from these lowly works that Dickens appropriated, in part, what I call the language of fortune.[7]

The popularity of these cheap productions among the poor is understandable. Chapbooks (from the Old English root *ceap*, meaning "cheap" or "bargain") were part of the deluge of ephemeral and affordable publications that began flooding city streets and villages after the English civil war—publications expressly directed to the interests, finances, and the education level of a peasant class (Ashton "Introduction"). Like "The World Turned Upside Down," chapbooks appealed to the private fantasies of the oppressed, who found comic relief in the thought of turning the tables on their oppressors. These books served as an antidote to poverty and the sheer drudgery of existence by always keeping open the possibility of "great expectations," which might materialize in a variety of forms. Thus there were many chapbooks that focused on fortune-telling and folk superstitions, or featured folk prophets like Mother Shipton or Robert Nixon, whose memory has been preserved from extinction largely by Dickensian references. Typical stories include the adventures of folk heroes like Dick Whittington (whose fortunate turn of fate is recalled in *The Old Curiosity Shop* by Dick Swiveller and through both of his names), who rises from humble circumstances to become Lord Mayor of London; or notorious reprobates like George Barnwell (whose tragical history becomes a leitmotif in *Great Expectations*), who falls, simultaneously, in love and into a life of crime, ultimately getting himself hanged. In almost every case, the overriding theme of these chapbooks is the omnipotence of fortune—as something external to character but largely in control of it. This theme has two corollaries: first, that fortune moves in a cyclical fashion and, second, thus has a tendency—ultimately—to reverse itself. As in classical and medieval iconography, chapbook Fortune is an all-powerful goddess who controls the fate of peasant and king alike, and takes pleasure in reversing their positions—whenever she wills—by spinning them about on her wheel.[8]

In *Great Expectations*, through the discourse of fortune that Dickens appropriates from the folk tradition and most recently located in the chapbooks and other street literature popular in his childhood, Dickens creates an autobiographical fantasy that is roughly based on all those heroes who are the minions of Fortune. His writing—here and elsewhere—is saturated not only with references but imaginative recreations of these heroes, as Harry Stone's *Dickens and the Invisible World* so convincingly demonstrates.[9] But the fate of one in particular bears such an uncanny resemblance to Dickens' own life that he could serve as the prototype for Pip.[10]

Like Dickens' own story, *The History of Fortunatus* begins with the birth of a son to an improvident father, who has lost not only his own wealth but his wife's as well (Ashton 124–37). Fortunatus must therefore seek his own fortune, which he does, according to tradition, by traveling abroad. After a series of prefatory adventures, he happens upon the goddess Fortune in a wood, who offers to bestow one of six gifts upon our hero. Of wisdom, strength, riches, health, beauty, and long life, Fortunatus chooses riches, for as long as he lives. "With that," so goes the story, "[the goddess] gave him a purse, saying, As oft as you put your hand into this purse, you shall find ten pounds of the coin of any nation thou shalt happen to be in" (Ashton 131).

Although the moral of the story—emphasized more in Thomas Dekker's play *Old Fortunatus* (1599), based on the same traditional romance—is that Fortunatus should have chosen wisdom rather than riches, the goddess's gift of this purse is the central moment of the plot and the chief interest of the narrative, as the woodcut on the cover of the chapbook illustrates (Ashton 125; see illustration). A blindfolded and barebreasted Fortune, standing on her wheel and holding one hand on her belly, presents, with the other hand, the magical purse to her beneficiary and namesake. The goddess's half-nude figure, which calls attention to her sexuality, suggests (as Machiavelli had suggested in *The Prince*) that Fortune's favors are sexual favors.[11] The goddess as donor thus figuratively stands in relation to the male recipient of her gift as mother or lover. Because her choice has nothing to do with merit—with the sterling character of a beneficiary selected through reason, virtue, or wisdom—it must have to do simply with chance or emotion, with the often cryptic logic of love.

This fantasy of becoming the darling of Fortune understandably captured the imagination of the poor and downtrodden just as it certainly made a permanent impression on Dickens, who refers to it in his fiction throughout his career. After all, Dickens was, in one sense, a Victorian Fortunatus: his own purse was constantly being filled by his writing but depleted by his enormous family, restless habits, and extravagant housekeeping. Similarly, Pip's status as a gentleman is defined by just such a continually renewable purse. But unlike Dickens, more like Fortunatus, and most of all like those fortunate Victorian gentlemen born into wealth and leisure, Pip does not have to *earn* his living: he simply takes it out of his purse, which has been magically filled by some secret, external power. Such wealth, derived without the exercise of reason or personal effort, is itself an aberration of nature, according to the self-help-loving Dickens. Pip's rise to gentility through such means can only be depicted as a monstrous parody, as well as a parable about the dangers of Victorian middle-class affluence not properly grounded in an ethic that holds work as a religious value.[12]

Discovering the identity of Pip's benefactor and concomitantly, the source of his wealth is, of course, the chief mystery around which the narrative pivots. Appropriately, Magwitch, the convicted thief, proves to be this benefactor, generously repaying the boy many times over for the bread taken from his pocket in the novel's opening scene. Dickens' plot thus demonstrates that Pip's wealth in fact derives from the boy's own merit. Nevertheless, Pip's ignorance about the source of his riches and, by extension, his blindness to his own and others' real value reveal themselves to be as destructive as unmerited fortune. Pip's long-held conviction that Miss Havisham has made his fortune while disregarding her own relations—imperiously ignoring a whole family of impecunious Pockets in order to fill his—reinforces the connection between *Great Expectations* and the story of Fortunatus. Certainly, Mr. Pumblechook's toast to Pip and Fortune underscores this connection: " 'Let us drink, Thanks to Fortune, and may she ever pick out her favorite with equal judgement!' " (180; Ch. 19). Judgment—as Pip, Miss Havisham, and Pumblechook understand it—has nothing to do with Pip's rise; and Fortune—rather perversely like Justice, but with more insidious implications—is a blind goddess.

Miss Havisham's role as Fortune in the novel again demonstrates that a naive view of economics is a grotesque and injurious anachronism. With her cronelike appearance and occasional wheeled chair, Miss Havisham transmogrifies in Pip's imagination from witch to fairy godmother; both of these fairy-tale female types are avatars of the goddess Fortune, for whom such shape-shifting is characteristic.[13] Like Mrs. Skewton and Mrs. Clennam before her, she is a type in Dickens' novels representing Fortune as a goddess more interested in wreaking revenge than in bestowing favors. Nevertheless, by encouraging Pip in his delusions, Miss Havisham promulgates the idea that money will come miraculously without hard work, an idea that can be seriously entertained only by those who have the luxury of leisure produced by inherited wealth, and therefore grotesquely depicted through her character as stagnation and decay. For a "common laboring boy" like Pip, such delusion proves to be disastrous. Miss Havisham's injunction to Pip simply to " 'Play, play, play!' " underscores her role as Fortune incarnate, the goddess who enforces leisure and pleasure; but (as her name suggests) the goddess as donor is a sham. It is an illusion that anything of real value comes from her hand.

By contrast and in an interesting gender reversal, the real author of Pip's fortune proves to be a male Mag*witch*—a magician/witch given also to disguise, but neither a female goddess nor a godmother. Magwitch makes his money (clearly like Dickens) through the prosaic but ultimately more valuable means of hard work and self-sacrifice. As he tells Pip, " 'I lived rough, that you should live smooth; I worked hard, that you should be above work' " (337; Ch. 39). That the source of Pip's fortune is not a woman and goddess is bad enough; that he turns out instead to be a "warmint," and a man of the lowest social caste, is even worse. Magwitch's pivotal role demonstrates that although no goddess presides over the distribution of wealth in the novel, Fortune's wheel represents a frightening economic truth: for Pip to be "high," Magwitch (and legions like him) must be "low." In effect, value in the Victorian world has reversed itself. The "low," common criminal working for his gentleman in the land Down Under elevates Pip to high noon on Fortune's Wheel, just as the mid-Victorian leisured class balanced itself on the backs and with the hands of the working class.

Through his personal experience of "The World Turned Upside Down" and his reenactment of the "The History of Fortunatus," Pip finally comes to understand that in the fully industrialized nineteenth-century world, "manly" and "gentlemanly" have ceased to be synonymous. The Wheel of Fortune, now operating in the Victorian world with accelerated motion, misplaces value, rewarding and punishing without regard to justice or merit. In so doing, Fortune emasculates all her minions because the high and the low are equally subject to her power. Thus, in his snobbishness, Pip becomes an effeminate fop; Joe is emasculated in Pip's eyes by his lowly occupation as blacksmith and in Dickens' eyes by a termagant wife; and Pip's self-proclaimed "second father" so violates Pip's equation of the manly with the gentlemanly that Magwitch seems not only like an asexual being, but one of another species.

On the other hand, even though women prove not to be the producers of fortune in a material sense, they in fact exercise control over Pip's fortune in the novel. As Michael Cotsell has said, *Great Expectations* can be defined as "a man's story of restless female characters" (13). Mrs. Joe has taken over household discipline, bringing Pip up by jerks and playing soldier to her

THE
WORLD
TURNED
UPSIDE DOWN
OR THE
FOLLY OF MAN
EXEMPLIFIED
IN TWELVE COMICAL RELATIONS
UPON
UNCOMMON SUBJECTS

*Illustrated with Twelve curious Cuts
Truly adapted to each Story*

from John Ashton's *Chap-Books of the Eighteenth Century*.

THE
HISTORY OF FORTUNATUS

CONTAINING

Various Surprising Adventures.

AMONG WHICH HE ACQUIRED A PURSE THAT
COULD NOT BE EMPTIED.

And a Hat that carried him wherever he
wished to be.

SUN, MOON, STARS AND EARTH TRANSPOSED.

THE OLD SOLDIER TURNED NURSE.

London: Chatto and Windus, 1882.

husband's role as nurse in true WUD-like fashion. Like Goneril in *King Lear*, Mrs. Joe represents the woman who "must change arms at home, and give the distaff / Into my husband's hands" (IV. 2:18–19), thereby perverting the presumably natural order of gender and domestic relationships. We have seen how Miss Havisham exercises control by demanding and exploiting the servile attentions of Pip as well as the Pocket family (parodied by Herbert's "highly ornamental, but perfectly helpless and useless" mother, who nevertheless controls the Pocket household through her haughty disregard for order—a comic representation of Fortune in reduced circumstances [212; ch. 23]).

But it is Estella who reigns as Fortune in *Great Expectations*. Through her tyrannical control over Pip's imagination and emotions, she is the "Star" of Pip's desiring, the sexy woman operating the cosmic emotional wheel that subjugates Pip in the present and around which he spins a dreamy future. Like Machiavelli's Fortune, Estella must be cuffed and mauled to be won by a lover. In a sinister inversion of the chapbook fantasy, Estella is not to be won (or if won, belatedly) by Pip as Fortunatus, but by Bentley Drummle, born gentleman and Machiavellian Prince, who knows how to manhandle Pip's goddess. Drummle maintains his position of ascendancy by subjugating Fortune herself.

Reluctantly, both Dickens and Pip demonstrate that the *gentle* man of *Great Expectations* is Joe Gargery, who always defers to women and remains at the bottom of Fortune's wheel, working away. Like Boethius, Joe accepts with philosophy a position that Pip (and perforce, even Dickens) can evaluate only in terms of fortune. This valuation reflects the not-quite tacit belief of the industrialized Victorian world that male power derives most clearly from capital rather than physical strength—that masculinity is indeed a function of control over one's fortune. Joe's gentle nature, humility, poverty, and inno-cence temper his masculinity and render his massive strength of character and body unmanly; and this most unsettling inversion of gender and value relations is the tragic reality underlying the topsy-turvy comedy of *Great Expectations*. In Havelock Ellis's terms describing what has happened in Pip's and Dickens' time, industrial civilization has made the world more "womanly," while men have become less "manly" (475–82).

Joe is the novel's embodiment of virtue—in its dual meaning of strength and goodness; but he is clearly not the role model for the nineteenth-century hero, as the novel has generically defined him. Joe's indifference to Fortune renders him uninteresting as the center of focus for readers more worldly-wise than he: he is as foolish as he is wise, in Dickens' terms, and humiliating in Pip's. In the gender reversal of the novel, Joe ultimately stands for the goodness and artlessness at the center of hearth and home that Dickens had habitually assigned (after Pickwick and Sam) to female characters like Agnes Wickfield, Florence Dombey, Esther Summerson, Sissy Jupe, or Little Dorrit—those spiritual women at the center of the Fortune's Wheel around which Dickens' heroes spin. The central, eternally *female* virtue that Joe represents had always been at the heart of Dickens' novels; but in *Great Expectations*, virtue undergoes a change of sex. Concomitantly, for the first time since *David Copperfield*, Dickens focuses almost exclusively (by way of first-person narration) on a male protagonist, thereby forcing to the periphery the womanly heart that serves as the moral center of his aesthetic vision.

NOTES

1. Dickens' use of inversion—under a variety of names—has been frequently (and eloquently) discussed by many critics analyzing the play of his imaginative genius. See, for example, Stoehr, 139; Carey, 174–75; Stone, 298–339. An excellent earlier examination of Dickens' use of this device in *Great Expectations* appears in E. Pearlman's "Inversion in *Great Expectations*."
2. All references to *Great Expectations* in this essay are taken from the Penguin Edition.
3. In literature, this motif is traceable to the Middle Ages (Curtius 94–98). Excellent book-length discussions of the history and the comic uses of this motif can be found in Babcock and Donaldson.
4. See Ashton, 265–72; and Collison, 112–14. The illustrations included here are taken from Ashton.
5. Tom Scott, the acrobatic boy who haunts Quilp's counting-house in *The Old Curiosity Shop* and spends most of his time in the novel walking on his hands or standing on his head, may serve to represent, by Dickensian shorthand, Quilp's perversely inverted world.
6. For excellent book-length studies of Dickens' relationship to illustrations and illustrators, see Steig and Cohen.
7. Dickens' familiarity with Shakespeare's dramas of course influenced his use of fortune as a central motif in his novels. For example, Mr. Dorrit plays out Lear's drama; Little Dorrit dramatizes Cordelia's natural, filial virtue; and Clennam as good but illegitimate son is a composite of Edgar and Edmund. Clennam gains insight only after he has been forsaken by Fortune, when for him as for Edmund, "The wheel is come full circle" (*King Lear* V. iii).
   Nevertheless, Dickens' visualizing technique draws equally from less literate sources: from chapbooks and probably from an oral, folk tradition still extant in the nineteenth century. The images of the goddess Fortune and her wheel that grace the tops of the monthly wrappers for *Nicholas Nickleby* and *David Copperfield* are reminiscent of chapbook art. For a related discussion, see Campbell.
8. It is fascinating to speculate on the effect that the 1840 discovery in Rochester Cathedral of a fresco, picturing Fortune and her wheel, may have had on Dickens'

imagination. According to the report in the *Gentleman's Magazine, New Series* 14 (August, 1840): 137–38, the painting was discovered in April of that year, when it was uncovered in the process of making interior renovations. A color plate of the fresco, showing Fortune turning her wheel with three men upon it, appears in Frank Kendon's *Mural Paintings in English Churches during the Middle Ages* (London: William Clowes and Sons), 1923, Plate XV.

9. See especially Chapter 3, "Dickens' Fabling Mind," 33–70.
10. Information about Dickens' life is largely drawn from Edgar Johnson's still-definitive biography.
11. ". . . Fortune is a woman and it is necessary, in order to keep her under, to cuff her and maul her. She more often lets herself be overcome by men using such methods than by those who proceed coldly; therefore always, like a woman, she is the friend of young men, because they are less cautious, more spirited, and with more boldness master her." *Machiavelli*, trans. Allan Gilbert, Vol. I, 92.
12. For an outstanding discussion of Dickens' belief in the Victorian work ethic, see Welsh, Chapter V, "Work."
13. For a full discussion of the early history of the goddess Fortune, see Patch.

WORKS CITED

Ashton, John. *Chap-books of the Eighteenth Century*. London: Chatto and Windus, 1882.

Babcock, Barbara A., Ed. *The Reversible World: Symbolic Inversion in Art and Society*. Ithaca: Cornell UP, 1978.

Boethius. *The Consolation of Philosophy*. Trans. Richard Green. Indianapolis, IN: Bobbs-Merrill, 1962.

Campbell, Elizabeth. "Minding the Wheel: Representations of Women's Time in Victorian Narrative." *Rocky Mountain Review of Language and Literature* 48 (1994): 45–60.

Carey, John. *The Violent Effigy: A Study of Dickens' Imagination*. London: Faber and Faber, 1973.

Cohen, Jane. *Charles Dickens and His Original Illustrators*. Columbus: Ohio State UP, 1980.

Collison, Robert. *The Story of Street Literature: Forerunner of the Popular Press*. Santa Barbara, CA: American Biliographical Center—Clio P, 1973.

Cottsell, Michael, Ed. *Critical Essays on Charles Dickens's 'Great Expectations.'* Boston: G. K. Hall, 1990.

Curtius, Ernst R. *European Literature and the Latin Middle Ages*. Trans. Willard Trask. New York: Pantheon, 1953.

Dekker, Thomas. "The Pleasant Comedie of Old Fortunatus." *Dramatic Works of Thomas Dekker*. Ed. Fredson Bowers. Cambridge: Cambridge UP, 1953.

Dickens, Charles. *Great Expectations*. Ed. Angus Calder. Harmondsworth: Penguin, 1963.

———. *Little Dorrit*. Ed. John Holloway. Harmondsworth: Penguin, 1967.

Donaldson, Ian. *The World Turned Upside-Down: Comedy from Jonson to Fielding*. Oxford: Clarendon, 1970.

Ellis, Havelock. *Man and Woman*. Boston: Houghton Mifflin, 1929.

Harvey, J. R. *Victorian Novelists and Their Illustrators*. New York: New York UP, 1971.

Hill, Christopher. *The World Turned Upside Down: Radical Ideas During the English Revolution*. Harmondsworth: Penguin, 1972.

Johnson, Edgar. *Charles Dickens: His Tragedy and Triumph*. New York: Simon and Schuster, 1952. 2 volumes.

Machiavelli, Niccolo. *The Chief Works and Others*. Trans. Allan Gilbert. Durham, NC: Duke UP, 1965, 2 Volumes.

Marten, Harry P. ''The Visual Imaginations of Dickens and Hogarth: Structure and Scene.'' *Studies in the Novel* 6 (1974): 145–64.

Patch, Howard R. *The Goddess Fortuna in Mediaeval Literature*. New York: Octagon, 1974.

Pearlman, E. ''Inversion in *Great Expectations*.'' *Dickens Studies Annual*, 7, 1978:190–202.

Stang, Richard. ''*Little Dorrit*: A World in Reverse.'' *Dickens the Craftsman: Strategies of Presentation*. Ed. Robert B. Partlow, Jr. Carbondale: Southern Illinois UP, 1970:140–64.

Steig, Michael. *Dickens and Phiz*. Bloomington: Indiana UP, 1978.

Stoehr, Taylor. *Dickens: The Dreamer's Stance*. Ithaca, NY: Cornell UP, 1965.

Stone, Harry. *Dickens and the Invisible World*. Bloomington: Indiana UP, 1979.

Welsh, Alexander. *The City of Dickens*. Cambridge, MA: Harvard UP, 1986.

"The Ring of Cant": Formulaic Elements in *Our Mutual Friend*

Rodney Stenning Edgecombe

At one point of *Our Mutual Friend* Dickens turns to the Podsnaps in his audience and attacks them for their reductive use of language, for the way in which they have blocked sentient human responses with unreal, inhuman formulae. The rebuke to some extent recalls the arraignment of Scrooge by the Spirit of Christmas Present—"Man . . . if man you be in heart, not adamant, forbear that wicked cant until you have discovered What the surplus is, and Where it is" (*Christmas Books*, 47; Stave 3):

> A surprising spirit in this lonely woman after so many years of hard working and hard living, my Lords and Gentlemen and Honourable Boards! What is it that we call it in our grandiose speeches? British independence, rather perverted? Is that, or something like it, the ring of the cant? (199; I, ch. 16)

"Ring" might at first glance seem to be inappropriate to the tiredness of cant, but Dickens seems to have chosen it for its monetary clink, an oblique pointer to an idea stated and restated ad infinitum throughout the novel—namely, that moral debility results from an obsession with wealth. Moral debility in this and in other instances also brings with it a linguistic debility that Dickens mimics and mocks repeatedly in *Our Mutual Friend*.

This authorially emphasized languor might account for the disfavor with which *Our Mutual Friend* has sometimes been viewed. For example, James's review objected to its putative "exhaustion" and factitiousness: "we should . . . congratulate [Dickens] on his success in what we should call the manufacture of fiction; for in so doing we should express a feeling that has attended us throughout the book. Seldom, we reflected, had we read a book so intensely *written*, so little seen, known, or felt" (32). Of course, James read *Our Mutual*

Friend with a polemical purpose, and, trying as he was to open up a new seam in nineteenth-century fiction, he probably felt compelled to announce the exhaustion of Dickens' particular mine. But even if we make allowance for this tendentiousness, it is possible that his dismissal might also have had something to do with the ''cant'' element in the novel. I shall argue, however, that far from being a defect, this ''cant'' (and the ''exhaustion'' it seems to evoke) is wholly controlled and put there to enhance the author's chief concerns.

Early on we find Lightwood using stereotypic phrases to reduce the story of Bella and the Harmon will to a sort of marionettish *commedia dell'arte*. His clichés trivialize and distance its human content, and reduce living persons to functions in a plot:

> ''. . . At this stage of the affair the poor girl respectfully intimated that she was secretly engaged to that popular character whom the novelists and versifiers call Another, and that such a marriage would make Dust of her heart and Dust of her life—in short, would set her up, on a very extensive scale, in her father's business. Immediately, the venerable parent—on a cold winter's night, it is said—anathematised and turned her out.''
>
> * * * * *
>
> ''The pecuniary resources of Another were, as they usually are, of a very limited nature. I believe I am not using too strong an expression when I say that Another was hard up. However, he married the young lady, and they lived in a humble dwelling, probably possessing a porch ornamented with honeysuckle and woodbine twining, until she died.''   (14; I, ch. 2)

Lightwood's offhand manner in telling the story registers above all in phrases so typical and conforming as to have been all but emptied of significance. Popular fiction might indeed characterize its stock patriarchs with the epithet ''venerable,'' but surely the phrase ought not to remain mindlessly in place when he is banishing a child. In the same way, the adverbs of habitude—''as they *usually* are'' and ''*probably* possessing''—sap the narrative of tension, and since narrative without tension conduces to boredom, boredom finally issues in languor. The clichés also infect and flatten the rhetorical surge of the Harmon girl's avowal. Since it contains *in ovo* parts of Bella's story, and since its metaphor is one that Dickens will orchestrate and augment throughout the novel, it deserves worthier treatment than Lightwood's indifferent paraphrase. Its disengaged, even tone is further secured by the upper case he gives to ''Dust,'' as though it were a stock item on a par with ''Another.'' If the speaker's witty detachment were set in abeyance, the story, even with all its archetypal components in place, could be made to register very differently.

Heinrich Heine's lyric "Ein Jüngling liebt ein Mädchen" dramatizes the way a narrator can, by a sudden shift from mechanical to engaged delivery, convert cliché to divine commonplace. After two stanzas of pat, formulaic delivery—Heine's "And're" is the exact equivalent of Lightwood's "Another"—he breaks open the stock triangle to reveal real suffering beneath the geometry—"dem bricht das Herz entzwei":

> Ein Jüngling liebt ein Mädchen,
> die hat einen Andern erwählt;
> der And're liebt eine And're,
> und hat sich mit dieser vermählt.

> Das Mädchen heirathet aus Aerger
> den ersten besten Mann,
> der ihr in den Weg gelaufen;
> der Jüngling ist übel dran.

> Est ist eine alte Geschichte,
> doch bleibt sie immer neu;
> und wem sie just passiret,
> dem bricht das Herz entzwei.

> [A youth oft loves a maiden,
> Who for another sighs,
> Perchance he loves another,
> And weds the blooming prize.

> The maiden thus neglected,
> Weds the first who comes that way,
> Then he who has been rejected,
> To grief doth become a prey.

> It is but an olden story,
> And yet it is ever new;
> The last fond youth who suffer'd
> He broke his heart so true.]   (Schumann, 204–05)

Only to the cynical and the world-weary—and Lightwood's stance is not dissimilar to that of the prophet in Ecclesiastes—is there nothing new under the sun. Having no emotional pulse, they cannot feel the recurrent force of the archetype.

A. O. J. Cockshut has remarked that although Lightwood "tells the story . . . as a stock comic melodrama; it is not that he really lacks sympathy; he is simply playing the Veneering game in the approved fashion" (172). That is so, but for the greater part of *Our Mutual Friend*, Dickens gives no hint that Lightwood and Wrayburn, his model, will undergo a conversion from degagé triviality to a life of purpose. They register primarily as characters of a type Dickens all but invented, and which Oscar Wilde later appropriated as his own persona. Because epigrams can be forged only by a cool, detached sensibility, wit often prides itself on being above the "vulgarity" of large emotion, as witness the Wildean dictum about a heart of stone and the death of Little Nell. Also, because epigrams often turn on inverting received wisdom and commonplaces, their purveyors have shown a contemptuous and guarded attitude towards ordinary human responses, and, equating ordinariness with cliché, have demonstrated their contempt by inverting it. Thus when Umberto Eco claims fastidiousness as a "note" of post-modernism, he seems to have forgotten a comparable rarefaction in the aesthetics of the Aesthetes: "I think of the postmodern attitude as that of a man who loves a very cultivated woman, and knows he cannot say to her, 'I love you madly,' because he knows—and she knows that he knows—that the words have already been written by Barbara Cartland" (67). In Eco's view such knowledge commits the speaker to an ironic, self-masking kind of declaration not unlike Lightwood's handling of the Harmon story.

This handling, however, while it establishes the dominant ethos of *Our Mutual Friend*, is not without precedent in the work of Dickens. The elder Chester in *Barnaby Rudge* provides a partial prototype for Lightwood and Wrayburn, expressing a dislike for "what are called family affairs, which are only fit for plebeian Christmas days," and evading the language of bereavement simply because—to find a pre-Romantic parallel for Barbara Cartland—Mrs. Radcliffe had already done it to death in *The Mysteries of Udolpho*:

> "You have me to thank, Ned, for being of good family; for your mother, charming person as she was, and almost broken-hearted, and so forth, as she left me, when she was prematurely compelled to become immortal—had nothing to boast of in that respect."   (118; ch. 15)

Because of his "witty" indifference to human feeling, the speaker shorthands a husband's grief with a "so forth" and thus reduces it to a tiresome predictability. At the same time, since he is the husband in question, he is manifestly (and impenitently) confessing his own inability to feel intense emotion.

There are many comparable instances of perfunctory dismissal in *Our Mutual Friend*, so many indeed that Lightwood's manner might be said to have provided a paradigm for Dickens' *own* narrative conduct in parts of the novel. J. Hillis Miller has pointed out that the "Veneering dinner parties are an elaborate theatrical ceremony resting on nothing, and the people who come to these parties have been so dehumanized by their submission to money that they exist not as individuals, but as their abstract roles, "Boots," "Brewer," and so on" (171). But even though these sections are written in a way that disengages them from the texture of the novel, they are not wholly *sui generis*. One can easily adduce other analogues for the disengaged, formulaic discourse of Lightwood. For example, Hillis Miller has also noted how the Veneering dinners are often "described in the present tense, in language that is cold and withdrawn, terse, with an elliptical economy new in Dickens. Sometimes verbs and articles are omitted . . ." (175). Much the same, *mutatis mutandis*, could be said of the compliments that Lightwood pays to Mrs. Boffin, though here the ellipticality seems not so much terse as debilitated:

> Mr. Lightwood murmured "Equal honour—Mrs. Boffin's head and heart."
> * * * * *
> Mr. Lightwood murmured "Vigorous Saxon spirit—Mrs. Boffin's ancestors—bowmen—Agincourt and Cressy. (90; I, ch. 8)

This is a languor too wan to turn up the volume, too tired to bother with conventional syntax, too bored by the predictability of its own formulae. Compare Dickens' own wearied impatience with blood lines at the start of Chapter 4 and the wholly unremarkable quality of their "remarkable facts":

> Reginald Wilfer is a name with rather a grand sound, suggesting on first acquaintance brasses in country churches, scrolls in stained-glass windows, and generally the De Wilfers who came over with the Conqueror. For, it is a remarkable fact in genealogy that no De Any ones came over with Anybody else. (32)

Chapter 4 is a chapter twice removed from the previous Veneering sequence, but some of the Veneering narrative habits have not been shed. Dickens characterizes William by function rather than by name, and he indifferently throws open the French patronymic to the "Any's," bored by the predictability of snobs as Lightwood had been bored by the predictability of the Harmon saga. The same sort of reader self-help occurs in a jibe at Mrs. Veneering. Having established a stock analogy, Dickens indifferently hands us the reins of the narrative for the moment, and says, "Do as you will": "[she] repeats in a distracted and devoted manner, compounded of Ophelia and any self-immolating female of antiquity you may prefer, 'We must work' " (244; II, ch. 3). Then again, at a moment of climactic "sincerity" in a Veneering speech, nonce words trivialize and open out the options to such an extent that meaning all but drains through the interstices: "for we couldn't think of spending sixpence on it, my love, and can only consent to be brought in by the spontaneous thingummies of the incorruptible whatdoyoucallums'' (250; II, ch. 3).

Indifference and ennui also register in other ways, as when Lightwood foregoes the effort of fresh speech, but at the same time apologizes for having offered a cliché instead:

> ''[. . .] You could put the whole in a cash-box to-morrow morning, and take it with you—say, to the Rocky Mountains. Inasmuch as every man,'' concluded Mr. Lightwood, with an indolent smile, ''appears to be under a fatal spell which obliges him, sooner or later, to mention the Rocky Mountains in a tone of extreme familiarity to some other man, I hope you'll excuse my pressing you into the service of that gigantic range of geographical bores.''
>
> (88–89; I, ch. 8)

To some extent this parallels Dickens' habit in *Our Mutual Friend* of invoking outmoded iconographic conventions which he clearly finds absurd, but applies notwithstanding. For example, in rendering Mrs. Wilfer's grotesque formality (comic antimasque to the formality of the Veneering world), he resorts to self-apologetic clichés à la Lightwood:

> As that was all the rum and water, too, or, in other words, as R. W. delicately signified that his glass was empty by throwing back his head and standing the glass upside down on his nose and upper lip, it might have been charitable in Mrs. Wilfer to suggest replenishment. But that heroine briefly suggesting ''Bedtime'' instead, the bottles were put away, and the family retired; she cherubically escorted, like some severe saint in a painting, or merely human matron allegorically treated.   (42; I, ch. 4)

This strategy is not unique to *Our Mutual Friend*. Dickens also resorts to mock history painting in earlier novels, as when Charity Pecksniff stages a domestic tableau for the elder Chuzzlewit:

> See the neat maiden, as with pen in hand, and calculating look addressed towards the ceiling, and bunch of keys within a little basket at her side, she checks the housekeeping expenditure! From flat-iron, dish-cover, and warming-pan; from pot and kettle, face of brass footman, and black-leaded stove; bright glances of approbation wink and glow upon her. The very onions dangling from the beam, mantle and shine like cherubs' cheeks.   (333; ch. 20)

Here the comedy is more oblique, for the various properties and postures of hagiographic painting have been *contained* in their domestic equivalents. Charity's eyeline recalls the beatific upward roll of such paintings as Raphael's ''St. Catherine of Alexandria'' (acquired by the National Gallery in 1839), her pen the emblem of an Evangelist or a martyr's palm, the onion swags the cherubim of sacred art. In the treatment of Mrs. Wilfer, on the other hand, the grandiose conventions engulf and swamp the domestic element altogether. Speaking like a bad translation of Sophocles, she can be said to have earned her formulaic treatment as an allegorization of motherhood—frigid and statuesque and far removed from the cosy images of maternity favored by bourgeois Victorian painters.

Perhaps because he could so effortlessly forge allegory from quotidian materials, Dickens seems to have felt antipathy for more solemn and self-conscious versions of the mode. We see this above all in his repeated mockery of neoclassic art. In *Great Expectations* Pip puts aside pre-Romantic allegory as a childish thing:

> This was always followed by Collins's Ode on the Passions, wherein I particularly venerated Mr. Wopsle as Revenge, throwing his blood-stained sword in thunder down, and taking the War-denouncing trumpet with a withering look. It was not with me then, as in later life, when I fell into the society of the Passions, and compared them with Collins and Wopsle, rather to the disadvantage of both gentlemen. (40; ch. 7)

In *Our Mutual Friend* Dickens disavows another aspect of neoclassic art—what he seems to conceive as the suave unreality of its loco-descriptive verse. At one point he incorporates a standard Thomsonian adjective-noun-adjective into a sentence as graceless and as gauche as he can make it. Thomson himself loses his poetic selfhood, crushed by a stampede of Cockney men for whom his seasonal idylls have no relevance at all:

> It was not summer yet, but spring; and it was not gentle spring ethereally mild, as in Thomson's Seasons, but nipping spring with an easterly wind, as in Johnson's, Jackson's, Dickson's, Smith's, and Jones's Seasons. (144;I, ch. 12)

Even the token symmetry of the disyllabic surnames that initially displace "Thomson" gets crushed and disarranged with the advent of Smith and of Jones, the last chosen for a possessive form harsh enough to make the cadence seem more ugly still.

Given this impatience with the "inert" heritage of neoclassic poetry, it is startling to find Silas Wegg surveyed by a personification that might have stepped from Collins's "Ode to Evening," duly draped in a "gradual dusky veil" (466): "But when night came, and with her veiled eyes beheld him stumping towards Boffin's Bower, he was elated too" (54; I, ch. 5). Dickens seems to have placed it there as a sort of residuum of the Veneering mode, where comparably dated formulae figure in Lady Tippins's rococo pastoral, her cupids and her "rough Cymons" dragged in from Boccaccio. Dickens also personifies Fashion in his account of the Boffin marriage, but because Fashion never figures in history paintings, and because the personification is cobbled from one of Mrs. Boffin's fashion plates, the effect is a touch more energetic: "Fashion, in the form of her black velvet hat and feathers, tried to prevent it; but got deservedly crushed in the endeavour" (56). Dickens nonetheless seems to be mocking the deific formulae and intercessory posture of a Collins ode when he observes that "Mrs. Boffin's Fashion" was a "less inexorable deity than the idol usually worshipped under that name" (57).

Dickens seems deliberately to have laced *Our Mutual Friend* with mock eighteenth-century prosopopoeia—the prosopopeia that Coleridge condemned as being forged from nothing more solid than the upper case. In Book I, Chapter 15, the curtain goes up on a tableau of Mr. and Mrs. Boffin in the Bower. Although there is no syntactic compulsion to use capital letters for "Care and Complication," the author has applied them as a sort of neoclassical cant, as though prosperity had brought a pretentious but exhausted literary mode with it, and forced it on its victims: "Mr. and Mrs. Boffin sat after breakfast, in the Bower, a prey to prosperity. Mr. Boffin's face denoted Care and Complication. Many disordered papers were before him . . ." (178). Bella's use of the uppercase at a later point of the novel also tends to formalize and flag the patness of her bestiary similes, much as Lightwood had commonplaced dust with a capital D: "for I am naturally as obstinate as a Pig" (528); "I chatter like a Magpie" (529; III, ch. 8).

Having claimed this sort of reductiveness for upper case nouns, I must point out that they tend to function reductively only when a "domestic" (i.e., cosy) prose texture throws them out as creatures unnative and unendued to their element. When, on the other hand, Dickens is working within his repertoire of universal symbols, or writing prophetically *in propria persona*, his afflatus imps the wing of capitalized abstractions. We can find an instance of this in one of Lizzie's reveries—"As she came beneath the lowering sky, a sense of being involved in a murky shade of Murder dropped upon her; and, as the tidal swell of the river broke at her feet without her seeing how it gathered, so, her thoughts startled her by rushing out of an unseen void and striking at her heart. . . . And as the great black river with its dreary shores was soon lost to her view in the gloom, so, she stood on the river's brink unable to see into the vast blank misery of a life suspected, and fallen away from by good and bad, but knowing that it lay dim before her, stretching away to the great ocean, Death" (70–71; I; ch. 6). Such passages are far removed from the sort of allegory we find in Gray or Collins. There it seems altogether more regulated, marked off into specific visual frames and clarifying tableaux. By contrast, we find nothing so premeditated in Dickens' treatment of "Murder" and "Death," and the spatial deixis and placement of neoclassical art (*ut pictura poesis*) bears little relation to his violent dynamism ("rushing") and inconceivable space ("the vast blank misery of a life suspected"). Cant has thus been subsumed by a vigorous imagination, and the languor of cliché galvanized by rampant energy.

We have seen how Dickens uses conventional phrases in his narrative of fashionable life to stress its emotional and moral enfeeblement. At such times he could be said to have followed the Lightwood/Wrayburn solution to cliché—viz., to tweezer it disdainfully. We see this, for example, in his perfunctory application of nuptial topoi to the Lammle marriage. Images once meaningful in the hands of Catullus or Spenser have here been reduced to pasteboard trimming:

> While the Loves and Graces have been preparing this torch for Hymen, which is to be kindled tomorrow, Mr. Twemlow has suffered much in his mind. It would seem that both the mature young lady and the mature young gentleman must indubitably be Veneering's oldest friends. Wards of his, perhaps? Yet that can hardly be, for they are older than himself. (114; I, ch. 10)

Having discarded these tired pseudo-Spenserian properties with contemptuous despatch, Dickens turns to an alternative tactic for exposing cant—that of interrogating its insincerity from an innocent viewpoint. One can reject a convention as an untenable cliché, crushing it wearily under the weight of such accumulated experience as says there is nothing new under the sun, or one can feign total innocence, and turn it into a ridiculous kenning, as in Dickens's faux-naif account of painterly cherubs:

> So the gridiron was put in requisition, and the good-tempered cherub, who was often as un-cherubically employed in his own family as if he had been in the employment of some of the Old Masters, undertook to grill the fowls. Indeed, except in respect of staring about him (a branch of the public service to which the pictorial cherub is much addicted), this domestic cherub discharged as many odd functions as his prototype; with the difference, say, that he performed with a blacking-brush on the family's boots, instead of performing on enormous wind instruments and double-basses, and that he conducted himself with cheerful alacrity to much useful purpose, instead of foreshortening himself in the air with the vaguest intentions. (454; III, ch. 4)

Dickens here effects a renovation of cliché by "innocently" confusing utilitarian and aesthetic functions. A cherub which stares and points might in fact have a real purpose in a pictorial design—that of *repoussoir*, say—and a foreshortened *putto* might indeed help to define a perspectival line. Only someone wholly ignorant of artistic function would so improbably cross lines.

Yet that is precisely Twemlow's mistake when he tries to root Veneering cant in sincerity and fact. The Veneerings and Podsnaps have founded their lives on phrases which they have severed from fact and emptied of meaning. Twemlow's difficulty centers on an unmeaning use of "oldest friend" and the contradictions that spring from that use:

> The abyss to which he could find no bottom, and from which started forth the engrossing and ever-swelling difficulty of this life, was the insoluble question whether he was Veneering's oldest friend, or newest friend.   (7; I, ch. 2)

The joke recurs again and again as Veneering fits the phrase to each new acquaintance in turn. While such cant might be a leitmotiv of the fashionable world, however, it also figures in its dark social antitype, the world of the watermen. Rogue Riderhood is quite as ready as Veneering to remove the substance of a phrase and traffic with its empty vessel. Dickens stresses its vacancy by rattling it again and again:

> "Lawyer Lightwood," ducking at him with a servile air, "I am a man as gets my living, and as seeks to get my living, by the sweat of my brow. Not to risk being done out of the sweat of my brow, by any chances, I should wish afore going further to be swore in."   (148; I, ch. 12)

Having thus mass-produced the cliché, Dickens even lets Eugene fit it into its predictable sockets. His languor recalls Lightwood's manner of story-telling:

> "Of seaman's pocket," said Mr. Riderhood. "Whereby I was in reality the man's best friend, and tried to take care of him."
> "With the sweat of your brow?" asked Eugene.
> "Till it poured down like rain," said Roger Riderhood.   (150)

And, as if to signal the start of Mr. Boffin's moral displacement, Dickens has him appropriate a stock element from the ballads that, by way of antimasque to the tired allusions and topoi of fashionable discourse, Silas Wegg is always forcing upon the circumstances of his own life:

> "[. . .] My literary man was so friendly as to drop into a charming piece of poetry on that occasion, in which he complimented Mrs. Boffin on coming into possession of—how did it go, my dear?'
> Mrs. Boffin replied:

' "The gay, the gay and festive scene,
The halls, the halls of dazzling light." '
* * * * *

"[. . .] To let him feel himself anyways slighted now, would be to be guilty of
a meanness, and to act like having one's head turned by the halls of dazzling
light. . . ." (181–2; I; ch. 15)

By interpolating H. S. van Dyke's verse into Mr. Boffin's bluff idiom, Dickens
on the one hand conveys his ingenuousness, but at the same time he also
seems to hint at a sort of mechanical adaptation of Veneeringspeak, and to
hint the imminent quenching of the dustman's spontaneity. It is only to be
expected, therefore, that when he needs to modulate into the *un*predictable
and *un*precedented intensity of Headstone's passion, he should effect the
transition by disavowing the sort of standard commonplace associated with
other parts of the novel: "Love at first sight is a trite expression quite suffi-
ciently discussed; enough that in certain smouldering natures like this man's,
that passion leaps into a blaze, and makes such head as fire does in a rage of
wind, when other passions, but for its mastery, could be held in chains" (341;
II, ch. 3). Those chains, reminiscent of the stock topos of the *vinculum amoris*,
enact the very ordinariness from which the man's intensity breaks free.

Tired iconography and empty phrases are one means by which Dickens
gives a character of listlessness to *Our Mutual Friend*, but there are many
additional devices of indifference and lassitude. Repetition is one of them. It
goes without saying that repetition is a key feature of Dickens' art, and it is
made to serve a multitude of thematic ends. In *Our Mutual Friend*, however,
the iterative patterns often seem more pronounced and insistent than usual,
helping to image the mechanical impulse behind every effort to conform. It
calls to mind the elder Chester's "so forth," that verbal "etc." sign which
lets the material generate itself on automatic pilot. The following extract from
Sketches by Boz provides a foil to its listlessness:

It was a neat, dull little house, on the shady side of the way, with new, narrow
floorcloth in the passage, and new, narrow stair-carpets up to the first floor. The
paper was new, and the paint was new, and the furniture was new; and all three,
paper, paint and furniture, bespoke the limited means of the tenant.
(42; *Our Parish*, ch. 7)

Context is everything, of course, and because the accumulated "new's" proceed here with the lively reportorial interest that the young Dickens takes in
his environment, the repetitions seem accordingly to bounce instead of dragging. Come *Our Mutual Friend*, however, and the iteration, as if by contact

with the deadening conformities of the society it analyses, levels the stylistic landscape for miles on end:

> Mr. and Mrs. Veneering were bran-new people in a bran-new house in a bran-new quarter of London. Everything about the Veneerings was spic and span new. All their furniture was new, all their friends were new, all their servants were new, their plate was new, their carriage was new, their harness was new, their horses were new, their pictures were new, they themselves were new, they were as newly married as was lawfully compatible with their having a bran-new baby, and if they had set up a great-grandfather, he would have come home in matting from the Pantechnicon, without a scratch upon him, French-polished to the crown of his head. (6; I, ch. 7)

In this passage the documentary newness in *Our Parish* has been stylized almost out of recognition, not only because Dickens has sustained the *heratio* with a more daring insistence, but also because he applies the epithet mechanically, and makes no attempt to distinguish between animate and inanimate items. The Veneerings develop a bright toy-like surface on the one hand, and on the other, a grandfather clock stands in as a nonce ancestor. Such flat, cumulative structures recall comparable moments in nursery rhymes—"The House that Jack Built," for example—and impart a sort of undifferentiated infantility to the Veneerings. (Part of the novel's distinctive color can be attributed to what John Robson has called its "remarkable series of references to nursery rhymes, games, and tales, songs, ballads, adages and images of childhood"—205). As a further token of this infantility, Wrayburn mentions the man from Tobago (from Marshall's *Anecdotes and Adventures of Fifteen Gentlemen*) at a Veneering dinner party, and makes the allusion doubly trivial by garbling it. (The implication is that it is hardly worth the effort of memory.) His *tibicines* (metrical prop lines) create an effect of indifference similar to the elder Chester's "so forth," and, by mangling both the invalid's diet and the diet of his cure, he makes nonsense of the entire poem:

> "Tobago, then."
> "Nor yet from Tobago."
> "Except." Eugene strikes in: so unexpectedly that the mature young lady, who has forgotten all about him, with a start takes the epaulette out of his way: "except our friend who long ago lived on rice-pudding and isinglass, till at length to his something or other, his physician said something else, and a leg of mutton somehow ended in daygo." (11; I, ch. 2)

Compare the purposeful "before" and "after" in the original: "There was a sick man of Tobago, / Liv'd long on rice-gruel and sago; / To his bliss /

The physician said this / 'To a roast leg of mutton you may go' " (Opie, pl. XIX, opp. 407). Although Lady Tippins rebukes Eugene on this occasion for forgetting his nursery rhymes, she herself makes heavy weather of an equally formulaic allusion to the Dunmow flitch of bacon: "And dear Mrs. Lammle and dear Mr. Lammle, how do you do, and when are you going down to what's-its-name place—Guy, Earl of Warwick, you know—what is it?—Dun Cow—to claim the flitch of bacon?" (409; II, ch. 16). The stock-figure unreality of folklore and nursery rhyme also pervades the treatment of the Podsnaps, one of whose conversations Dickens renders in the manner of Simple Simon's exchange with the Pieman:

> Said Mr. Podsnap to Mrs. Podsnap, "Georgiana is almost eighteen."
> Said Mrs. Podsnap to Mr. Podsnap, assenting, "Almost eighteen."
> Said Mr. Podsnap then to Mrs. Podsnap, "Really I think we should have some people on Georgiana's birthday."
> Said Mrs. Podsnap then to Mr. Podsnap, "Which will enable us to clear off all those people who are due." (130; I, ch. 11)

Relief is promised to the woodenness of this conversation by the author's adding a variant ("assenting") to the mirrored *verba dicendi*—but that variant, being tautological, cannot offer variety. As G. W. Kennedy has pointed out, there are moments in *Our Mutual Friend* when "language tends to perish almost completely, becoming totally disconnected from any human or physical reality" (169).

Since the whole ethos of Podsnappery centers on conventionality, it is not surprising that Dickens should also use repetition to render the joyless exigence of its forms. He even paraphrases a recreational quadrille chez the Podsnaps as a dance to the Protestant work ethic:

> Then the discreet automaton who had surveyed his ground, played a blossomless tuneless "set," and sixteen disciples of Podsnappery went through the figures of—1, Getting up at eight and shaving close at a quarter-past—2, Breakfasting at nine—3, Going to the City at ten—4, Coming home at half-past five—5, Dining at seven, and the grand chain. (137–38; I, ch. 11)

Only the final section of the Lancers escapes the paraphrase, but by contagion with the other sections, it has by now acquired the dead weight of a manacle. If life is a lifeless inventory for Podsnap, it is no less so for Bradley Headstone as he aspires to enter the "respectable" world. In this instance, the uniformity of repetition becomes the verbal icon of a literal uniform. What in early Dickens had been a trope of exuberance is recreated here (as in the fog sequence in *Bleak House*, and the "red brick" proem to *Hard Times*) as the vector of ennui and disaffection:

> Bradley Headstone, in his decent black coat and waistcoat, and decent white shirt, and decent formal black tie, and decent pantaloons of pepper and salt, with his decent silver watch in his pocket and its decent hair-guard round his neck, looked a thoroughly decent young man of six-and-twenty.... He could do mental arithmetic mechanically, sing at sight mechanically, blow various wind instruments mechanically, even play the great church organ mechanically.
>
> (217; II, ch. 1)

Just as Dickens imparts an additional mechanicality to the Podsnap party by cancelling the spontaneity of dance, so here he gives Headstone a superadded harshness by subsuming the spontaneity of music to mental arithmetic and uniting the disciplines through a mechanical adverb. Peter Sucksmith has also pointed out how, by "repeating 'mechanical', Dickens draws attention to the way the instinctive man in Bradley Headstone has been repressed beneath a difficultly acquired veneer of culture; by repeating 'decent,' the novelist stresses that the professional *persona* of the schoolmaster is overcompensating for his social origin" (64–65).

Few verbal structures could be more mechanical than the rote lessons of Victorian primary schools, with their preformulated responses and preformulated questions. As if further to satirize a lifeless, formulary outlook in *Our Mutual Friend*, Dickens turns several sections into a catechism. He himself uses a question-and-answer antiphony in his satire on shares:

> Where does he come from? Shares. Where is he going to? Shares. What are his tastes? Shares. Has he any principles? Shares. What squeezes him into Parliament? Shares.
>
> (114; I, ch. 10)

In a lighter vein, the improbable exchanges between Miss Peecher and Mary Anne relay gossip about Bradley Headstone and Lizzie via labyrinthine grammatical interrogations:

> "They say she is very handsome."
>
> "Oh, Mary Anne, Mary Anne!" returned Miss Peecher, slightly colouring, and shaking her head, a little out of humour; "how often have I told you not to use that vague expression, not to speak in that general way? When you say *they* say, what do you mean? Part of speech They?"
>
> Mary Anne hooked her right arm behind her in her left hand, as being under examination, and replied:

"Personal pronoun." (220; II, ch. 1)

Then there also is Riderhood's lesson on river, in which he torments Headstone (who alone knows the right answer) by asking a Sphinxian question of his pupils. Their innocently formulaic minds cannot begin to encompass its horror:

> "[. . .] Wot is it, lambs, as they ketches in seas, rivers, lakes, and ponds?"
> Shrill chorus (with some contempt for the ease of the question): "Fish!"
> "Good agin!" said Riderhood. "But what else is it, my lambs, as they sometimes ketches in rivers?"
> Chorus at a loss. One shrill voice: "Weed!" (794; IV, ch. 15)

And, finally, there is Podsnap's patronage of his French dinner guest:

> "It merely referred," Mr. Podsnap explained, with a sense of meritorious proprietorship, "to Our Constitution, Sir. We Englishmen are Very Proud of our Constitution, Sir. It Was Bestowed Upon Us by Providence. No Other Country is so Favoured as This Country."
> "And ozer countries," the foreign gentleman was beginning, when Mr. Podsnap put him right again.
> "We do not say Ozer; we say Other; the letters are "T" and "H;" you say Tay and Aish, You Know;" (still with clemency). "The sound is 'th'—'th!'"
> (133; I, ch. 11)

At the same time as Dickens uses the uppercase to register the patronizing, schoolmasterly distinctness of Podsnap's articulation, he also uses it to draw a separative line round each element of the lesson. Words no longer have the flexibility and litheness that they would ordinarily bring to human discourse, but lead a lifeless, discrete existence as counters in a formulary world view.

And although his outlook is very different, and his mental process diametrically opposed, Eugene Wrayburn is as guilty as Mr. Podsnap is of using capital letters in a reductive way. By means of the "institutional" uppercase, and by means of a world-weary desire to abbreviate, he devitalizes into frigid capitals the otherwise significant bond of father and son. Because, on Eugene's half-reliable testimony, the father does not himself escape the taint of Podsnappery, there is some justice in the reduction:

> "With some money, of course, or he would not have found her. My respected father—let me shorten the dutiful tautology by substituting in future M. R. F., which sounds military, and rather like the Duke of Wellington."
> "What an absurd fellow you are, Eugene!"
> "Not at all, I assure you. M. R. F. having always in the clearest manner provided (as he calls it) for his children by pre-arranging from the hour of the

> birth of each, and sometimes from an earlier period, what the devoted little victim's calling and course in life should be. . . .'' (146; I, ch. 12)

Several allusions lie under the languid becalmment of this speech. The Duke of Wellington was, of course, the icon for the reactionary forces that had tried to obstruct social progress in Britain after the defeat of Napoleon, a fact which makes the conformity of militarism seem all the more airless and unprogressive. There is also a fleeting allusion to Gray's ''Ode on a Distant Prospect of Eton College''—''Alas, regardless of their doom, / The little victims play!'' (59)—bringing with it a whiff of the neo-classicism that Dickens approaches so distrustfully here and elsewhere in his novels. It also brings with it the memory of the final line (''No more; where ignorance is bliss / 'Tis folly to be wise''), a gesture of effacement which Dickens would probably have aligned with Podsnap's.

In taking Lightwood's narrative as point of departure for this article, and in suggesting that it offers a sort of prototype for a calculated and subversive languor affected in many parts of his novel, I have really been speaking about levels of engagement, levels which are crucially bound up in the choice of narrative vantage. Just as the elder Wrayburn foreknows the destiny of each of his children, and so figures as a dark Calvinistic deity preordaining the fate of each, so too Lightwood, by his offhand use of the third-person omniscient, turns prompter to a set of squeaking marionettes. A narrator can alienate us from his characters be denying us direct access to their thoughts, omitting *verba dicendi*, and smoothing a once impassioned utterance into an unpersuasive flatness. The terrible anagnorisis of the Lammles' marriage provides a case in point. Their lives henceforth will mask an unrehearsed private hell with a public script. This disparity is caught in the rendering, for the apparent immediacy of the historic present makes the third person mode seem all the more manipulative and remote:

> She bursts into tears, declaring herself the wretchedest, the most deceived, the worst-used of women. Then she says that if she had the courage to kill herself, she would do it. Then she calls him a vile impostor. Then she asks him why, in the disappointment of his base speculation, he does not take her life with his own hand, under the present favourable circumstances. Then she cries again. Then she is enraged again, and makes some mention of swindlers.
>
> (125; I, ch. 10)

In that relentless anaphoraic chant of ''then's,'' which stylize living reactions into an inventory of postures, and in that muffled relay of passion where hyperbole, cut off from the power of the speaking voice, must necessarily issue as cliché—in these and in many other features of *Our Mutual Friend*, we hear that characteristic "ring of the cant."

In his pioneering essay on Dickens, George Orwell concluded that what one might term the "narrative face" of the author is

> the face of a man who is always fighting against something, but who fights in the open and is not frightened, the face of a man who is *generously angry*—in other words, of a nineteenth-century liberal, a free intelligence, a type hated with equal hatred by all the smelly little orthodoxies which are now contending for our souls.
> ("Charles Dickens," *Decline of the English Murder and Other Essays*, 140–41)

Some of those "smelly little orthodoxies" were also abroad in the nineteenth century, and they figure as stagnant bywaters in *Our Mutual Friend*, cut off from the energetic momentum of the novel by their formulaic listlessness. Orthodoxies are based on creeds, and creeds, themselves the most summary reduction of imponderables, are shored up by the preformulated antiphons of the catechism, whether cut to the Gospel of Christ or of Marx or of Mao. Writing of one kind of orthodoxy—the political—Orwell also noted that its "language—and with variations this is true of all political parties, from Conservatives to Anarchists—is designed to make lies sound truthful and murder respectable, and to give an appearance of solidity to pure wind" ("Politics and the English Language," *Inside the Whale and Other Essays*, 156). No better epigraph could be adduced for the world of Podsnap and Veneering.

WORKS CITED

Cockshut, A. O. J. *The Imagination of Charles Dickens*. London: Collins, 1961.

Dickens, Charles. *Barnaby Rudge: A Tale of the Riots of 'Eighty*. Introduced by Kathleen Tillotson. London: Oxford UP, 1954.

———. *Christmas Books*. Introduced by Eleanor Farjeon. London: Oxford UP, 1954.

———. *Great Expectations*. Introduced by F. W. Pailthorpe. London: Oxford UP, 1953.

———. *Martin Chuzzlewit*. Edited by Margaret Cardwell. Oxford: Clarendon, 1982.

———. *Our Mutual Friend*. Introduced by E. Salter Davies. London: Oxford UP, 1952.

———. *Sketches by Boz Illustrative of Every-Day Life and Every-Day People*. Introduced by Thea Holme. London: Oxford UP, 1957.

Eco, Umberto. *Reflections on "The Name of the Rose."* London: Secker and Warburg, 1985.

Gray, Thomas. *The Poems of Gray, Collins and Goldsmith.* Edited by Roger Lonsdale. London: Longman, 1969.

James, Henry. *Selected Literary Criticism.* Edited by Morris Shapira. 1963; Rpt. Harmondsworth: Penguin, 1968.

Kennedy, G. W. "Naming and Language in *Our Mutual Friend,*" *Nineteenth-Century Fiction* 28 (1973): 165–78.

Miller, J. Hillis. "Our Mutual Friend," in *Dickens: A Collection of Critical Essays.* Edited by Martin Price. Englewood Cliffs: Prentice-Hall, 1967.

Opie, Iona and Peter. *The Oxford Dictionary of Nursery Rhymes.* Oxford: Clarendon, 1951.

Orwell, George. *Decline of the English Murder and Other Essays.* Harmondsworth: Penguin, 1965.

———. *Inside the Whale and Other Essays.* Harmondsworth: Penguin, 1957.

Robson, John M. "*Our Mutual Friend*: A Rhetorical Approach," *Dickens Studies Annual* 3 (1974): 198–213.

Schumann, Robert. *Songs by Schumann.* London: Boosey and Company, No Date.

Sucksmith, Harvey Peter. *The Narrative Art of Charles Dickens: The Rhetoric of Sympathy and Irony in his Novels.* Oxford: Clarendon, 1970.

Drood Redux: Mystery and the Art of Fiction

David Parker

Scholars with academic reputations to uphold tend to be wary of speculation about how Dickens might have ended *The Mystery of Edwin Drood*.[1] To say no more, it is unfashionable. Voicing current fashion, Steven Connor sees, at the root of all such speculation, a demand for closure and a fixation upon plot, both rendered redundant by postmodernist understanding of narrative. Recommending acceptance of the novel's incompleteness, he draws attention to types of incompleteness presented by the text, and submits that death did no more than set the seal upon Dickens' own growing resistance to closure.

Connor's revealing analysis of textual detail, however, is married to a reading of cultural history, not easy to substantiate. Considering the taste for narrative closure, he is firm about blame:

> from the nineteenth century onwards, narrative, and the novel in particular, is precisely the means employed to enact and enforce the continuity of beginnings and ends, the establishing of organic forms of connection in a newly complex, disjoined world in which such principles were far from being apparent. (89)

Perhaps, but it was no nineteenth-century commentator who wrote,

> just as in the other imitative arts one imitation is invariably of a single thing, so in poetry the story, as an imitation of an action, must represent one action, a complete whole; and it must connect the various incidents in such a way that the whole will be disjoined and dislocated if any one of them is transposed or removed. (Aristotle 17)

The taste for narrative closure precedes the nineteenth by some twenty-three centuries at least. No great knowledge of literature is needed to reveal that

Aristotle speaks for consumers of narrative down the ages, and that closure is the norm from which anything contrary is a deviation.

Narrative openness, to be sure, mirrors aspects of experience, and acceptance of it permits analysis of an expanded range of texts, in a way that can be exhilarating. But this permission is at the expense of evaluation, and no amount of theorizing diminishes the force of Aristotle's prescription. It would be worth asking how often narrative dispensing entirely with closure is not freakish, sportive, or simply bad. For the purposes of this essay, however, it is enough to point out how odd it is to imagine that Dickens might have contemplated abandoning unity of plot, in an effort to shed an unfortunate habit recently picked up by his contemporaries.

Yet it is hard not to share Connor's irritation with some Droodists. They dispute upon a battlefield where the first casualty is judgment. That is not to say, however, that speculation about the ending of the novel must always be at the expense of judgment. It need not be.

I shall try to justify this proposition by exploring the hypothesis that, at the end of the novel, Dickens intended to reveal Edwin Drood still to be alive. My method will be substantially Aristotelian, and unrepentantly pre-postmodernist. Needless to say, I do not suppose Dickens knew the *Poetics* (there is no evidence for that): only that it supplies prescriptions for the construction of narrative which have not been superseded, and which explain most good practice. For the time being, at any rate, I postulate that Dickens intended to achieve unity of plot through causal connections, resulting chiefly from moral choice or moral error. This will lead me to examine both plot and character. In place of a theoretical defence of the method, I urge readers to accept that my assumptions about narrative reflect Dickens' practice, and ask them to defer judgment until they see what the method yields. It offers, I suggest, a useful means for scrutinizing some of the intricacies of the book, and for revealing difficulties created by mystery for the art of fiction. A place can be made for mystery in the carefully crafted novel, I submit, only through the exercise of some skill.

It is possible to argue Edwin was to survive, there can be no doubt about that. He disappears; he is separated from his personal trinkets; various hints are thrown out about motives, means, and opportunity for murder; but more than that we do not know. Indeed, the case to be made for his survival is so strong, I believe, that it is scarcely to be repudiated, except in a way to which I shall eventually come.

Arguments about what was to happen in *Drood* fall into three main categories. The first I shall call the biographical: arguments, that is, about what

Dickens wrote in private papers, or is reported to have said. The second I shall call the forensic category: arguments treating what we find in the book as if it were evidence about a real-life mystery. The third category I shall call the aesthetic: arguments seeking to determine what might be a satisfactory conclusion to a coherent work of art.

The third category is the one I am chiefly concerned with. I am spending little time on the second, forensic arguments, because these are demonstrably inconclusive. During nearly a century and a quarter of debate, no generally accepted conclusion has been reached. The book supplies no evidence that would lead to a verdict beyond reasonable doubt, in a real-life tribunal.

Biographical arguments, however, clearly have to be dealt with. If it can be shown that Dickens the private man acknowledged Drood was murdered, then there is an end to all speculation. But I do not believe he did acknowledge that. That there was a murder, he certainly acknowledged. Number plans he jotted down for the novel contain such phrases as "Murder very far off," and "Lay the ground for the manner of the Murder, to come out at last" (Cardwell, 221, 225). None indicates Drood was the victim. It is usually supposed the murder was committed on a dark, tempestuous, bewildering night, by someone half-mad with passion, possibly dazed by opium. We cannot be sure it was the intended victim who was murdered. Neither the final title for the book, nor any of the titles Dickens toyed with in notes, demands that we believe it was Edwin who died. These titles include ambiguities such as "The Loss of Edwyn Drood," "The Flight of Edwyn Drood," and "The Disappearance of Edwin Drood." They include the tantalising 'Dead? Or alive?" And they include one that it is hard not to see as verification of my hypothesis: "Edwin Drood in hiding" (*Drood*, Appendix A, 218).

Turning to what Dickens is reported to have said, we find three important pieces of testimony, none of them entirely satisfactory. I am ignoring the testimony, I should say, of Charles Collins, Dickens's son-in-law, who designed the wrapper for the parts. It is far from clear he was not simply following John Forster's or someone else's account.[2]

Forster's version is encapsulated at the point in the *Life* of Dickens where he speaks of a letter, in which Dickens told him of "a very curious and new idea for my new story. Not a communicable idea (or the interest of the book would be gone), but a very strong one, though difficult to work." "The story, I learnt immediately afterward," Forster says, "was to be that of the murder of a nephew by his uncle" (808). There is clearly a contradiction here. Dickens told Forster his idea for the story was incommunicable. "Immediately afterward," according to Forster, it was communicated. Forster was saddened by a cooling in his relationship with Dickens, towards the end of his friend's life, and strives sometimes, in the biography, to conceal it. It is tempting to ascribe the contradiction to Forster's claiming a privileged disclosure in fact denied him.

The second piece of testimony is that of Charles Dickens Jr. who, in the introduction to the Macmillan edition of the novel, written twenty-five years after its first publication, recalls speaking to his father during its composition. "Of course, Edwin Drood was murdered?", Charley had suggested. He describes his father's response in this way: "he turned upon me with an expression of astonishment at my having asked such an unnecessary question, and said: 'Of course; what else do you suppose?' " (xv). Is not a false note struck here? The response, if truly his, seems to devalue Dickens' art. It relegates *Drood* to the status of the kind of formula mystery allowing clever readers to make instant judgments about character, to detect the author's intentions early on, and thereafter chiefly to enjoy the elegance with which they are worked out. I find it hard to believe the Dickens who declared his idea for the story incommunicable and difficult to work, would have devalued his art in quite this way. I can believe he might have said something of the kind to Charley, but evasively. Dickens' relations with his adult children were often constrained. It would not have been beyond him to tease Charley on this issue. Charley, of course, had much to gain from encouraging the idea that his father expected him always to be clever.

The third piece of testimony is more difficult to ignore, because it is more difficult to detect in it any contradiction or ulterior motive. Sir Luke Fildes's contribution to the debate can be represented by a letter the illustrator of *Drood* wrote to *The Times Literary Supplement* in 1905. In it, Fildes speaks of questioning Dickens about Jasper's long scarf, or "neckerchief" as he calls it on this occasion, and of being told he must show it, "for Jasper strangles Edwin Drood with it" (373). Fildes had no very obvious axe to grind. Even so, there are reasons for being cautious about what he says. He was remembering words uttered thirty-five years earlier. Soon after Dickens' death, someone whom Fildes would have regarded (probably rightly, despite cooling) as the author's closest friend, and as his greatest biographer, had gone on record saying Jasper murdered Drood. The Macmillan edition was not published till 1923, but Fildes had known Charley, and would inevitably have discussed the intended ending with him. And there were opportunities for error to have crept in. Dickens could have told Fildes that Jasper commits the murder with the scarf, but not who is murdered—that being filled out in Fildes's mind by other sources of information. Or Dickens could have told him Jasper strangled Edwin, without revealing the strangling to be incomplete—that Edwin survived it. If I seem to be laboring the point about this testimony, let me reiterate that nothing Dickens himself wrote demands that we suppose it was Drood who died.

Biographical arguments, then, offer testimony supporting the notion that Drood was murdered, but none of it is entirely satisfactory, and I feel little compunction in disregarding it in favor of evidence I find more compelling.

And so I come to aesthetic arguments. "I call my book the Mystery, not the History, of Edwin Drood," Dickens reminded his sister-in-law, Georgina Hogarth.[3] But he was not, I suggest, claiming a licence arbitrarily to mystify, something effectively forbidden by Aristotelian precept. Diminish the roles played by causality and closure in the novel, to be sure, and the way is open for arbitrary mystification. That, as I understand it, is a problem for postmodernism, which admits random and disjunctive events to narrative, making judgment of such matters difficult.

In fiction designed primarily to mystify—some detective fiction, for instance—writers can drag red herrings across the reader's path, and then abandon them. Not so, the craftsman novelist, bound by chains of causality. In a novel worthy of the name, next to nothing should happen not caused by something else that has already happened. Next to nothing should happen that does not cause other things to happen in their turn. We are entitled to complain about mystification designed merely to distract. I think it unlikely Dickens would have trailed red herrings at this stage in his career. What we know of his artistry permits us to suppose everything is significant, everything needing development would have been developed. If there are things designed to put us off the scent, we can suppose he intended to develop them and show them to be significant, not just abandon them. I say this, not least because I am convinced that, when he died, Dickens had by no means finished with the character of Edwin. Without Edwin's survival, I submit, a completed *Mystery of Edwin Drood* would have been imperfect.

The clearest indication Dickens planned to develop him further is to be found in Edwin's attraction to Helena Landless, growing, we surmise, into love. A feature of this attraction, easy to miss but scarcely possible to deny, is that not a single character in the novel knows of it, other than Edwin himself. In chapter 8, the narrator tells us Edwin is "already" impressed by Helena (55). In chapter 13, when he and Rosa break off their engagement, we are told "he did already entertain some wandering speculations whether it might ever come to pass that he would know more of Miss Landless" (119). Uses of the word "already," alone, seem to demand development of plot and character. And in chapter 14 we learn that, while doubting he is worthy of her, Edwin has "that handsome figure of Miss Landless in the background of his mind" (124). Apart from an observation to Jasper and Neville, that he could paint a good portrait of her (58), the only comment upon Helena ever uttered by Edwin is to Mr Grewgious, in chapter 11. "She is a strikingly handsome girl, sir," Edwin tells him, "and I thought she might have been described to you, or presented to you, perhaps?" (92). This attraction of Edwin's will lead nowhere, and can have no consequences, if he is dead.

One hesitates to imagine Dickens, at this stage in his career, writing in this genre, using duplicitous devices such as a disclosure subsequently revealed, or a confessional document subsequently discovered. He might have intended the narrator to make something of the attraction, I suppose, but the narrative's sketching of bare facts surely foreshadows no elegaic lament, and being told cannot compare with being shown the pathos of thwarted hopes. If Edwin dies, this potential character development dies with him, and we must look upon it as separable, dangling and unintegrated.

If Edwin's feelings for Helena Landless call for development of his story, how much does the broad presentation of his character? There is an impetus, as I see it, towards development in a particular direction. Dickens' options, I believe, were limited and defined by the craft of fiction itself, which offers templates for shaping novels, ignored by writers at their peril, and available, not just because they are familiar, but because they are fundamental, structured by causality, and morally interesting.

There were three such patterns that Dickens could have used in further shaping the story of a morally imperfect character such as Edwin. Two would require his dying, one his surviving. One is the poetic justice template. This would entail Edwin's being so wicked that readers would be satisfied by his death, ironically caused by that very wickedness. The second is the tragic template. This would entail his being seen as a fundamentally good man, spoiled by a tragic flaw, or misled by tragic error, and doomed because of this. The third is the sentimental education or *Bildungsroman* template, which would entail Edwin's learning from his mistake, or being transformed in some way, to survive, a better man.

Certain templates were not available to Dickens, I think it fair to say, including one he has made especially his own. Edwin was not being shaped into a doomed Dickensian innocent, like Little Nell, or Jo, the crossing sweeper. He is too old, too complex, too imperfect, and if he is destroyed, presumably it is by one man's wickedness, not neglect that might have been prevented or repaired, which is what always destroys the Dickensian innocent. Nor do I think we can suppose Dickens was planning for Edwin what Thomas Hardy might have planned: destruction, despite promise, by an indifferent or hostile fate. That never happens in Dicken' works. It is anachronistic to suppose it might have.

My contention is that Dickens was clearly using the sentimental education template. Edwin, I submit, is presented to us, at first as a character in need of a sentimental education, then as one embarking upon a sentimental education, but never as one who has completed a sentimental education.

Undoubtedly, Edwin has good qualities. He is "always kindly," we are told (126). And when he is first introduced in chapter 2, we cannot but notice his open and easy manner. But for all that, he is full of himself and insensitive to the feelings of others. Almost his first words are a demand that Jasper cease to "moddley-coddley" him, and the narrative draws attention to the "check upon" Jasper, "of being unsympathetically restrained in a genial outburst of enthusiasm" (7). Edwin quibbles with Jasper's innocent ban of the terms "uncle" and "nephew" from their discourse. He patronises Jasper: "What a dreadfully conscientious fellow you are, Jack!'"; "Have you lost your tongue, Jack?" He speaks carelessly of Rosa without noticing Jasper's pain (9). For all her indulgence and scandalised pleasure, Edwin's manner to Mrs. Tope is still impertinent. "Give me a kiss," he demands, "because it's Pussy's birthday" (8–9).

Towards the end of the chapter, when Jasper reveals how unhappy he is, Edwin pinpoints his own deficiency:

> I am afraid I am but a shallow, surface kind of fellow, Jack, and that my headpiece is none of the best. But I needn't say I am young; and perhaps I shall not grow worse as I grow older. At all events, I hope I have something impressible within me, which feels—deeply feels—the disinterestedness of your painfully laying your inner self bare, as a warning to me. (12)

There is irony at work here, but there is also evidence of a moral self-consciousness, indicating that the poetic justice template is not being used. We could not rejoice in the death of someone so open to experience and to improvement. The same self-consciousness indicates that the tragic template is not being used. We neither see a tragic flaw in Edwin, nor witness a tragic error. What we see is youth. Tempting though it might be, to see youth as a flaw or an error, it is a temptation to be resisted. Edwin's confession, however, is entirely appropriate to the sentimental education template. It reveals moral awareness, to be sure, but it is also a kind of excuse for not changing yet. He has much to learn, the reader concludes. This judgment is reinforced.

We next see Edwin in chapter 7, at the soirée after Mr. Crisparkle's dinner party. When, under Jasper's merciless scrutiny, Rosa breaks down during her song, we cannot but be struck by the way Edwin misinterprets, not only Jasper's part in the collapse, but also both Rosa's and Helena's response:

> "Pussy's not used to an audience; that's the fact," said Edwin Drood. "She got nervous and couldn't hold out. Besides, Jack, you are such a conscientious master, and require so much, that I believe you make her afraid of you. No wonder."
>
> "No wonder," repeated Helena.
>
> "There, Jack, you hear! You would be afraid of him, under similar circumstances, wouldn't you, Miss Landless?"
>
> "Not under any circumstances," returned Helena.   (51)

Rosa and Helena understand Jasper. Edwin does not. How can he be so blind, we ask ourselves.

In the succeeding chapter, Edwin's self-absorption and self-assertiveness offend Neville Landless, prompted to antagonism anyway, by jealousy of Edwin's prospects with Rosa. For all that, Neville brings himself to congratulate Edwin on his betrothal, only to meet with an ungracious rebuff: "By George! . . . Everybody in this chattering old Cloisterham refers to it. I wonder no Public House has been set up, with my portrait for the sign of The Betrothed's Head. Or Pussy's portrait. One or the other" (55). Later, provoked by Jasper's insinuations and confused by wine, probably drugged, Neville becomes overtly antagonistic, but he is goaded. Edwin is the patronizing and indifferent goader. Neville suggests Edwin might be the better for having known hardships, "Because they might have made him more sensible . . . of good fortune that is not by any means necessarily the result of his own merits." Not a friendly thing to say, certainly, but friendlier than Edwin's deliberate provocations: "You may know a black common fellow, or a black common boaster, when you see him (and no doubt you have a large acquaintance that way); but you are no judge of white men" (59–60). By now, though, we know enough of Edwin to attribute his behavior to youth, rather than to unforgivable wickedness or tragic imperfection.

This judgment is reinforced by chapter 11, in which Edwin discusses his betrothal to Rosa with Mr. Grewgious, and shows clear signs of becoming conscious of others' feelings. Mr. Grewgious is indignant that Edwin should "make a plaything of a treasure" (96), and our attention is repeatedly drawn to Edwin's embarrassment and indecision. "Edwin had turned red and turned white . . . ," we are told. "He now sat looking into the fire, and bit his lip"

(95). He is uneasy about accepting the token of their betrothal: "Some trouble was in the young man's face, and some indecision was in the action of his hand, as Mr Grewgious, looking steadfastly at him, gave him the ring"(97).

With Edwin steadied by Mr. Grewgious's advice, in chapter 13 the young couple are able to break off their engagement, without loss of respect for each other, and for both this is a major step in sentimental education:

> This pure young feeling, this gentle and forebearing feeling of each towards the other, brought with it its reward in a softening light that seemed to shine on their position. The relations between them did not look wilful, or capricious, or a failure, in such a light; they became elevated into something more self-denying, honorable, affectionate, and true. (115)

Edwin, however, remains not only insensitive to the complexities of Jasper's attitude towards him, but complacent about it. "Can you suppose," he asks Rosa of all people, "that anyone so wrapped up in another—Mrs Tope's expression: not mine—as Jack's in me, could fail to be struck all of a heap by such a sudden and complete change in my life?" (117).

Edwin's attitudes are clearly changing. Difficulties between him and Rosa are resolved. Not at his initiative, though. The engagement ends because of Mr. Grewgious's admonition, and Rosa's instinct. Edwin can recognize what is right, but not yet initiate a change in relationships. There is not only the insensitivity towards Jasper still to be corrected. What is wrong between him and Neville has yet to be put right. His sentimental education is incomplete.

Dickens made Edwin youthfully insensitive and annoying, in order both to explore how such blemishes are unlearned, and to yield action. That is how this kind of narrative is constructed. Edwin has to be insensitive, or he would see through Jasper and precipitate the wrong sort of crisis. He has to be annoying, to antagonize Neville and motivate another potential murderer. But Dickens refrained from making him so insensitive, so annoying, that the reader's sympathy is lost. That, on the contrary, is sustained by a moral improvement which makes us look for more. The option of having Edwin murdered is forfeited, not because it would wound readers' sensibilities too much, but because it would destroy the dynamic of the plot.

When we turn our attention from Edwin's character to the more general unfolding of plot, another of Aristotle's concepts reinforces the argument. Giving utterance, as so often, to the perception of every alert theater-goer or reader, he observes that one of the most powerful mechanisms in plot is discovery, "a change from ignorance to knowledge." Among other things, characters and readers can discover "whether someone has or has not done something'' (20), whether, we can gloss, something has or has not been done to someone. In considering this, it is important to recognize that, after a certain point, every character in *Drood*, not even excepting Jasper it would seem, supposes Edwin to be dead. Was Dickens planning no discovery, in the Aristotelian sense? Was everyone at the end in effect going to say, ''Yes, we were all right. No one got it wrong. What we supposed to have happened did happen. Edwin is dead. Let us get on with our lives''? The novel is the *Mystery* of Edwin Drood, and Dickens did remind Georgina Hogarth of this. What other mystery might there be, awaiting discovery?

The chief possibility is that Edwin is dead, murdered by someone other than Jasper. But if that was to be the discovery, why did Dickens let no body be found? If the mystery was to be the identity of Edwin's killer, what difference could the lack of a body make, at the stage the novel reaches? It might as well be found on Christmas day. Little narrative advantage could have been gained, by delaying its discovery until later. No, the major mystery is whether Edwin is dead or alive and, since everyone supposes him dead, the most likely discovery is that he is alive.

Edwin's final appearance in what we have of the novel is in chapter 14. He is in a valedictory mood: ''His wonted carelessness is replaced by a wistful looking at, and dwelling upon, all the old landmarks. He will soon be far away, and may never see them again, he thinks. Poor youth! Poor youth!'' The manuscript, but not the published version, adds the sentence, ''And he little, little knows how near a case he has for thinking so'' (125 and n.). Danger clearly threatens. But for all the valedictory mood, for all the menace of death, there is no unambiguous foreshadowing of it, such as we find before the deaths of Little Nell, Montague Tigg, or Paul Dombey. The danger, I suggest, is of suffering, not of death. To complete his sentimental education, Edwin is to be scourged, like Pip and Estella in *Great Expectations*, like Mrs. Joe, Miss Havisham and Magwitch too, like Eugene Wrayburn in *Our Mutual Friend*. We cannot be sure about the form his scourging will take, but we have an idea of what it will fit him for. He will become worthy of Helena Landless.

I have said the case for Edwin's survival is almost too strong to be repudiated but, in the course of arguing this, I have imagined only two ways for Dickens to have written his book: the way of the craftsman, shaping an aesthetically coherent narrative; or the way of the literary speculator, abandoning principle to mystify with cheap tricks. There is, however, a third possibility. Integrity undimmed, but tired and ill, and working in a genre only just beginning to take shape, it could be that Dickens allowed a desire to mystify, to clash irreconcilably with his acquired novel-writing skills. Both W. H.

Wills and Dion Boucicault are reported to have suggested something of the kind.[4] Perhaps Dickens had set himself tasks impossible to achieve in the unwritten numbers. It may be that that biographical evidence suggesting Edwin is dead is right, and that Dickens' death aborted an artistic failure.

We shall never know. However intriguing it is to speculate about Dickens's intentions, there is no end to it, because intentions can be contradictory and self-defeating. What speculation can do, however, is make us think how a novel develops, and show how what he has already written must constrain a novelist worthy of the title, and working properly. If postmodernism cannot accommodate such speculation, I suggest it is because there is something wrong with postmodernism.

NOTES

1. This paper is based on a lecture delivered during the Dickens Universe, at the University of California Santa Cruz, in 1993. That was based on an earlier paper read as part of a symposium organized by the Dickens Fellowship in London, in 1987.
2. See Charles Forsyte, pp. 42–44.
3. See "Edwin Drood and the Last Days of Charles Dickens, by his younger daughter Kate Perugini," *Pall Mall Magazine*, June 1906.
4. See Introduction, *Drood*, ed. Cardwell, xxvii.

WORKS CITED

Aristotle. *Aristotle's Poetics*. Trans. John Warrington. London, 1963.

Connor, Steven. "Dead? Or Alive?: Edwin Drood and the Work of Mourning." *The Dickensian* LXXXIX (1993): 85–102.

Dickens, Charles. *The Mystery of Edwin Drood*. Ed. Margaret Cardwell. Oxford: Oxford UP, 1972.

Dickens, Charles, Jr. Introduction. *The Mystery of Edwin Drood*. By Charles Dickens. London: Macmillan, 1923.

Fildes, Sir Luke. Letter. *The Times Literary Supplement* 3 Nov. 1905:373.

Forster, John. *The Life of Charles Dickens*. Ed. J. W. T. Ley. London: Cecil Palmer, 1927.

Forsyte, Charles. *The Decoding of Edwin Drood*. London: Gollancz, 1980.

Perugini, Kate. "Edwin Drood and the Last Days of Charles Dickens." *Pall Mall Magazine* 37 (June 1906).

References in Longfellow's *Journals* (1856–1882) to Charles Dickens

Edward L. Tucker

Edward Wagenknecht stated of the Longfellow-Dickens relationship: "Whatever reservations may have been made upon either side, there is no room for doubt that for Henry Wadsworth Longfellow, Charles Dickens was the most important of all novelists" (19). Andrew Hilen, in agreement, concluded that Dickens was Longfellow's "closest literary friend in England."[1]

Henry Wadsworth Longfellow was born at Portland, Maine, 27 February 1807, and died at Cambridge, Massachusetts, 24 March 1882. The two men met four times: Dickens visited Boston twice and saw Longfellow, first in 1842 and then in 1867–68; Longfellow visited England and saw Dickens twice, first in 1842 and then in 1868, shortly before Dickens' death. At the time of their first meeting, between "the most widely read English novelist and the most widely read American poet of that day" (Dana 55), Longfellow was 34 and Dickens 29.

By 1842, the date of the first trans-Atlantic visit, Dickens had written some successful novels, was married, and the father of four children. By this same date, Longfellow had written two prose works of some interest: *Outre-Mer* (1835) and *Hyperion* (1839). Although his popular, full-length poems were to appear after 1842, he had received much acclaim for some short selections, notably "A Psalm of Life" and "The Beleaguered City" in *Voices of the Night* (1839) and "The Skeleton in Armor," "The Wreck of the Hesperus," "The Village Blacksmith," and "Excelsior" in *Ballads and Other Poems* (1841). He was made an early widower. He had married Mary Storer Potter (1812–35) on 14 September 1831, and she had died on a trip to Rotterdam on 29 November 1835. There were no children by the marriage.

Although this article concentrates on the 1867–68 visits, a few comments about the earlier ones seem appropriate. In September 1841 Dickens wrote:

"I HAVE MADE UP MY MIND (WITH GOD'S LEAVE) TO GO TO AMERICA—AND TO START AS SOON AFTER CHRISTMAS AS IT WILL BE SAFE TO GO." One reason for the trip was that he had an enormous following in the United States. He gave another reason a few days later: "I wrote to Chapman and Hall asking them what they thought of it, and saying I meant to keep a note-book, and publish it for half a guinea or thereabouts, on my return."[2] One result of the trip was *American Notes* (1842), which, according to Longfellow, contained "a grand chapter on Slavery"; other "topics of censure" were "*spitting* and *politics* at Washington."[3]

Dickens and his wife set sail for America on 4 January 1842; they arrived on Saturday, 22 January, and stayed at Boston's leading hotel, Tremont House, until 5 February. The visit was a huge success with "the greatest possible enthusiasm" existing "among all classes"; Dickens did not have "a moment's rest" because of the "calls innumerable" and the "invitations innumerable."[4]

It was a considerable honor for Longfellow to meet Dickens; he described him as "a glorious fellow," "a gay, free and easy character" with "a good constitution," who was enjoying "the fun of the thing." Longfellow was also attracted to Dickens' wife, "a good-natured—mild, rosy young woman—not beautiful, but amiable."[5] Longfellow and Dickens were together on four different occasions during Dickens' 1842 visit. On Wednesday, 26 January, the two met for the first time in Dickens' rooms at the Tremont House; others present were Cornelius Felton and Jared Sparks. The next meeting was an extended one: on Sunday, 30 January, Longfellow and his friend, Charles Sumner, took Dickens to the Seamen's Bethel, to hear Father Edward Taylor preach to seamen; then they "walked ten miles; namely, *to* town, *through* town, and *out* of town," going to the waterfront of Boston, the wharves where the Boston Tea Party took place, North End, the Old North Church, the Copp's Hill Burying Ground, the Bunker Hill Monument. On Tuesday, 1 February, Longfellow attended the famous Dickens Dinner at Papanti's Hall, for which the tickets were fifteen dollars apiece and at which there were ten courses with countless toasts and tributes. Finally, on Friday, 4 February, Longfellow entertained Dickens at a breakfast in the upstairs rooms of the Craigie House, where he was living; the other guests were Cornelius Felton and Andrews Norton. After breakfast Dickens and Longfellow went on a walking tour of the Harvard College campus. On Saturday, 5 February, Dickens left Boston by train for Worcester. Dickens' best friend during this stay was Cornelius Felton, who went with the novelist on a portion of the remainder of this American visit.[6]

Dickens knew that Longfellow was planning a trip to Europe. He wrote him that when he was in London: "Have no home but mine . . . let me be your London host and cicerone."[7] Longfellow, eager to see Dickens again, arrived at the novelist's London residence, No. 1 Devonshire Terrace, York Gate, Regent Park, on Wednesday, 5 October 1842. The poet described Dickens' household as "a delightful one" with the wife "a most kind, amiable person and his four children beautiful in the extreme." On Thursday, 6 October, Dickens and Longfellow attended a performance of *As You Like It*, starring the famous tragedian, William Charles Macready. During the next two weeks, Longfellow met a number of distinguished people. Dickens had at his dinner table "artists and authors," such as "Cruikshank, a very original genius" and "Maclise the painter." Longfellow "breakfasted and dined with Mr. Rogers," and "met at his table Tom Campbell, and Mr. Moxon the publisher and Sonneteer." Lady Blessington "cheered" his eyes "by her fair presence."[8] In addition, Dickens took him to Rochester, where the novelist had spent his childhood, and at night exposed him to "the tramps and thieves" of the slums of London (Dana 73).

On Thursday, 20 October, Longfellow left London; Dickens and John Forster accompanied him to Bristol, via Bath, where they visited with Walter Savage Landor. On Friday, 21 October, Longfellow set sail for America. All in all, for the poet the visit was "charming," "a memory of delight forever."[9]

It was twenty-five years before the two men were to meet again. During this time much had happened in their professional and personal lives. Dickens had written other successful novels, had become the father of six more children, had lost two children, and had separated from his wife.[10] Longfellow had written his most famous full-length poems: *Evangeline: A Tale of Acadie* (1847), *The Song of Hiawatha* (1855), *The Courtship of Miles Standish* (1858), and *Tales of a Wayside Inn* (1863), and had translated *The Divine Comedy of Dante Alighieri* (1865–67). He married Frances Appleton (1817–61) on 13 July 1843. There were six children: Charles (1844–93), Ernest (1845–1921), Fanny (1847–48), Alice (1850–1928), Edith (1853–1915), and Annie (1855–1934). The baby Fanny died in 1848, and Longfellow's wife was severely burned in a fire on 9 July 1861 and died the next day. Longfellow had become a widower for the second time.

They met again because Dickens decided to give a series of public readings. He made this decision because he wanted to keep "his entire large family forever beyond the fear of want" and to relieve his "emotional needs" (Johnson 548). Dickens had long been interested in the theater: he had written some works to be staged, had often acted in amateur theatricals, and sometimes had directed performances.

His earliest public readings from his own works were for charity, the very first being on 27, 29, 30 December 1853 at the Birmingham Town Hall in aid of the Literary and Scientific Institute, at which he read *A Christmas Carol* twice and *The Cricket on the Hearth* on the 29th. The first of a series of public readings for profit was at St. Martin's Hall on 29 April 1858, when he performed *The Cricket on the Hearth.* In all there were four series of public readings for profit: 1858–59, 1861–63, 1866–67, and 1868–70. During the last series he came to the United States. Dickens' itinerary for the 1867–68 visit, emphasizing his contacts with Longfellow, is as follows: [11]

Tuesday, 19 November 1867: Dickens arrived in Boston and registered at the Parker House Hotel, Suite 338, with a parlor, a bedchamber for himself, and one for George Dolby, his manager. The "enthusiam" for Dickens and "for his Readings" was "immense"; every "ticket was sold for the whole course and the public clamorous for more."[12]

Wednesday, 20 November: Longfellow, on the way to dine with Holmes, stopped by to see Dickens early in the afternoon. He found that he had "the same sweetness and flavor as of old," with "only greater ripeness." After dinner, Longfellow, Oliver Wendell Holmes, and the other two guests at the dinner—Agassiz and Emerson—came to see Dickens at the Parker House.[13]

Thurday, 21 November: James Fields gave a dinner party to welcome Dickens; the guests included Longfellow.[14]

Friday, 22 November: Longfellow had a supper party for Dickens at the Craigie House, this time downstairs.

Tueday, 26 November: Charles Eliot Norton gave a dinner party for Dickens; the guests included Longfellow.[15]

Thursday, 28 November: Dickens had Thanksgiving dinner at Longfellow's house. The poet showed Dickens the works by the English novelist in his bookshelves, and Dickens remarked, "Ah, I see you read the good authors."[16]

Saturday, 30 November: Dickens was a guest of the Saturday Club. The members included Longfellow.

On Monday 2 December, Dickens began the first of his eighteen Boston readings, all given in the Tremont Temple.[17] His innate sense of the dramatic, plus his own experience and advice from Dolby, helped him in arranging the programs. For this American tour, he always had the two-part division. The first selection "consisted of one long item (about seventy to eighty minutes)," which "though it might be predominantly comic," also "found a place for other effects, pathetic or dramatic." After intermission, there was a "short item (about thirty to forty minutes),'' which was "usually comic, and had something of the effect of a theatrical 'afterpiece' " (Collins xxvii). In the American tour, the first item was always one of the following: "A Christmas Carol," "David Copperfield," "Nicholas Nickleby," "Dombey and Son," or "Dr. Marigold." The second item was always one of the following: "Trial from Pickwick," "Bob Sawyer's Party," "Boots at the Holly Tree Inn," or "Mrs. Gamp."

Monday, 2 December (1st reading): "A Christmas Carol" and "Trial from Pickwick."

Tuesday, 3 December (2nd reading): "David Copperfield" and "Bob Sawyer's Party."

Thursday, 5 December (3rd reading): "Nicholas Nickleby" and "Boots at the Holly Tree Inn."

Friday, 6 December (4th reading): "Dombey and Son" and "Trial from Pickwick."

Longfellow reported that Boston had been "not Galvanized, but Dickinized, into great activity, very pleasant to behold"; the "Readings, or rather Actings," had been "immensely successful."[18]

Saturday, 7 December: Dickens left Boston to give readings in New York.

Saturday, 21 December: Dickens returned to Boston from New York and registered for the same suite at the Parker House Hotel.

Monday, 23 December (5th reading): "David Copperfield" and "Bob Sawyer's Party."

Tuesday, 24 December (6th reading): "A Christmas Carol" and "Trial from Pickwick."

Wednesday, 25 December: Dickens left Boston for New York. Longfellow and others were at the station to tell him farewell and to extend Christmas greetings.

Saturday, 4 January 1868: He returned to Boston and accepted an invitation to stay with Mr. and Mrs. Fields, who became his best friends during this American visit.[19]

Sunday, 5 January: Mrs. Fields had a dinner party for Dickens; Longfellow, one of the guests, told an anecdote about Dr. John White Webster, Professor of Chemistry at Harvard, who was hanged for murdering Dr. George Parkman.

Monday, 6 January (7th reading): "Nicholas Nickleby" and "Boots at the Holly Tree Inn."

Tuesday, 7 January (8th reading): "David Copperfield" and "Trial from Pickwick."

Wednesday, 8 January: Dickens left Boston for New York, Phildelphia, Brooklyn, Baltimore, Washington, Hartford, and Providence.

Sunday, 23 February: Dickens returned to Boston and the Parker House Hotel.

Monday, 24 February (9th reading): "Dr. Marigold" and "Trial from Pickwick."

Tuesday, 25 February (10th reading): "David Copperfield" and "Bob Sawyer's Party."

Thursday, 27 February (11th reading): "A Christmas Carol" and "Boots at the Holly Tree Inn." Mrs. Fields had a birthday party for Longfellow afterwards; Dickens was too ill to go, but he sent a letter in which he wished for Longfellow "all earthly happiness and prosperity"; this day was "a precious one to the civilized world" because Longfellow was born on 27 February. Dickens hoped to "welcome" the poet "at Gad's Hill next Summer," and he would give him "the heartiest reception."[20]

Friday, 28 February (12th reading): "Nicholas Nickleby" and "Trial from Pickwick."

Saturday, 29 February: (In spite of bad health, Dickens walked a number of miles almost every day.) On this day, a contest was held, called the "Great International Walking Match," in which James R. Osgood, Dolby, Fields, and Dickens took part. In the evening there was an elaborate dinner at the Parker House; Longfellow was one of the guests.[21]

Because the discussion of impeachment proceedings against President Andrew Johnson discouraged business, Dickens cancelled a series of four scheduled readings during the week of Monday, 2 March—Friday, 6 March.

Tuesday, 3 March: Dickens gave a dinner for some friends at the Parker House; the list included Longfellow.

Wednesday, 4 March: Longfellow gave a dinner party at the Craigie House for Dickens.

Friday, 6 March: Dickens left Boston for Syracuse, Rochester, Buffalo, Albany, Springfield, Worcester, New Haven, Hartford, New Bedford, and Portland.

Tuesday, 31 March: Dickens returned to Boston and stayed at the Parker House Hotel.

Wednesday, 1 April (13th reading): "A Christmas Carol" and "Trial from Pickwick."

Thursday, 2 April (14th reading): "Nicholas Nickleby" and "Boots at the Holly Tree Inn."

Friday, 3 April (15th reading: "Dr. Marigold" and "Mrs. Gamp." Earlier on this day Longfellow and others went to his suite at the Parker House and tried, without success, to persuade Dickens, because of his bad cold, not to appear that evening.

Monday, 6 April (16th reading): "David Copperfield" and "Bob Sawyer's Party."

Tuesday, 7 April (17th reading): Longfellow and others called on Dickens at the Parker House and urged him, again without success, not to read that night because of his poor health. "Dombey and Son" and "Trial from Pickwick."

Wednesday, 8 April (18th reading): "Dr. Marigold" and "Mrs. Gamp."

Thursday, 9 April: Longfellow and others called to say goodbye.

Friday, 10 April: Dickens departed for the farewell trip to New York.

Wednesday, 22 April: Dickens sailed for England.

Financially, the "American tour had been successful beyond all expectations"; receipts totalled "$228,000 and the expenses not quite $39,000." This latter figure included "hotels, travelling, rent of halls, and a 5 per cent commission to Ticknor and Fields on the receipts in Boston." There were also "preliminary expenses in England" and a "commission" for Dolby (Johnson 548). The novelist "made a fortune in America, where his average nightly profit was nearly three times as much as even his Farewells brought him in Britain." All the readings taken together "earned Dickens about £45,000—nearly half the estate which he left (£93,000)" (Collins xxix, 2).[22] There was a horrible cost, however. Though he received much "pleasure" from this career, the results "were purchased at the dear cost of the sacrifice of his health" (Dolby 451).

Although Longfellow in 1867 described Dickens as being "as vivacious and genial as on his former visit in 1842," he eventually changed his mind and wrote after the novelist's death: "How suddenly Dickens vanished from our sight! And yet I was not much surprised; for when he was last here, he seemed very restless, as if driven by fate."[23] The Dickens of 1867–68 was different from the man of 1842. "The gay young dandy had become a careworn, middle-aged man" who needed much solitude. "It was decided that there was to be no repetition of the 1842 round of receptions," and Dickens, although "he desired to renew old friendships, was to make no new ones" (Payne 139, 153). In his biography Johnson includes this American tour in a section entitled "The Bottom of the Cup, 1865–1870," with an emphasis on his poor health, especially his "dismal cold," the "American catarrh," and problem with his feet (2:532–46).[24]

Once Dickens was at sea after the American tour, he began to feel better. Longfellow took advantage of the offer extended to him in the birthday message of 27 February 1868, and he, his three daughters, and his brother-in-law, Thomas Gold Appleton, visited Dickens at Gad's Hill on 4–6 July 1868. Although there is no reference to this visit in the Longfellow *Journals*, in his letters the poet spoke of "the pleasant days" spent at Dickens' home and of the "hospitality" he and his family received.[25] This was the fourth and final meeting between Dickens and Longfellow.

At the beginning of 1856, Henry Wadsworth Longfellow was 48 years old. He lived to the age of 75. The years 1856–1882, then, are approximately the last one third of his life. During this period, he kept extensive *Journals*, numbering 1,146 pages; they are now housed in the Houghton Library, Harvard. Although selected passages from the *Journals* referring to Dickens have been previously published, this article, for the first time, contains *all* the references Longfellow made to the English novelist during the period.[26]

In editing these passages, I have on rare occasions silently emended confusing punctuation, mechanical, or paragraphing practices for the convenience of readers. Words have not been changed. If a change has been made in spelling for improved comprehension, I have included it in brackets. If I have added a word for clarity, I have included it in brackets. In the manuscripts, the year for a set of entries appears only once, at the beginning of the year. To improve readability, I have supplied the appropriate year before each individual entry.

1856, Friday, March 21. Evening, another chapter of "Little Dorrit"—not so good as the last: and not helping the story on much.[27]

1857, Thursday, January 22. Evening, read Dicken[s'] "Wreck of the Golden Mary." Too tragic, too tragic. The boys rebelled against it, and called for Cooper's "Wyandotté" which was given them instead.[28]

1860, Monday, March 12. Evening, "Barnaby Rudge." Dickens is always prodigal, and ample; but what a set of vagabonds he contrives to introduce one to.

1860, Wednesday, March 21. Evening, went to Mrs. Colburns's to see some of the characters of the Dicken[s] fancy-dress Party, given by Mrs. Chs. Lowell. Tom as Capt. Bunsby. Darley as Turvy-drop; Mrs. Darley as Mrs. McStringer. Miss Colburn as Pocahontas of the Jarley Wax-works. After all, what a collection of vulgarities these will be.[29]

1861, Thursday, March 7. Read "Dombey and Son," which is a dismal book, though rich in character and with a great deal of fun in it. "Pride goes before a Fall" is the meaning and moral of it. The description of Dr. Blimber's school is capital.[30]

1861, Saturday, March 9. Darley made his appearance this morning; looking unchanged. He is here for a few days. Is illustrating the new edition of Dickens's works.[31]

1861, Thursday, March 21. Passed the day writing letters, and reading Dickens.

1861, Thursday, March 28. Afternoon and evening, read "Pickwick"—It contains all Dickens in embryo, as an Overture does an Opera: themes and motives just touched upon, which are more elaborately developed in later works.

1865, Saturday, September 23. Lowell came in; and after that I read "Our Mutual Friend" till dinner.[32]

1867, Monday, November 18. Dickens is expected tomorrow by steamer, now at Halifax. A great crowd at Fields', to buy tickets for his Readings.[33]

1867, Wednesday, November 20. Dined with Dr. Holmes. On my way stopped at Parker House to see Dickens, whom I found very well and most cordial. It was right pleasant to see him again, after so many years; twenty five! He looks somewhat older, but as elastic and quick in his movements as ever.

1867, Thursday, November 21. Dined with Fields—a dinner of welcome for Dickens. Guests to meet him, Emerson, Agassiz, Holmes, Judge Hoar, Norton, Greene and myself. A beautiful dinner.[34]

1867, Friday, November 22. Evening, Dickens came out to a little Supper. Had to meet him Darley, Lowell, Fields, Howells, U. S. and E. W. L. and Greene. It was very pleasant and satisfactory.[35]

1867, Tuesday, November 26. Dined with Norton to meet Dickens. The other guests were Lowell, Mr. James, Miss Sarah Sedgwick, Miss Ashburner, and. . . .[36]

1867, Thursday, November 28. Thanksgiving Day. Dickens came out to a quiet family dinner at 2.30. No one out of the house but Mrs. Pierce and Hattie Spelman.[37]

1867, Saturday, November 30. Dined at the Club, with Dickens on one side of me and Richard Dana, Senior, on the other. Next to Dickens sat Dr. Holmes, and next to him Bigelow, the handsome man. On the left, next to Dana, Greene; then Fields, then Norton, Lowell, Strutt the Englishman &c.

Mr. Holland also there; and a dozen more; Emerson, Whipple, Prof. Wyman, Dr. Howe. A delightful dinner; we stayed till near ten o'clock.[38]

1867, Monday, December 2. Dickens's First Reading. We all went; a pleasant moonlight drive; and a triumph for Dickens. It is not Reading exactly; but acting, and quite wonderful in its way.[39] He gave the "Christmas Carol" and "Trial from Pickwick." I never saw anything better. The old Judge was equal to Dogberry.

1867, Thursday, December 5. Dickens's Readings; 'Nicholas Nickleby" and "Boots at the Holly Inn," a beautiful little story from one of the Christmas Books.

1867, Friday, December 6. Dickens's Readings; "Dombey & Son," and "Trial from Pickwick." Audience not very demonstrative, which is a pity; as it throws a chill over the reader.[40]

1868, Sunday, January 5. Take a long walk in the morning. Another in the afternoon on my way to dine with Fields; a dinner for Dickens, who is staying with him. Very pleasant. The other guests Mr. and Mrs. Thaxter, and T. G. A.[41] We sat from 6 o'clock till 11. There being no car so late, walked out with Mr. Thaxter in the bright moonlight. Very tired. It seemed as if I should never reach home; and then that I should never get to bed.

1868, Monday, February 24. Called on Dickens, who arrived on Saturday. . . . Evening at Dickens' Reading.

1868, Tuesday, February 25. Evening, Dickens again.

1868, Thursday, February 27. Evening, Dickens reads "The Carol" and "Boots at the Holly Tree Inn." Then a Supper at Fields' in honor of the day! Emerson, Holmes, Norton, Howells, Akers, Uncle Tom and brother Sam.[42] Dickens had too bad a cold to go; but he wrote me a nice letter on the occasion.

1868, Friday, February 28. Evening, Dickens again. Took Edie with me. "Nicholas Nickleby" and "Trial from Pickwick."

1868, Saturday, February 29. Alice and I dined with Dickens at the Parker house; a grand banquet given to Mrs. Fields. We were eighteen in all. Dickens, Mr. and Mrs. Lowell, Mr. and Mrs. Norton, Mr. and Mrs. Fields, Mr. and Mrs. Ticknor, Mr. and Mrs. Aldrich, Holmes, Osgood, Schlesinger, Dolby, and Alice and myself, and Mabel Lowell. Here are the card from my plate and the Bill of Fare.[43]

1868, Wednesday, March 4. Gave a dinner to Dickens. The guests were: Dickens, Dolby, Palfrey, Lowell, Fields, Osgood, Uncle Sam; which added to Charley, Erny and myself made ten.[44]

1868, Wednesday, April 1. Took Mr. and Mrs. Spelman and Mrs. Alex. to hear Dickens read the "Carol" and the "Trial." He was in great force.[45]

1868, Thursday, April 2. Dickens read "Nich. Nickleby" and "Boots at the Holly Tree Inn." Took Mrs. Alex., Edie and Annie.

1868, Friday, April 3. Dickens read "Dr. Marigold" and "Mrs. Gamp." Took with me A. L. P.[46]

1868, Sunday, April 5. Took tea with the Nortons. Dickens too ill with a cold to come.

1868, Monday, April 6. Dickens reads "David Copperfield" and "Bob Sawyer."

1868, Tuesday, April 7. Dickens, "Little Dombey" and "Trial from Pickwick."

1868, Wednesday, April 8. In town; muddy, sloppy, drippy. . . . Dickens' last Reading, and a triumphant one, with abundant flowers, and a "Little Speech."[47]

1870, Tuesday, June 14. Greene has been here for some days, and left me yesterday in the rain for Newport. During his stay we heard the news of the sudden death of Chas. Dickens! I can think of nothing else; but see him lying there dead in his house at Gad's Hill; silent, motionless, / "The colde death, with mouth gaping upright." / I have written to Forster and to Miss Hogarth.[48]

1870, Friday, June 17. "La Tribune de la Nouvelle Orléans" says: ["Charles Dickens, le grand romancier américain, est mort hier d'apoplexie. Il était le Walter Scott de l'Amérique."][49]

1870, Wednesday, November 16. Went with Fields to the Globe Theatre at 3 o'clock to hear Miss Kate Fields lecture on Dickens.[50]

1870, Thursday, December 8. Went in the evening to hear Geo. Curtis lecture on Dickens.[51]

1871, Wednesday, August 30. Go to see Sumner. On my way back stop at Mr. Beal's and sit half an hour with Fields. Urge him to suppress certain things in his account of Dickens in the "Whispering Gallery."[52]

1871, Wednesday, December 20. Fields sends me Dickens's Life by Forster. It looks interesting, but I have not time to read it to-day.[53]

1871, Friday, December 22. Read Forster's Life of Dickens. It is very interesting, but it makes me profoundly melancholy.

1872, Wednesday, December 4. Went to town on business. Saw Fields, who promised me the second volume of Forster's life of Dickens.

1872, Thursday, December 5. Read Forster's Dickens. Very interesting. The most restless of mortals. No repose in anything. Always at full speed. It is a wonder he lived so long.[54]

1872, Friday, December 6. Finished Dicken[s'] Life. Evening, read some chapters of "David Copperfield."

1877, Friday, December 7. Called at the Brunswik to see Mrs. Caird, who brings a letter from Mary Dickens.[55]

NOTES

1. Introduction to "The Virtuous Man 1870–1871" (*Letters* 5:316).
2. CD to John Forster, 19 Sept. 1841 (*Pilgrim* 2:386; CD to Forster, 22 Sept. 1841 (*Pilgrim* 2:388).
3. HWL to Charles Sumner, 16 Oct. 1842 (*Letters* 2:473–74). Both Moss (80–173) and Meckier (39–74) discuss in detail reactions to *American Notes*, the American episodes in *Martin Chuzzlewit*, and Dickens' role in the copyright controversy.
4. HWL to Stephen Longfellow, 30 Jan. 1842 (*Letters* 2:380–81).
5. HWL to Stephen Longfellow, 30 Jan. 1842 (*Letters* 2:380–81).
6. HWL to Samuel Ward, 30 Jan. 1842 (*Letters* 2:382–83); HWL to Stephen Longfellow, 30 Jan. 1842 (*Letters* 2:380–81). Payne (122–27) and Page (30–35) are valuable sources for the chronology of this visit. Cornelius Felton (1807–62), professor of Greek, was president of Harvard (1860–62). Jared Sparks (1789–1866), professor of History, was president of Harvard (1849–53). Charles Sumner (1811–74), American statesman, was U.S. senator (1851–74). Father Edward Thompson Taylor (1793–1871), earlier a seaman, had a pulpit style similar to that of Father Mapple in Herman Melville's *Moby-Dick*. Andrews Norton (1786–1853), Unitarian theologian, was professor of Sacred Literature at Harvard Divinity School (1819–30).
7. CD's note to HWL is quoted in full in HWL to Stephen Longfellow, 27 Feb. 1842 (*Letters* 2:387–88).
8. HWL to Ferdinand Freiligrath, 6 Jan. 1843 (*Letters* 2:495–98). William Charles Macready (1793–1873), who was manager of Drury Lane (1841–43), was famous for his performances as Macbeth and Lear. George Cruikshank (1792–1878) was an English illustrator. Daniel Maclise (1806–70) was an Irish historical painter. Samuel Rogers (1763–1855), English poet, author of *The Pleasures of Memory* (1792), was long considered a literary dictator. Thomas Campbell (1777–1844), English poet, is remembered chiefly for his stirring patriotic and war lyrics. Edward Moxon (1801–58) was an English publisher and writer of verse. Lady Blessington (1789–1849), born Marguerite Power, an Irish woman of letters, attracted to her soirées distinguished persons of art, letters, and fashion.
9. HWL to Forster, 17 Oct. 1848 (*Letters* 3:183). Walter Savage Landor (1775–1864), English poet and prose writer, wrote *Imaginary Conversations* (1824–29). Of all the people HWL saw during the 1842 visit, John Forster (1812–76), English historian, journalist, and biographer, became his closest friend.
10. Of this sensational episode in Dickens' life, HWL makes no direct reference in the *Journals*. He does have an indirect reference to it in the entry for 30 Aug. 1871. HWL to Sumner, 3 June 1858 (*Letters* 4:82): "What a sad affair is this of Dickens. Immensely exaggerated no doubt; but sad enough at least. How discouraging it is, and disgusting, to see how eagerly and recklessly a fair reputation is dragged through the mire of the streets."
11. The sources for this itinerary are Dana 86–96, Dexter *Dickensian* 158–60, Dolby 145–272, Forster 2:355–91, Johnson 2:533–48, Moss 331–33, Page 127–30, Payne 139–262, Wagenknecht 15–17.

12. HWL to Forster, 23 Nov. 1867 (*Letters* 5:188).
13. HWL to Forster, 23 Nov. 1867 (*Letters* 5:188). Oliver Wendell Holmes (1809–94). Jean Louis Rodolphe Agassiz (1807–73) was professor of Natural History, Lawrence Scientific School, Harvard (1848–73). Ralph Waldo Emerson (1803–82).
14. James Thomas Fields (1817–81), American author and pulisher of the firm Ticknor and Fields, helped persuade Dickens to make the trip.
15. Charles Eliot Norton (1827–1908), translator and author, was editor with James Russell Lowell of the *North American Review*, beginning in 1864.
16. HWL to Elizabeth Stuart Phelps, 7 Mar. 1879 (*Letters* 6:456).
17. The schedule of Boston readings is taken from the 76 performances in the American tour given in Moss 331–33. The listing in Moss includes Date, City, Hall, Reading. Dexter in the *Dickensian* lists 74 performances. Moss adds appearances on 30 and 31 December. The only differences in the Boston performances given in Moss are in the programs for 6 and 7 January; Dexter lists "A Christmas Carol" and "Trial from Pickwick" for 6 January, and "Nicholas Nickleby" and "Bob Sawyer's Party" for 7 January. The number of times Dickens read each work in Boston is as follows: "Trial from Pickwick," 8; "David Copperfield," 5; "A Christmas Carol," 4; "Bob Sawyer's Party," 4; "Nicholas Nickleby," 4; "Boots at the Holly Tree Inn," 4; "Dr. Marigold," 3; "Dombey and Son," 2; "Mrs. Gamp," 2. The most successful combination during the entire American tour was "A Christmas Carol" and "Trial from Pickwick"; it was the initial (or only) reading in every American city with the exception of New Haven. CD to William Henry Wills, 21 Nov. 1867, about the first appearance in Boston: "If I can only hit them hard with the Carol and Trial, I think our expectations may be far overpassed" (*Selected Letters* 157). The texts for all the nine American readings are in the twenty-one readings in Collins. Dickens "took immense pains with the texts he selected for reading. He chose each piece with care, reworking the narrative to heighten its dramatic appeal, tightening the dialogue, and adding special stage directions to remind himself of points to emphasize during each performance" (*Selected Letters*, "I. Introduction," 14). "Dr. Marigold's Prescriptions" was first published in *All the Year Round* (Christmas 1865). "Trial from Pickwick" is sometimes listed as "Bardell and Pickwick." "Bob Sawyer's Party" is from *Pickwick Papers*. "Boots at the Holly Tree Inn" was first published in *Household Words* (Christmas 1855). "Mrs. Gamp" is from *Martin Chuzzlewit*. Dolby (160) explained one reason for beginning the tour in Boston: "Mr. Dickens always regarded Boston as his American home, inasmuch as all his literary friends lived there, and he felt it to be only due to them that he should make that his starting-place."
18. HWL to Sumner, 8 Dec. 1867 (*Letters* 5:191).
19. For a description of the interesting bond between Annie Adams Fields (1834–1915) and CD, see Meckier 147–82.
20. CD to HWL, 27 Feb. 1868 (*Nonesuch* 3:626).
21. James Ripley Osgood (1836–92) became senior partner in James R. Osgood and Company, successor to Ticknor and Fields, in 1870. George Dolby (d. 1900, aged 70) had been a theatrical manager.
22. Meckier ix: "Had the ticket speculators been thwarted, receipts could easily have swelled into the bonanza that this venture is wrongly assumed to have been. Collectively, scalpers made more from Dickens's performances in 1867–68 than he did."
23. HWL to Henry Arthur Bright, 5 Dec. 1867 (*Letters* 5:190); HWL to William Charles Mark Kent, 20 Apr. 1878 (*Letters* 6:350).

24. Meckier questions the traditional belief that Dickens was in almost unendurably poor health during the American tour: "Typically for Dickens's contemporaries but contrary to his modern biographers, Annie [Fields] beheld no suicidal workaholic in the spring of 1868; as the American tour neared its end, her 'dear great man' seemed in better condition than posterity has been willing to allow" (167).

25. HWL to Georgina Hogarth, 13 June 1870 (*Letters* 5:354); HWL to William Charles Mark Kent, 20 Apr. 1878 (*Letters* 6:350).

26. The five sources that have printed portions of the *Journals* are Samuel Longfellow, Payne, Wagenknecht, Dana, and *Letters*.

The following entries in Samuel Longfellow are essentially the same as they are in the manuscripts: 1857, Jan. 22; 1860, Mar. 12; 1867, Nov. 20; 1867, Dec. 2; 1868, Apr. 8; 1872, Dec. 5. Samuel Longfellow also prints a portion of the following entries: 1867, Nov. 21 (the list of guests is omitted); 1867, Nov. 22 (the list of guests is omitted); 1867, Dec. 5th and 6th (the notation is "Dickens's Readings" without the actual readings given and no reference to the audience as being "not very demonstrative"; 1868, Feb. 24th, 25th (listed simply as "Dickens Reading"); 1868, Feb. 27 (there are references to the titles of the readings, the supper, and the letter sent by CD, but the list of guests is not given); 1868, Feb. 29 (the list of guests is omitted); 1868, Mar. 4 (the list of guests is omitted); 1870, June 14; 1871, Dec. 22.

The following entries in Payne are essentially the same as in the manuscripts: 1867, Nov. 20; 1867, Nov. 21 (the list of guests is given); 1867, Nov. 22 (the list of guests, with the exception of "Greene," is given); 1867, Nov. 28 ("and Hattie Spelman" is omitted); 1867, Nov. 30 (the list of guests is given; Payne reads the wording of a portion as follows: "and next to him Bigelow. The handsome man on the left next to Dana, was Greene. . . ."); 1867, Dec. 2 (Payne moves the position of "We all went; a pleasant moonlight drive"); 1867, Dec. 5; 1868, Jan. 5; 1868, Feb. 25; 1868, Feb. 27 (the list of guests is given); 1868, Apr. 1 (the name "Spelman" is read by Payne as "Speilman" and 'Mrs. Alex." becomes "Mr. Allyn"; instead of "force," Payne has "form"); 1868, Apr. 2 ("Mrs. Alex." is read by Payne as "Mrs. Allyn"); 1868, Apr. 5. Payne prints a portion of the following entry: 1868, Feb. 29 (the list of guests is omitted). One of the most interesting liberties taken by Payne is the entry for 1867, Nov. 18. The manuscript reads simply: "Dickens is expected tomorrow by steamer, now at Halifax. A great crowd at Fields', to buy tickets for his Readings." Payne, with all the information he had collected from newspapers, other journals and diaries, embellished the entry to the following: "I saw great crowds waiting, in line, outside of Ticknor and Fields at Tremont Street, to buy tickets for Dickens' readings. Dickens himself being expected tomorrow, as the steamer was at Halifax on this day."

Wagenknecht transcribes accurately the following entries: 1856, Mar. 21; 1860, Mar. 12; 1861, Mar. 28. In addition, he transcribes accurately portions of two other entries: 1861, Mar. 7; 1871, Aug.30.

Dana, the poet's grandson, transcribes accurately the following entries: 1867, Nov. 18; 1867, Nov. 20 (Dana omits "as"); 1867, Nov. 21; 1867, Dec. 2; 1868, Apr. 8. In addition, Dana transcribes accurately portions of two other entries: 1867, Nov. 28; 1870, June 14.

The *Letters* transcribes accurately the following: 1867, Nov. 21; 1868, Feb. 27; 1870, June 17. In addition, the *Letters* transcribes accurately a portion of 1867, Nov. 18.

In summary, of the 44 entries given here, 15 are being published for the first time; 21 entries have been previously published, sometimes with inaccurate renderings. Of the remaining 8 entries, portions are being published for the first time.

The passages from the *Journals* are printed by permission of the Houghton Library, Harvard University. I am indebted to Nancy A. Metz, Jean L. Aroeste, and Walter R. Robinson for their aid in the preparation of this article.

27. *Harper's Monthly* serialized *Little Dorrit* (Janury 1856–July 1857). "Much of Dickens's continued success as a popular writer was due to Harpers. . . . [B]eginning with *Bleak House* most of what he wrote . . . first reached American readers in the pages of one of the Harper periodicals" (Bracher 246–47).

28. "The Wreck of the Golden Mary" was published in *Household Words* (Christmas 1856). *Wyandotté* (New York, 1834).

29. Jenny (Jane) Colburn, widow of Warren Colburn (1793–1833), teacher of mathematics. Anna Cabot Jackson Lowell (1811–74), a minor author, was headmistress of a girls' school in Boston. Thomas Gold Appleton (1812–84), HWL's brother-in-law and close friend, wrote several volumes of poems and essays. Captain Jack Bunsby, skipper of the *Cautious Clara*, is in *Dombey and Son*. Felix Octavius Carr Darley (1822–88) was a noted illustrator of American classics. Prince Turveydrop is the dancing master in *Bleak House*. Jane Darley (d. 1916, aged 88) was the daughter of Warren and Jenny Colburn. Mrs. MacStringer, a landlady in *Dombey and Son*, eventually married Captain Bunsby. Miss Colburn was the sister of Jane Darley. Mrs. Jarley was the owner of a traveling wax-works show in *The Old Curiosity Shop*.

30. Doctor Blimber was principal of the school at Brighton in *Dombey and Son*, to which Paul Dombey was sent.

31 Frederic G. Kitton, *Dickens and His Illustrators* (London, 1899), 223: "Perhaps the best of Dickens's American illustrators was Felix Octavius Carr Darley, a most eminent and successful 'character' draughtsman, whose productions are both original and clever."

32. James Russell Lowell (1819–91). *Harper's Monthly* serialized *Our Mutual Friend* (June 1864–December 1865).

33. HWL to Fields, 18 Nov. 1867 (*Letters* 5:187): "What a lively tune you had at your door this morning! You must be glad it is over."

34. Ebenezer Rockwood Hoar (1816–95) was judge of the Massachusetts Supreme Court in 1867. George Washington Greene (1811–83), American historian, was the grandson of General Nathanael Greene (1742–86) of Revolutionary fame.

35. William Dean Howells (1837–1920). U. S. Is Uncle Samuel Longfellow (1819–92), clergyman and HWL's younger brother. E. W. L. is Ernest Wadsworth Longfellow, HWL's younger son.

36. Henry James, Sr. (1811–82), American philosopher and author, was the father of William James (1842–1910), Henry James, Jr. (1843–1916), and Alice James (1848–92). On this occasion, the novelist, Henry James, Jr., and his friend, Arthur Sedgwick (1844–1915), brother of Mrs. Charles Eliot Norton, were invited to meet CD after dinner. Henry James, Jr., records the experience in *Notes of a Son and Brother* (New York, 1914), 248–56: the meeting was "but of a moment," and yet James "trembled . . . in every limb" as he "saw the master"; this brief encounter he "always superlatively cherished." Sarah Price Ashburner Sedgwick (b. 1839) and Mrs. Charles Eliot Norton were daughters of Theodore Sedgwick (1811–59), a lawyer. Probably Grace Ashburner (1812–93), who became

the guardian of Sarah Sedgwick after the death of Theodore Sedgwick in 1859. The manuscript has dots.

37. Anne Longfellow Pierce (1810–1901), HWL's sister and widow of George Washington Pierce (1805–35). Harriet Maria Spelman (1848–1937) married Ernest Longfellow in 1868.

38. The Saturday Club, so named in 1857, had as a chief project the founding of the *Atlantic Monthly* in 1857. Richard Henry Dana, Sr. (1787–1879), was a founder of *The North American Review*. John Bigelow (1817–1911), for many years an associate of William Cullen Bryant on the *New York Evening Post*, had been U.S. minister to France (1865–66). An entry in the *Journals* for 19 Nov. 1867 states: "Mr. Holland and Mr. Strutt with a letter from Motley"; otherwise, Holland and Strutt are unidentified. John Lothrop Motley (1814–77), American historian, had been U.S. minister to Austria (1861–67). Edwin Percy Whipple (1819–86), American critic and essayist. Jeffries Wyman (1814–74), professor of anatomy, Harvard. Estes Howe (1814–87), who received an M.D. from Harvard, was treasurer of the Cambridge Gas Light Company.

39. HWL to Sumner, 20 Dec. 1867 (*Letters* 5:196): CD "is in great force; and his Readings, or rather Recitations, are wonderful."

40. HWL to Sumner, 8 Dec. 1867 (*Letters* 5:191): "Boston audiences are proverbially cold. The Gulf Stream itself would hardly raise their temperature a degree."

41. Celia Laighton Thaxter (1835–94), New Hampshire poet, had married Levi Lincoln Thaxter (d. 1884) in 1851. T. G. A. is Thomas Gold Appleton.

42. The "day" was HWL's sixty-first birthday. Charles Akers (1836–1906) was a sculptor and portrait painter.

43. This was the day of the "Great International Walking Match." Frances Dunlap Lowell (1825–85). Susan Ridley Sedgwick Norton (1838–72). George Ticknor (1791–1871), educator and historian, and his wife Anna Eliot Ticknor. Thomas Bailey Aldrich (1836–1907), local color author, and his wife Lilian Woodman Aldrich (1841–1927). Sebastian Benson Schlesinger (1837–1917), German-born composer, who became German consul in Boston (1872–89). Mabel Lowell (1847–98), daughter of James Russell Lowell and his first wife. In addition to the place card, HWL attached to the entry the menu, which was arranged according to soup, fish, entrees, roast, releves, game, entremets, and dessert, with several items under each. For example, one soup was Terrapin; and under *game* were Canvas Back Duck and Larded Quails.

44. John Gorham Palfrey (1796–1881) was a Unitarian cleryman and professor of sacred literature at Harvard.

45. Israel Munson Spelman (1816–1907) was a Cambridge neighbor and president of the Boston and Maine Railroad. He and his wife, Martha Hubbard Choate Spelman, were the parents of Hattie Spelman, who married Ernest Longfellow. Alexander Longfellow (1814–1901), HWL's younger brother, had married Elizabeth Clapp Porter (b. 1822).

46. A. L. P. is Annie Longfellow Pierce, HWL's sister.

47. HWL pasted in the *Journals* a newspaper account of the speech. In the speech, CD said: "My gracious and generous welcome in America, which can never be obliterated from my remembrance, began here. My departure begins here too. . . . I cannot conceal from you . . . that it is a sad consideration with me that in a few moments from this time this brilliant hall and all that it contains will fade from my view forevermore. . . . [P]rivate friendships . . . have for years upon years made Boston a memorable and beloved spot to me" (Payne 256–57).

48. HWL to Forster, 12 June 1870 (*Letters* 5:353): "The terrible news from England fills us all with inexpressible grief. Dickens was so full of life, that it did not seem possible he could die. . . . I hope his book is finished. . . . I never knew an author's death cause such general mourning. It is no exaggeration to say that this whole country is stricken with grief." The book was *The Mystery of Edwin Drood*; six of the projected twelve parts were published in monthly installments (April–September 1870). HWL to Georgina Hogarth (1827–1917), CD's sister-in-law and the manager of his household after his separation from his wife (*Letters* 5:354): "The melancholy news from Gad's Hill has reached us, and filled all our hearts with the deepest sorrow. In truth I may say it is a universal grief. The whole country is filled with it."

49. HWL to Greene, 19 June 1870 (*Letters* 5:355–56): "Here is something odd from a French newspaper of New Orleans—La Tribune. The writer was evidently thinking of Cooper. What a comment on Literary Fame!" HWL pasted the clipping (the portion in brackets) in the *Journals*. "Charles Dickens, the great American novelist, died yesterday of apoplexy. He was the Walter Scott of America."

50. Mary Katherine Keemle Field (1838–96), journalist and lyceum lecturer known professionally as Kate Field, wrote *Pen Photographs of Charles Dickens's Readings* (Boston, 1868).

51. George William Curtis (1824–92) was editor of *Harper's Weekly*, author, and lecturer.

52. William James Beal (1833–1924) was an American botanist and educator. Fields, "Some Memories of Charles Dickens," *Atlantic Monthly*, 26 (Aug. 1870): 235–45, and a series of later articles were incorporated into a chapter on CD in *Yesterday with Authors* (Boston, 1900), 125–250, with no hint of scandal.

53. John Forster, *The Life of Charles Dickens* (London, 1872–74). The reference is to Volume I.

54. HWL to Forster, 18 June 1873 (*Letters* 5:670): "I have read the two volumes with deepest interest and sympathy. You give an exact portrait of Dickens; and have had the courage not to conceal some things, that others might have hidden, but which make the likeness true and life-like."

55. Although the identification of Mrs. Caird is uncertain, the reference possibly is to Mrs. Mona (Alison) Caird, a romantic novelist, who also wrote on medical subjects.

WORKS CITED

Bracher, Peter School. *Dickens and His American Readers, 1834–1870: A Study of the American Reception, Reputation, and Popularity of Charles Dickens and His Novels During His Lifetime*. Diss., U of Pennsylvania, 1966.

Collins, Philip, ed. *Charles Dickens: The Public Readings*. Oxford: Clarendon, 1975.

Dana, Henry Wadsworth Longfellow. "Longfellow and Dickens: The Story of a Transatlantic Friendship." *Cambridge* [MA] *Historical Society Publications*, 27 (1943): 55–104.

Dexter, Walter. "Mr. Charles Dickens Will Read. V." *Dickensian*, 38 (Summer 1942): 158–60.

Dolby, George. *Charles Dickens As I Knew Him: The Story of the Reading Tours in Great Britain and America (1866–1870)*. New York: Scribner's, 1912.

Forster, John. *The Life of Charles Dickens*. 2 vols. Philadelphia: Lippincott, 1905.

Johnson, Edgar. *Charles Dickens: His Tragedy and Triumph*. 2 vols. New York: Simon and Schuster, 1952.

The Letters of Charles Dickens, Nonesuch Edition, ed. Walter Dexter. 3 vols. Bloomsbury: Nonesuch, 1938. Cited as *Nonesuch*.

The Letters of Charles Dickens, Pilgrim Edition, ed. Madeline House, Graham Storey, and Kathleen Tillotson. 12 volumes projected. Oxford: Clarendon, 1965– Cited as *Pilgrim*.

The Letters of Henry Wadsworth Longfellow, ed. Andrew Hilen. 6 vols. Cambridge: Harvard UP, 1966–82. Cited as *Letters*.

Longfellow, Samuel, ed. *Life of Henry Wadsworth Longfellow with Extracts from His Journals and Correspondence*. 3 vols. Boston: Houghton, Mifflin, 1891.

Meckier, Jerome. *Innocent Abroad: Charles Dickens's American Engagements*. Lexington: UP of Kentucky, 1990.

Moss, Sidney P. *Charles Dickens' Quarrel with America*. Troy, NY: Whitston, 1984.

Page, Norman. *A Dickens Chronology*. Boston: G. K. Hall, 1988.

Payne, Edward F. *Dickens Days in Boston*. Boston: Houghton, Mifflin, 1927.

Selected Letters of Charles Dickens, ed. David Paroissien. London: Macmillan, 1985. Cited as *Selected Letters*.

Wagenknecht, Edward. "Dickens in Longfellow's Letters and Journals." *Dickensian*, 52 (Dec. 1955): 7–19.

The Rake, The Writer, and *The Stranger*: Textual Relations between *Pendennis* and *David Copperfield*

Mark Cronin

There have been few suggestions that Charles Dickens ever appropriated structures of character and plot, as well as themes and motifs, from the novels of William Makepeace Thackeray. In contrast, Thackeray himself openly acknowledged the profound influence that Dickens had on his writing, stating, Dickens "knows that my books are a protest against his—that if one set are true, the other must be false" (Lippincott 107). An examination of this "protest" reveals that in a deliberate attempt to distinguish his work from his rival's, Thackeray parodied and transformed elements from Dickens' novels in his early fiction.[1] The literary relationship between Dickens and Thackeray changed, though, with the publication of *Vanity Fair* (1847–48). Inspired by his critical success, Thackeray wrote to his mother that he had become a "great man in my way—all but at the top of the tree: indeed there if truth be known and having a great fight up there with Dickens" (Ray, *Letters* 2:333). Critics and the public alike acknowledged the battle. The contemporaneous monthly publications of *Pendennis* (Nov. 1848 to Dec. 1850) and *David Copperfield* (May 1849 to Nov. 1850) by the firm Bradbury and Evans produced so frequent comparisons that David Masson declared in the May 1851 *North British Review*, "Thackeray and Dickens, Dickens and Thackeray—the two names almost now necessarily go together" (Collins 249). Thackeray even claimed that Dickens had learned a stylistic lesson from *Vanity Fair* that improved the prose in *David Copperfield*.[2] Despite such pronouncements, the significant influence that Thackeray's *Pendennis* had on *David Copperfield* has gone unnoted.

Explicitly sustained intersections and parallels between the two novels indicate that Dickens may have shaped characters and events from *David Copperfield* in response to Thackeray's *Pendennis*. Three major points of textual relations can be established. First, similarities between Arthur Pendennis and James Steerforth suggest that Dickens was not only shadowing Thackeray's portrayal of the gentleman-rake, but that he also modelled the Steerforth-Mrs. Steerforth-Rosa Dartle triangle after Thackeray's Pendennis-Mrs. Pendennis-Laura Bell household. Second, Thackeray and Dickens provide competing depictions of the artist as hero. Although traditional comparisons between the two novels have focused on this similarity in subject matter—the development and maturation of a young author—few readers have argued that Dickens' silence about the writing life was a response and "protest" to Thackeray's effusiveness. Third, the eponymous title characters share similar theatrical experiences: both Pendennis and David Copperfield attend a production of August von Kotzebue's *The Stranger*.[3] These intersections not only reveal Dickens and Thackeray as authors who were aware of and responsive to the artistic productions of a competitor, they also offer a compelling case of literary engagement, one in which connections and relationships between the plots and characters of contemporaneous serial novels can be established. Such textual relationships, Jerome Meckier argues, were characteristic of the age: "Many of the classic Victorian novels were double-barreled documents, written not just for their own sakes but to revise another novelist's views; their authors wrote to pass judgment on society and, at the same time, to offer systematic revaluations (revaluative parodies) of the ideas, characters, and techniques of an established competitor" (3).

The issue of structural similarities between the Pendennis and Steerforth households requires elaboration. Dickens' predilection for structural repetition and narrative doubling is evidenced throughout his novels: plot patterns are paralleled and replicated; a character's physical, social, or mental composition is reflected or embodied by another character in the novel. *David Copperfield* is no exception to this practice, and many critics have noted both the role of patterned parallel events as well as the presence of intratextual doubles in the novel.[4] For example, Steerforth and Uriah Heep seem to act out the unconscious sexual impulses of David. Thus, David's professed guilt over Steerforth's seduction of Emily suggests that he too may have wished to perpetrate the same crime. Similarly, we also see the danger in David's effort "to form Dora's mind," for such an attempt clearly echoes Murdstone's severe methods in molding David's mother. I will argue in addition that Dickensian doubling is intertextual as well as intratextual in *David Copperfield*: the novel extends outward, containing characters and events patterned after Thackeray's *Pendennis*.

Dickens' device of intertextual doubling functions as a clear but cloaked recognition of the relevance of Thackeray's characterization of sexuality and male power within the family. The Pendennis and the Steerforth households have many points of comparison: a widowed, doting mother indulges and idolizes her arrogant, dandified son. In the background, the orphaned ward of the family keeps the mother company, faithfully waiting for the prodigal son to return home after his bachelor dalliances so that she may marry him and return the domestic sphere to the wholeness missing since the death of the father. A family crisis in both works is precipitated by or results from the near-seduction/seduction of a lower-class girl who has been dazzled and class-struck by the attentions of a charming gentleman. Pen's near-seduction of Fanny Bolton is completed, so to speak, by Steerforth's successful seduction of Little Em'ly. By replicating the Pendennis household with the Steerforths, Dickens not only highlights the essential vulnerability of the domestic sphere, he also offers a competing (and complementary) picture to Thackeray's novel. Both novelists counterpoint portraits of domestic purity and innocence with suggestions of the potential perverseness of mother-love. Yet *Pendennis* approaches and then retreats from exposing the almost incestuous nature of the domestic arrangement, whereas *David Copperfield* points to the inherent danger of the structure by presenting the darker, destructive aspects of these suffocating, obsessive relationships in the Steerforth family.

The similarities between the Pendennis and the Steerforth households are signalled by the presence of the orphaned ward, a figure who is thus both sister and potential love object for the young men. Laura Bell is the orphaned daughter of Mr. Francis Bell, who was the cousin and thwarted lover of Helen Pendennis. We learn that Laura "was neither related to his [Major Pendennis's] own family of Pendennis, nor to any nobleman in this empire, and she had but a couple of thousand of pounds for her fortune" (112; ch. 8). Rosa Dartle is described in similar terms by Steerforth: "She was the motherless child of a sort of cousin of my father's. He died one day. My mother, who was then a widow, brought her here to be company to her. She has a couple of thousand of pounds of her own, and saves the interest of it every year, to add to the principle" (252; ch. 20). Laura and Rosa are literally valuable additions to the household: both bring two thousand pounds (money that ostensibly goes to their dowry); both function as companions to the widows. Furthermore, the orphaned ward's presence allows the mother to groom her successor in her son's affections and to control, in part, her son's future. Laura's and Rosa's domestic circumstances are strikingly similar; their personalities clearly are not. Laura is younger and gayer than Rosa, and considers herself fortunate to be a member of the household. Rosa recognizes that she has been used and manipulated by the Steerforths, but is helpless to alter her situation.

Both *Pendennis* and *David Copperfield* examine the mother's adulation of the son, the son's love for and indifference to the mother, and the son's assertion of independence through illicit sexual dalliance. And although Thackeray claims that "the maternal passion is a sacred mystery to me" (55; ch. 2), he points to the profane complexities of the mother-son bond by suggesting that maternal devotion is often complicated by possessiveness and sexual jealousy. The death of the father initiates Pen's maturation; it is a rite of passage that leaves Pendennis in the enviable and uncomfortable position as his mother's son and master. Thackeray writes: "I am not sure that in the very moment of grief, and as he embraced his mother, and tenderly consoled her, and promised to love her for ever, there was not springing up in his breast a sort of secret triumph and exultation. He was the chief now and lord" (55; ch. 2). Neither Pen nor Steerforth can successfully navigate the path between his doting mother and the orphaned ward who has come into their house. In one of his few moments of candor, Steerforth admits the need for paternal influence: "I wish to God I had a judicious father these last twenty years! . . . I wish with all my soul I had been better guided!" (274; ch. 22). Pen soon abuses his position, encouraging the cloying attentions of his mother, who caters to his every whim. His proposal to Laura virtually announces the incestuous ties that bind the family: "Will you take me, dear Laura, and make our mother happy?" (301; ch. 27). Laura gently declines and will not succeed Mrs. Pendennis until she is dead. For these young men, the Victorian home becomes claustrophobic, the maternal embrace suffocating; and as the path and pattern of their later sexual transgressions will suggest, they cannot wholly efface the mother's presence through an affair.

Helen Pendennis quickly adapts to her changed role: as concerned mother, she anxiously frets over her son's relationships with other women; as fervent admirer, she blindly believes that his every action manifests some aspect of high genius. Yet in matters of courtship this Victorian mother refuses to relinquish control. Pen's flirtation with Miss Fotheringay forces his mother to enlist Pen's uncle, Major Pendennis, in her campaign against the actress. Class issues and family reputation are at stake, for an actress is necessarily associated with promiscuity, and Pen's mother wishes to keep him free from the taint of illicitness. Helen Pendennis harbors a sexless fantasy of the perfect son:

> she had made up her mind that he was to marry little Laura: she would be eighteen when Pen was six-and-twenty; and had finished his college career; and had made his grand tour; and was settled either in London, astonishing all the metropolis by his learning and eloquence at the bar, or better still in a sweet country parsonage surrounded with hollyhocks and roses, close to the delightful romantic ivy-covered church, from the pulpit of which Pen would utter the most beautiful sermons ever preached.   (64; ch. 3)

Helen Pendennis wants to choose the non-threatening domestic woman as her son's lover and wife. She reacts to Pen's flirtation with Blanche Amory by watching "the pair with that anxiety with which brooding women watch over their sons' affections—and in acknowledging which, I have no doubt there is a sexual jealousy on the mother's part, and a secret pang" (264; ch. 24). This sexual jealousy threatens the stability of the household, for both Pendennis and Steerforth rebel against domestic entrapment: Pen initially resists his mother's choice of bride; Steerforth's self-imposed exile urges him to foreign shores.

The widowed mother seeks an emotional wholeness and closure missing since the death of the father. Thus, a sense of urgency informs the son's return because his marriage to the ward completes and encloses the family circle once more. *David Copperfield* teems with forward-looking parents who await the marriages of their children to restore their broken homes to wholeness. The Wickfield home is incomplete until the child Mr. Wickfield once took into his home returns to marry his daughter. Mr. Peggotty's reconstructed family waits for Ham and Emily's pre-ordained union. Both Uriah and Mrs. Heep greedily hope to acquire the graceful and dignified Agnes for their hearth. Similarly, Traddles keeps his bride and her sisters waiting until he is financially solvent, and a frustrated Rosa Dartle believes James Steerforth will return to her after he finishes his sexual conquests among the lower classes. The parents' fear that the home may never be whole proves warranted; only David and Traddles return to marry the waiting daughter.

Dickens makes explicit the potential for familial betrayal and sexual violence that was implicit in Thackeray's domestic paradigm. By recasting the Steerforths as extremes of the petty selfishness and self-centeredness that characterized the Pendennises, he magnifies the flaws of the Pendennis household: Pen's shallow egotism becomes Steerforth's overbearing self-centered pride; Helen Pendennis's adoration of her son becomes Mrs. Steerforth's near idol worship; and Laura's patient self-righteousness becomes Rosa's embittered and caustic haughtiness.

Mrs. Steerforth and Rosa Dartle are extremes of insularity and possessiveness. They are snobs—passionately and destructively jealous, equally afraid that someone will violate the sacred bond that ties them together. Like Helen Pendennis, Mrs. Steerforth dotes on her son. Yet Helen Pendennis adores Pen with a mother's prejudice; Mrs. Steerforth cultivates in her son his essential superiority, and then believes the myth of his greatness that she has created. David reports:

> It was no matter of wonder to me to find Mrs. Steerforth devoted to her son. She seemed to be able to speak or think about nothing else. She showed me his picture as an infant, in a locket, with some of his baby-hair in it; she showed me his picture as he had been when I first knew him, and she wore at her breast his picture as he was now. All the letters he had ever written to her, she kept in a cabinet near her own chair by the fire.   (252; ch. 20)

The relationship between mother and son borders on obsession; Mrs. Steerforth acts more like a faithful lover than a loving mother. Yet, like Rosa and Emily, she too will be abandoned by James.

Dickens replaces Thackeray's innocent, gentle ward with the bitterly caustic Rosa Dartle. Laura is a worthy choice as bride for Pendennis: she is selfless, devoted, and generous, "a paragon of virtue and excellence" (769; ch. 75). She even donates her savings (i.e., dowry) to extricate Pen from financial difficulties accrued through extravagant spending. Carol Hanbery MacKay observes that Laura is in many ways like Dickens' Agnes: "Agnes and Laura are indeed comparable: they both seem associated with love and truth, and they provide their mates with a second chance at happiness—David through remarriage, Pen through marriage to someone realistic enough to have turned him down when his first proposal was insincere" (257).[5] Rosa, on the other hand, is a twisted and tainted siren, physically scarred by a hammer Steerforth threw at her as a child, emotionally wounded by his open disregard for her. David concludes that

> she was about thirty years of age, and that she wished to be married. She was a little dilapidated—like a house—with having been so long to let; yet had, as I have said, an appearance of good looks. Her thinness seemed to be the effect of some wasting fire within her, which found a vent in her gaunt eyes.
> (249–50; ch. 20)

Pen recognizes Laura's worth, yet must struggle to accommodate himself to his mother's choice. Steerforth, by all indications, has already seduced Rosa and is willing to abandon her as well. Unlike Laura, who rejects Pen's insincere proposal with grace and dignity, Rosa reponds to Steerforth's taunts with enraged animosity: "Steerforth had left his seat, and gone to her, and had put his arm laughingly about her, and had said, 'Come, Rosa, for the future we will love each other very much!' And she had struck him, and had thrown him off with the fury of a wild cat, and had burst out of the room" (372; ch. 29). With this violent display Dickens exposes the vicious sexual aggression between the son and ward and offers a sharp contrast to Thackeray's restrained portrait of domestic sexual jealousy. Steerforth and Rosa, who are wrought to a higher pitch than Pen and Laura, are full of energy and life, but have found no direction to channel this vitality; they merely dissipate it in bursts of unpremeditated passion.

At the center of these domestic triangles stand Pendennis and Steerforth. These pampered sons become dandified rakes, enamored only of their own image and driven by narcissistic sexual desire. They are Byronic figures: alternatively arrogant, brooding, and charming, as well as handsome and wealthy. Both resist early marriage and choose instead to indulge the liberties of university life; as such figures, Steerforth and Pendennis offer competing depictions of the celebrated university dandy. They affect boredom with academic life, but still manage to cut impressive social figures. Pendennis neglects his studies in order to cultivate the lifestyle of a gentleman. He becomes "famous to behold" and "one of the men of fashion in the university" (204; ch. 18). Like Steerforth, he even attracts a following, who "wonder at him, and love him, and imitate him" (204; ch. 18). Pen is rewarded with such youthful admiration and by being "plucked" at the University. Steerforth proves equally proficient in neglecting his studies. He responds to David's innocent assertion, "You'll take a high degree at college," by admitting "I have not the least desire or intention to distinguish myself in that way. I have done quite sufficient for my purpose. I find that I am heavy company enough for myself, as I am" (249; ch. 20). Thackeray mocks Pen's Byronic pretension as self-important, immature posturing. Dickens, though, presents split attitudes toward Steerforth: he makes him destructive and manipulative, but he also has David idolize and dote on him.

Although Thackeray repeatedly invokes Richardson's Robert Lovelace as a literary prototype for Pendennis, James Steerforth is much closer to the villain of *Clarissa*. The amoral Steerforth presents a far greater threat to domestic wholeness than Pendennis, for Pen is more concerned with presenting the appearance of the sensitive poet and dangerous rake than he is with actually playing the part. Steerforth plans and plays at the seduction of Little Em'ly as if it is an elaborate game; he discards her when he become disenchanted and then offers her to his butler. He willingly destroys the home of the Peggottys—a reconstructed family unlike his own in that the members genuinely care about one another—because he believes the lower classes have no worth:

> "Why, there's a pretty wide separation between them and us," said Steerforth, with indifference. "They are not to be expected to be as sensitive as we are. Their delicacy is not to be shocked, or hurt very easily. They are wonderfully virtuous, I dare say—some people contend for that, at least; and I am sure I don't want to contradict them—but they have not very fine natures, and they may be thankful that, like their coarse rough skins, they are not easily wounded." (251; ch. 20)

Steerforth's notions of superiority not only remain unchallenged, they are fostered by those around him: by an overly devoted, insensitively snobbish mother; by Creakle's school system, which honors Steerforth's code of class discrimination against Dr. Mell; and by David, who worships him unreservedly. Mrs. Steerforth, who imagines that the bond between her and her son is far greater than that between Mr. Peggotty and Emily, audaciously demands of Peggotty: "What compensation can you make to *me* for opening such a pit between me and my son? What is your love to mine? What is your separation to ours?" (400–01; ch. 32). If Helen Pendennis harbors fantasies about the moral worth and high intellect of her son, Mrs. Steerforth perpetuates a far more damaging false ideal of class worth and natural superiority.

Although Thackeray began *Pendennis* six months before Dickens started *David Copperfield*, Dickens introduces the seduction of a lower-class girl earlier: Steerforth seduces and flees with Emily two months (Feb. 1850) before Pendennis decides to leave his affair with Fanny unconsummated (April 1850).[6] In the article, "Who Was the Imitator—Dickens or Thackeray?" an early anonymous critic addressed the similarities between the seductions: "As I reread the two situations side by side, it seemed impossible not to feel that the treatment of the one was advisedly based on the treatment of the other" (140). This critic then argues: "My theory is that Thackeray seized the idea of recasting the whole situation on what he considered a truer and fairer model" (140), and thus, "without question the follower was Thackeray" (141). I disagree. The ultimately diverging paths of Pendennis and Steerforth had been scripted early in each book: that Pen will remain chaste until marriage is as clearly foreshadowed as Steerforth's seduction of Emily. Dickens' manuscript notes document Steerforth's plans.[7] So too, the original wrapper to the 1848 edition of *Pendennis* illustrates the choice Pen faces: he is flanked by both the dangerous siren and the domestic angel. The outcome though is never in doubt: the innocent Laura is reserved for Pen's bride; no suitor ever poses a legitimate threat. Bachelor Pen does indeed sow his wild oats—becoming a spendthrift, getting plucked at school, and cultivating such vices as gambling and cigar-smoking—yet he can still be redeemed in marriage because he remains free from the stigma of illicit sexual experience. J. I. M. Stewart remarks that Thackeray was disposed "to bring his heroes, whenever possible, virgins to their brides" (12). Gordon Ray explains why:

> the world of *Pendennis* is for the most part the world of real life, where a young man in Pen's situation would in all probability have made Fanny his mistress. But as a character in a novel, by seducing Fanny Pen would become a villain, and since he is Thackeray's hero, not an expendable figure like Steerforth, this is *impossible*.   (*Thackeray: Age of Wisdom* 125)

More than Dickens, Thackeray felt constrained by the moral strictures of the day. In the 1850 preface to *Pendennis*, he complained: "Since the author of *Tom Jones* was buried, no writer of fiction among us has been permitted to depict to his utmost power a MAN. We must drape him, and give him a certain conventional simper. Society will not tolerate the Natural in our Art." Thackeray's justification of his central character, which may have been written with Steerforth in mind, suggests that he is responding to society's moral prohibitions as well as a rival's text. Nevertheless, his restraint indicates that both he and Dickens were probing an issue still sensitive to their Victorian audience. In the December 1850 *Scotsman*, J. R. Findlay responded to this preface by praising Thackeray's delicate treatment of the near-seduction and assailing Dickens':

> Mr. Thackeray's "frankness" in the instance alluded to has not been too great, neither has he constrained himself too much. The fact is, that his very excellence as a delineator of modern life and manners, imposes on him peculiar limitations. He paints so closely, and deals so little in the vague and general, that some subjects which can only be treated in a vague and general style, are in a manner to him forbidden. Thus, though Mr. Dickens introduced, in his last novel, a seduction of the worst character, aggravated by every accessary, and episodical and needless as regards the main current of his tale, we should very much question if with him "ladies remonstrated and subscribers left," and we doubt it simply because he enveloped the whole in a cloud of sentiment, fancy, and fine writing.   (Tillotson and Hawes 96)

Findlay echoes a debate central to the age: whether morally suspect characters should be made attractive, romantic figures.

Pen nearly completes his 'education" as a young bachelor when he begins an affair with the star-struck Fanny Bolton, a young girl in awe of his "dandified protecting air, his conceit, generosity, and good humour" (502; ch. 47). But Pen is warned away from the deed by his conscience, his duty to his family, and the advice of friends and acquaintances. Because he has not placed himself above the influence of others, even Mr. Bows, the former manager of the Fotheringay and current friend of the Boltons, can confront Pen with his intentions:

> And my belief is that you came to steal a pretty girl's heart away, and to ruin it, and to spurn it afterwards, Mr. Arthur Pendennis. That's what the world makes of you young dandies, you gentleman of fashion, you high and mighty aristocrats that trample upon the people. It's sport to you, but what is it to the poor . . . I know your order, sir. I know your selfishness, your arrogance, and your pride. (518; ch. 49)

Bows's speech is as applicable to Steerforth as it is to Pendennis. And Pen does learn discretion and restraint, which is not unlike the prudence which Tom Jones must acquire.

In both novels the dalliance with the lower-class girl has devastating effects on the household. The mother and adopted daughter feel betrayed. However, the smug, self-righteous reproach of Helen and Laura cannot match the unrestrained hatred that explodes from Mrs. Steerforth and Rosa when they learn of James's flight with Emily. Mrs. Steerforth rails against her son's actions:

> to take up in a moment with a miserable girl, and avoid me! To repay my confidence with systematic deception, for her sake, and quit me for her! To set this wretched fancy, against his mother's claims upon his duty, love, respect, gratitude—claims that every day and hour of his life should have strengthened into ties that nothing could be proof against! (401; ch. 32)

There is something pathetic in Mrs. Steerforth's short-sightedness, for she cannot see the inevitability of James's sexual maturation, nor does she recognize that the monster she has created has turned on her. James's betrayal and subsequent death tear the fabric of the family apart, exposing the implicit jealousy that exists between mother and ward. Rosa attacks Mrs. Steerforth as the "proud mother of a proud false son!" She unsympathetically cries: "Moan for your nurture of him, moan for your corruption of him, moan for your loss of him, moan for mine!" (685; ch. 56); and she avers that

> I loved him better than you ever loved him! . . . I could have loved him, and asked no return. If I had been his wife, I could have been the slave of his

caprices for a word of love a-year. I should have been. Who knows it better than I? You were exacting, proud, punctilious, selfish. My love would have been devoted—would have trod your paltry whimpering underfoot.

(685; ch. 56)

Bitterness consumes the house; Mrs. Steerforth is reduced to a moaning shell of a woman, left only with Rosa to comfort her.

In both works, the ward, a potential surrogate and replacement for the mother, reproaches the fallen woman, the girl who has replaced her by fulfilling the son's desires. Such confrontations not only provide narrative drama, they also underscore the explicit class tension inherent in these depictions of domesticity and male sexuality. In her country estate, Laura was a model of propriety, dignity, and humility, yet when she and Mrs. Pendennis confront Fanny, they rely on their assumed class superiority to silently scorn and dismiss her. Fanny is so intimidated by the haughtiness and disdain of the "fine ladies" that she meekly retreats home. Laura allies herself with Mrs. Pendennis to defeat a perceived common enemy; Rosa Dartle, though, turns on both Mrs. Steerforth and Little Em'ly. Her unrestrained attack on Emily expresses not only the overwhelming hatred she feels for James's mistress, but for the lower classes altogether. As David listens, she brands Emily a "purchased slave," an "earth-worm," a "piece of pollution," "carrion," a "broken toy," and a 'worthless spangle" (614–16; ch. 50). Such sexual antagonism is learned behavior; Rosa undoubtedly gives voice to the maltreatment she has felt at James's hands.

Pendennis averts a family tragedy by conveniently falling ill. Since Thackeray cannot let Pen's physical desires pursue their potentially ruinous course, the unspent fever of his passions is rechanneled: "he tried to drive the thoughts of that fascinating little person out of his head, by constant occupation, by exercise, by dissipation and society. He worked then too much; he walked and rode too much; he ate, drank, and smoked too much" (528; ch. 51). A real fever soon follows. Helen Pendennis and Laura arrive in town, fearing the worst, but prepared to nurse Pen back to health. The fever does consume Pen's ardent passions, but the aborted seduction and the near-family tragedy at first cast a shadow over the mother-son relationship, which Pen attempts to dispel:

poor Pen was most constant and affectionate in waiting upon his mother, whose wounded bosom yearned with love towards him, though there was a secret between them, and an anguish or rage almost on the mother's part, to think that she was dispossessed somehow of her son's heart, or that there were recesses in it which she must not or dared not enter. She sickened as she thought of the sacred days of boyhood when it had not been so—when Arthur's heart had no secrets, and she was his all in all: when he poured his hopes and pleasures, his childish griefs, vanities, triumphs into her willing and tender embrace.

(582; ch. 56)

Pen and his mother return to the relationship of his childhood. Through the help of Warrington and the revealed knowledge that Pen has remained chaste, the family is reconciled just prior to Helen Pendennis's death from a failed heart. She dies, not only secure in the belief that her son has remained pure, but with her final image of Pen praying the "Our Father" at her knees as he did as a boy: "as he spoke the last words of the supplication, the mother's head fell down on her boy's, and her arms closed round him" (598; ch. 57). Unlike Dickens, Thackeray has come full circle, and has made Pen return to his unambiguous role as his mother's innocent child.

After Steerforth's flight and later his death, the narrative opposition to Pendennis shifts from the rake Steerforth to the writer David. Dickens distinguishes David as the ideal, middle-class worker from the idle, aristocratic Steerforth and Pendennis. Pendennis's casual, gentleman-like approach to writing is answered by David's steadfast industry.

II

The opening line of *David Copperfield*, "Whether I shall turn out to be a hero of my own life, or whether that station will be held by anybody else, these pages must show," echoes several strains of Victorian thought. The notion of the artist as hero recalls Thomas Carlyle's influential "Hero as Man of Letters" lecture; it also reflects Dickens' assistance of the literary man in England through the Guild of Literature and Art; and it is a repudiation of Thackeray's recent novels, *Vanity Fair* (originally subtitled: "A Novel Without a Hero") and *Pendennis*, which openly declare that the flawed characters found in their pages in no way deserve the status of hero. Indeed, *Pendennis* closes by responding to the opening lines of *David Copperfield*: "Let us give a hand of charity to Arthur Pendennis, with all his faults and shortcomings, who does not claim to be a hero, but only a man and brother" (788; ch. 75).

Both Thackeray and Dickens engage in the contemporary discourse about the status of the man of letters, a figure who was undergoing a necessary reevaluation in the Victorian age. The diverging representations of the artist in *Pendennis* and *David Copperfield* reflect this ongoing debate: while Thackeray portrays the writer as a prose laborer, Dickens depicts the writer as hero. Thackeray attempts to demystify the man of letters, because as Peter Shillingsburg suggests, "a considerable mythology about writing has developed around words like imagination, fancy, creativity, genius, inspiration, the Muse, and artistic integrity. . . . Such a mythology demands of authors that they conceal the sweat" (2). In *Pendennis*, Thackeray dispels such romantic notions: writers are not portrayed as innate geniuses who respond to the irresistible call of a beckoning muse; they do not have sensitive, colorful temperaments; indeed, they are not unique in any way. George Warrington perhaps best characterizes the literary profession when he remarks:

> A fiddelstick about men of genius! . . . I deny that there are so many geniuses as people who whimper about the fate of men of letters assert there are. There are thousands of clever fellows in the world, who could, if they would, turn verses, write articles, read articles, read books, and deliver a judgment on them; the talk of professional critics and writers is not a whit more brilliant, or profound, or amusing, than that of any other society of educated people.
> (354–55; ch. 32)

Thackeray's perception is both democratic and elitist: he reveals that the writing class is comparable to many other segments of the working population, and thus does not innately demand special recognition; yet he also hints that a gentleman must descend from his natural sphere to join the ranks of the literati, for a literary man is "just like any other daily toiler" (380; ch. 36). Such de-romanticizing of the writing life offended some of London's literary elite. Dickens' reticence, reserve, and almost decidedly close-lipped portrayal of the novelist's profession in *David Copperfield* was very likely the expression of an intense disapproval of Thackeray's view.

Thackeray reviews with bemused nostalgia the arrogant aspirations of the literary youth. He parodies the young Pendennis, who writes poetry filled with "Byronic afflatus," and is partial to over-dramatic, sensationalized artistic productions:

> His genius at this time was of a decidedly gloomy cast. He brought his mother a tragedy, at which, though he killed sixteen people before the second act, Helen laughed so, that he thrust the masterpiece into the fire in a pet. He projected an epic poem in blank verse, 'Cortez, or the Conqueror of Mexico, and the Inca's Daughter.' He wrote part of 'Seneca, or the Fatal Bath,' and 'Ariadne in Naxos,' . . . and began a 'History of the Jesuits,' in which he lashed that Order with tremendous severity.   (60; ch. 3)

Thackeray's impulse in parodying Pen is not merely to deflate his self-important hero, but to delight in the follies of the developing artist. What must have disturbed Dickens, though, is the apparent ease and lack of interest with which Pen condescendingly takes to the literary profession. After wasting his mother's generous support at Oxbridge, Pen decides to make his fortune in London through writing:

> "I shall take chambers," he said, "and enter myself at an Inn of Court. With a couple of hundred pounds I shall be able to carry through the first year doing very well; after that I have little doubt my pen will support me, as it is doing with several Oxbridge men now in town. I have a tragedy, a comedy, and a novel, all nearly finished, and for which I can't fail to get a price. . . . Then, someday I will come back and make her [his mother] happy by marrying Laura. She is as good and sweet-tempered a girl as ever lived, besides being really very good-looking. (297; ch. 27)

Pen's virtually self-parodic description of his projected career almost prefigures the course that David as proctor-turned-writer will choose. And although Pendennis seemingly suffers none of the difficulty involved in becoming an author, Pen's route to success is not wholly straightforward. Like Thackeray, he begins by composing light verses for magazines and by writing reviews and short literary articles. Pen does serve a discernible literary apprenticeship, which is more than we learn about David Copperfield.

The August and September 1849 numbers of *Pendennis* (chapters twenty-nine through thirty-five) provide one of the most complete and unadorned depictions of literary societies in all of Victorian fiction. Once again, Thackeray's attitude towards the writing profession seems ambivalent: he recognizes the power of the press and marvels at the intricate workings of the writing class, the "Corporation of the Goosequill"; yet he also conveys the unpopular sentiment that a true gentleman doesn't write to earn a living. For example, George Warrington praises the press as a powerful machine, a "great engine," yet he shuns association with this vital vehicle, preferring to keep himself free from the taint of middle-class journalistic labor: " 'I write,' said Warrington, 'I don't tell the world that I do so,' he added, with a blush. 'I do not choose that questions should be asked; or, perhaps, I am an ass, and don't wish it to be said that George Warrington writes for bread' " (339; ch. 31). Major Pendennis will voice similar sentiments while marvelling at Pen's new found popularity:

> You have got yourself a little reputation by your literary talents, which I am very far from undervaluing, though in my time, begad, poetry and genius and that sort of thing were devilish disreputable. There was poor Byron, for instance, who ruined himself, and contracted the worst habits by living with poets and newsaper-writers, and people of that kind. But the times are changed now—

there's a run upon literature—clever fellows get into the best houses in town, begad!   (392; ch. 36)

The snobbish Major's speech encompasses the diverging view points about literature: although it has become socially acceptable and even gains people access to the best houses, it is, nevertheless, a middle-class pursuit.

Thackeray's satire peaks with the depiction of the sacred literary banquet, which he reduces to something quite common. He gives us "The Honourable Percy Popjoy," the artist who doesn't know his own work; Captain Sumph, an "ex-beau still about town," who will only tell anecdotes about Byron; and Miss Bunion, whose appearance resembles her name instead of the young flower who adorns the cover of her poetry volumes. Also present are the hostess, Mrs. Bungay, who is more concerned with class status than literary achievement, and the infamous Captain Shandon, a brilliant writer who spends more time in debtor's prison than at the press. Warrington remarks to Pen after the dinner: "And now . . . that you have seen the men of letters, tell me, was I wrong in saying that there are thousands of people in this town, who don't write books, who are, to the full, as clever and intellectual as people who do?" (374; ch. 34). We learn, as Craig Howes has suggested, that "writers don't respect each other, or care much about writing at all—like everyone else, their concerns tend to be money and social reputation" (285). Perhaps Dickens took offense at this scene, for he had a penchant for giving such gatherings, and only three months before Thackeray's satire appeared in print, on May 12, 1849, he had given such a literary banquet to celebrate the start of *David Copperfield*. The guests included Thackeray, the Carlyles, John Forster, Douglass Jerrold, Mrs. Gaskell, and Hablot K. Browne.

Thackeray was criticized for his unflattering depictions of the literary world in the January 3, *Morning Chronicle*, and by John Forster's January 5 article in *The Examiner*, "Encouragement of Literature by the State." It is possible to see Forster representing Dickens' point of view in this debate not only because *David Copperfield* was a suitably noble portrayal of the writing life, but also because Forster believed that Thackeray's satiric depictions hindered attempts to establish the Guild of Literature and Art—a cause Dickens had aligned himself with. The context for the dignity of literature controversy was in part prefigured by the 1847 Thackeray-Forster quarrel, which stemmed from Thackeray's previous satires and fictional caricatures.[8] During this dispute, in which Dickens acted as a mediator, Dickens informed Thackeray that his literary parodies in *Punch* "did no honor to literature or literary men, and should be left to very inferior and miserable hands" (Ray, *Letters* 2:297).

Thackeray was particularly offended that the *Morning Chronicle* charged him with "fostering a baneful prejudice" against literary men and that John Forster accused him of "stooping to flatter" and "condescending to caricature . . . literary-labourers, in order to pay court to 'the non-literary class.' " Believing that such comments were tantamount to calling him a "rogue" or a "cheat," Thackeray responded to both papers with "The Dignity of Literature," written to the editor of the *Morning Chronicle* on January 12, 1850 (Ray, *Letters* 2:629–35). He replied that he never had "been ashamed of his profession" (630); he suggested that the nation daily demonstrates a "generous faith in men of letters" (631); and that "the literary profession is not held in disrepute" (632). Thackeray continued: "I believe that the social estimation of the man of letters is as good as it deserves to be, and as good as that of any other professional man" (632).

Thackeray argued on two fronts throughout the letter: he asserted, as he does in *Pendennis*, that literary men are no better or no worse than their fellow man, and thus deserve no special treatment in fiction; he also claimed that in characterizing a few writers he was not defining the behavior of all writers. Thackeray, implicitly recognizing that Dickens may have been the silent voice behind Forster's attack, stated that it was clear that Stiggins of *The Pickwick Papers* was not intended "as an insult to all Dissenters" (635). Thackeray thus argued for his inherent right of artistic liberty:

> And if every character in a story is to represent a class, not an individual—if every bad figure is to have its obliged contrast of a good one, and balance of vice and virtue is to be struck—novels, I think, would become impossible, as they would be intolerably stupid and unnatural, and there would be a lamentable end of writers and readers of such compositions.   (635)

Craig Howe has suggested that Thackeray further answers his critics in chapter 41 of *Pendennis*, "Contains a Novel Incident" (Feb. 1850).[9] In this chapter, Pen dusts off an old manuscript written "under the influence of youthful embarrassments," gives it a more modern air, and "promotes" all of his characters at the request of his publishers. Although he admits to Warrington that his fashionable novel *Walter Lorraine* may be flawed, Pen defends it as an honest production: "a poet sets down his thoughts and experiences upon paper as a painter does a landscape or a face upon a canvas, to the best of his ability, and according to his particular gift. If ever I think I have the stuff in me to write an epic, by Jove I will try. If I only feel that I am good enough to crack a joke or tell a story, I will do that" (435; ch. 41). This response characterizes Thackeray's attempt at what his preface labels "a certain truth and honesty." Successful novels, like Pen's, are not always products of high genius and hard work; they are as much the result of good fortune, a good family, and a favorable market. Pen is successful, in part, because he writes "like a gentleman" (376; ch. 35) and because he is "known both in literary and polite circles" (382; ch. 36). Warrington is able to sell Pendennis's manuscript for more money because of his upper-class associations. To his credit, though, Pen never believes

> that the story he was writing was a masterpiece of composition, or that he was the equal of the great authors whom he admired; and when he now reviewed his little performance, he was keenly enough alive to its faults, and pretty modest regarding its merits. It was not very good, he thought; but it was as good as most books of the kind that had the run of circulating libraries and the career of the season.   (435; ch. 41)

Such a passage documents Pen's development as a person and writer. He no longer takes himself or his work too seriously and has achieved a level of clear-sightedness. Just as he becomes aware of his artistic shortcomings, so too, he will recognize his personal flaws.

If the first response to the depiction of the writing class in *Pedennis* occurs with the *Morning Chronicle* and *The Examiner*, then I think that Dickens' portrayal of the author in *David Copperfield* must also be considered a response to Thackeray's novel. Dickens counters Thackeray's unflattering portrait of the artist with his own vision of the writing life. And while *Pendennis* depicts Pen's literary development and critiques the literary societies of Victorian England, *David Copperfield* chronicles the private life of a dedicated artist.

The role of novels and writing is clear in *David Copperfield*. David sings the praises of books, from Peggotty's crocodile book to his list of childhood favorites, which he will later obligingly recount to Steerforth. His exploration of the writing life includes a job as a reporter, his idiosyncratic work as an aide in the compilation of Doctor Strong's dictionary, and as a welcome ear to Mr. Dick's muddled account of the testimonial. As Murray Baumgarten comments, "At one time or another most of the characters in *David Copperfield* commit their thoughts to paper" (39); thus, by "presenting characters who are writers and displaying the products of their work as well, *David Copperfield* explores some of the meanings of writing for its time" (39). Nevertheless, for all this attention to writing, David rarely speaks of his own artistic career.

David's willful decision not to elaborate on the nature of his writing distinguishes Dickens' novel from Thackeray's. David informs the reader:

> It is not my purpose, in this record, though in all other essentials it is my written memory, to pursue the history of my own fictions. They express themselves, and I leave them to themselves. When I refer to them, incidentally, it is only as part of my progress.   (588–89; ch. 48)

These "incidental" references to his novels define David's approach; he will only allude to his professional work when it appears as a necessary part of his history. Thus, we cannot fail to see that David's career as a novelist sharply contrasts with Pendennis's. Pendennis appears, at times, to embody the worst excesses of the Romantic artist: he is flippant, insincere, and arrogant about his ability, success, and artistic production. David, who counters this Romantic image of the self-involved, egocentric writer, believes "nature and accident has made me an author." He approaches the profession as if he were an unworthy devotee approaching a sacred art: "I have taken with fear and trembling to authorship. I wrote a little something, in secret, and sent it to a magazine" (535; ch. 43). The secrecy that surrounds his first submission forecasts the mystery that will enshroud the rest of his fictions. For an autobiographical narrative written by a successful novelist, *David Copperfield* is remarkably devoid of commentary on writing as a profession; and, ironically, writing is frequently portrayed as a private activity, one that demands that the self be concealed. Alexander Welsh comments: "So lightly does the narrator of his own life touch upon his career that as readers we are a little taken aback and have to remind ourselves that this is a novel about a novelist" (109).

Dickens "corrects" or balances Thackeray's portrait of the developing author: David is everything that Pen is not. Pen's arrogance and half-hearted commitment are rebuked by David, who first proclaims that "there is no substitute for thorough-going, ardent, and sincere earnestness" and then vows: "Never to put one hand to anything, on which I could throw my whole self; and never to affect depreciation of my work, whatever it was" (518; ch. 42). Class issues largely compel this debate: Pendennis disparages the gentility of the very profession that David pursues so fervently because of its favorable class associations. Dickens thus attempts to redefine the image of the artist as David repeatedly describes his own work habits in terms of such Victorian middle-class virtues as "determination," "order," "perseverance," "diligence," and "earnestness." He offers this outlook: "whatever I have tried to do in my life, I have tried with all my heart to do well; that whatever I devoted myself to, I have devoted myself to completely; that, in great aims and small, I have always been thoroughly in earnest" (518; ch. 42) David only gradually reveals hints of his success and attributes it to his unwavering, disciplined work: "my success had steadily increased with my steady application" (567; ch. 46).

The notion of artistic heroism is only implied in *David Copperfield*. Although David's decidedly successful career seems to answer the question of heroism posed in the opening line of the book—that is, David is the hero of his own life—we must discern from David's behavior what constitutes a "literary hero." Certainly Dickens suggests that this hero is a humble, hardworking, earnest and committed writer, who with quiet dignity graciously accepts his worldly success. Furthermore, a consideration of the third-person narrative of *Pendennis* allows us to perhaps recognize that the autobiographical act itself—David's writing of his own life—constitutes a form of artistic heroism.

It becomes apparent that the dignity of literature controversy was not an isolated incident: it was largely prefigured in the 1846 Thackeray-Forster quarrel; the dispute influenced both Thackeray's *Pendennis* and Dickens' *David Copperfield*; and the debate resurfaced in their later fiction. Traces of the quarrel can be found in the depictions of the painters Clive Newcome in Thackeray's *The Newcomes* (1853–55) and Henry Gowan in Dickens' *Little Dorrit* (1855–57). Still later, while writing the eulogy, "In Memoriam," for Thackeray in *Cornhill Magazine*, Dickens could not resist a final pronouncement on the issue: "We had our differences of opinion. I thought that he too much feigned a want of earnestness, and that he made a pretence of undervaluing his art, which was not good for the art that he held in trust" (Tillotson and Hawes 321).

III

As part of their shared experiences, both Pendennis and David Copperfield attend the theatrical production, *The Stranger*, a play which affects them profoundly. *The Stranger*, Benjamin Thompson's 1798 adaptation of August von Kotzebue's *Menschenhass und Reue* (1788), played in London consistently throughout the 1840s and was included in a series of plays performed at Windsor Castle in 1848–49.[10] The play occupies a more central place in Thackeray's novel than in Dickens', for at this play the young Pendennis first becomes infatuated with the actress Miss Fotheringay. In Dickens' novel the allusion to *The Stranger* is brief and perplexing. Given that Pendennis sees the play in chapters three and four (Nov. and Dec. 1848) and that David Copperfield does not attend the drama until chapter twenty-six (Jan. 1850), we are left to speculate about why Dickens sent David to the same play as Pendennis. Yet as a point of intersection between *Pendennis* and *David Copperfield*, Thackeray's and Dickens' use of *The Stranger* offers another instance of intertextual doubling, one in which a third text—a contemporay dramatic production—becomes part of a shared cultural context for the eponymous characters, as well as for their authors.

In an earlier nineteenth-century novel, Jane Austen's *Mansfield Park* (1814), Kotzebue's "Lover's Vows" provides a source of controversy: Edmund and Fanny question whether the overwrought romance is too indecorous and immodest for them to perform. Kotzebue's plays were known for their sentimental excesses; however, they were also enormously popular. Thomas Carlyle described Kotzebue as "once the darling of theatrical Europe," whose plays were acted "in every theatre from Kamtschatka to Cadiz" (360). This popularity did not lead to critical acclaim, though, as evidenced by Thackeray's mockery of the play:

> Those who know the play of the 'Stranger' are aware that the remarks made by the various characters are not valuable in themselves, either for their sound sense, their novelty of observation, or their poetic fancy.
> Nobody ever talked so. If we meet idiots in life, as will happen, it is a great mercy that they do not use such absurdly fine words. (72; ch. 4)

Nevertheless, Pendennis is captivated by the actress Miss Fotheringay, who plays the role of Mrs. Haller. Ironically, when Pen attempts to discuss *The Stranger* with Miss Fotheringay after a performance, she displays a marked lack of knowledge about the author and the German drama. Pen's immaturity and inexperience become further apparent when he begins to court her. Unable to distinguish between Miss Fotheringay and her theatrically created personas, Pen falls in love with Mrs. Haller from *The Stranger* and is blind to her off-stage self.

David Copperfield's enigmatic reference to the play would be easy to overlook: "I went to see 'The Stranger' as a Doctors' Commons sort of play, and was so dreadfully cut up, that I hardly knew myself in my own glass when I got home" (330; ch. 26). Undoubtedly, as Alexander Welsh suggests, the reference is a "sly hit at Thackeray's novel" (124). Certainly David's reaction recalls Pendennis's, for at the conclusion of the performance Pen "did not quite know what he felt yet; it was something overwhelming, maddening, delicious; a fever of wild joy and undefined longing" (74; ch. 4). Dickens follows the pattern that Thackeray had established: he allows his hero to be overpowered by a sensationalized production of undying love. Immediately after mentioning the play, David reports that Mr. Spenlow has invited him to his house: in his narration, *The Stranger* is linked with his first meeting Dora. Thompson's play has prepared both fictional authors for their first engagements.

The Stranger appeals to the unrefined sensibilities of the maturing authors because it articulates and enacts their own desire to lead a romantic life. We know from David's and Pendennis's nostalgic listing of their favorite writers and books that as aspiring artists they were impressionable and receptive to literary works. It is not surprising, then, that Pen and David are vulnerable to theatrical productions. After the play, Pen "was as much in love as the best hero in the best romance he ever read" (75; ch. 4). David's earlier response to the Covent Garden Theatre's production of *Julius Caesar* suggests that he is equally as impressionable: "when I came out into the rainy street, a twelve o'clock at night, I felt as if I had come from the clouds, where I had been leading a romantic life for ages" (244–45; ch. 19). Kotzebue's play so profoundly affects Pen and David because it indulges and inflames these literary-induced longings.

The Stranger portrays the noble suffering of Mrs. Haller and the unnamed Stranger. Unknown to each other, both characters live in quiet isolation, performing acts of charity in the nearby countryside. Though they have renounced the world, they still hope to alleviate the suffering of their fellow man. The audience learns that Mrs. Haller had once fell prey to the seductions of her husband's "friend," who had deceived her into believing her husband was unfaithful. And thus, "she plunged an honourable husband into misery. She ran away with a villain" (226). The Stranger remains a mystery for much of the play, suffering from some unspeakable agony that torments him daily (though it is obvious that he is Mrs. Haller's husband).

The popular appeal of such a play lies in the noble, generous, and widely admired lead characters. The "wretched outcast" Stranger and the "lovely penitent" Mrs. Haller are refined, sensitive souls who embody the ideal of the estranged, suffering lovers. The Stranger appears deep and unfathomable to his servant, who early in the play describes him:

> A man kind and clear—though I cannot understand him. He rails against the whole world, and yet, no beggar leaves his door unsatisfied. I have now lived three years with him, and yet, I know not who he is. A hater of society, no doubt; but not by Providence intended to be so. Misanthropy in his head, not in his heart.   (195)

This Byronic, tortured soul may have attracted Pendennis and David because the Stranger is precisely what they are not: worldly, experienced, above the petty concerns of everyday life, and struggling nobly in the face of some grave wrong. As an early outcast himself, a child "abandoned" by his mother, David may have imagined that he too faced life's trials with the dignity of the Stranger.

The play's complications ensue when the Count and Countess Wintersen return to their castle with the Baron Steinfort (the Countess's brother and the Stranger's oldest friend). The Baron falls in love with Mrs. Haller, who resists his advances. Meanwhile, the Stranger saves the Count's only son from drowning, but refuses to accept a reward, even rejecting a dinner invitation. When the Baron recognizes the Stranger as his closest friend, and later learns through a plot twist that Mrs. Haller is his wife, the Baron attempts to reconcile the two. The stoical Stranger, though, only agrees to see his penitent wife so that she may receive his forgiveness. Of course, this meeting produces the necessary melodramatic catalyst to restore the estranged lovers:

> Their hands lie in each other: their eyes mournfully meet each other, they stammer another "Farewell" and part. But, as they are going, she encounters the Boy and the Girl. They press the children in their arms with speechless affection; they tear themselves away—gaze at each other—spread their arms, and rush into an embrace. The children run and cling around their parents. The curtain falls.   (251)

The play scandalized its audiences, who believed that the adulterous wife did not deserve a happy ending to her story. Oscar Mandel writes that "audiences absolutely expected from their serious plays—and paintings—a representation of horrid punishment for the least sexual deviation of their heroines.... A single slip, and the lady was undone. She must commit suicide ... flee to some Australia, turn prostitute" (35). Mandel suggests that Kotzebue's play can be bracketed between Nicholas Rowe's *Fair Penitent* (1703) and Dickens' *David Copperfield* in its concern with the penitent, fallen woman.

Neither Pen nor David appear scandalized; instead, they are profoundly touched by the melodramatic pathos, which invites an overwrought indulgence of grief. Thackeray provides one explanation: he qualifies his mockery of the play by admitting that "in the midst of the balderdash, there runs the reality of love, children, and forgiveness of wrong, which will be listened to wherever it is preached, and sets all the world sympathising" (72; ch. 4). Alexander Welsh insightfully offers another reason for Pen's and David's reaction:

> What Kotzebue's "Doctors' Commons sort of play" allowed them [Pen and David] to glimpse or imagine was a beautiful woman who had married at

sixteen, who had coupled and uncoupled with her husband, had an affair with another man, and returned as a lovely penitent—after examples of charity on both sides—to her husband and children. The foreign play, in short, invited a young man to contemplate what men and women can do together whether married or unmarried.   (124)

This discussion can be advanced further. Certainly both Pen and David are more than ready to play the part of the suffering, heroic lover, and will soon do so. The play teaches them that patience and perseverance are necessary elements of romance, for like Mrs. Haller, Pen and David will realize the danger in following "the first mistaken impulse of an undisciplined heart." More important, though, the play is an appropriate precursor for what happens to Steerforth-Emily-Ham, for Emily and Steerforth's flight occurs in the next monthly number of *David Copperfield*. Perhaps David is so "cut up" becaue he intuits or senses Steerforth's forthcoming seduction of Emily. Indeed, Emily Peggotty plays the real life role that Emily Fotheringay acted so well: little Em'ly foolishly runs away with a treacherous "friend" of the family; she flees to foreign parts to escape the condemnation of her behavior; and she returns penitent and wiser. Thus, the play offers more than an opportunity for Pen and David to contemplate sexual dalliance; *The Stranger* serves as a subtle omen to David and Pendennis, who must learn to navigate the perilous course of romantic entanglement and to understand that compassion some-times defines love as much as passion does. It further allows them to examine the pattern of transgression and reconciliation that will occupy such a large part of both works.[11]

As an instance of shared attention, *The Stranger* allows readers to examine a text that influenced both Dickens and Thackeray, David and Pendennis. This detail, as well as the larger critical locuses of intertextuality, suggest that Dickens and Thackeray were responsive not only to cultural texts of the day, but to each other's current rival publication.

David Masson, who had first compared *Pendennis* and *David Copperfield* in 1851, provides a fitting conclusion, writing in *British Novelists and Their Styles* (1859) that Thackeray and Dickens "are so closely associated in the public mind, that whenever the one is mentioned the other is thought of. It is now Dickens and Thackeray, Thackeray and Dickens, all the world over" (Ford and Lane 26).

NOTES

1. Specifically, Thackeray's *Yellowplush Correspondence* (1838) rewrites aspects of *The Pickwick Papers* (1836–37); *Catherine* (1839–40) parodies *Oliver Twist*

(1838) as well as the Newgate novels of Bulwer and Ainsworth; even Thackeray's Christmas books can be seen as anti-Dickensian in content and tone.

2. In a letter to his mother, dated May 4, 1849, Thackeray commented on *David Copperfield*'s opening number: "Have you read Dickens?—O it is charming. Bravo Dickens. It has some of his prettiest touches—those inimitable Dickens touches w^h make such a great man of him. And the reading of the book has done another author a great deal of good. In the first place it pleases the other Author to see that Dickens who has long left off alluding to his the O A's works has been copying the O A, and greatly simplifying his style and foregoing the use of fine words. By this the public will be the gainer and David Copperfield will be improved by taking a lesson from Vanity Fair" (Ray, *Letters* 2:531).

3. Stanley Friedman, Carol Hanbery MacKay, and Alexander Welsh have pointed this out: Friedman in "Kotzebue's *The Stranger* in *David Copperfield*," *Dickens Studies Newsletter* 9 (1970): 50; MacKay in "Surrealization and the Redoubled Self: Fantasy in *David Copperfield* and *Pendennis*," *Dickens Studies Annual* 14 (1985): 261; and Welsh in *From Copyright to Copperfield: The Identity of Dickens* (Cambridge: Harvard UP, 1987) 124. However, the implications of this connection have not been fully explored.

4. See, for example, Carol Hanbery MacKay's previously cited article, "Surrealization and the Redoubled Self: Fantasy in *David Copperfield* and *Pendennis*."

5. George Orwell, in *Critical Essays*, (London: Secker and Warburg, 1951.) also associated Laura and Agnes, but was not as complimentary, stating that "Agnes is the most disagreeable of his heroines, the real legless angel of Victorian romance, almost as bad as Thackeray's Laura" (58).

6. It is worth noting that Thackeray suspended his novel from Oct. to Dec. 1849 because of illness.

7. John Butt and Kathleen Tillotson state in *Dickens at Work* (London: Methuen, 1957) that from early in the book Steerforth is designed for Emily. They write: "He is the only possible seducer for Little Em'ly, and that he was already destined for the role may be guessed from a hint of the young libertine, underdeveloped as yet, but casual and untrustworthy in his approaches to women" (123).

8. See Ray, *Letters*, 2:294–303, for a complete account of this dispute between Thackeray and Forster, which requires Dickens to act as a mediator.

9. Howes writes, "Introducing 'Walter Lorraine'" allows him [Pen] to discuss past experience as a suitable source of material for the professional writer. Warrington's and Pen's conversation about this novel will stand as Thackeray's answer to his critics" (291).

10. *The Stranger* played in the following London theaters in the 1840s: Victoria, November 1841; Sadler's Wells, June 1844; Haymarket, October 1840, July 1848; Princess's, March 1845, May 1847; Olympic, April 1848; Drury Lane, December 1849. This information was found in Donald Mullin, comp., *Victorian Plays: A Record of Significant Productions on the London Stage, 1830–1901* (New York: Greenwood, 1987) 363.

11. Stanley Friedman makes a similar point about *The Stranger*: "the references to the play help direct us to the idea of forgiveness of sexual transgression, an important concern in *David Copperfield*" (50).

WORKS CITED

Baumgarten, Murray. "Writing and *David Copperfield*." *Dickens Studies Annual* 14 (1985): 39–59.

Butt, John and Kathleen Tillotson. *Dickens at Work*. London: Methuen, 1957.

Carlyle, Thomas. *Critical and Miscellaneous Essays*. Vol. 1. London: Chapman and Hall, 1899. 5 vols. Rpt. New York: AMS, 1969.

Collins, Philip, ed. *Dickens: The Critical Heritage*. New York: Barnes and Noble, 1971.

Dickens, Charles. *David Copperfield*. Ed. Nina Burgis. Oxford: Clarendon, 1981.

―――. "In Memoriam." *Cornhill Magazine* 9 (1864): 129–32. Rpt. in *Thackeray: The Critical Heritage*. Eds. Georffrey Tillotson and Donald Hawes. London: Routledge and Kegan Paul, 1968. 320–24.

Ford, George and Lauriate Lane, Jr. eds. *The Dickens Critics*. Ithaca, New York: Cornell UP, 1961.

Friedman, Stanley. "Kotzebue's *The Stranger* in *David Copperfield*." *Dickens Studies Newsletter* 9 (1970): 49–50.

Howes, Craig. "*Pendennis* and the Controversy on the 'Dignity of Literature.' " *Nineteenth Century Fiction* 41 (1986): 269–98.

Lippincott, A. Z. "Some Recollections of Thackeray." *Lippincott's Magazine* 7 (1871): 106–10. Rpt. in *Thackeray: Interviews and Recollections*. 2 vols. Ed. Philip Collins. New York: St. Martin's, 1983. 1:178–85.

MacKay, Carol Hanbery. "Surrealization and the Redoubled Self: Fantasy in *David Copperfield* and *Pendennis*." *Dickens Studies Annual* 14 (1985): 241–65.

Mandel, Oscar. *August von Kotzebue: The Comedy, The Man*. University Park: Pennsylvania State UP, 1990.

Masson, David. "*Pendennis* and *Copperfield*: Thackeray and Dickens." *North British Review* May 1851:57–89. Rpt. in *Dickens: The Critical Heritage*. Ed. Philip Collins. New York: Barnes and Noble, 1971. 249–59.

―――. *British Novelists and Their Styles*. 1859. Rpt. in *The Dickens Critics*. Eds. George Ford and Lauriate Lane, Jr. Ithaca, New York: Cornell UP, 1961, 25–37.

Meckier, Jerome. *Hidden Rivalries in Victorian Fiction: Dickens, Realism, and Revaluation*. Lexington: UP of Kentucky, 1987.

Mullin, Donald, comp. *Victorian Plays: A Record of Significant Productions on the London Stage, 1830–1901*. New York: Greenwood, 1987.

Orwell, George. *Critical Essays*. London: Secker and Warburg, 1951.

Ray, Gordon, ed. *The Letters and Private Papers of William Makepeace Thackeray*. 4 vols. Cambridge: Harvard UP, 1945–46.

―――. *Thackeray: The Age of Wisdom, 1847–1863*. New York: McGraw-Hill, 1958.

Shillingsburg, Peter. *Pegasus in Harness: Victorian Publishing and W. M. Thackeray.* Charlottesville: UP of Virginia, 1992.

Stewart, J. I. M. Introduction. *The History of Pendennis.* By William Makepeace Thackeray. Ed. Donald Hawes. London: Penguin, 1986.

Thackeray, William Makepeace. *The History of Pendennis.* Ed. Donald Hawes. London: Penguin Classics, 1986.

Thompson, Benjamin. *The Stranger, The Series of Dramatic Entertainments Performed before Her Majesty the Queen, His Royal Highness Prince Albert, The Royal Family and the Court at Windsor Castle. 1848–49.* Ed. Benjamin Webster. London: Mr. Mitchell, Royal Library, 1848–49.

Tillotson, Geoffrey and Donald Hawes, eds. *Thackeray: The Critical Heritage.* London: Routledge and Kegan Paul, 1968.

Welsh, Alexander. *From Copyright to Copperfield: The Identity of Dickens.* Cambridge: Harvard UP, 1987.

"Who Was the Imitator—Dickens or Thackeray?" *Atlantic Monthly* 78 (1896): 139–41.

Who Are You, Lucy Snowe? Disoriented *Bildung* in *Villette*

Margaret Soenser Breen

"Bunyan must have been closer to [Bronté] . . . than to any other novelist, often as he stands in the background of English novelists." Q. D. Leavis's comment (1:212), made in reference to *Villette* (1853), is equally applicable to *Jane Eyre* (1847), with its innovative adaptation of *The Pilgrim's Progress* (1678; 1684) at the novel's end. There Jane calls up the image of a Greatheart protecting pilgrims from Apollyon. The description pays tribute to St. John Rivers, the cold-hearted clergyman whose insistence that Jane's understanding of her faith be mediated by his own perpetuates St. Paul's problematic construction of femininity, whereby the belief in woman's indirect relation to God denies her the spiritual center inside herself:

> . . . He may be stern; he may be exacting; he may be ambitious yet; but his is the sternness of the warrior Great-heart, who guards his pilgrim convoy from the onslaught of Apollyon.
> . . . No fear of death will darken St. John's last hour: his mind will be sure; his faith steadfast. His own words are a pledge of this—
> "—My Master," he says, "has forewarned me. Daily He announces more distinctly, "Surely I come quickly" and hourly I more eagerly respond—"Amen, even so I come, Lord Jesus!" (Bronté 398)[1]

The metaphor of Bunyanesque pilgrimage is a deliberate one; the writer whom one reviewer described as "protestant to the last fibre of her being"[2] reverts to it again in a key closing moment in *Villette*. It is also equivocal praise for St. John the Christian hero. Bronté's use of Bunyan refocuses the annihilatory capacity of the would-be suitor and spiritual taskmaster.

Apollyon and Greatheart belong respectively to Parts 1 and 2 of *The Pilgrim's Progress*; the two characters never actually meet. The resolute Christian, who divorces himself from family, friends, and community, fights and

defeats Apollyon in Part 1; Greatheart, Christian's stand-in and his wife Christiana's guide in Part 2, certainly finds no such violent threat as the one
Apollyon presents for Part 1's hero. The "false prince," a figure of conventional secular authority *cum* monstrosity, embodies the assault on Christian's
faith from without. From the vantage point of Part 1, Greatheart complements
Christian. He personifies the assurance of spiritual victory that the individualistic Christian would have welcomed. For this reason, Greatheart actively
seeks out his enemies. His faith promotes an aggression from within. At the
same time, from the vantage point of Part 2, Apollyon anticipates and doubles
for Christiana, for the greatest difficulty and most tenacious opposition that
Greatheart faces comes not from overt enemies whom he encounters along
the way to the Celestial City but from the female pilgrim whom he must
take there.

Christiana in her propensity to improvise and so interpret her progress for
herself threatens to defy the Pauline requirement of female subordination. She
begins her journey without a male guide, only to be told shortly after starting
out that she will be held accountable for any assault that a man may make
on her. Spiritual other rather than protagonist of her own narrative, Christiana
discovers that harassment takes the shape of evildoers and church patriarchs
alike. If the near rape that she suffers at the outset of pilgrimage teaches her
the utility of male protection, her own attempt to cast Greatheart as travel
companion rather than overseer and to suggest the terms of her *Bildung* is
enough to incite his chastisement. That Christiana fades into the background
of Part 2 is therefore unsurprising. The woman who resists her prescribed
identity is too risky a subject for sustained spiritual contemplation. The narrative's shift to the generic concerns of Christian community effectually cen-
sures her.

Such are the configurations that Jane Eyre's splicing together of Parts 1
and 2 calls forth. The imagined encounter between Apollyon and Greatheart
discloses the aggressive quality of the spiritual guide and the implications of
that quality for the female pilgrim. Jane, in contrast to Christiana, is an avid
reader of character, not the least her own. She studies Rochester's physiognomy and behavior. When she discovers her own slavish veneration of him,
she goes away. And to St. John, that inverted parody of the Word incarnate,
who is himself "no longer flesh" (361), she responds: "If I were to marry
you, you would kill me" (363). Throughout her autobiography, Jane is her
own guide and interpreter. The final chapter reiterates this message of inner
resourcefulness. Whereas Greatheart prevents Christiana from validating her
spiritual and social autonomy, Jane in effect claims hers by pitting Greatheart

against Apollyon. Jane's comparison of the suitor whom she rejects to the guide whom Christiana could not reject is as gracious as it is cautionary.

Jane Eyre's ambivalent tribute to St. John is indicative of Brontë's resistance to constructions of femininity that deny women spiritual as well as social autonomy. *The Pilgrim's Progress*, along with the Bible and *Paradise Lost* all essential parts of nineteenth-century England's cultural and imaginative life, provides one such construction.[3] Popular Victorian representations concede women an interiority where Bunyan does not. The more striking difference, however, lies not in any overturning of the female pilgrim's selflessness but in the Victorian's *idealization* of that selflessness. Christiana, whose effacing inclusion within a community of faithful leaves her the reverberation of her husband's vocation, proves the precursor of the Victorian woman whom John Ruskin exalts via the negation of her inner and outer life: she is not "for rule, not for battle, and her intellect is not for invention or creation, but for sweet orderings" (Gilbert & Gubar 24). The ornamental function that Ruskin denominates as woman's work indicates an extension of, rather than a departure from, Bunyan's vision of femininity.[4]

Brontë, like so many Victorians, caught between a middle-class ideology that pronounced working women "redundant" and a pressured economic reality that, increasingly, required women to earn livelihoods away from home, rebels against passive constructions of femininity such as Ruskin's.[5] Jane tells Rochester, "I had rather be a thing than an angel" (230). And, significantly, in *Villette*, the man whom Lucy Snowe's imagination grows to reject as its male ideal, John Graham Bretton, etherealizes both of the women to whom he is attracted. The one is a "graceful angel" (222); the other is "divine" (Brontë, *Villette* 529). In contrast to narrator-protagonist Lucy's own insights, these assessments only register the surface of the women's characters. Dr. John, in other words, does not adore these women so much as the conventional image of femininity that they evoke for him.

In the wake of the contemporary veneration of woman as the sympathetic sounding board of male action, Brontë and her heroines insist that self-reliance is a necessary posture for both their spiritual and social lives. In the words of Lucy Snowe, "self-reliance and exertion were forced upon me by circumstances, as they are upon thousands besides" (95). Jane Eyre and Lucy Snowe both acknowledge that companionship without the possibility for self-reliance threatens the "inner life"; conversely, self-reliance without companionship yields isolation. In *Jane Eyre* this latter threat is minimal. The difficulties Jane faces after she leaves Rochester are external, material rather than psychological. Importantly, they are also temporary: within a year of her separation she has discovered cousins whom she never knew she had and has inherited the family fortune. But in *Villette* the threat is potentially devastating. In contrast to Jane, Lucy is in danger not simply of becoming a social outcast. The biblical phrases that she uses to describe herself are suitably ominous. Lucy risks being buried alive within the "snow-sepulchre" (348) of her own consciousness, which conventional patterns of thought have "whited" for her.[6]

Two impossible love stories frame Lucy's narrative: the one with John Graham Bretton, the other with M. Paul Emmanuel. The initial chapters depict the youthful meeting between Bretton and Lucy. (Lucy is the goddaughter of John's mother). This opening serves both an anticipatory and a retrospective purpose. Lucy's childhood familiarity with John is the ground for her adult attraction to him. The first section also looks forward to the relation between the two when they reencounter one another some ten years later in Villette. Importantly, there is no mention of any direct interaction between young Bretton and Miss Snowe. As an effective indicator of her remove from him, narrator Lucy recalls John's easy dismissal of the housewifely attentions of little Polly, a distant family relation who later becomes his wife. In one instance, Polly lays her head at his feet. The posture is reminiscent of adoring, submissive Victorian femininity. John, though, remains oblivious. How much more so is he to the scene's onlooker, Lucy, who, much later, equates her submissive double with a cocker spaniel. When Graham sees Lucy again in Villette, he remarks that then as now, she was "a being inoffensive as a shadow" (403). John Bretton's lack of awareness either as a boy or as a man that Lucy holds any romantic interest in him is counterbalanced by the disappearance of husband-to-be M. Paul Emmanuel at the end of novel. The fiery teacher at the girls' school where Lucy comes to work confesses his love, but further involvement is suspended by *Villette*'s ambiguous conclusion. It is unclear what happens to M. Paul—whether or not he is drowned in a storm at sea. In any event, he is *not* an agent for narrative closure or resolution; Lucy Snowe stands alone at the end of her autobiography, much as she does at its beginning.

In sharp contrast to Harriet Martineau's assertion that "there is an absence of introspection, an unconsciousness, a repose in women's lives" (Allott 173), Lucy Snowe is maddeningly introspective; she imagines emotional connections or possibilities that cannot be readily translated into worldly plots. Still—and this is *Villette*'s particular contribution to realism—the remove of Lucy's inner life figures a critique of those plots, fictional as well as social, that have left her the marginalized heroine of her own love story. The reserve that Margaret Oliphant has cited as the conventional attitude of female protagonists in pre-Bronté novels is recalled in *Villette* to uphold the validity of Lucy's particular experience.[7] This narrative reserve—what Mary Jacobus calls "the discursive activity of Lucy's (over)heated imagination"—marks Lucy's separation from conventional romance plots but also comments on the incapacity of those plots to contain her experience.[8] Within *Villette* the authority of character and narrator Lucy rests on her consciousness of a relation between God and community that, rather than harmonious, is disjunctive and, above all, disorienting.[9]

This disorienting experience bespeaks the importance of *The Pilgrim's Progress* as a crucial source text for the English *Bildungsroman* in general and for *Villette* in particular.[10] Bunyan's text consists of a two-part narrative whose principal interest throughout is the pilgrim Christian. The first, linear narrative follows him as a solitary believer; the second, circular narrative recognizes him as the founding father of a new Israel. At first, Part 2 suggests another protagonist, Christian's wife, Christiana; but interest in her is structural rather than dramatic: she is a testimony to Christian's authority rather than a witness to her own. Considered apart from his, her progress—partially effaced, narratively submerged—lacks aesthetic and spiritual integrity. Christiana is thus a problematic figure for her literary granddaughters, the novel heroines who follow in her wake: Christiana celebrates Christian's pilgrimage seemingly at the expense of her own.

Lucy Snowe is one such inheritor, disoriented by the vexed possibilities for female progress, offered and withheld by Bunyan's account. *Villette* repeats the configurations of *The Pilgrim's Progress*. Lucy Snowe may be the novel's heroine, but as her own biographer, she cannot tell her history without recounting that of her godbrother John Graham Bretton. The two characters are linked together by Christian rite, which in turn provides the basis for Lucy's self-eradicating investment in Graham. With one subject but two focal points, *Villette* studies the threat of effacement and the ineluctable disorientation—social as well as psychological—that Lucy's leading man poses for her once she insists on the integrity of her own story.

John, or Graham as he is called by his family, is one of the many characters in Victorian fiction whose secular travel recalls the resilient quality of Christian's pilgrimage. His progress begins in fatherlessness and necessitates his expatriation; it passes through the loss and retrieval of social status, and culminates in marriage and the realization of a felicitous circle of domesticity. In many ways, these events parallel and clarify Lucy's. Importantly, though, the language of her experience differs widely from his. Graham's personal as well as worldly misfortunes are put down in a brisk, pragmatic language that mirrors his elastic capacity to rebound from loss and make good of it. At the novel's opening we hear that Graham's mother "had been left a widow, with one son. . . ; her husband, a physician, having died while she was yet a young and handsome woman" (61). And a bit later: "the handsome property of which she was left guardian for her son . . . had melted . . . to a fraction of its original amount. Graham . . . had adopted a profession" (94–95). Autobiographer Lucy does not dwell on Graham's hardships. The above sketches serve as a backdrop for her own difficulties in overcoming personal loss. At the same time, Graham in a nutshell is not very different from the Dr. John who receives an extensive character analysis over the course of the novel. Of his marriage Lucy remarks,

> This pair was blessed indeed. . . . Doubtless they knew crosses, disappointments, difficulties; but these were well borne . . .
> In short, I do but speak the truth when I say that [this life] of Graham . . . [was] blessed with "blessings of Heaven above" . . .　　(532–33)

Summary representations remain possible for Graham: the biblical language of the above passage identifies him as a pilgrim and underlines his generic character. Adversity does not break or complicate him; rather, as with Carlyle's Teufelsdrockh, it "compresses" him.[11]

Adversity does, however, disclose Lucy's inability to answer and overturn her personal trials through outward action. At the novel's beginning she compares her childhood stay at the Brettons' to "the sojourn of Christian and Hopeful beside a certain stream" (62). In *The Pilgrim's Progress* that stream is called both "the River of God" and "the River of the Water of Life" (Bunyan 148). The Bretton household, in other words, attests to the harmonious balance between heaven and earth. Misfortunes disrupt that balance for both Lucy and Graham; but whereas Graham regains it in his heaven-blessed marriage, Lucy does not. After the loss of family and fortune, she travels through an allegorically-charged landscape that is uniformly bleak, more reminiscent of Bunyan's Slough of Despond than River of God. The country of Labassecour, where she goes to find work, its principal port Boue-Marine, and Rue Fossette, the street of the pensionnat where she comes to teach—all suggest a world pervaded by mud and muck. This stagnancy without mirrors the absence of any transformative link between her inner and outer lives, the deadening disparity between her "life of thought, and that of reality . . . [between] the strange necromantic joys of fancy, [and] the privileges . . . [of] daily bread, hourly work, and a roof of shelter" (140).

Lucy may be propelled on her journey to Villette by the very same questions that initiate Christian's linear progress. "Whence did I come? Whither should I go? What should I do?" (107). Yet, in the same moment she concedes, "I lie in the shadow of St. Paul's" (107), where the shadow of the cathedral blocks out assurance of her capacity for self-direction—challenges the authority of her subjectivity. Unsurprisingly, then, "Who are *you*?" (emphasis added) is the most resonant of the questions continually put to Lucy and that she, within the whole of the novel, must ask of herself. In its first-person form it is a central question of pilgrimage (Qualls 75), but of a pilgrimage divorced from any recognizable, outwardly affirming scheme. (How much more so is this the case when the question displaces the I with the audacious second person!) "Who are you?" is an entirely appropriate query for the traveller who, in contrast to Graham, not only cannot claim the patrimony she has lost, but is also a disorienting figure within the plots that promote patriarchal renewal.

Tellingly, Lucy recounts her loss of family in veiled, religious language:

> For many days and nights neither sun nor stars appeared; . . . a heavy tempest lay on us; all hope that we should be saved was taken away. In fine, the ship was lost, the crew perished.
> . . .
> . . . Thus, there remained no possibility of dependence on others; to myself alone could I look.   (94–95)

Lucy draws on the metaphors of shipwreck, which within the tradition of Protestant meditation signal spiritual abandonment and, with it, the necessity of conversion. Thus, the gloss attests to the profundity of Lucy's experience of bereavement and focuses the imperative of her inner, spiritual development. At the same time, in its sharp contrast to the matter-of-factness accorded Graham, the retreating prose style here mimics Lucy's position of social marginality. Graham and Lucy are from the same class, but whereas the self-reliant Graham may become a doctor like his father before him and so retrieve his paternal inheritance and validate the family line, self-reliant Lucy cannot. The position immediately available to her is as the companion to an elderly invalid. Upon accepting this work, Lucy finds that "I still felt life at life's sources" (96); but this testament to inner fortitude only meets with "[t]wo hot, close rooms" that become "my world" (97). Even after Miss Marchmont's death, when Lucy travels to Villette and becomes a teacher in Madame Beck's school, her more active duties can only guarantee her present comfort. They cannot refigure her vivid inner life as social inheritance. The gender division between her and her godbrother reduces her socially to the "inoffensive shadow" not only of him but, more importantly, of herself.

During a sheltered moment in childhood, Lucy equates herself to Bunyan's Christian. Yet, gender restrictions do not readily permit an adult Lucy to secularize her pilgrim's progress. Like Christiana, she is dependent on outside, masculine intervention, if she is to claim her inherited social position. Importantly, narrator Lucy's definition of her godbrother as both a male guide and a potential husband raises the possibility for critiquing the conflation of spiritual and social direction that is at the core of Part 2 of *The Pilgrim's Progress*. Writing of Bunyan's work, Ronald Knox distinguishes between its two types of journeying: "Christian goes on pilgrimage, Christiana on a walking tour" (Knox 206). The assessment, which mirrors the prevalent dismissal of Christiana's travel as a model for genuine spiritual development,[12] does not consider that the detached authority of the male guide Greatheart (who accompanies Christiana for almost all of her journey) is the primary vehicle for rendering the female pilgrim a mere extension of the husband who has gone before her. Within *Villette*, Graham may lead Lucy through the streets of the foreign city. But precisely the ease with which he does so focuses his detachment from (if not indifference to) her. The "cool young Briton" (341) proves incapable of being either her spiritual or social guide.

The adult Graham's ability to act as Lucy's guide is initially considered when the two reencounter each other as strangers. Upon her arrival in Villette, Lucy asks a fellow traveller if he knows of an inn where she might stay the night. Because it is "too late and too dark for a woman to go ... alone" (124–25), he offers to accompany her part of the way. Lucy is ready to rely completely on Graham. He is willing to lead her. The exchange assumes conventional gender roles, which in turn invest Graham with more than social authority. Following him, Lucy is reminded of her own spiritual journey: "as to distrusting ... I should almost as soon have thought of distrusting the Bible" (124). Much as Greatheart in *The Pilgrim's Progress* is made the protector of Christiana and other weak pilgrims, the man whom Lucy later calls "Good, gallant heart" (306) is here imagined as "chivalric to the needy and feeble" (125). In a description that recalls Psalm 23.4 ("Yea, though I walk through the valley of the shadow of death, I will fear no evil"), she reveals the easy association of her gendered dependence with the need for spiritual assistance: "In the double gloom of trees and fog, I could not see my guide; I could only follow his tread. Not the least fear had I; I believe I would have followed that frank tread, through continual night, to the world's end" (125). In contrast to *The Christian Remembrancer*'s criticism that she "rejects all guides but her Bible" (Allott 206), Lucy here demonstrates her readiness to invest men, even under the most mundane circumstances, with Biblical authority. The mature Graham appears to Lucy as an inspired guide to whom she may consign her spiritual as well as worldly cares.

Ultimately, though, Graham only proves a tour guide, even while Lucy's emotional susceptibility prompts her to defer to him as omniscient male authority. "Under his *guidance*," she notes, "I saw, in one happy fortnight, more of Villette . . . than I had seen in the whole eight months of my previous residence" (271–72; emphasis added). Within this parodic role he remains removed from Lucy's inner life, impervious in particular to her interpretive capacities. Thus he takes her to an art gallery but is not with her when she is "happy, not always in admiring, but in examining, questioning, and forming conclusions" (274). His absence actually allows the gallery to become a kind of Bunyanesque Interpreter's House: much as the domestic emblems that Christiana is shown affirm the gender specificity of her spiritual travel, the paintings in the Villette gallery invite Lucy to define herself against them. When confrontational fellow teacher M. Paul distinguishes between the paintings "Cleopatra" and "*La vie d'une femme*" by pronouncing the one suitable for a male, the other for a female audience, Brontë's pilgrim is able to counter with her own assessment, which deems the two pictures alter egos of one another. They are companion pieces for the stereotypical idolatry of passive femininity: woman is either a voluptuous queen or a selfless handmaiden. According to Lucy, the second painting depicts a series of "insincere . . . bloodness, brainless nonentities," as bad as "the indolent gipsygiantress" (278) of the first. Tellingly, Graham's reappearance curtails Lucy's analysis. His "bright handsome head" (282), or, more precisely, Lucy's adoration of it, instates the very gender distinctions upon which the choleric professor had unsuccessfully insisted. Under Graham's active patronage, Lucy's thoughts become "a woman's rather obscure and stammering explanation" (282), an updated version of Christiana's muted reception of the Interpreter's lesson.

In the end, Lucy will not be silenced by Graham. She rebels against women's objectification, in particular against her own exclusion from the conventionally gendered models of [English] secular progress, whereby the male pilgrim all but overshadows his female counterpart. Lucy's second impossible love story (with Catholic teacher M. Paul Emmanuel) authorizes this protest. Importantly, though, Lucy and Paul's involvement can effect no conventional happy end, which celebrates the heroine's integration into community through marriage. The bond furthers Lucy's private and social lives, but the link between these two remains an unstable one, governed by Lucy's imaginative and narrative disorientation.

Ironically, the testimony of M. Paul's love for Lucy is his separation from her. He upholds their religious differences: she is his "little English Puritan" (594), Protestantism "the sole creed for Lucy" (595). He also provides her with the means for establishing her own school and so with the opportunity of reentering, economically speaking, the class into which she was born. But if his three-year stay in Antigua allows Lucy to deem "myself the faithful steward of his property" (593) and to find him "more my own" (595), Paul's authority, to which this romantic and quasi-spiritual language appeals, is never actually sealed; it is in fact held off by the novel's ambiguous finale. Whether M. Paul drowns upon his voyage home or returns to marry Lucy as "sunny imaginations hope" (596) is not the issue; that their outcome remains veiled in uncertainty is.

Like the speaker in Ecclesiastes, tight-lipped narrator Lucy is fundamentally uneasy the desires that bind us to this world. "Sorrow is better than laughter: for by the sadness of the countenance the heart is made better," the Bible tells us (Eccles. 7.3). This is the end determination of *Villette* with regard to possibilities of marriage, even while Lucy during Paul's absence experiences "a wonderfully changed life, a relieved heart" (594). Only the uncertain outcome of her male guide's travel can balance the disoriented female pilgrim between this world and the next.

M. Paul holds a problematic appeal for Lucy; as his name suggests, he is a Pauline hero, whose relation to women is inherently ambivalent. If self-sacrificing, he is also aggressive; toward his female pupils, and Lucy especially, he is dogmatic, baiting, and interfering; together, these traits signal his protectiveness. As many critics have noted, this combination of abrasiveness and concern holds a certain attraction for Lucy.[13] Early in the novel he locks her in a rat-filled attic without anything to eat that she might learn a part for the school play. Yet, she does not respond with resentment. Rather than a physically oppressive tyrant, he becomes a kind of psychological liberator for her. During her performance she realizes "it was not the crowd I feared, so much as my own voice" (209); by the end, she acts 'to please [herself]'' (211). Thus M. Paul's antagonistic mediation functions for Lucy much as Rochester's does for Jane: it is a spur to affirmatory self-discovery.

This pattern, whereby harshness becomes the vehicle for emotional intimacy, does not abate once M. Paul and Lucy begin their "biblical romance" (Qualls 80). His acerbic expressions of care only increase and intensify. Verbal reprimands announce his attraction to her. Coming upon her as she is mourning her one-sided love for Dr. John, he chastises her for her "malade de coeur" (310). This exchange plays on Isaiah 5.20—"Woe unto them . . . - that put bitter for sweet, and sweet for bitter"—even as it also recalls the opening of Part 2 of *The Pilgrim's Progress*. There the divine [male] messenger Secret responds to Christiana's wish for a trouble-free journey to the Celestial City with a caution: " 'The bitter is before the sweet' " (Bunyan 226). If, after all, Christiana's pilgrimage is filled with singing, marriage celebrations, and much leisure time, such sweetness signals her inscription within a patriarchal community that does not allow her to dictate the terms of her own spiritual development. Determined where Christiana is subdued, Lucy argues that "I never liked bitters; nor do I believe them wholesome. And to whatever is sweet, be it poison or good, you cannot, at least, deny its own delicious quality—sweetness. Better, perhaps to die quickly a pleasant death, than drag on long a charmless life" (311). For this part, M. Paul sounds much like God's emissary in Bunyan's book: "you should take your bitter dose duly and daily, if I had the power to administer it" (311). That M. Paul in fact regularly supplies Lucy with chocolates and sweets only buttresses his corrective stance. As in *The Pilgrim's Progress*, so in *Villette*: sweetness is a function of male prerogative not of female desire.

Importantly, though, Lucy's desires exist in part without the Pauline framework in which M. Paul attempts to locate them. On the issue of women's education, the professor's mixture of benevolence and contentiousness does not suffice either to entice or intimidate Lucy into intellectual submission. She readily admits that she has not benefitted from the academic training available to men; but, for her, doing so only confirms that her own intelligence must be apprehended apart from gender prescriptions—social as well as religious—that align knowledge with masculinity; ignorance with femininity. Lucy remains discerning of but curiously untouched by her French tutor's efforts to instruct her simultaneously in the grammar of language and the grammar of gender.

M. Paul is both the greatest suporter of and most obdurate barrier to Lucy's academic progress. In his role as all-knowing guide he may brag to his male colleagues of Lucy's accomplishments; but he is also very wary of her potential to overreach "that lovely, placid, and passive feminine mediocrity . . . the only pillow on which manly thought . . . could find rest" (443), and become his intellectual match. The lessons he offers her inevitably devolve into lessons in humiliation. As with Bunyan's own Pauline hero Greatheart, intellectual harassment becomes M. Paul's means for attempting to contain the development of a woman's mind. Lucy notes:

when I voluntarily doubled, trebled, quadrupled the tasks he set, to please him as I thought, his kindness became sternness; . . . he fretted, he opposed, he curbed me imperiously; the more I did, the harder I worked, the less he seemed content. Sarcasms of which the severity amazed and puzzled me, harassed my ears . . . I was vaguely threatened with I know not what doom, if I ever trespassed *the limits proper to my sex*, and conceived a contraband appetite for *unfeminine* knowledge . . .   (439–40; emphasis added)

The euphemisms that Lucy ascribes to M. Paul—"the limits proper to my sex" and "unfeminine knowledge"—have an origin in Christianity's definition of woman as an inferior being. Lucy, however, understands them as prescriptions for mediation, which obstruct the relation between God and the individual. Ultimately, they incite her own religiously-charged protest. "Whatever my powers," she insists, "—feminine or the contrary—God had given them, and I felt resolute to be ashamed of no faculty of His bestowal" (440). Her conviction of an unimpeded bond between the female worshipper and God sanctions a knowledge apart from M. Paul's (and, for that matter, Graham's) formulations of women's inferiority. M. Paul's "injustice" only gives "wings to [Lucy's] aspiration" (440). Her conviction grants her "a knowledge of my own" (444).

Lucy's assertion of her intellectual independence in Protestant terms throws M. Paul's own mediated station within Catholicism into relief. The man of whom Lucy notes above, "he opposed, he curbed me" (439) may himself "detest spur or curb" (410); within the context of his practiced faith, however, he is "permitted to withhold nothing; suffered to keep no corner of his heart sacred to God and to himself" (508). His submissive relation to his Father-Confessor recalls Lucy's own social marginalization—so much so that he remarks, "you are a strict Protestant, and I am a sort of lay Jesuit: but we are alike—there is affinity" (457). That affinity lies in their shared experience of interiorized disenfranchisement or "the buried life." Painfully aware of the imbalance between her affection for Graham and his benign regard for her, Lucy buries the letter he has written her and so attempts to sever her capacity to feel—her potential to love—from her everyday existence. Similarly, M. Paul's veneration of the memory of his first lover, the nun Justine Marie, exacts the sacrifice of his own desire for profound human connection. Passion, he tells Lucy, "is alien to my whole life and views. It died in the past—in the present it lies buried— . . . in the future there will be a resurrection . . . it will rise, not for earth, but for heaven" (433). Much as Lucy Snowe has been whited out of the world of Bretton and its inhabitants, M. Paul has been "overwrought" (515) by the Catholic community of Villette. His constructions of selfhood a disparate function of his capacity to serve Church interests, the virginal Paul inhabits a feminized position that mirrors Lucy's own schismatic experience of self.

More than his insistence on his gendered authority vis-à-vis women in general and Lucy in particular, M. Paul's own history of personal sacrifice and mediation within the context of his faith inspires Lucy to revitalize her investment in the Protestant paradigm for social as well a spiritual identity. Their romance answers Graham's with childhood playmate Paulina Home, who, as her name and her oft-repeated line "Put me down, please" suggest, is perfectly at home in her submission to men. The respective ending and beginning of consecutive chapters "Sunshine" and "Cloud," which sharply juxtapose the plots of development allotted these two women, proves a case in point.

Paulina, whom the reviewer for the *Spectator* termed "nearly as perfect as mortals ever can be" (Allott 183), may be accorded a kind of Genesis, "for God saw that it was good" (533); Lucy, by comparison, endures a kind of apocalypse in which proof "of a life to come must be given . . . [i]n fire and blood if needful" (534); however, the joyous mood of the one and the bleakness of the other are overturned by the women's relations to the men who accompany them. While Graham as Paulina's husband transforms himself into the male guide and protector that he is so utterly incapable of being for Lucy, Paulina all but disappears from the tribute to her own hymeneal rebirth: "Dr. Bretton saw himself live again in a son who inherited his looks and his disposition; he had stately daughters, too, like himself" (533). Exiled from this androcentric plot, which paradoxically celebrates Paulina by effacing her, Lucy addresses herself in the second person: "Tired wayfarer, gird up thy loins, look upward, march onward. Pilgrims and brother mourners, join in friendly company. Dark through the wilderness of this world stretches the way for most of us: equal and steady be our tread: be our cross our banner" (534). Yet, Lucy's vision of individual progress, while care-ridden, is not without "friendly company." As is suggested a few chapters earlier, she finds in M. Paul a "brother mourner": in maintaining the family of his dead lover, "those once dear to her he prized—he had . . . *taken up a cross*" (490; emphasis added). Though a Catholic, M. Paul becomes Lucy's "Christian hero" (491). His actions do not overshadow hers as Graham's do Paulina's. For Lucy, Paul's Catholic self-sacrifice validates her own Protestant solitariness.

Because their "theological difference" is acknowledged and sustained, Paul and Lucy reach a "mutual understanding" whereby "feelings of union and hope made themselves profoundly felt in the heart" (537). This romance invests Lucy's Protestantism with a figurative richness that bewilders the conventional gender relations celebrated within her own religious heritage. Nowhere is this disorientation more apparent than in her gloss of the religious and social opposition that their love encounters. Like the ending of *Jane Eyre*, the passage splices together Parts 1 and 2 of *The Pilgrim's Progress* and critiques the paradigms for progress available to women:

> Oh! *I* would be ready, but could that longed-for meeting really be achieved? the time was so short, the schemers seemed so watchful, so active, so hostile; the way of access appeared straight as a gully, deep as a chasm—Apollyon straddled across it, breathing flames. Could my Greatheart overcome? Could my guide reach me?   (542)

In *Jane Eyre*, the closing tribute to rejected suitor St. John Rivers makes no mention of the individual [female] pilgrim. It rather focuses on the confrontation between Greatheart and Apollyon, where the zealous ministry of the one is challenged by the intrusive violence of the other. The scene sanctions the guide's aggression insofar as the latter is directed against another, usurpatory male figure who is entirely distinct—that is, physically and even narratively removed—from the female pilgrim. By comparison, in *Villette*'s reworking of Bunyan, Greatheart is once again imagined as the potential vanquisher of Apollyon; but, importantly, the individual pilgrim in the form of the first-person narrator is also present. Because she imagines herself opposing Apollyon and so conventional worldly authority (specifically, the Catholic opponents to her romance with M. Paul) *and* being aided by the guide (M. Paul himself), Lucy becomes, within the gloss, a stand-in for both Christian and Christiana. In contrast to the Old Testament and *The Pilgrim's Progress*, where to look back is to ally oneself with destruction, Greatheart Paul's turn toward wayfarer Lucy—the guide appears on the other side of Apollyon—is a condition of her progress.

The *anticipated* union between guide and pilgrim disrupts *The Pilgrim's Progress*'s delineation of gender hierarchy. The pilgrim does not follow the guide. Her steps are not an image of his. Nor is destruction any longer a function of linear backtracking. Greatheart faces Apollyon in order to move toward and so join the travelling I. The turn sanctions both her self-reliance and her desire for human connection. Approaching yet not overtaking the pilgrim, Greatheart bewilders the signifying capacity of linear advance. Disorientation within linear schemes, whereby the pilgrim is imagined simultaneously alone and accompanied, figures Lucy's progress.

Lucy's application of Bunyan's paradigm to her second love relationship may radicalize his vision of female progress; yet, as its series of questions suggests, Lucy's reading is a testimony to the anxiety-ridden position of the novel heroine who insists on the autonomy of her experience, on the authority of her own story by disrupting conventional paradigms of progress. That is, Lucy's subversions cannot readily translate her understanding of her spiritual and social *Bildung* (centered in part in her individualist faith, in part in her love for M. Paul) into a neat secular outcome. Tellingly, the gloss continues,

> I waited my champion. Apollyon came trailing his Hell behind him. I think if Eternity held torment, its form would not be fiery rack, nor its nature, despair. I think that . . . an angel entered Hades. . . . His legacy was suspense—a boon worse than despair.   (542)

Lucy's union with M. Paul only momentarily occupies the level of imaginative possibility.[14] Apollyonic forces, the conventions that in *Villette* propel plots, order resolutions, and, importantly, determine much of the lovers' combative interaction, suspend realization of Lucy's potential orientation outside a conventional androcentric grid.

This reconfiguration of *The Pilgrim's Progress* prepares the novel's ambiguous finish where Lucy abruptly breaks off her narration, having just cited M. Paul on a storm-driven sea. If "sunny imaginations" (596) are left to hope for Paul's safe return and marriage to her, Lucy herself stifles knowledge of her fate. "Peace, be still! . . . Here pause: pause at once" (596). Lucy is in the end as "at sea" as M. Paul. In the tradition of Christian spiritual narrative, she manages to define herself apart from Villette, a latter-day City of Destruction at which the novel's final paragraph looks back. Yet, unlike Bunyan's pilgrims who progress toward the Celestial City and whose place at the marriage feast is secure, Lucy is an uncertain wanderer. She may achieve economic independence through Paul's aid and through her own application transform a day school into a pensionnat. She may uphold the Protestantism that spiritualizes her self-reliance. Even so, the suffocation of her narration has been determined by these apparent triumphs. An estranged pilgrim within conventional plots, Lucy finds that her own capacity to disorient the signifying power of those plots and instead measure divine placement in terms of personal revelation is itself but one more "vanity of vanities."

NOTES

1. All subsequent page references to the novel refer to this edition.
2. Eugene Forcade. Review in *Revue des deux mondes* 15 March 1853, tome 1, 1084–86. Qtd. in Allott.

3. For comprehensive discussions of Victorian revisions of Puritanism in general and Bunyan in particular, see Janet Larson, *Dickens and the Broken Scripture* (Athens: U of Georgia P,) 1985 and Qualls.

4. *David Copperfield* (1850) captures this shift in perspective, whereby pliant passivity gives way to introspective docility as the popular expression of femininity. David's two marriages, first to Dora and then to Agnes, mark no change in the submissive posture of his wife. But Dora is David's "child-wife": she lacks the moral centeredness that makes Agnes, "ever-pointing upward," the ministering angel of David's progress. Her interior gravity acknowledged, Agnes does not assert her independence from male authority, but rather reinscribes herself within it. She is its devoted muse and caretaker, one example of that iconic "angel in the house" popularized by Victorian culture.

5. See W. R. Greg, "Why are Women Redundant?" *National Review* 14 (1862) and Mary Poovey, "The Anathemized Race: The Governess and *Jane Eyre*," *Uneven Developments: The Ideological Work of Gender in Mid Victorian England* (Chicago: U of Chicago P, 1988), 126–63.

6. Lucy's self-description plays on Matt. 23.27 and in so doing asserts the hypocrisy of conventional definitions of womanhood that hold very little of independent female experience: "Woe unto you, scribes and Pharisees, hypocrites! for ye are like unto whited sepulcres, which appear beautiful outward, but are within full of dead men's bones and unclean." All biblical quotations in this essay are from the King James version.

7. Margaret Oliphant, writing at the turn of the century, remarked that before *Jane Eyre* novels were governed by "the instinct of primitive humanity which . . . decided that the woman should be no more than responsive, maintaining a reserve with respect to her feelings." See Margaret Oliphant, *Women Novelists of Queen Victoria's Reign. A Book of Appreciations* (London: Hurst & Blackett, Ltd., 1897; rpt. Folcroft, 1969) 23.

8. See Mary Jacobus, "The Buried Letter: *Villette*," *Reading Women* (New York: Columbia UP, 1986) 46: ". . . what the novel cannot say is eloquently inscribed in its subtext . . . and in the agitated notation and heightened language which signal it."

9. *Bildung* in *Villette* only partially resembles the "plot of inner development" that, according to Marianne Hirsch, is characteristic of nineteenth-century heroines. Lucy does follow the "discontinuous and circular path which . . . culminates in return to origins." She leaves England for Labassecour only to find that her childhood haven, that microcosm of Great Britain, the Bretton household, has preceded her. At the same time, the protagonist who grows from godchild to solitary individual, from social dependent to independent schoolmistress, also charts out the linear scheme of social acquisition founded on individualism that brings to mind the dominant pattern of the male-centered *Bildungsroman*. See Marianne Hirsch, "Spiritual *Bildung*: The Beautiful Soul as Paradigm," *The Voyage In. Fictions of Female Development*, eds. Elizabeth Abel, Marianne Hirsch, and Elizabeth Langland (Hanover, N.H.: Dartmouth; UP New England, 1983) 23–48, 26.

10. In contrast to Goethe's *Wilhelm Meisters Lehrjahre* (1795), which Marianne Hirsch cites as the prototypical *Bildungsroman*, Bunyan's work does not assign a one-to-one correspondence between gender and pattern. Instead, it maps out gender through the configuration of the two patterns. See Hirsch 23–48.

11. In *Sartor Resartus* the harmonious relation between the godlike and nature enables Teufelsdrockh simultaneously to affirm his specificity and his universality. Consciousness of himself validates consciousness of his human connectedness. In

nature he discovers his mirror image: it is "godlike and my *Father's*" (emphasis added); he sees himself again in the totalizing representative of human community, "Man," who is his "Brother." Importantly, it is the Wertherian experience of unrequited love that awakens Teufelsdrockh to his universalized and universalizing identificatory power. He is rejected by Blumine (whose actual name we never learn), the "little Blossom" who, tellingly, shares this allegorical name with Copperfield's Dora: she is barely distinguishable from nature. Blumine is the personification of Teufelsdrockh's own natural-spiritual imbalance. (The editor implies as much with his assurance that "if [Teufelsdrockh's] sudden bereavement in this matter of the Flower-goddess is talked of as a real Doomsday and Dissolution of Nature, [his] own nature is nowise dissolved thereby; but rather compressed closer.") She has only evoked his "empfindliche Empfindsamkeit," the "sick" Romanticism that, divorced from work *and* overtly feminized, was denounced by Goethe, Carlyle, and Dickens alike. Lucy Snowe, by comparison, suffers from unrealized love, which serves not so much as the point of departure as the context for her consciousness of a divinely charged self. See Thomas Carlyle, *Sartor Resartus, A Carlyle Reader*, ed. G. B. Tennyson (New York: Cambridge UP, 1985) 227–228.

12. Like St. Paul, Bunyan insists on woman's essential impurity. See "A Case of Conscience Resolved" (1683). See John Bunyan, *The Miscellaneous Works of John Bunyan*, gen. ed. Roger Sharrock (Oxford: Clarendon, 1976–), vol. 4, ed. T. L. Underwood (1989), 4:291–330, 306.

13. See, for example, Nina Auerbach, *Communities of Women* (Cambridge: Harvard UP, 1978) 112; Sandra Gilbert and Susan Gubar, *The Madwoman in the Attic* (New Haven: Yale UP, 1979) 438; Kate Millet, *Sexual Politics* (Garden City, NY: Doubleday & Co., 1970) 146; Margot Peters, *Charlotte Brontë: Style in the Novel* (Madison: U of Wisconsin P, 1973) 37.

14. Much as actress Vashti's passionate self-expression is confined to the theater.

WORKS CITED

Allott, Miriam, ed. *The Brontés: The Critical Heritage*. London: Routledge, 1974.

Bronté, Charlotte. *Jane Eyre*. New York: Norton, 1971.

———. *Villette*. Harmondsworth: Penguin, 1979.

Bunyan, John. *The Pilgrim's Progress*. Harmondsworth: Penguin, 1984.

Gilbert, Sandra and Susan Gubar. *The Madwoman in the Attic*. New Haven: Yale UP, 1979.

Knox, Ronald A. *Essays in Satire*. London: Sheed and Ward, 1928.

Leavis, Q. D. "Villette," in *Collected Essays*. 3 vols., ed. I. G. Singh. Cambridge: Cambridge UP, 1983.

Qualls, Barry V. *The Secular Pilgrims of Victorian Fiction*. New York: Cambridge UP, 1982.

Who's Doing It? Fifteen Years of Work on Victorian Detective Fiction

Anne Humpherys

Let's begin with the plot. Detective fiction has what Dennis Porter calls "backward construction." It starts with the crime and continues with the observations and deductions of the detective which finally result in his reconstruction of the actions that led to and followed from the crime. That is, in the detective fiction plot, we start in the "present", and then move back into a reconstruction of the past, and come back to the present when the detective makes meaning of past events by analyzing motive, discarding false or misleading clues, ordering events, and ultimately revealing the only possible explanation of the crime. There can be at closure several reconstructions, but only one will be "true," the one that accounts for all the events in an orderly, cause-and-effect way.

Recent work on Victorian detective fiction[1] follows a similar "backward construction"—that is, from a contemporary perspective critics see a "crime," usually an ideological one, and proceed to "reveal" it by a careful reconstruction of the contexts and omissions of the text. So I too begin this review with the discovery of a "crime" in fifteen years of work on Victorian detective fiction, namely the exclusion of the majority of such fiction (a good deal written by women) from critical attention in favor of an obsessive return of critical analysis to a handful of canonized texts by three male writers—Charles Dickens, Wilkie Collins, and Arthur Conan Doyle.

There were dozens of other Victorian detective writers,[2] including Arthur Morrison, whose detective Martin Hewitt replaced Sherlock Holmes in *The Strand* when Conan Doyle killed him off in episode 24. Steven Knight, in "Radical Thrillers" (in *Watching the Detectives*, ed. Ian A. Bell and Graham Daldry [St. Martin's, 1990:172–87]) argues that Morrison's detective is actually "a deliberate answer to Sherlock Holmes" (176). James Sutherland has estimated that "by the mid-1890s . . . of the 800 weekly papers in Britain, 240 were carrying some variety of detective story."[3]

Nonetheless, in a survey of some 170 items on Victorian detective fiction from 1980 through 1992, we found over 80 of them were separate pieces on Sherlock Holmes.[4] In addition, most general histories and book-length analyses of a detective fiction say something about the Holmes stories, but not much if anything about anyone else except Dickens (with 10, the next largest number of pieces on a single author, mostly *The Mystery of Edwin Drood*) and Collins (10 or so on *The Woman in White* and *The Moonstone*; we found not a single piece on Collins's woman detective in *The Law and the Lady*, though I did hear a paper at the 1993 Dickens Universe conference by Theresa Magnum on "Detection and Deformity" in this novel).

To reconstruct this pattern of criticism, the following general review begins with an opening survey of general material on Victorian detective fiction followed by sections on recent works on the Sherlock Holmes stories; on Wilkie Collins's and Charles Dickens' detectives, and finally closes with a survey of contemporary detective novels that are set in late Victorian England.

1. MOTIVE, MEANS, AND OPPORTUNITY

The standard history of Victorian detective fiction usually starts with Edgar Allan Poe's Dupin stories, followed by the detectives of Charles Dickens and Wilkie Collins, and culminating in the first appearance of Sherlock Holmes in *A Study in Scarlet* in 1887. Though there are sometimes references to other Victorian detective fiction writers after Sherlock Holmes, most serious critical works jump from Conan Doyle to Agatha Christie. The rise to prominence in the last decade of Elizabeth Braddon's *Lady Audley's Secret* reflects the rise in critical interest in the sensation novel which sometimes overlaps an interest in detective fiction and sometimes does not.[5]

We are lucky to have in the *Dictionary of Literary Biography* series (vol. 70), *British Mystery Writers 1860–1919*, edited by Bernard Benstock and Thomas F. Stalley, with entries for 35 writers.[6] But for the most part, the dozens of detective writers of the 1890s and early 1900s are mentioned, if at all, mainly in general descriptive histories of the genre, and then only briefly. For example, Audrey Peterson, in a popularly written survey *Victorian Masters of Mystery: From Wilkie Collins to Conan Doyle* (Ungar, 1984), focuses on Collins, Dickens, and LeFanu, citing Elizabeth Braddon, James Payn, and the American Anna Katherine Green only to contrast with the more well-known figures. Her book does contain a useful checklist of detective fictions by these latter writers, however. Leroy Lad Panek, in a good general survey, *An Introduction to the Detective Story* (Bowling Green Press, 1987) has, in addition to a whole chapter on Collins and the sensation novelists, one on "Turn-of-the-Century Writers" focusing on the influence of and advances over the Sherlock Holmes stories, but none of his analyses of individual writers is longer than a paragraph or two. A collection of essays edited by Clive Bloom, Brian Docherty, Jane Gibb, and Keith Shand entitled *Nineteenth-Century Suspense: From Poe to Conan Doyle* (Macmillan, 1988) treats only Poe, Dickens, Collins, Doyle, *Dracula*, and Jack the Ripper. T. J. Binyon's, *'Murder Will Out': The Detective in Fiction* (Oxford, 1989) has a few paragraphs devoted to Morrison's Martin Hewitt and George R. Sims's Dorcas Dene. In a naively written book on the theological implications of detective fiction, Robert S. Paul (*Whatever Happened to Sherlock Holmes: Detective Fiction, Popular Theology, and Society* [Southern Illinois, 1991]) adds to the obligatory discussion of Poe, Collins, and Doyle some remarks about H. F. Wood's Inspector Bryce in *Passenger from Scotland Yard* (1888). A more sophisticated analysis is Martin Priestman's in *Detective Fiction and Literature* (St. Martin's, 1991) which seeks to articulate the relationship between popular culture and "established literature" using *The Moonstone* and the Holmes stories.

Thus, even though there has certainly been an increase of interest in Victorian detective fiction in the last decade, as evidenced by three Oxford University Press anthologies that appeared in 1992,[7] the critical picture is a little unbalanced.

Certainly part of the reason for the failure to pay attention to the majority of Victorian detective fiction is the difficulty of getting the texts. Many of the early detective fictions have not been collected from the periodicals in which they first appeared, and most individual volumes have been long out of print and even when in print were not collected by research libraries.[8] Elizabeth Braddon is an example; only *Lady Audley's Secret*, of all her 100 or more novels, is most libraries. There are, however, additional reasons for the concentration on Sherlock Holmes and Collins's two detective novels and the marginalization of other writers in the surveys. To return to a point I have made elsewhere,[9] late-twentieth-century critics have a good deal of difficulty finding a position from which to analyze the popular fiction of the last century. Our interest in Wilkie Collins began as an extension of our interest in Dickens, and we now treat his works as though they *are* by Dickens, that is of major literary importance. On the other hand, we turn to the Sherlock Holmes stories for a cultural and mythic resonance we have also found in *Frankenstein* and *Dracula*, two other texts which have been canonized over the past two decades (*Lady Audley's Secret* has now become the most recent popular text to achieve that status) and thus a fertile ground for various structural and cultural critical projects.[10] With pulp literature, we have much more difficulty in finding a critical vocabulary and analytical method that does not automatically denigrate the materials.

Given their limitation of reference, many recent works specifically on Victorian detective fiction have nonetheless had an interesting revisionist project, that is, to reveal various "crimes" of omission, namely the marginalization of women; the denial of brutality, sexuality, and violence in the upper and middle classes; a naiveté about the rationality and scientism of the detective process itself, and the social conservatism revealed in the return to order inevitable in the detective plot. Take for example, the survey, *The Lady Investigates: Women Detectives and Spies in Fiction* (St. Martin's, 1981) by Patricia Craig and Mary Cadogan, which has as its main virtue its insistence on the centrality of women as detectives and detective story writers. This work contains two opening chapters that sumarize both British and American works up until WWI which have women detectives at their center, including the first (predating Sherlock Holmes by over 20 years) Mrs. Paschal's *The Revelations of a Lady Detective* (1861), and *Lady Molly of Scotland Yard* by Baroness Orczy as well as Catherine L. Pirkis's *The Experiences of Loveday Brooke, Lady Detective* (1894), Fergus Hume's *Hagar of the Pawn-Shop* (1898), McDonnell Bodkin's *Dora Myrl, the Lady Detective* (1900), and the novels of Anna Katharine Green (1846–1935). (A recent book on Green is Patricia Maida, *Mother of Detective Fiction: The Life and Work of Anna Katherine Green* [Bowling Green Popular Press, 1989]).

Approaching the same topic from a different angle, Catherine Belsey, in "Deconstructing the Text: Sherlock Holmes" from *Critical Practices* (excerpted in *Popular Fiction: Technology, Ideology, Production, Reading* edited by Tony Bennett [Routledge, 1990]), discusses among other cultural attitudes the mysogony in the Sherlock Holmes stories and concludes "in the Sherlock Holmes stories classic realism ironically tells a truth, though not the truth about the world which is the project of classic realism . . . [but] the truth about ideology, the truth which ideology represses, its own existence as ideology itself" (285). Susan Katz gave a paper on "Dispossession and Self-Creation: The Case of the Female Sleuth" at the 1993 Dickens Universe Conference in which she examined the way in which the women sleuths of the late

Victorian period (Loveaday Brooks and Bella Thorne) invite an examination of the problems of women's identity.

Beth Kalikoff, *Murder and Moral Decay in Victorian Popular Literature* (UMI Research Press, 1986), argues that "both men and women return to the bestial in late-century crime literature" (129) and uses among her sources three Victorian detective novels: Fergus Hume, *The Mystery of a Hansom Cab* (1880), Robert and Marie Leighton, *Michael Dred, Detective* (1899), and Israel Zangwill, *The Big Bow Mystery* (1892), supposedly the first locked room detective fiction. Jeanne F. Bedall turns to issues of class in "Melodrama and Manners: Changing Attitudes toward Class Distinction in English Detective Fiction, 1868–1939" (*Clues: A Journal of Detection* 1:15–23 1980), while Ronald R. Thomas's article in the first volume of *Victorian Literature and Culture*, "Minding the Body Politic: The Romance of Science and the Revision of History in Victorian Detective Fiction" (1991:233–254), turns to politics. Inevitably using the Sherlock Holmes stories as a paradigm for all Victorian detective fiction, Thomas argues that "the tendency to suppress political facts with scientific theory in the Holmes canon recapitulates a recurring narrative pattern in Victorian detective fiction" (245), and that "Victorian detective fiction commonly acknowledged . . . political 'crimes' only to then obscure and excuse them with a scientific investigation that focused attention on the criminal body" (252 n.2).

Robin Woods in " 'His Appearance Is Against Him': the Emergence of the Detective" (in *The Cunning Craft: Original Essays on Detective Fiction and Contemporary Literary Theory* edited by Ronald G. Walter and June M. Frazer [Western Illinois UP, 1990]: 24–40) uses Foucault to show that "In his role as mediator the detective [of Poe, Collins, and Doyle] embodies a code of 'professional' behavior that both enables the solution of mystery and distances us from the crime itself." Finally, Marie Christine Leps argues in her excellent study of the shift from an environmental explanation of crime to a biological one at the end of the century, *Apprehending the Criminal: The Production of Deviance in Nineteenth-Century Discourse* (Duke, 1992), that "if the basic plot development sequence (problem-investigation-solution) and the theoretical postulates of the [Science of Deduction and Analysis] reproduce and reinforce the age's positivist faith in science as a solution to social problems, the general hermeneutic quest for truth led by Holmes and the other characters calls into question the basic epistemological presuppositions of contemporary methods of knowledge production" (201).

Not all the recent works on Victorian detective fiction focus on what is not there, however. One useful bibliographical essay by Ayresome Johns,

"Detective Fiction in Periodicals" (*Antiquarian Book Monthly Review* 17:386–91, 1991), aimed at collectors, identifies the Victorian periodicals that published a large number of detective stories, and names many of the contributors. There is the *Strand* of course, which, in addition to the Sherlock Holmes stories also published some by Grant Allen, Arthur Morrison and L. T. Meade, and later those by E. C. Bentley. *Pearson's Weekly* published R. Austin Freeman. Other magazines publishing detective fiction in the 1890s included *Windsor*, the *Harmsworth*, and *London Magazine*.

But the majority of articles and chapters of books treating Victorian detective fiction in the last fifteen years focus only on Arthur Conan Doyle's Sherlock Holmes.

2. SHERLOCK HOLMES: "ELEMENTARY, MY DEAR WATSON"

The standard edition of the Sherlock Holmes stories is now the nine volume *Oxford Sherlock Holmes* edited by Owen Dudley Edwards (1993) and reviewed in *TLS* by John Bayley (12 November 1993:6–7). *Sherlock Holmes: The Major Short Stories with Contemporary Critical Essays* edited by John A. Hodgson, (St. Martins, 1994) is for classroom use. One journal is completely devoted to Holmesiana: *Baker Street Journal*, a chatty quarterly made up of short articles that range from informative notes for Sherlock buffs (Applewhite Mineyard, "The Religious Views of Sherlock Holmes" 39 [1989]: 198–202) to more scholarly topics, such as Bonnie Plummer, "Meta-fiction in the Sherlock Holmes Saga" (40 [1991]: 78–82).

On the other hand, general reference works tend to ignore what Michael Hardwick calls "higher scholarship." Bibliographies subsequent to the magisterial Ronald DeWaal, *World Bibliography of Sherlock Holmes* (N.Y. Graphic Society, 1972) include Richard Lancelyn Green and John Michael Gibson, *A Bibliography of Arthur Conan Doyle* (Clarendon, 1983), 600 pages that cover every conceivable version of the primary sources but none of the secondary material. Hardwick's *The Complete Guide to Sherlock Holmes* (Weidenfeld, 1986) includes outlines of the life and work, indexes of characters and places (as does Scott Bullard and Michael Collins, *Who's Who in Sherlock Holmes* [Taplinger, 1980]), and illustrations from magazines in which many of the stories were originally published, but deliberately eschews academic articles. An exception to the determinedly non-scholarly bent of much reference work on Holmes is Philip A. Shreffler, ed. in *The Baker Street Reader: Cornerstone*

Writings about Sherlock Holmes (Greenwood, 1984) which surveys 50 years serious Holmes scholarship.

General biographical works include Julian Symons, *Conan Doyle: Portrait of an Artist* (Whizard/Deutsch, 1979), Don Richard Cox, *Arthur Conan Doyle* (Ungar, 1985), and Jacqueline Jaffee, *Arthur Conan Doyle* (Twayne, 1987). Collections of essays on Holmes include Allen Eyles, comp., *Sherlock Holmes: A Centenary Celebration* (Harper, 1986), which examines the influence of the Doyle canon on popular culture and includes copious illustrations and photographs and an annotated chronology of "Sherlock Holmes in Performance" from 1899 to 1986. Studies of origins and sources include Michael Harrison, *A Study in Surmise: The Making of Sherlock Homes* (Gaslight, 1984); Walter Klinefelter, *Origins of Sherlock Holmes* (Gaslight, 1983), and Donald Aitcheson Redmond, *Sherlock Holmes: A Study in Sources* (McGill-Queen's U.P., 1982).

Perhaps because of Doyle's medical training, doctors seem particularly fascinated with Holmes, there being six articles either by doctors or published in medical journals. Psychiatrist Michael Shepherd in *Sherlock Holmes and the Case of Dr. Freud* (Tavistock, 1985) has written a short and entertaining monograph arguing that Holmes and Freud share a form of scientific method connected with the power of "mythopoetic imagination." In his discussion, he cites detective fiction, medical history, art connoisseurship, psychoanalytic material and literary criticism. More medical perhaps, Pasquale Accardo (*Diagnosis and Detection: the Medical Iconography of Sherlock Holmes* [Fairleigh Dickinson, 1987]) explores the literary and medical sources of the stories. Alvin E. Rodin and Jack D. Key have a similar focus in *Medical Casebook of Doctor Arthur Conan Doyle: From Practitioner to Sherlock Holmes and Beyond* (Krieger, 1984). The most quirky perhaps is another piece of these two authors, "Arthur Conan Doyle's Thesis on Tabes Dorsalis" for the *Journal of the American Medical Association* (247 [1982]: 646–50).

Most of the more than 80 pieces we identified concerning the Sherlock Holmes stories are products of buffs and odd connections. (My personal favorite among these is Madeleine B. Stern, *The Game's A Head: A Phrenological Study of Sherlock Holmes and Arthur Conan Doyle* [Green, 1982]). There are a few more scholarly pieces that focus on cultural attitudes about race, class, and gender as revealed in the stories. Chapters or long discussions on Holmes appear in the following works: Stephen Knight, *Form and Ideology in Crime Fiction* (Indiana, 1981); Dennis Porter, *The Pursuit of Crime* op. cit., and various references throughout Glenn W. Most and William W. Stowe, eds., *The Poetics of Murder: Detective Fiction and Literary Theory* (Harcourt, 1983).

Of scholarly articles on Holmes, one of the most interesting is "Detecting the Beggar: Arthur Conan Doyle, Henry Mayhew, and 'The Man with the Twisted Lip' " by Audrey Jaffe (*Representations* 31:96–117, 1991). Focusing on the anxieties about "false beggars" and Holmes's passion for disguise, Jaffe examines Doyle's story as a metaphor for the problem of identity within the hierarchy of Victorian laborers. She also considers Doyle's and Mayhew's anxieties over their own identities as authors and their fictional representations of other work-related identities, showing how these identities are used in the fiction of Doyle and Mayhew both to define and undermine social categories as they are constructed through work. In another critical study ("Sherlock Holmes Codes the Social Body," *ELH* 57:685–708, 1990), Rosemary Jann has as her main objective to consider "Doyle's use of various nineteenth-century typologies to give 'scientific' support to a particular social order and to focus on instabilities in the classification of class and gender that betray Doyle's ideological investments" (687). She also examines the way in which Holmes's "positivistic science" works to soothe anxieties over "the disruptive power of the irrational and the unconscious" (705).

Lydia A. Fillingham (" 'The Colorless Skein of Life': Threats to the Private Sphere in Conan Doyle's *A Study in Scarlet*", *ELH* 56:667–88, 1990) examines the theme of Mormonism, exotic and heathen in Victorian eyes, and how it plays into the Victorian issues of the private-public spheres. Christopher Clausen ("Sherlock Holmes, Order, and the Late Victorian Mind," *Georgia Review* 38:104–23, 1984) accounts for Holmes's status as a popular hero because, by solving crimes against the rich and famous as well as property crimes against the middle class, he defends the social order of the privileged who have come to feel threatened because of the perceived growth of poverty, social unrest, and the rise of socialism. In the collection *The Cunning Craft* (op. cit.) Thomas J. Farrell "deconstructs" "The Final Problem" using Derrida, concluding that "the textuality of 'The Final Problem' virtually mandated the revival of Holmes" ("Deconstructing Moriarity: False Armageddon at Reichenbach," 66).

Two articles in the journal *Clues* (published by Bowling Green Popular Press) focussed on structure and genre in the Holmes stories: Paul F. Ferguson, "Narrative Vision in 'The Hound of the Baskervilles' " (1:2 [1980]: 224–30), and Michael Atkinson "Virginity Preserved and the Secret Marriage of Sherlock Holmes: The Theory of Popular Romance Applied to Detective Fiction" ["A Scandal in Bohemia"] (2:1 (1981): 62–69). But in the last decade the most important study of form in the stories—specifically Holmes's use of logic—is the collection of essays edited by Umberto Eco and Thomas A. Sebeok, *The Sign of Three: Dupin, Holmes, Peirce*, (Indiana, 1983). To over-simplify a complex and interesting set of essays, the central focus of this collection is the exemplification through the Dupin and Holmes stories of a type of logic formulated by the philosopher C. S. Peirce, namely "abduction," that is, a form of inference in explanatory hypotheses. In the process, the authors in this collection try to counter the general assumption that Holmes's method of logic hovers somewhere between deduction and induction.[11] On the other hand, abduction, as defined by Peirce, "depends on our hope, sooner or later, to guess at the conditions under which a given kind of phenomenon will present itself" (2). So "we often derive from observation strong intima-tions of truth, without being able to specify what were the circumstances we had observed which conveyed those intimations" (18). Sherlock Holmes, as the best example of this logical process, becomes a "consulting semioti-cian" (19).

The centrality of the Sherlock Holmes stories to any study of Victorian detective fiction, or detective fiction in general, is not likely to change. Unlike other previously popular texts like *Frankenstein* and *Dracula*, however, the Holmes stories have maintained their fascination for non-specialists, and the professional academic critics have come to them only recently. But this is not true for the next set of materials, those on Wilkie Collins and Charles Dickens, whose detectives have, until recently, essentially defined academic interests in the genre.

3. COLLINS AND DICKENS: THEY DOES THE POLICE IN DIFFERENT VOICES

Academic literary interest in the Victorian detective has traditionally fo-cussed on three novels: *Bleak House* by Dickens, and *The Woman in White* and *The Moonstone* by Wilkie Collins. In addition, there has been a minor industry in speculation about the development and conclusions to *The Mystery of Edwin Drood*, culminating in Carlo Fruttero and Franco Lucentini, *The D. Case, or The Truth about The Mystery of Edwin Drood* (Harcourt, 1992). A nice commentary on this trend in scholarship, though unfortunately poorly plotted and not very well-written, are the two detective novels by William J. Palmer, *The Detective and Mr. Dickens* (Ballantine, 1992) and *The Highway-man and Mr. Dickens* (St. Martin's, 1992), which purport to be secret journals of Wilkie Collins which recount the detective work of Dickens and cast Collins in the role of his Dr. Watson. For Victorianists, perhaps the most amusing part of these books will be the discovery that the author gives various workers and low-life characters in the novels the names of eminent twentieth-century Victorian scholars.

In *The Pursuit of Crime: Art and Ideology in Detective Fiction* (Yale, 1981) Dennis Porter discusses *The Moonstone* in terms of its structure. But, of the articles and books on detectives and detection in Collins and Dickens in the last fifteen years, most have been influenced by Foucault and are concerned with processes of "surveillance" and "detection" in terms of issues of professionalization, the conflict between the public and private sphere, and, under the influence of the feminist re-visioning of Victorian literature and culture, the interplay of these issues in the construction of gender and the role of women in Victorian society. In his dissertation, "The Way of the Labyrinth: Mystery and Detection in the Novels of Charles Dickens" (Toronto, 1980), Patrick Joseph Kelly argues that "the mystery in many of Charles Dickens's novels is ultimately unsolvable, although it can usually be approached by detectives." Characteristically, Kelly expands the label "detective" to include David Copperfield, Pip, Esther, John Harmon, and John Jasper.

The most significant of the published works is D. A. Miller, *The Novel and the Police* (University of California, 1988), a Foucauldian reading of Victorian fiction (including *Bleak House* and *The Woman in White*) which brilliantly demonstrates the ways in which Victorian strategies of surveillance and incarceration are part of the project of Victorian fiction itself. His chapter on *Bleak House* demonstrates how "the themes of power and social control are passed accordingly from the abyssmal filiations of the law into the capable hands of the detective police" (66), while that on *The Moonstone* demonstrates that this novel "displaces the structures of detective fiction only to restage its ideology of everyday life in more ambitious ways" (49).

Increased interest in Wilkie Collins in the last ten years or so has resulted in a noticeable increase of books and articles about this author. Some general works include Audrey Peterson, *Victorian Masters of Mystery: From Wilkie Collins to Conan Doyle* (Ungar, 1984) and a chapter on Collins by Jeanne F. Bedell in *Twelve Englishmen of Mystery* edited by Earl F. Bargainnier (Popular, 1984). Many of the most recent scholarly works on Collins are outgrowths of interest in the sensation novel and its role in issues of gender construction and resistance to gender, as also indicated by a number of articles on the women in Collins's novels. An example of this interest in Collins's sensation novels is the large role that an analyses of these novels plays in Thomas

Boyle's well-received *Black Swine in the Sewers of Hampstead: Beneath the Surface of Victorian Sensationalism* (Viking, 1989). Boyle also has a charming chapter on his own "detecting"—"Adventures of a Scholar Detective."

The scholarly book-length studies of Collins began with Sue Lonoff's *Wilkie Collins and His Victorian Readers: A Study in the Rhetoric of Authorship* (AMS, 1982) and have included, most recently, Nicholas Rance, *Wilkie Collins and Other Sensation Novelists: Walking the Moral Hospital* (Fairleigh Dickinson, 1991) and Tamar Heller's *Dead Secrets: Wilkie Collins and the Female Gothic* (Yale, 1992) with a chapter on "Blank Spaces: Ideological Tensions and the Detective Work of *The Moonstone*."

But surprisingly, pieces specifically on the detectives in Collins's work are few. Rather, most pieces on detectives in Collins, as in Boyle's *Black Swine*, use the term metaphorically as a way of calling attention to the critical project itself. For example, Mark M. Hennelly Jr., in "Reading Detection in *The Woman in White*" (*Texas Studies in Literature and Language* 30:449–67, 1980) analyzes Collins's novel from the perspective of reader-response criticism, showing how modern readers are similar to and different from the original Victorian audience. Hennelly's critical stance looks both back and forward: he rather old-fashionedly considers Collins's novel "escapist fiction" (his piece was written in 1980), but he also shows how the text illuminates the problem of the divided self and the realities of Victorian life. Another example of this metaphoric use of "detection" is in the chapter entitled "The Critic as Detective: Mystery and Method in *The Moonstone*" in W. David Shaw's *Victorians and Mystery: Crises of Representation* (Cornell, 1990). Shaw examines theories of criminal detection in Collins's novel in this chapter (and in Browning's *The Ring and the Book*) in the context of theories of history and compares the role of the historian as an "historical agent" to that of the reader/critic of detective fiction.

However, it is contemporary detective fiction writers who really shine the bull's-eye on the Victorian detective himself (and herself) and illuminate for us what the issues of class and gender and the roles of sex and violence in crime might "really" have been like as well as what contemporary writers like Conan Doyle distorted or omitted.

4. CONTEMPORARY DETECTIVE FICTION: THE RETURN OF THE REPRESSED

The trend towards setting current detective novels in Victorian Britain probably started with the 'additions" to the Sherlock Holmes canon in the

1970s—*The Seven-Per-Cent Solution* by Nicholas Meyer (1974)[12] (though there had been many earlier parodies and plagiarisms, and in 1902 Mark Twain wrote *A Double Barrelled Detective Story* in which Sherlock Holmes singularly fails to solve the mystery[13]). Such play-offs of the Sherlock Holmes stories continue apace, a recent one being Meyer's fiction, *The Canary Trainer: From the Memoirs of John H. Watson* (Norton, 1993) and *The List of 7* by Mark Frost (Morrow, 1993) in which Conan Doyle tackles the Jack the Ripper case. Sena Jeter Naslund writes about *Sherlock in Love* (Godine, 1993), bringing Holmes and Irene Adler back together. That leads to what is the most interesting and ambitious of these resurrections of Holmes, the three books by Carole Nelson Douglas in which Irene Adler herself is the detective. *Good Night, Mr. Holmes* (1990) retells "The Scandal in Bohemia" as Irene experienced it. Two subsequent novels, *Good Morning, Irene* (1991) and *Irene at Large* (1992) bring Holmes and Irene together again, though Holmes detection continues to be inferior to Irene's. Nelson Douglas's project in setting her novels in the midst of the Holmes canon is to introduce the woman's perspective into both detective fiction *and* the unqualifiedly Victorian male world represented by the Sherlock Holmes stories.

In fact, a number of these recent Victorian detective fictions are like the critical analyses surveyed above, efforts at a re-evaluation of class and gender, particularly in their relationship to sex and violence, in the Victorian period. Of course, some of these contemporary novels are not serious about this project of recuperation, and mainly use the Victorian setting as a device to vary the formula. The detective fictions by Peter Lovesey (*Bertie and the Tinman* [1987] and *Bertie and the Seven Bodies* [1990]), have the Prince of Wales as the detective, and though there are some revelations about the scandalous lives of the rich and famous and some titillation about homosexuality, the main use of the Victorian setting is to complicate the solution—how can the Prince of Wales do his detecting without being seen to do it? Similarly, the fictions of Emily Brightwell (*The Inspector and Mrs. Jeffries* [1993] and *Mrs. Jeffries Dusts for Clues* [1993]) have a faint comment on class and gender. Basically simple puzzles, the stories are complicated by the relationship between an incompetent inspector at Scotland Yard (promoted beyond his capacity) who is repeatedly saved from failure and embarrassment by the detective work of his housekeeper and her staff. The interest is mainly in the way Mrs. Jeffries manages to do her detecting without anyone knowing who she is, particularly her employer, and her ability to make sure he thinks he actually solved the crime. Another series that has a marginal comment on Victorian gender arrangements is that by Elizabeth Peters, whose woman detective, Amelia Peabody, solves most of her crimes on archeological digs with her husband.[14] The main interest here, however, is in the ways in which the details of archaeology fit into the solutions of the crimes.

The series of Victorian detective novels by Ray Harrison (the first is *Why Kill Arthur Potter?* [1983] followed by five more) is between the surface use of Victoriana and the more serious projects of recuperation and social criticism of Ann Perry and Carole Nelson Douglas. His novels feature a Scotland Yard team of Sergeant Bragg and Constable Morton, who reverse the class relationships in Ann Perry's novels. Constable Morton is an aristocrat while his immediate boss Sergeant Bragg is working-class. The feminist figure is Catherine Marston, an upper-class woman working as a journalist. These differences allow for some indirect exploration of class relations in the 1890s, but more compelling is the "presence of the present" in Richard Altick's phrase—the way the details of late Victorian England can be experienced as current. For example, in *Counterfeit of Murder* (1986), characters talk about what we know (but they don't yet) are the Jack the Ripper murders.

The detective fiction of Ann Perry, however, has the most serious project of re-writing the Victorian detective novel in terms of race, class, and gender. This project is achieved in her novels through two main devices: one, the class difference between her husband-and-wife detective team—Inspector Thomas Pitt of Scotland Yard, who as a policeman is clearly lower-middle-class, and Charlotte Ellison Pitt who comes from an upper-class family—and by the location and type of crimes. Perry has started a second series that has Monk, born in a humble Northumberland fishing village and now secretly suffering from amnesia, who works with Hester Letterly, of a higher class but impoverished and more importantly, an ex-Crimean nurse, as well as Oliver Rathbone, a very upper-class barrister. The varieties of tensions, misunderstandings, and tentative accommodations generated by these class differences are no small part of the interest in her novels.

Almost all the crimes in Ann Perry's novels take place in upper-middle or aristocratic families. In addition to the murder of members of this class by their own (never the "dangerous classes"), there is adultery, homosexuality, and lesbianism; violent sexual crimes of sodomy, child-abuse rings, incest, and rape; abortion; financial depredations, such as one where upper-class parents of dead Crimean officers are bilked by a charming son of one of their own, who is in turn murdered by his own brother (*The Face of a Stranger* [1990]); devastating miscarriages of justice—a female servant is dismissed without references because she is made pregnant from a rape by the son of her employer, and a servant is hanged for a crime he did not commit because his employers wish to avoid the scandal of a daughter's suicide (*A Dangerous Mourning* (1991). Figures of authority (whether they be the higher-ups in Scotland Yard or the hospitals) want only to look good to the upper classes and have no hesitation in sacrificing their underlings to their social desires. In one case, (*Silence in Hanover Close* [1988], Superintendent Ballarat, Pitt's superior, allows Pitt himself to be charged for the crime of murder because he does not want to ruffle the feathers of an aristocratic family, whose matriarch has set Pitt up after murdering two people. Other issues in this novel include treason, transvestitism, manslaughter, blackmail, and male prostitution, all in one powerful upper-class family.

Beyond these crimes of upper-class sex and violence, an attack on the social constraints on women are part of the fabric of Perry's novels. The worst enforcers of female repression are the matriarchs of the families, but, on the other hand, a couple of widowed women with aristocratic backgrounds and money become sources of support and liberation. While there is nothing startling for Victorianists about these and the other social emphases in Perry's novels, they do draw stark attention to the absences in the Sherlock Holmes and other Victorian detective fictions. One could think about them as "meta-Victorian detective fictions." There is also something to be said about the popularity of these works with late twentieth-century readers, but I must leave that for another place.

Michael Holquist has remarked that "what the structural and philosophical presuppositions of myth and depth psychology were to modernism . . . the detective is to post-modernism."[15] And it is the late Victorian period that essentially produced the detective that has become so central in the works of Juan Luis Borges, Alain Robbe-Grillet, Ishmael Reed, and Robert Coover among others. What I hope and expect is that the next fifteen years of work on Victorian detective fiction will move beyond the Sherlock Holmes stories, *Bleak House*, and *The Moonstone* to a thorough recovery and serious analysis of the dozens of other texts that contributed to the shape of this enduring and problematic figure.

NOTES

1. The books, chapters, and articles discussed in this review are those which are concerned with Victorian detective fiction in and of itself. There are of course other closely related genres of fiction—mysteries, crime stories, and ghost stories.

There also continues to be an abiding interest in the true life crime story, particularly Jack the Ripper. Since the focus in the recent works of Victorian true crime is seldom on detectives and detection, I do not cover this material in this review.

The category "Victorian detective fiction" includes British stories written between 1860 and 1905. The highpoint for detective fiction during the Victorian period was the 1890s.

2. For example, preceding Sherlock Holmes are the fictional *Recollections of a Detective Police-Officer* by "Thomas Waters" [William Russell] (1856) and Mrs. Paschal, *The Revelations of a Lady Detective* (1861). Some other detective fiction authors, mostly of the 1890s, include Grant Allen, Robert Barr, Frank Barrish, M. M'Donnel Bodkin, Milton Danvers, B. L. Farjeon, André Forester Junior, R. Austin Freeman, Major Arthur Griffiths, Headon Hill, William Hope Hodgson, Fergus Hume, Robert and Marie Leighton, Laurence Lynch, Richard Marsh, L. T. Meade and Robert Eustace, Arthur Morrison, J. E. P. Muddock (Dick Donovan), E. P. Oppenheim, Baroness Orczy, Hugh Owen, James Payn, Catherine L. Pirkis, Hesketh Prichard, Clarence Rook, George R. Sims, Hawley Smart, Victor L. Whitechurch, Florence Warden, Mrs. Henry Wood, H. F. Wood, and Israel Zangwill. *Victorian Detective Fiction* (Bodley Head, 1966), a catalogue of a collection put together by Grahame Green and Dorothy Glover, has over 400 entries covering the period 1840–1900.

3. *The Stanford Companion to the Victorian Novel.* Stanford, 1989.

4. My research assistant Lisa Green did a bibliographical search and some summaries. I am indebted to her for her thorough and professional work on this project.

5. See for example Anthea Trodd, *Domestic Crime in the Victorian Novel* (St. Martin's, 1989), especially her chapter on "The Policeman and the Lady" which discusses the transgression in this relationship of the public and private spheres.

6 There are entries of varying length for Grant Allen, Robert Barr, E. C. Bentley, M. McDonnell Bodkin, Mary Elizabeth Braddon, Ernest Bramah, John Buchan, G. K. Chesterton, Erskine Childers, Wilkie Collins, Charles Dickens, Sir Arthur Conan Doyle, J. S. Fletcher, R. Austin Freeman, H. Rider Haggard, William Hope Hodgson, E. W. Hornung, Fergus Hume, Sheridan Le Fanu, William Le Queux, Marie Belloc Lowndes, A. E. W. Mason, Arthur Morrison, E. Phillips Oppenheim, Emma Baroness Orczy, Sir Max Pemberton, Eden Phillpotts, Angus Reach, Saxe Rohmer (Arthur Henry Sarsfied Ward), Joseph Shearing (Gabrielle Margaret Vere Campbell), George R. Sims, Bram Stoker, Edgar Wallace, H. G. Wells, and Victor L. Whitechurch.

7. Jack Adrian, ed. with an Introduction by Julian Symons, *Detective Stories from the Strand* (1992); Michael Cox, ed. *Victorian Tales of Mystery and Detection* (1992); Michael Cox, ed. *Victorian Detective Stories: An Oxford Anthology* (1992). See also Patricia Craig, ed. *The Oxford Book of English Detective Stories* (1990), Edward Wagenknecht, ed. *Murder by Gaslight: Victorian Tales* (Prentice-Hall, 1949), E. F. Bleiler, ed. *A Treasury of Victorian Detective Stories* (Scribner's 1979), and Isaac Asimov, Charles G. Waugh, and Martin H. Greenberg, eds. *The Best Crime Stories of the Nineteenth-Century* (Dembner, 1988).

8. In the 1970s, Hugh Green edited a number of volumes that collected some of these stories. See *The Rivals of Sherlock Holmes: Early Detective Stories* (Bodley Head and Pantheon, 1970); *More Rivals of Sherlock Holmes: Cosmopolitan Crimes* (Bodley Head, 1971); *The Crooked Counties* (Bodley Head, 1975) or *The Further Rivals of Sherlock Holmes* (Pantheon, 1973), and *The Americn Rivals of Sherlock Holmes* (Bodley Head and Pantheon, 1976). See also Alan K. Russell,

ed. *Rivals of Sherlock Holmes* (Castle, 1978), 40 stories in facsimile from late Victorian magazines, and *The Rivals of Sherlock Holmes Two* (Castle, 1979), with 46 more stories. There are ten Victorian detective stories in Michele B. Slung, ed. *Crime on Her Mind: Fifteen Stories of Female Sleuths from the Victorian Era to the Forties* (Pantheon, 1975).

9. See my article "Locating the Popular Text" in *Victorian Literature and Culture* 19 (1991): 351–59.

10. A good example of this is the chapter "*Frankenstein*, Detective Fiction, and *Jekyll and Hyde*" in *Dr. Jekyll and Mr. Hyde After One Hundred Years*, ed. William Veeder and Gordon Hirsch ([Chicago, 1988]: 223–46) Hirsch argues that *Jekyll and Hyde* is structurally a detective novel, and then argues that it deconstructs the form. Hirsch thus cancels his argument out, though I take his point that structurally there are similarities between the classic detective novel and Stevenson's work.

11. For example, William Stowe's original contribution to *The Poetics of Murder*, "From Semiotics to Hermeneutics: Modes of Detection in Doyle and Chandler" (366–83) contrasts Chandler's complicated relationship of detective and situation to what Stowe sees as a simple model in the Holmes stories, where Holmes treats sensuous data as signs which can be read to reveal hidden facts about events in the past and truths about people's lives.

12. In *Murder . . . by Category: A Subject Guide to Mystery Fiction* by Tasha Mackler (Scarecrow Press, 1991), the author identifies under the category "Victorian", in addition to the detective fictions discussed here, single works by Ray Blach and André Norton, John Dickson Carr, Richard Freeborn, Marion J. A. Jackson, Alanna Knight, Gillian Linscott, and three by H. R. F. Keating. All but two of these were published in the late 1980s and early 1990s.

13. I am grateful to Betty Anselowitz for pointing out Twain's parodies of Sherlock Holmes to me.

14. *The Crocodile on the Sandbank* (1988); *The Curse of the Pharaohs* (1988); *Lion in the Valley* (1990); *The Mummy Case* (1992); *The Deeds of the Disturber* (1992), and *The Snake, The Crocodile, and the Dog* (1993).

15. Michael Holquist, "Whodunit and Other Questions: Detective Stories in Postwar Fiction" in *The Poetics of Murder*, 150.

Recent Dickens Criticism: 1993

Barry V. Qualls

> I had meant to ask some solemn questions about the genre
> or genres of *A Christmas Carol*. Re-reading it has put all
> that out of my mind. As is always the case for me when I
> read anything by Dickens, the inordinate linguistic exuber-
> ance of *A Christmas Carol* makes all formal questions seem
> beside the point. . . . Perhaps all that can be done is to put
> "Wow!" in the margin of the text or adjacent to a citation.
>
> J. Hillis Miller

Hillis Miller's "Wow!" in *The Dickensian*'s celebration of the 150th anniversary of *A Christmas Carol* recalls Barbara Hardy's remark to me many years
ago when, as a graduate student, I first began to read Dickens *seriously*:
"You don't like Dickens. You like Hillis Miller's Dickens." One of the great
teachers of the novel I have encountered, she was of course right: I tended
then to write "Wow" in the margins of my copy of Miller, and return to my
(closet) laughter in reading Dickens. As a reader, I giggled uproariously about
Guppy, the Pecksniffs, and Pumblechook; as a writer, I turned solemn.

Reading the Dickens critics of 1993 reminded me of Barbary Hardy's
remark, reminded me too how difficult it is for critics to enjoy Dickens'
exuberance, how easy it is for the thesis and its theoretical foundations to
smother that exuberance, the wonderful *play* of the novels. It is clear from
my survey that Dickens criticism, and perhaps literary criticism in general,
are at a turning point. The work of Foucault and of D. A. Miller continues
as the major influences in critical thinking about Victorian fiction. But the
thinness and derivativeness of most writing should give us all pause. Much
of this work seems warmed-over and repetitive, lacking either the freshness
or profundity of its critical or theoretical models, and well-nigh never engaged
compellingly with Dickens as a marvelously creative exuberant *writer*. Studies
with a historical, or historicizing, focus have much more of critical interest

to offer than the character studies. But few critics seem tempted to write "Wow!" in the margins of their Dickens; nor are their readers likely to have that impulse in *their* margins.

Not surprisingly, then, in 1993 there were no major books focused only on Dickens. There were no articles in *Victorian Studies* or in *Nineteenth-Century Literature*. There were major critical editions. *The Dickensian* celebrated the 150th anniversary of *A Christmas Carol*, and *Dickens Quarterly* celebrated the 150th anniversary of *Martin Chuzzlewit*. Important chapters did appear in books. And a year that boasts such compelling work as the essays by Mary Poovey and Hillis Miller is not a waste for the Dickens reader.

The Clarendon Press's attention to Dickens continued in 1993. Margaret Cardwell edited *Great Expectations*, choosing the 1861, three-volume edition for her copy-text, and giving generally brief attention to the manuscript and to the installments in *All the Year Round*. Like earlier Clarendon Dickens volumes, this one will excite debate because of the editorial choices. Suffice it to say, it still remains an impressive achievement. Volume 7 of the Pilgrim Edition of the letters, covering 1853–57, is a stunner. (It also offers, in an appendix, additional letters not included in volumes 1–6, or else not printed correctly or completely.) Dickens' letters from 1853 to 1857 show him busy completing *Bleak House*, writing *Hard Times*, and beginning *Little Dorrit*. In fact, the letters show Dickens busy at everything. There are over 130 letters to Angela Burdett Coutts about the Home for Homeless Women. There are over 120 letters to the assistant editor of *Household Words*, W. H. Wills. There are letters about politics, about travel in England and on the continent, about family matters, about friends and fellow-writers. Here too are more of Dickens' proclamations about spontaneous combustion (in a new letter to G. H. Lewes), pleasure about his representations of Allen Woodcourt and Harold Skimpole, and an explanation about the necessity of destroying Lady Dedlock. Dickens' letters provide a rich source of information about his daily and imaginative lives. The Pilgrim Edition, offering new letters and unexpurgated versions of older ones published elsewhere, is the *sine qua non* for anyone who cares about Dickens. It is beautifully edited and beautifully produced.

Ruth Glancy's annotated bibliography of *A Tale of Two Cities* is a cornuco- pia on the novel that was once a staple of the American public school curricu- lum. Editions, film and television adaptations, and critical discussions are all surveyed. Glancy also offers a section called "Topography and Character Prototypes," another on "Literary Influences, Parallels, and Other Sources," even one on "Study Guides and Handbooks." Her annotations are judicious and succinct, and the thoroughness and care of her work generate confidence in its completeness.

In turning to the criticism and theoretical discussions of Dickens, it is important to note at once that most criticism focusing on Dickens in 1993 uses some kind of historical basis or context. Only a few studies concentrate solely on characters, and these almost inevitably continue to use psychological tools developed in Freudian analysis. No essay published in 1993 matches, in complexity and exemplary signifiance, Mary Poovey's "Reading History in Literature: Speculation and Virtue in *Our Mutual Friend*." In this essay Poovey is at once literary scholar-critic and historian, at once a nuanced reader of Dickens' text and an historian of Victorian economic history, of race and gender and their figurations in nineteenth-century England, and of cultural ideas and ideals that produced the social and cultural environment in which Dickens worked. Because she knows how to listen to a text, Poovey is able to chart the "network of connotations and associations," the "field of cultural meanings," that shaped the readings of *Our Mutual Friend* in 1864–65 and that shape our readings now.

The emphasis of Poovey's title, "Reading History in Literature," is on the *in*, and it tells much about her method. Neither literary historian (in the older sense) nor new historicist, Poovey sees her "new history" as one that focuses on

> the extent to which the work involved in constructing a historical narrative can alert the reader to a network of connotations and associations to which the language of the literary text also belongs. In so doing, this work enables the reader to identify the ideological projects in which the text participated at its moment of production. . . . This model also suggests that one important literary-critical practice will abandon the pursuit of "complete" readings of discrete texts in favor of analyses that reconstruct the debates and practices in which texts initially participated as well as the contemporary interpretive practices that make these debates visible now. The privileged sites for this analysis will be textual details that (also) belong to (other) contemporary vocabularies and discussions, textual contradictions or symbolic solutions that reveal the presence of the text's "outside" in the fabric of textuality itself, and the features of the text that coincide with contemporary critical preoccupations. (pp. 43, 46–47)

In this work, everything around the novel is also available for interpretation—as itself, and as it moves into Dickens' text through its connotations, amplifications, and implications. "Reading" Dickens alongside discussions of financial speculation in Parliamentary debates, newspaper articles, and essays from *All the Year Round*, Poovey shows how the issues of "scrip" money and speculation work in *Our Mutual Friend*. In the speculation manias of the period and in the rage for both international and domestic investment, Poovey locates the "issues of national (or 'racial') otherness and gender anxiety" (p. 55) that become very much a part of Dickens' novel. Through Poovey's explorations and suggestions, we see the ways "Englishness" works as a coin of value in the novel. And we see how "the John Harmon plot works to rewrite 'value,' to exchange the false currency of literal money for the 'true,' metaphorical coin of love" (p. 57). More tellingly, we see the "infiltration of economic motives into the domestic sphere" (p. 56), and the ways Dickens works to "cordon" off such infiltration, figured in the John Harmon plot, from the rest of the novel in order to insure that "recognizing the metaphorical nature of money facilitates exchanges that enhance domestic relations and bring out the humanity in people" (p. 57).

Here Poovey's argument moves to two central assumptions about women that determine the novel's gender politics and its representations of Bella Wilfer and Lizzie Hexam.

> The first is that that "true" woman desires only what the man who (legally) represents her desires, that the law of coverture does not so much bind the wife's desires to those of the husband as recognize a community of interests that really does exist. The second assumption is that women can themselves stand in for the inhuman systems that control men. Literal women, in other words, can function like metaphors, which represent and displace something they are not. (p. 58)

The discussion of Lizzie Hexam, in Poovey and other critics in this survey, bids to make her the central Dickensian heroine of the 1990s, more complex and "authentic" (Holbrook) than all of his women and most of his men. For Poovey, Lizzie's status as a working-class woman who is economically independent confers on her a kind of masculine independence (not to mention the want of leisure to think about femininity) and paradoxically brings into the novel central Victorian preoccupations about "women and figuration." In a brilliant section of her essay, Poovey traces the ways women came to be connected with morality and truth—*and* thus outside or beyond politics and its contagions. The connection of women with the novel and novel reading in the nineteenth-century (we might remember here Dickens' emphasis on the purity of his fiction) leads directly, for Poovey, to Dickens' most radical gesture in his representation of Lizzie, his "reanimation" of traditional anxieties about the link between women and figuration: his portrayal of Lizzie "ties what most Victorians thought to be the natural capacity of women to incarnate morality and value to a series of threats posed to the male characters" (p. 64). Dickens sees instinctively that the "naturalization of womanly virtue'' is threatened by a woman who actually works, and thus he must erase as much as possible attention to Lizzie working. After all: ''if Lizzie can be like a man when Eugene needs to be pulled from the water and like a woman when he is ready for a wife, then is it possible that her character is *not* an expression of some underlying female nature but merely the effect of a man's needs?'' (p. 65).

The concluding part of Poovey's essay examines the crucial question raised by the representaion of Lizzie Hexam: Is female virtue natural, inherent? Or is it ''only a figment of men's desire''? Does the ''sexed body'' not ''guarantee moral difference''? Is ''real'' difference no more than metaphor? If so, what is possible, likely, in a world without women? The moral chaos that *Our Mutual Friend* approaches and avoids grows out of these interrelated questions posed about economics, about gender, and about colonial expansion that were so much a part of the cultural noise of the lives of Dickens and his readers in the late 1850s and the 1860s. For Poovey, what allows Dickens to avoid the chaos of the questions his text raises is ''the difference of race.'' ''Dickens's textually marginal, but ideological central, invocation of racial difference holds the key to his ability to recuperate the moralized image of woman.'' No matter how long it had been a part of English consciousness, race was a newly visible difference in the 1860s because of the Indian Mutiny of 1857 and the Jamaica uprising of 1865. Poovey's discussion of three small racialized moments in the text shows how Dickens re-secures, for the moment, the natural superiority of being English and the natural morality inherent in being (born) female.

If my summary of Poovey threatens to take over this survey, I intend that. The complexity of argument, the density of her network of illustrations, the nuanced voices speaking from all over the world that she hears in *Our Mutual Friend* make her study exemplary. Here the text is not strained to illustrate a theory; nor is it swamped in historical specifics. It is seen anew. The reader has the opportunity to meet the novel as Victorian readers met it, even as the critical preoccupations of our own period—race, class, gender—determine many of the emphases. The essay is the work of one of our major critics, working as always to expand the boundaries of what constitutes criticism and history.

Nothing else matches the work of Poovey this year, but there are essays and chapters in books that suggest the value of attending to Victorian culture and history and of listening to Dickens' voice. Chief among these is the work of Miriam Bailin, *The Sickroom in Victorian Fiction: The Art of Being Ill.*

Bailin (who offers a salutary explanation of why she provides "scant reference" to Foucault's work on medical discourse) tellingly focuses on what has seemed so characteristic of Victorian fiction and life as to be taken for granted and asks questions about the pervasiveness of sickrooms and invalidism and about their relation to the realist aesthetic so central to the ideological positioning of the novel. She notes the continual need of novels, whether their protagonist be male or female, to go through illness on the way to the ending, and adds: "Illness in Dickens's fiction is the *sine qua non* both of restored or reconstructed identity, and of narrative structure and closure." What makes her study significant is that her analogy between the representation of illness and the work of realism is never facile, never used to force an argument. She shows convincingly, in the work of Charlotte Brontë, Dickens, and George Eliot, that the sickroom scenes "serve, in themselves and in their relation to the larger narrative structure, as an adaptive strategy to encode and mediate competing personal, social, and aesthetic imperatives" (p. 1). Her chapter on "Life in the Sickroom" is a marvelous compendium of Victorian attitudes towards illness and novelistic anxieties about plot and closure. She shows how illness indeed became a "social role" in the nineteenth-century, introducing a new "corporeal language" into common discussion and privileging conditions of frailty, suffering, and morbidity. To watch the Victorians, whether Harriet Martineau or Florence Nightingale or a host of lesser known figures, almost celebrating the sickroom because it separated them from the "real" conditions of daily life—conditions of work, duty, responsibility to social decorums and gender definitions—is to understand fully the appeal of invalidism. Nightingale declared that "a patient wants according to his wants," his desires are not mediated by consideration for the needs of others. For her, invalidism freed her to work—prodigiously, as Bailin shows.

In discussing Dickens, Bailin notes the way his sickrooms contest the "manic restlessness and profusion of the narratives they conclude" (p. 80), studies how the scenes focus the strands of narrative concern with identity and the dread of having none, and traces how they also bring to the fore individual career and class anxieties that the thrust of the text, towards domestic harmony and sanctity, often obscures. Her test cases are *The Old Curiosity Shop* and *Our Mutual Friend*, though she offers insightful discussion of sickrooms and sick souls in many of the other novels. Like Poovey and other critics in 1993, she singles out Eugene Wrayburn for particular attention, charting the roles of Jenny Wren and Lizzie Hexam in his cure, and noting the ways that cure insures that he will be "too wan and worn for excess" (p. 104). For Dickens, Bailin says, the sickroom was "a place where vigilance could be suspended, desire and invention stilled, the feverish journey ended. His idealization of incapacity expresses the yearning of his aspiring and restless age for exemption and surcease as acutely as the convergence of the delirium expresses its feverish desire to 'get on' " (p. 108).

Kevin McLaughlin's study of "Displacement and Domesticity" in *Bleak House* also emphasizes the domestic spaces in British novels and how they "organize themselves by analogy to the home." For him, *Bleak House*, in the ways it links the home and the subject, defines essential ideas about sources of order in the larger world. Using Hegel's *Phenomenology* as the basis of his definition of subjectivity, McLaughlin suggests how Esther Summerson, "both homeless and a woman," is a "paradigmatic autobiographical subject." To define "what kind of subject" she is, he reads the great scene in which Esther looks at herself in the mirror for the first time after her illness. Here, Esther, in the very indefiniteness she discovers, "makes herself the subject and predicate of her narrative" (p. 879). Within it contagion, self-consciousness, and domesticity congregate. Yet institutionally (and here McLaughlin rewrites D. A. Miller's discussion of *Bleak House*), the very fact that Esther in the end inhabits a newly constructed Bleak House suggests that for Dickens institutions are not fixed forever, that one is *not* condemned to "hold one's place" forever because of an institution's assumed disciplinary power. This is a challenging discussion, and one that suggests new ways of considering "the link between aesthetic and institutional questions" in Victorian fiction.

Wendy Lesser's "Defending Dickens" offers added support to McLaughlin's insights about Esther Summerson, though her damning judgment of Esther—even as she elevates Eugene Wrayburn to new complexity—is to place her among the grotesques of Dickens, alongside Uriah Heep. Beginning her argument in the truism that "the 'problem' of Dickens' characters" (are they round? or grotesque? or. . . ?) "is intimately linked to the nature of Dickens' urban vision, which uses superficiality as both an aesthetic and moral instrument" (p. 227), Lesser considers the familiar issue of the ways Dickens animates inanimate objects. She observes: "Metaphor purportedly seeks to describe by comparing like to different; but in Dickens' world, the 'different' has already been converted to the 'like' (the non-human to the human, or vice versa), so the metaphor simply brings the described object back to itself" (p. 229).

Lesser finds Wrayburn unlike any other character in Dickens, and Esther all too much like others. For her Wrayburn is a Dickens manqué, and certainly a stand-in for Dickens at many points in *Our Mutual Friend*. He knows that "the only access we can have to interiority is through the superficial" (p. 236). His perspective is the novel's urban perspective, the notion "that if external views are certainly suspect, they are still the best we have" (p. 235). Needless to say, Esther Summerson's difference from Wrayburn guarantees her fall from critical grace in this argument: "Esther is a Dickensian caricature masquerading as a self . . . a character who is portrayed *too* completely for what she is, which is a version of the Dickensian grotesque. Esther has no self precisely because she cannot see herself from the outside" (p. 235). Like Micawber, Bounderby, Uriah Heep, and others, Esther sees nothing beyond her own self, hears nothing beyond her own voice. Though there is much here to challenge (and though, in the brief space, little is demonstrated), Lesser should stimulate fresh discussions of Dickens' characterizations.

Natalie McKnight will not. Her *Idiots, Madmen, and Other Prisoners in Dickens* has some of the same emphases as do Poovey and Bailin. She notes the many fools, madmen, and idiots in Dickens; she locates their sources and analogues in literature and history; she traces concerns with such figures in *Household Words* and in *All the Year Round*. But though she insists, at the outset, on distinguishing these figures ("Holy idiots and wise fools differ"), as she discusses individual novels, they finally become one and the same with almost all of Dickens' eccentrics, and—surprisingly—also with his women: all represent marginalized figures. We end up, then, with a study of imprisoned characters as seen through a Foucauldian lens. Characters connected to chaos or foolishness, McKnight declares, escape the surveillance of Society, the oppressions of life in a regimented world. But then the same thing seems true of objects. In *Dombey*, she even connects the railway's energy to "chaos and its related folly, nonsense, and idiocy" (p. 95). In *Little Dorrit*, she finds Maggie "neither a holy nor a wise fool"; but "Dickens advocates, through her, foolishness for its own sake" (p. 120). Amy Dorrit is for McKnight the best representative of the "holy fool." A "freak of *littleness*," Amy uses her foolishness to escape the effects of her society's surveillance. She, Arthur, and the small group around them at the novel's end are misfits, escapees from a panopticon world. In arguments like this, definitions lose all specificity: small women and large fools are one and the same; foolishness is all.

What makes this argument dispiriting are its porous definitions and its Procrustean application of Foucault. "In Foucault's terms," McKnight writes continually about Dickens. She finds that "Barnaby's history recapitulates the history of the treatment of the insane, as Foucault presents it in *Madness and Civilization*," and that Dickens' characterization "bears out this analysis." Of course it does not, though it may parallel or anticipate it. At her best,

McKnight sees this, and places Dickens within his own century, working alongside Carlyle (she has insightful things to say about the use of clothes on the idiots and fools). Dickens may be comparable to Foucault in his representations; he may often "prefigure" Foucault's analyses. But to reduce the novelist to illustration is to miss the life of the novels and to ignore their conflicted relationships to the social culture that surrounded Dickens.

Equally dispiriting, though not at all influenced by Foucauldian ideas, is David Holbrook's *Charles Dickens and the Image of Woman*. (The book also depresses because of the slackness of its editing and proofreading. Surely the author or someone at the NYU Press might have checked the spelling of the names of characters and critics, and might have caught mistakes like "Dicken's," used often as a possesive?) Holbrook, who labels his method a "modern phenomenological interpretation" (p. 30), is unapologetically a Freudian reader, though he also uses Klein, D. W. Winnicott, and others. For him, both author and characters, not to mention Victorian readers and modern critics, come in for examination and correction because they praised false psychology and worse representation, because they believed those incredible "religiose" scenes Dickens produced ("How could they believe in. . . ?" he asks repeatedly, rhetorically). *Little Dorrit* particularly dismays Holbrook, while *Our Mutual Friend* achieves Shakespearean status. "Little Doormat" is an angel. "But that is the trouble with her: as an embodiment of Christ's forgiveness she is too much inclined to condone and so to forfeit her authenticity: she becomes an idealized all-pardoning submissive" (p. 75). "The protagonists are not selfish enough," they care nothing "for their own self-realization and fulfillment" (p. 77). And Mr. Dorrit "ought to be ashamed of himself" (p. 78) for his exploitation of the "Euphrasia motif." It will surprise no one that Holbrook finds F. R. Leavis psychologically deficient for his championing of the "life" represented in this novel. What does surprise is the language in which Holbrook exalts *Our Mutual Friend* and Lizzie Hexam. For Holbrook, Lizzie confronts "the ultimate questions of existence" (p. 148) and in doing so finds her authenticity. In her marriage to Wrayburn, Holbrook sees rewritings of Beatrice and Benedict and of Elizabeth Bennet and Darcy: "tangible lovers [not angels and enervated men] who discover their possibilities for freedom and equality in their mutual plight" (p. 163). Dizzying. Michael Slater's *Dickens and Women* will help readers wanting sane consideration of this topic.

After this, it is bracing to turn back to criticism where history and culture matter in the ways we read. Like other critics inspired by Foucault, Jeremy Tambling finds textual repressions throughout *Dombey and Son* and evaluates them as the direct result of the modernity that threatens the text. Like Poovey, he hears the various discourses of mercantilism and international trade, and the imperialism they supported, adding their own powers to the text. Opposing this modernity is "the increased prominence of the older form of caricatural writing (Toots, Cuttle, Mrs. MacStringer)" (p. 313). Change and the desperate need to reverse it are everywhere in *Dombey*, and Tambling compellingly locates in the repressions of "the patriarchal narrative" the effort to control these double movements. Best of all in this study is the discussion of the famous passage from chapter 47, "Oh for a good spirit who would take the house tops off. . . ." Here Tambling finds both the novel's appeals to nature and its repressions of class and other differences for the sake of "one 'common end' " (pp. 325–26).

The most complex, interesting, and perplexing of the Foucault-inspired readings of the novels is William Cohen's "Manual Conduct in *Great Expectations*." Densely argued, always clever, it is certain to enrage traditional Dickensians, bemuse "common readers," provide fodder for academic bashers, and leave even the most accepting of critical readers uncertain whether to ask for "more" or to give up criticism forever. A quotation will serve best to introduce the idea and the method:

> If one were writing the masturbator's guide to the English novel, certain correspondences would soon become evident. Like the novel, the discourse that constitutes masturbation (as a medical condition, a moral sin, a personal identity, a psychological stage) first arose early in the eighteenth century; like the novel, too, it achieved full cultural currency by the Victorian period and began its decline early in the present century. . . . Through famously repressive techniques, medical authorities sought to control the onanistic vice that, as we now suppose, they thereby invented; the novel, meanwhile, so perilously implicated in encouraging kindred forms of imaginative self-abuse, had to find ways of managing the erotic reveries it was accused of arousing in its readers. . . . In the masturbator's guide to the English novel, at least under the heading "men's bodies," Charles Dickens would doubtless merit a good deal of attention.
>
> (p. 217)

Needless to say, *Oliver Twist*'s Charley Bates—"Master Bates"—will serve for more than pun in this argument.

And he does, along with Pip, Jaggers, Herbert Pocket, and Magwitch, whose tendencies towards pedophilia begger description. Handkerchiefs, bread and butter—any things that can be put in one's trouser pockets lose all their actual materiality as they bespeak sexuality in this argument about hands and manual labors. The result: "*Great Expectations* manages to anatomize whole species of erotic dispositions without ever mentioning sex" (p. 219).

Cohen's argument derives from pondering what a text says as it represses culturally forbidden topics: "One of the nineteenth-century novel's principal accomplishments is to formulate a literary language that expresses eroticism even as it designates sexuality the supremely unmentionable subject" (p. 220). For Cohen, *Great Expectations* has at its center "a deeply saturated perversity." "The novel both arouses and coerces its readers' desires; tracing the productive interplay of pleasure and power allows not only a reconception of this classic work but a charting of Victorian sexual ideology's formidable operations" (pp. 220–21).

Here *in excelsis* is argument by analogy. I confess to finding it so clever and so uninterested in Dickens' tone and its emotional range that the novel loses any sense of historical embeddedness and becomes a verbal gym for the critic's imaginative aerobics. Of course the Victorians did not, like John Updike, turn soup into an obvious metaphor for sexual play. They did have many codes for expressing the overflows of powerful feeling. The metaphorical possibilities of hands are certainly "generalizable," as Cohen insists; and there may sometimes be a "metonymic association of hands with autoerotic functions as a conduit between representation and sexuality." But this argument is so relentlessly focused on its subject that the rich possibilities of *Great Expectations*, including inscriptions of sexuality, are lost. Cohen allows no class issues and few gender issues to interrupt the progress of his ideas and his expression. In reading his pages, I wanted to remind him of the ways John Kucich argues about psychological issues in Dickens; or the ways Bruce Robbins, in *The Servant's Hand*, focuses on the representation of the hand and its connection to the issues of class representation in fiction. I do not want Cohen to repeat arguments already made. He is clearly too intelligent for such derivative work. But he needs to set his argument in conjunction with other possibilities, other arguments, and let these inflect his own readings. Those readings will doubtlessly remain, but enlarged because they acknowledge the richness of Dickens' text. They recognize that play, even sexual play, is richly varied, or unduly restricted, in Dickens' novels. Listening to Dickens, as Mary Poovey might say, provides immense rewards.

After such argumentative strategies, it is a pleasure to turn to Richard Dunn's study of *Oliver Twist*. Writing for the Twayne's Masterworks Studies, Dunn discusses the novel's literary and historical context, its reception, and the characteristics that have given it almost mythic status. In his "reading" of the novel, he constrasts its "romantic fable," its story of Oliver himself and the middle-class characters who want to surround him, with the contrasting world that focuses on "those who face Oliver and how they cope with the challenges his very existence raises for them'' (p. 51). For Dunn, ''The novel's opposing sets of forces have in common the desire to possess Oliver, and their ways of seeing him—most literally what they face with him—reveal their own varied conditions, their way stations on 'The Parish Boy's Progress' '' (p. 51). The chapter on Fagin is equally fresh (though his assertion that ''Fagin is not the principal villain'' and is a victim like Oliver [p.75] will surprise some readers into disagreement). Dunn concludes his discussion with commentary on Cruikshank's illustrations (which he sees as determining future theatrical representations of the characters) and on stage and film versions of the novel, each of which constitute for Dunn a ''reading'' of the novel. The discussion in this small volume, conducted genially and providing really useful background information and solid critical insight, is always illuminating.

Steven Michael also finds the contrasts of *Oliver Twist* essential to a full reading of the novel, particularly to understanding the ways power is figured around these contrasts. Following Foucault and Pierre Macherey, he locates things unsaid in things said, focusing on the slang of the novel's criminal characters in order to indicate how criminals ''were becoming a social class unto themselves'' (p. 49). Noting how the criminal characters sometimes translate their particular patois for auditors they find sympathetic, Michael writes that the Artful Dodger ''uses language—whether translating flash language or dropping it altogether—to sustain his identity, to separate himself from a society whose Principle of Good is a gossamer morality having little to do with humanity'' (p. 59). Not surprisingly, in examining Oliver's impeccable speech, Michael hears the language of a principle, not a person. Still: his insight leads to brilliant discussions of Oliver as the novel's ''disruptive—even destructive—force'' and of the novel's final chapters. Michael notes that ''Oliver's arrival in the criminal world sets in motion a relentless chain of suffering and death'' (p. 51) even as goodness becomes increasingly ''passive and illogical,'' thus revealing the ways ''the dominant order'' guards its laws and property.

Cates Baldridge also focuses on Oliver's perfections—on the nature/nurture issues raised by his natural goodness—in order to address what he calls Dickens' ''precarious political fantasy fraught with embarrassing contradictions'' (p. 186). For Bates, Oliver's perfection and thus Dickens' insistence on ''blood-inheritance as the sole and sufficient explanation of character [are], to some extent, both anti-novelistic *and* anti-bourgeois'' (p. 187). Perhaps. But while I agree that the ''quasi-Wordsworthian discourse of the novel'' (p. 189) lacks the cogent representation or vigorous writing that distinguishes the

Bumble, Fagin, and Sikes sections, it is important to remember that Dickens mixed genres with abandon, stirred allegory into the realistic novel, combined Bunyan's progress and Wordsworth's, and created the perfect orphan in Oliver. It is true that in the half-brother Monks Dickens finds vices—and upper-class ones at that—which amazingly do not infect Oliver. Still: in early Dickens good people and bad people are not so allied as they will be in *Great Expectations* and *Our Mutual Friend*.

After so much focus on the play of power and the panopticon in Dickens, turning to *Dickens Quarterly* and *The Dickensian* and their celebrations of the 150th anniversaries of the publications of *Martin Chuzzlewit* and *A Christmas Carol* may recall simpler days indeed. In *Dickens Quarterly*, Nancy Metz offers a lively, and happily illustrated, discussion of the speculations that Samuel Carter Hall, founder of the *Art Journal*, and Sir Robert Peel were the inspirations for Pecksniff. Jerome Meckier teases out the ways Dickens used James Fenimore Cooper and Natty Bumppo in chapters 33–34 of *Martin Chuzzlewit*. In *The Dickensian*, Kathleen Tillotson discusses the *Carol*'s background, Philip Collins looks at its "reception and status," Michael Slater considers Dickens' uses of wit and humor (and the very English nature of the humor), and Edwin Eigner connects the *Carol* to Victorian pantomime.

Best of all is Hillis Miller discussing the "hyperbolic superabundance" (p. 196) of the *Carol*. Miller can never be dull or uninteresting. Here he is positively exuberant. After admitting, as I noted, that the very reading of Dickens' pages "makes all formal questions seem beside the point," he offers in a few pages a stunning discussion of the grab-bag nature of Dickens' art. Noting the extravagant catalogues of edibles in the text, Miller not only finds this "superabundance of good things to eat" astonishing, but he finds the personification of the inanimate—of all these edibles—part of the "ubiquitous personification" that makes Dickens' world teem with unthreatening energy; this inanimate world is "not threatening or other" (p. 195). Even what is bad is "superlative" (p. 196). From the hyperbolic nature of language and action (Miller notes that Baudelaire, describing pantomime, spoke of "vertige de l'hyperbole": the "dizziness of hyperbole"), Miller turns to the generic boundaries that are constantly broken in the *Carol*. Allegory or parable, pantomime text or conversion narrative, dream vision or melodrama, ghost story or Gothic tale—*A Christmas Carol* is all of these, its methods beyond realism, and uninterested in its strictures, even as it is also, surely, a short novel (pp. 202–03). Everything about it speaks to its "hyperbolic generosity." Reading it finally becomes "a performative as well as a cognitive event" (p. 206).

Whatever its ideological conflicts, *A Christmas Carol* will be satisfied to help us erase Ignorance and Want.

One more exuberant performance needs mention before this survey ends. Daniel Pool, political scientist and lawyer, has no critical theories from which to construct Dickens or any Victorian novelist, and not much concern about the ideological repressions and silences imposed on and by their novels. In *What Jane Austen Ate and Charles Dickens Knew*, Pool simply wants to tell us something about the questions he asks when he reads Victorian fiction: questions about shillings and puddings, wife-selling and baronets, Puseyites and nobs. The book, composed of short essays, a substantial glossary, and a bibliography, makes no claim to accuracy, and has less than it should. Do we really want to hear Dorothea Brooke named "Dorothy Brook" or "Dorothy Casaubon" (p. 254)? Is there really a "Eugene Hexam" in *Our Mutual Friend* (p. 47) or a "Eugene Lydgate" in *Middlemarch* (p. 247)? Why has Wemmick's wondrous "portable property" become "personal property" (p. 139)? The brief essays focus on such topics as "Local Government," "Life on the Farm," "Money," and "Sex." The glossary runs from *abigail* ("a lady's maid") to *Your Worship* ("The correct form of address to a magistrate, e.g., a justice of the peace").

What Jane Austen Ate and Charles Dickens Knew, used cautiously (if assigned to students), is simply fun: a happy complement to reading Victorian novels, an ideal volume for bedside browsing after a multitudinous day. It is one long "Wow!" by a reader who loves Victorian fiction—a perfect antidote to criticism that refuses to listen to the hyperbolic superabundance of Charles Dickens.

WORKS CITED/WORKS CONSULTED

Articles not mentioned but considered for this review are also listed here. When necessary, a brief annotation explains their focus.

Great Expectations. The Clarendon Dickens. Ed. Margaret Cardwell. Oxford: Clarendon, 1993.

The Letters of Charles Dickens. The Pilgrim Edition: Volume 7:1853–55. Ed. Graham Storey, Kathleen Tillotson, and Angus Easson. Oxford: Clarendon, 1993.

Arms, G. D. "Reassembling *Bleak House*: 'Is there *three* of 'em then?' " *Literature and Psychology* 39 (1993): 84–96.

Bailin, Miriam. *The Sickroom in Victorian Fiction: The Art of Being Ill*. Cambridge: Cambridge UP, 1993.

Baldridge, Cates. "The Instabilities of Inheritance in *Oliver Twist*." *Studies in the Novel* 25 (1993): 184–95.

Barnes, James and Patience. "Solitude and Ghosts in Dickens's Christmas Books." *The Dickensian* 89 (1993): 218–25.

Callahan, Charles V. Jr. "Tiny Tim: The Child with a Crippling Fatal Illness." *The Dickensian* 89 (1993): 214–17.

Cohen, William. "Manual Conduct in *Great Expectations*." *ELH* 60 (1993): 217–59.

Collins, Philip. "The Reception and Status of the *Carol*." *The Dickensian* 89 (1993): 170–76.

Cunningham, John. "The Figure of the Wedding Feast in *Great Expectations*." *Dickens Quarterly* 10 (1993): 87–91.

Cronin, Mark. "Thackeray's First Fashioned Response to Dickens: *The Yellowplush Papers* Cast a Cynical Eye on the 'Admiral Boz's' *Pickwick Papers*." *Dickens Quarterly* 10 (1993): 191–202.

Dickens, David. "Dickens Was Dead: To Begin With." *The Dickensian* 89 (1993): 207–18. Reminiscence of family readings of *A Christmas Carol* by great-grandson of Dickens.

Dunn, Richard J. *Oliver Twist: Whole Heart and Soul*. Twayne Masterwork Studies. New York: Twayne, 1993.

Easson, Angus. "From Terror to Terror: Dickens, Carlyle and Cannibalism." In *Reflections on Romanticism: Images of Revolution*. Ed. Alison Yarrington and Kelvin Everest. London and New York: Routledge 1993.

Edgecombe, R. S. "Locution and Authority in *Martin Chuzzlewit*." *English Studies* 74 (1993): 143–53.

Eigner, Edwin. "On Becoming Pantaloon." *The Dickensian* 89 (1993): 177–83.

Glancy, Ruth. *A Tale of Two Cities: An Annotated Bibliography*. New York: Garland, 1993.

Golden, Morris. "Politics, Class, and *Martin Chuzzlewit*." *Dickens Quarterly* 10 (1993): 17–32.

Holbrook, David. *Charles Dickens and the Image of Woman*. New York and London: New York UP, 1993.

Hollington, Michael. "The Live Hieroglyphic: *Physiologie* and Physiognomy in *Martin Chuzzlewit*." *Dickens Quarterly* 10 (1993): 57–68.

Hornback, Bert G. "*New American Notes* by Charles Dickens." *Dickens Quarterly* 10 (1993): 68–75. Dickens "returns" to discuss America 150 years later.

Innes, Christopher. "Adapting Dickens to the Modern Eye: *Nicholas Nickleby* and *Little Dorrit*." In *Novel Images: Literature in Performance*. Ed. Peter Reynolds. London and New York: Routledge, 1993.

Kusnetz, Ella. " 'This Leaf of My Life': Writing and Play in *Great Expectations*." *Dickens Quarterly* 10 (1993): 91–103, 146–60.

Lesser, Wendy. "Defending Dickens." *Western Humanities Review* 47 (1993): 226–36.

Maynard, John. *Victorian Discourses on Sexuality and Religion*. Cambridge: Cambridge UP, 1993. Though only Hardy, among the major novelists, is considered at length, Maynard's is a wide-ranging and important study that bears significantly on the absence of explicitly interrelated sexual and religious languages in Dickens' novels. (This is also a beautifully produced and edited book, a rarity now.)

McKnight, Natalie. *Idiots, Madmen, and Other Prisoners in Dickens*. New York: St. Martin's, 1993.

McLaughlin, Kevin. "Losing One's Place: Displacement and Domesticity in Dickens's *Bleak House*." *MLN* 108 (1993): 875–90.

Meckier, Jerome. "Charles Dickens's *Great Expectations*: A Defense of the Second Ending." *Studies in the Novel* 25 (1993): 28–58.

———. "Hannibal Chollop's Offensiveness: Natty Bumppo and Chapters 33–34 of *Martin Chuzzlewit*." *Dickens Quarterly* 10 (1993): 33–57.

Metz, Nancy Aycock. "Dickens, *Punch*, and *Pecksniff*." *Dickens Quarterly* 10 (1993): 6–17.

Michael, Steven. "Criminal Slang in *Oliver Twist*: Dickens' Survival Code." *Style* 27 (1993): 41–62.

Miller, J. Hillis. "The Genres of *A Christmas Carol*." *The Dickensian* 89 (1993): 193–206.

Pool, Daniel. *What Jane Austen Ate and Charles Dickens Knew: From Fox Hunting to Whist—The Facts of Daily Life in 19th-Century England*. New York: Simon and Schuster, 1993.

Poovey, Mary. "Reading History in Literature: Speculation and Virtue in *Our Mutual Friend*." In *Historical Criticism and the Challenge of Theory*. Ed. Janet Levarie Smarr. Urbana: U of Illinois P, 1993.

Potau, Mercedes. "Notes on Parallels between *The Pickwick Papers* and *Don Quixote*." *Dickens Quarterly* 10 (1993): 105–110.

Simpson, Margaret. "*Hard Times* and Circus Times." *Dickens Quarterly* 10 (1993): 131–46.

Slater, Michael. "The Triumph of Humour: The *Carol* Revisited." *The Dickensian* 89 (1993): 184–92.

Smith, Grahame. "Dickens and Adaptation: Imagery in words and pictures." In *Novel Images: Literature in Performance.*" Ed. Peter Reynolds. London and New York: Routledge, 1993.

Tambling, Jeremy. "Death and Modernity in *Dombey and Son.*" *Essays in Criticism* 43 (1993): 308–329.

Tillotson, Kathleen. "A Background for *A Christmas Carol.*" *The Dickensian* 89 (1993): 165–69.

Trezise, Simon. "Dickens and Critical Change: The Making of Dickens: Three Themes in the Criticism of 1837–1939." *Dickens Quarterly* 10 (1993): 161–70.

Wall, William G. "Mrs. Affrey Flintwinch's Dreams: Reading and Remembering in *Little Dorrit.*" *Dickens Quarterly* 10 (1993): 202–06.

Westland, Ella. "Dickens and Critical Change: The Making of Dickens: Conflicts in Criticism 1940–1970." *Dickens Quarterly* 10 (1993): 208–18.

Index